Public Relations Worktext

A Writing and Planning Resource

Second Edition

Joseph M. Zappala, APR
Cornell University

Ann R. Carden, APR
State University of New York College at Fredonia

LEA
2004

LAWRENCE ERLBAUM ASSOCIATES, PUBLISHERS
Mahwah, New Jersey   London

Acquisitions Editor:	Linda Bathgate
Assistant Editor:	Karin Wittig Bates
Cover Design:	Sean Trane Sciarrone
Textbook Production Manager:	Paul Smolenski
Full-Service Compositor:	TechBooks
Text and Cover Printer:	Hamilton Printing Company

This book was typeset in 10/12 Times, Italic, Bold, Bold Italic. The heads were typeset in ACaslon Regular, Bold, Italic, and Bold Italic.

Lawrence Erlbaum Associates, Inc., Publishers
10 Industrial Avenue
Mahwah, New Jersey 07430
www.erlbaum.com

Library of Congress Cataloging-in-Publication Data

Zappala, Joseph M.
    Public relations worktext : a writing and planning resource / Joseph
M. Zappala, Ann R. Carden.—2nd ed.
      p.   cm.
    Rev. ed. of: Public relations workbook / Raymond Simon, Joseph M. Zappala. c1998.
    Includes bibliographical references and index.
    ISBN 0-8058-4263-2 (pbk.: alk. paper)
    1. Public relations.   2. Business writing.   I. Carden, Ann R.   II. Simon, Raymond.
Public relations workbook.   III. Title.
HM1221.Z37 2004
659.2—dc22

                                                    2003023118

Printed in the United States of America
10 9 8 7 6 5 4 3 2 1

Brief Table of Contents

Table of Contents

List of Exhibits

Preface

About the Book

When Ray Simon and I (Zappala) began work on the first edition of *Public Relations Workbook*, we did so with the intent of creating a practical "how-to" text, a training manual, if you will, for the aspiring public relations writer. We wanted to keep the format of the book fairly simple—brief introductory text sections that focused on key concepts and explained the subject in easy-to-read language, followed by several case studies in each chapter that would give students the chance to apply principles by writing actual public relations materials.

Many of the cases were based on our on-the-job experiences as practitioners, or on the experiences that other public relations professionals shared with us, making the written work completed by students true-to-life. We also thought that instructors would find our book to be "teacher-friendly," since it comes ready-made with a variety of practical assignments, something that seemed to be missing from many of the other public relations writing textbooks at that time. The first edition, then, could be an excellent supplement to another public relations writing textbook or, for some, it might even be able to stand alone as the primary text.

The second edition of the book retains the same approach as the first edition, but there have been a number of changes that we think will have value to both students and instructors and will better position the newly-titled *Public Relations Worktext: A Writing and Planning Resource* as a primary course text:

- Expanded text sections with more detailed content on subjects such as research, planning, ethical and legal considerations, and crisis communications.
- More focus on writing for the Web and electronic media, including an entire chapter entitled "Online Writing and Communication."
- More and updated examples and reprints of effective public relations writing by leading companies in a variety of organizational settings, including Procter & Gamble, Ben & Jerry's, Mattel, the U.S. Golf Association, Kodak, Heinz, and many more.
- Easy-to-read summaries in each chapter and an appendix including more than 30 checklists for students to reference when working on assignments.
- Q&A pieces featuring comments and insights from public relations and media professionals on important topics such as pitching the media, planning events, and developing intranet sites.
- An original illustration showing the integration of public relations, advertising, and marketing, and a chart to help students select the most appropriate research methods for their project(s).

The book is divided into four sections:

Section I provides an introduction to public relations and writing. Chapter 1 includes information on public relations as compared to marketing and advertising and introduces the different forms of public relations writing, as well as the concepts of communication and persuasion. Chapter 2 focuses on the basics of writing—spelling, punctuation, grammar, and style—as well as ethical and legal considerations.

Section II introduces the four-step public relations process. Chapter 3 reviews the importance of research and the various methods used. Chapter 4 outlines the components of program planning and execution.

Section III provides in-depth information on the various writing formats and techniques used in implementing strategic public relations plans, from memos and proposals (chap. 5) and news releases (chap. 6) to brochures (chap. 10) and special events (chap. 13). Chapter 14 focuses on crisis communications.

Section IV completes the public relations process with a comprehensive look at evaluation in Chapter 15.

Our Vision

This book provides students both the fundamental knowledge required for public relations writing as well as the critical writing practice they need, allowing them to make mistakes in the classroom and receive feedback on written pieces before they enter a professional setting. Without this experience, students will have difficulty succeeding in field assignments and in that first job, both of which will require them to do a lot of writing. Internship supervisors and employers want students and graduates who can "hit the ground running," and that means having the ability to write a variety of public relations materials competently and with minimal direction. We think this book will give students basic writing preparation to get started in their careers and will also be a useful resource "down the road" when they need a refresher on some aspect of public relations writing.

Although this book is primarily targeted to college students, we kept another audience in mind while preparing the text—the many people who, with no training, have found themselves in the position of performing public relations tasks. Before organizations make the decision to hire a public relations practitioner, they often turn to other people within the organization to write a news release, design a flier, or plan a special event. Civic, professional, and religious organizations often turn to volunteers to complete tasks that fall within public relations expertise. Although we do not suggest that this book replaces proper training in the field, it is hoped that it will provide some professional guidance to people who find themselves in these situations.

Acknowledgments

No book is assembled by the authors alone. There are many people involved in the writing process from beginning to end, and many people to thank for their contributions.

We are grateful to Lawrence Erlbaum Associates, Inc., for seeing the value of publishing a second edition of the text, and to our editor, Linda Bathgate, for her direction and flexibility. Other members of the publishing team at Lawrence Erlbaum Associates included Karin Wittig Bates, assistant editor, and Paul Smolenski, the liaison with the book production house, TechBooks, where project manager Joanne Bowser oversaw the production process that made this book a reality.

Practitioners and educators throughout the country generously agreed to review the first draft of the manuscript. We are grateful for their time and comments.

We recognize the contributions of the many practitioners and educators who have developed, and continue to develop, a body of knowledge for public relations through books of their own, other publications, research, and practice. Their work, listed under "References and Suggested Reading" following each chapter, serves as a basis of this text as well as future works in the field of public relations.

This edition of *Public Relations Worktext* includes dozens of excellent, and often award-winning, examples and reprints from leading companies. We thank these companies for providing access to their work and for their willingness to share.

Of course, there would be no book at all without readers. We are grateful to the instructors who selected the first edition of *Public Relations Workbook* for use in their classrooms and expressed interest in a second edition. We appreciate their confidence in the material presented in the text and thank them, as well as future instructors and students, who will use the book.

On a Personal Note . . .

A few years ago, when I was teaching full time at Utica College of Syracuse University, I began work on this edition, having the good fortune to secure a sabbatical in the fall of 1999 to devote my full energy to research and writing. Shortly after completing the first draft of the manuscript, I was faced with "publisher limbo." The original publisher decided to sell its college text division, and it was unclear if this new edition would find a publishing home and eventually make its way to college bookstore shelves.

When I finally learned, almost two years later, that Lawrence Erlbaum Associates, Inc., had purchased the rights to this book, it was truly a day of celebration, almost as big as the day I made that last college loan payment. It has been such a great pleasure to work with Erlbaum, Linda Bathgate, and its professional staff; I couldn't be happier to call LEA "our publisher."

Just when I thought there would be no more surprises, I made a major life and career decision. After 13 years as a college instructor, I made the momentous (and some would say, foolish) choice to go back "into the trenches" by taking on a new challenge as director of communications for Cornell University's alumni affairs and development division. It has been interesting to complete the second edition of the book now as a practitioner, as I apply concepts shared in the book each and every day on the job—whether I am writing a presidential letter, consulting with staff on Web strategy and content, or working on a communications plan.

There are several people I need to acknowledge and whose guidance and support made it possible for me to complete this project. First, Ray Simon, someone to whom I owe a debt of gratitude. When Ray asked me to assist him with the first edition, I was deeply honored, and a little scared. But his confidence in me made a huge difference, and I am thankful to him for all he did for me, both as a mentor and a friend. Ray stepped away from his co-author role for this edition to enjoy the leisure of his well-deserved retirement, but his spirit and his wisdom lives on in the book nonetheless.

My new co-author, Ann Carden, has been an outstanding collaborator, and completing the second edition would not have been possible without her advice and planning expertise, writing and editing skills, and overall positive outlook. There were many times that I lagged behind on a deadline, or when the demands of my new job made it difficult to focus on the book. Ann was always there to keep the project on track and to pick up the slack when things got a bit crazy on my end. This is a much better book than it would have been because of Ann's contributions and hard work.

I also want to thank my former colleagues at Utica College, especially Kim Landon and Cecilia Friend, who saw me through both the first edition and the first draft of the second edition, and whose friendship meant a lot to me during those Utica years. I miss seeing them every day. And, of course, my thanks goes to all the students I have taught over the years, some of whom still keep in touch with me and still insist on calling me "professor." (At this point in time, I let them know that "Joe" is just fine.) I learned a lot from my students, both inside and outside the classroom. I hope this book proves to be a useful learning tool for the next generation of public relations students.

Finally, thank you to my parents, who over the past two years kept saying "So, what's happening with the book?" Their faith in my abilities and constant encouragement kept me motivated. I'm lucky to have such terrific parents.

—*J.Z.*

I would not be writing this section had it not been for my co-author, Joseph Zappala, who graciously invited—with only a reference from a mutual friend to go on—a stranger to help with his textbook. Thank you, Joe, for your confidence in me and especially for your willingness to let me be a full partner in the writing process, which can be a deeply personal thing for the original author.

While my co-author was leaving academe to return to the professional world, I was leaving daily practice to enter academe. It has been my lifelong dream to teach at the college level and to someday publish a writing text. Knowing how important writing is to the practice of public relations, I wanted to do my part to ensure that future public relations practitioners developed strong writing skills. It is an area I'm passionate about, to which my students, both former and present, will attest. I thank them for letting me know (eventually) that although I demanded much from them and made grade deductions for misspellings and poor grammar, they are now better writers.

My deep appreciation goes to my faculty colleagues in the Department of Communication at the State University of New York College at Fredonia, who always expressed an interest in how the book was going, even though they must have gotten tired of my frenzied "I'm on deadline!" banter. Thank you for your support and indulgence.

As with everybody, my path to this point is the culmination of varied experiences and many influences along the way, beginning with my high school English teacher who talked me out of studying nursing in college because she thought I had a talent for writing. My father, T. Guy Reynolds, Jr., instilled in me a strong work ethic, a thirst for knowledge, the belief that job satisfaction comes before money, and the attitude that there wasn't anything I couldn't do—all attributes that allowed me to stretch my wings and try new things.

My thoughts on the practice of public relations have been honed through the years by every organization for which I have worked, by each coworker in those organizations, and especially others in the public relations field. Whether it was a formal presentation, casual conversation, or a discussion over lunch (and there were many of those), I have learned much from my colleagues and am grateful to the members of the Buffalo/Niagara chapter of the Public Relations Society of America for sharing their expertise. Special thanks goes to Ronald D. Smith, APR; Stanton H. Hudson, Jr., APR, Fellow PRSA; Donald J. Goralski, APR; and Bill Sledzik, APR, Fellow PRSA.

A project of this size takes time—time that is taken away from other things and, more importantly, other people. This book is dedicated to my family, who sacrificed their time so I could fulfill this dream. I cannot express how much their understanding has meant to me. Thank you to my children, Maggie and Stephen. I love you and am so proud of the adults you are becoming. And to my husband, Michael, a special thank you—I love you for all the things you have been, and all the things you are.

—A.C.

An Invitation

A textbook is much like a snapshot in time. Different trends develop, theories evolve, and new case studies are introduced almost as soon as the book is published. With this in mind, we encourage our readers to provide us with feedback on the text so we may continue to develop it into a useful tool in the future. Please send your comments to:

Joseph Zappala, APR
Director, Communications
Alumni Affairs & Development
Cornell University
55 Brown Rd.
Ithaca, NY 14850
jz76@cornell.edu

Ann Carden, APR
Assistant Professor, Communications
SUNY Fredonia
304 McEwen Hall
Fredonia, NY 14063
ann.carden@fredonia.edu

Public Relations Worktext

A Writing and Planning Resource

Second Edition

1

What Is Public Relations Writing?

"I don't know what real childbirth is like, but writing songs seems as close as I'm going to come."

—Billy Joel[1]

"I refuse to slap some stupid words on the stupid paper just so we have a stupid song finished."

—Suzanne Vega

You may think that songwriters and public relations writers have little in common. But songwriters, poets, novelists and other writers, including public relations writers, will tell you that writing is hard, even painful. Most writers know the frustration of staring at an empty computer screen or a blank sheet of paper, waiting for the right words to come, and public relations writers are no exception.

The songwriter faced with writer's block might take a long drive or meditate to stimulate the writing process. As a public relations writer, you don't always have that luxury. In a crisis, when you need to communicate quickly and accurately about a threatening situation, there's little time for leisurely drives or meditation. Consider, as well, that public relations professionals write for many different audiences, for many different media, and in many different forms and styles, sometimes all in the same day. This is no easy task.

Songwriters, like poets, novelists, sculptors and other artists, often create works that are deeply personal; they are not always creating a work of art to please someone else, but more so to express something important they need to say. This is not so for public relations writers. Public relations writing has an organizational purpose. It cannot just be "some stupid words on the stupid paper." You must write with the interests of a specific group of people in mind, and balance that with the interests of the organization you represent. Public relations writing succeeds when people respond by doing something your organization wants them to do, whether that be learning something you want

[1] *The Great Rock 'N' Roll Quote Book* (pp. 148–149), edited by Merritt Malloy, 1995, New York: St. Martin's Griffin.

them to learn, adopting an attitude or position you want them to adopt, taking a positive action you want them to take, or simply thinking good thoughts about the organization. Writing without such a purpose is a waste of time.

As a public relations writer, you are not aiming to create works of art. Don't make the mistake of thinking that good public relations writing is like a song, or like poetry or prose, full of descriptive phrasing and obscure thoughts. There are times when creative writing is necessary, but creativity should never overshadow what's most important about a public relations message: its ability to communicate information in a way that people will understand. It's about simple words and clear messages that inspire a desired change in thinking or behavior.

While those brochures and news releases you write may not be on the artistic level of a classic novel or an Academy Award-winning film script, they do require special skill and finesse. And that makes public relations writing a fine art.

What Is Public Relations?

Before discussing the role of a public relations writer, it's important to give that role some perspective by first defining the public relations function, and then explaining how public relations differs from and integrates with marketing and advertising (as illustrated in Exhibit 1.1). While each of these functions has a distinct purpose, they also work together and share the common goal of helping an organization communicate to its publics—groups that are critical to the organization's survival. Exhibit 1.2 presents some of the most current definitions of public relations by some of the industry's most respected educators and professionals. In sum, *public relations* is a strategic function that manages and builds relationships with an organization's publics through two-way communication. Public relations professionals promote two-way communication by providing an open flow of idea exchange, feedback, and information between an organization and its publics. They counsel management on how to best shape policy and establish programs that are mutually beneficial and sensitive to public concerns. Public relations builds goodwill and an understanding of organizational goals among various internal and external publics, to help the organization operate smoothly and conduct its business in a cooperative, conflict-free environment.

The goal of *marketing*, by contrast, is to develop, maintain and improve a product's market share; attract and satisfy customers; and cause a transaction in order to build profitability. Public relations professionals support marketing staff by providing promotional services. One common marketing communications activity is *publicity*, which may involve placing news stories in the media about products and services or arranging photo opportunities. The most common form of publicity is the news release, an announcement from an organization written in news style.

If a newspaper publishes your product news release, it does so at no cost to you. Once your publicity material is received by the media, however, you lose control of the content. The media is free to use it in any form they choose, or they can decide not to use it. This differs from *advertising*, which is paid promotional messages that you can control. When you supply an advertisement to the media, they run it as you've written

Exhibit 1.1 The Integration of Public Relations, Marketing, and Advertising

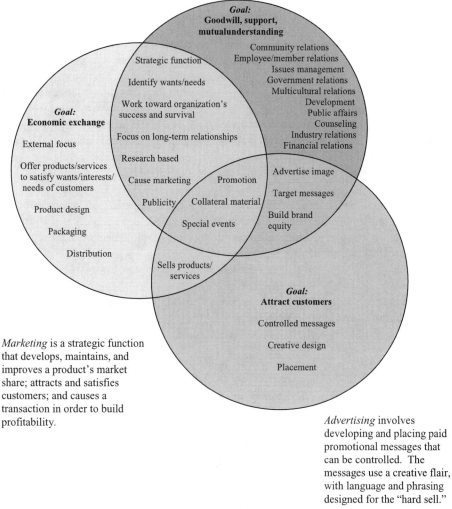

Public relations is a strategic function that manages and builds relationships with an organization's publics through two-way communication.

Goal: Goodwill, support, mutualunderstanding

Strategic function

Identify wants/needs

Work toward organization's success and survival

Focus on long-term relationships

Research based

Community relations
Employee/member relations
Issues management
Government relations
Multicultural relations
Development
Public affairs
Counseling
Industry relations
Financial relations

Goal: Economic exchange

External focus

Offer products/services to satisfy wants/interests/needs of customers

Product design

Packaging

Distribution

Cause marketing

Publicity

Promotion

Collateral material

Special events

Advertise image

Target messages

Build brand equity

Sells products/services

Goal: Attract customers

Controlled messages

Creative design

Placement

Marketing is a strategic function that develops, maintains, and improves a product's market share; attracts and satisfies customers; and causes a transaction in order to build profitability.

Advertising involves developing and placing paid promotional messages that can be controlled. The messages use a creative flair, with language and phrasing designed for the "hard sell."

it. Advertising copy has a creative flair, with language and phrasing designed for the "hard sell." Publicity materials are more subtle and read more like news articles. To illustrate the difference, look at the headline and lead from a product news release that appeared on Intel's Web site (www.intel.com/pressroom/archive/releases/nh040699.htm), and the headline and lead copy from an advertisement for the same Intel product:

Exhibit 1.2   Defining Public Relations

"Management of communication between an organization and its publics."

—Grunig and Hunt, *Managing Public Relations*

"The management function that establishes and maintains mutually beneficial relationships between an organization and publics on whom its success or failure depends."

—Cutlip, Center, and Broom, *Effective Public Relations*

"Public relations is a distinctive management function which helps establish and maintain mutual lines of communication, understanding, acceptance and cooperation between an organization and its publics; involves the management of problems or issues; helps management keep informed on and responsive to public opinion; defines and emphasizes the responsibility of management to serve the public interest; helps management keep abreast of and effectively utilize change, serving as an early warning system to help anticipate trends; and uses research and sound ethical communication techniques as its principal tools."

—Harlow, "Building a Public Relations Definition," *Public Relations Review*

"(1) Management function, (2) relationships between an organization and its publics, (3) analysis and evaluation through research, (4) management counseling, (5) implementation and execution of a planned program of action, communication and evaluation through research, and (6) achievement of goodwill."

—Simon, *Public Relations Concepts and Practices*

"(1) deliberate, (2) planned, (3) performance, (4) public interest, (5) two-way communication, and (6) management function."

—Wilcox, Ault and Agee, *Public Relations Strategies and Tactics*

"Public relations is the management function which evaluates public attitudes, identifies the policies and procedures of an individual or an organization with the public interest, and plans and executes a program of action to earn public understanding and acceptance."

—*Public Relations News*

Source: Joye C. Gordon, Public Relations Review, Spring 1997. Reprinted with permission of Public Relations Review.

Product News Release:

Intel Brings Powerful, Simple PC Networking to the Home

Intel Corporation today introduced the AnyPoint™ Home Network product line, which helps makes it easy for families with more than one PC to share Internet access, printers, files and games.

Product Advertisement:

Now, everyone gets to hog the Internet.

The AnyPoint™ Home Network connects all your PCs to the Internet simultaneously. So your entire family can surf at the same time. And you don't need a new Internet account. Or a new phone line . . . .

In addition to supporting the marketing function with promotional efforts, public relations practitioners offer advice on the social implications of products and help counter attacks from consumer and special interest groups. For example, some years ago tuna companies faced protests from environmental groups concerned about the number of dolphins getting trapped and killed in nets used by tuna fishermen. Protests and negative media headlines created a serious public relations problem which, in turn, had an impact on product sales. To regain public trust, tuna companies opened up dialogue with environmentalists and began making changes in their fishing practices to avoid doing harm to dolphins. After these changes were made and communicated, tuna companies began declaring their products "dolphin safe" and restoring their reputations through good public relations, while avoiding a marketing disaster.

Types of Public Relations Writing

Public relations writers are among the most versatile of writers. While a magazine journalist writes each article for a single mass audience—the people who read that magazine—the public relations writer prepares many pieces with many distinct publics in mind. A corporate public relations professional, for example, writes for employees, customers, media, and stockholders, all requiring different writing formats and message content. Among the types of writing assignments handled by public relations professionals are:

- *Business correspondence*—internal memos that inform others in the organization about the status of projects and other subjects, external business letters that confirm agreements and solicit support, and proposals to clients and internal supervisors that outline recommended public relations campaigns.
- *Corporate and internal communications*—news and feature stories for publication in newsletters, company magazines, and other employee publications; scripts for training and corporate video programs; content for Web sites and intranets; and annual reports directed to shareholders and the financial community.
- *Publicity writing*—news releases, background materials, and other written pieces designed to produce print and broadcast media coverage.
- *Marketing communications*—written materials that support marketing efforts, product promotion, and customer relations such as product publicity, product brochures and catalogs, posters and fliers, sales literature, direct mail pieces, and customer newsletters.

- *Advocacy writing*—writing that establishes a position or comments on an issue, endorses a cause or rallies support such as letters to the editor and articles sent to the opinion pages of print media; speeches written for executives that are delivered at industry conferences, media events, or business meetings; and corporate or "image" advertising that "sells the company," not a specific product (e.g., a corporate ad from a utility company publicly thanking the community for its patience during a power outage).

Communication and the Public Relations Writer

Public relations writing, regardless of what the specific piece is or who it is written for, is always purposeful. Its primary goal is to communicate information that will influence people. Mass communication literature identifies four mass communication goals that also have relevance to public relations writing:

- To *inform* people of threats and opportunities and to help them better understand their environment;
- To *teach* skills, knowledge, and appropriate behavior that help people adapt to their environment and feel accepted;
- To *persuade* people to adopt desired behaviors and see them as acceptable; and
- To *please* people by providing entertainment and enjoyment.

These goals have much in common with those of the public relations writer, especially the first three—to inform, to teach, and to persuade. Some public relations writing certainly has entertainment value. For example, many college public relations and communication programs across the country produce alumni newsletters. Graduates say they enjoy reading the newsletter and especially like knowing what former classmates are doing, if they have changed jobs, gotten engaged or married, had babies, or received an award for their work.

But, in addition to entertainment, this information has greater value. Publishing alumni updates helps graduates stay connected to one another and to the program. Over time, this builds loyalty and support and increases the perceived value of their college degree. The newsletter is more than just an interesting, entertaining read. It has a positive, long-term influence as a communication vehicle.

Like any good communicator, public relations writers must get feedback from their targeted publics to measure the true success of their efforts. The receiver of the message must respond in some way to indicate the message was received, processed, and understood. If you send a news release to a newspaper and the newspaper publishes the release, have you communicated with your public? Not necessarily. You have merely interested an editor enough in the subject to use the material. You can estimate the potential number of people who may have read the story by looking at the circulation figures for the newspaper. But you cannot assume that communication took place, or that people even saw your message, unless they tell you. If the goal of your news release is to inform and to encourage people to learn more about a subject, include a toll-free number in the release and ask them to "call for more information." This technique generates feedback you can measure and provides some assurance that communication occurred.

Public relations theorists and behavioral scientists point out that the traditional S-M-R communications model—sending a message through a specific channel to a desired receiver—is not effective if the intent of communication is to change behavior. They say this model is best used for publicity and awareness building. It is most effective when sending information to people who have little resistance to your message, like consumers who already use and like your product and whose positive feelings are simply reinforced through the communication. But if the goal is to get people to form an opinion, or to reduce negative public opinion, building awareness alone is not enough.

According to the diffusion of innovations theory, people adopt new ideas as the result of a five-step process that begins with *awareness*. They must first learn about the idea. Next, they must develop further *interest* in the idea and gather additional information on the subject. Then come *evaluation* and *trial*, weighing the pros and cons of the idea and discussing it with others, followed by testing the idea to see how well it fits into their lives. If the trial is successful, the result is *adoption* of the idea.

Think about buying a car. You might first see a television ad or article in the "Auto" section of the newspaper about a particular model (awareness). Thinking this car has potential, you visit a Web site, collect brochures, and read *Consumer Reports* to get more details (interest). With more information in hand, you talk to associates at work, people you know who own the car, and maybe parents to get their opinions of the car's quality, value, and performance. You also look carefully at your budget to determine if this is a realistic purchase (evaluation). Their positive remarks may motivate you to visit a dealer, talk to a salesperson about the car, and take a test drive (trial). After negotiating an agreeable price, you buy the car (adoption). The late Patrick Jackson, one of the most widely known and respected public relations practitioners, developed a behavioral model of communication to explain this process as it relates to public relations (see Exhibit 1.3). According to this model, once people are aware of a product, service, or issue, they will begin to formulate a readiness to act; an event then triggers this readiness into actual behavior.

As the car example shows, publicity and public relations writing have the greatest impact in the awareness and interest stages. Well-placed media articles about the car, a creative Web site, and informative brochures, all produced by public relations writers,

Exhibit 1.3   Jackson's Behavioral Communication Model

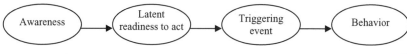

Note: Reprinted with permission of *pr reporter*, Ragan Communications, Inc.

play a significant role. However, these written tools become less influential in the later stages when personal communication and the opinions of family, friends, and peers have the most impact; it is important to keep this in perspective. Public relations writing plays a part in the acceptance of new ideas and behavioral change early in the process, but face-to-face communication and personal experience make the difference in the end. In addition, your written materials are competing with those of other organizations for someone's attention, so these pieces must do more than just communicate—they must communicate persuasively.

Persuasion and the Public Relations Writer

Persuasion is not a dirty word. "Persuade" means influence, move, motivate, convince, win over. Those aren't bad words. When you think about it, many of the things you say or do as a college student in an average day—asking your roommate if you can borrow her car, calling your parents in hopes they will send money, convincing your professor to extend an assignment deadline—are all done in an effort to influence, motivate, or persuade. Persuasion "goes bad" when you purposely mislead someone or tell a lie to get what you want. If you tell your parents you need extra cash to buy some textbooks, but they find out you used the money to buy a DVD player for your dorm room, those checks from home will probably stop coming.

Some people may perceive persuasion as negative because they confuse it with propaganda. While persuasion and propaganda may use similar techniques, such as symbols, stereotypes, and testimonials, the goal of *persuasion* is to provide new information or existing information in a fresh light to enable people to make up their own minds. *Propaganda*, on the other hand, seeks to manipulate the public's thinking by deliberately providing misinformation.

Public relations professionals are in the persuasion business. They are advocates for their organizations; every conversation, every proposal, every media event, and every piece of writing is intended to influence, build rapport, and win support. But winning support at any cost is never an option. There may be pressure to twist facts, omit details, or say something that just isn't true, but *do not bow to that pressure*. Once trust is lost, it is hard to regain. In a statement made at Utica College when he delivered the Harold Burjon Distinguished Lecture, John Reed, an international public relations consultant and veteran practitioner, defined public relations as "ethical persuasion." Keep that definition in mind as a writer, communicator, and protector of an organization's reputation—and your own.

There are honest and reasonable techniques to make communication more persuasive. Messages that genuinely appeal to a public's self-interests, that come from trusted sources, and that suggest a beneficial course of action can be highly persuasive. These principles are illustrated in The Air Bag Safety Campaign launched by the National Safety Council. In response to an increasing number of automobile air-bag-related fatalities, the campaign stressed the importance of properly restraining children under 12 when riding in a car.

Public opinion research showed that many parents did not know the risks air bags posed to their children, and that the majority of parents did not take the necessary steps to buckle up their children. In addition, national crash test data confirmed that the greatest risk was not the air bags themselves but the potential for injury should an air bag deploy when someone is riding without a seat belt. The campaign appealed to the most fundamental of interests: parents' desires to protect the lives of their children.

The campaign, "Air Bag Safety Means: Buckle Everyone! Children in the Back," or the ABC's of air bag safety, communicated a simple and clear call to action. The key message was, if you and your children use seat belts, you can avoid injury and a possible air-bag-related fatality. Information provided to adult drivers also clearly explained how air bags work and what can happen if someone is unrestrained and too close to the air bag when it deploys. To strengthen message impact, the National Safety Council partnered with professional organizations such as The American Academy of Family Physicians, The National Highway Traffic Safety Administration, and respected safety groups to help educate drivers about air bag safety. The campaign led to a significant increase in the number of adult drivers properly restraining children before transporting them in cars and thus to a reduced number of air bag fatalities. Follow-up surveys indicated greater awareness of the risks of air bags. Here are other tips for persuasive communication that are supported by behavioral research:

- Use a blend of rational and emotional messages. The National Safety Council's campaign shared facts, statistics, and results of air bag safety public opinion research, but it also used the media to publish stories about individual tragedies. This made the problem real; it added a human face to the problem to which other families could relate. Generally, messages directed to high-involvement audiences—those already connected to or inclined to support your organization or cause—might call for a more rational or factual approach. Low-involvement groups may need to be targeted with more emotional messages.

- Select the most appropriate media based on message content and the preferences of your target publics. Print media is best when attempting to explain complex subjects, but visual messages usually have greater influence on attitude change. Know your public and how it prefers to receive information. The fire department of a northeast city, concerned about the growing number of inner-city fires, provided information to local newspapers in hopes of educating residents about fire safety, but with minimal effect. Upon closer inspection, the department discovered a high rate of illiteracy among residents in those areas of the city where fires broke out most often. This prompted a change in strategy that involved using more face-to-face communication and broadcast media.

- Begin and end your writing with the most important messages. Studies indicate that people have higher recall of information that appears in the opening and closing of a message.

At the start of this chapter, we described public relations writing as a fine art, one requiring special skill—a skill that can be learned. To hone that skill, public relations writers must know all aspects of their organizations; have in-depth understanding of their publics and the media that reach those publics; possess finely tuned research skills and expertise in communication and persuasion theory; and be creative, strategic thinkers who can take complex, detailed material and make it simple and easy to understand. Despite their differences, the art of public relations writing and the art of songwriting may not be so different after all. As country musician and songwriter Steve Earle points out: "It's important to me to make sure the average person can understand what I'm trying to say. Songwriting at its best is very rarely poetry; it's usually narrative and practically journalism. It's a form of literature, but one you can consume while you're driving your car" (Malloy, 1995).

References and Suggested Reading

Caywood, C.L. (1997). *The handbook of strategic public relations and integrated communications*. New York: McGraw Hill.

Cutlip, S., Center, A., & Broom, G. (1999). *Effective public relations* (8th ed.). Upper Saddle River, NJ: Prentice Hall.

Gordon, J.C. (1997). Interpreting definitions of public relations: Self assessment and a symbolic interactionism-based alternative. *Public Relations Review, 23 (1)*, 57–66.

Grunig, J.E. (Ed.) (1992). *Excellence in public relations and communication management*. Hillsdale, NJ: Lawrence Erlbaum Associates.

Jackson, P. (1990). *Pr reporter, 33 (30)*, 1–2.

Kitchen, P.J. (1997). *Public relations: Principles & practice*. Stamford, CT: International Thomson Business Press.

Lesly, P. (1998). *Lesly's handbook of public relations and communications* (5th ed.). St. Louis, MO: McGraw Hill/Contemporary Books.

Malloy, M. (Ed.). (1995). *The Great Rock 'N' Roll Quote Book*. New York: St. Martin's Griffin.

Newsom, D., Turk, J.V., & Kruckeberg, D. (2000). *This is PR: The realities of public relations* (7th ed.). Belmont, CA: Wadsworth.

Seitel, F.P. (2001). *Practice of public relations* (8th ed.). New York: Prentice Hall.

Smith, R. (2002). *Strategic planning for public relations*. Mahwah, NJ: Lawrence Erlbaum Associates.

Wilcox, D., Ault, P.H., Agee, W.K., & Cameron, G.T. (2001). *Essentials of public relations*. New York: Longman.

Wilson, L. (2000). *Strategic program planning for effective public relations campaigns* (3rd ed.). Dubuque, IA: Kendall/Hunt Publishing Company.

Tips from the Top[2]

"The Art of Public Relations Writing"
Christopher Dobens

Christopher Dobens is former head of the Los Angeles office of Creamer Dickson Basford, a leading public relations firm. He discusses his views on the art of effective public relations writing, and offers practical advice on how to be a better writer.

Q: Describe the different types of public relations writing you have done in your career.

A: Of all the communications skills in public relations, writing is the most important. I have written such a variety of things that it is impossible to remember all of them. Here's what I can recall: memos and letters; press releases, backgrounders, fact sheets and media alerts; newsletters, bylines and technical articles; position papers, speeches, and presentations; brochures, ads, and annual report copy; and video scripts.

Perhaps the lesson to be learned is everything you write is important. I recently wrote an e-mail to a particular management level within our company. I spent a lot of time crafting it because I wanted to influence specific individuals without offending others. No matter what you write, it should be given an equal amount of thought and effort.

Q: How do you know when you have read a good piece of writing? What distinguishes it from not-so-good writing?

A: In general, when writing is good, you won't even notice it. It is unobtrusive—much like a good PR person. It is also clear and concise, so that the reader isn't left with any uncertainty as to the focus or meaning. Unfortunately, that last sentence is a bad example!

However, there are occasions where it makes sense for writing to stand out, such as when it is clever. For example, I once spiced up a headline simply by playing off a famous Elvis Presley album title. Instead of saying that the company sold its 100,000th cable modem, I suggested that it read "100,000 Cable Modem Users Can't Be Wrong." This works because it communicates the same message in a more memorable way—without sacrificing clarity.

Q: In a *Public Relations Tactics* article, you claim that writing and, specifically, good public relations writing, is a "lost art." What do you mean by that statement?

A: Good writing is an art because, unlike a science, formulas and rules don't always apply. Yes, one must abide by the accepted rules of grammar and things

---

[2] All "Tips from the Top" pieces are interviews conducted by J. Zappala.

like AP style, but there is much more to creating good writing. It's the clear and concise communication of ideas, preferably in an enlightening manner.

You can teach someone chemistry, but painting can't be taught—at least not in the same way. I look at writing as an art, in that you can learn the fundamentals but the rest must be developed on your own. How? Practice, practice, practice.

I call it a lost art because people seem to think writing is a science. In science, one simply must follow rules to find a logical conclusion. That's not the path to great writing. It's really sad what I am seeing these days. It's all "connect the words" writing, as if everything can be written by formula. That makes writing difficult to teach. That's why good writers are scarce these days. PR writers need to learn how to write by more than "formula" alone.

Q: How has the growth of the Internet and online communication affected the art of writing?

A: I think that the Internet has damaged the art of writing. It's ironic, because you'd think a writer would welcome the return of communication between individuals. The telephone had rendered the letter nearly obsolete. But now, with e-mail, people are once again using writing to communicate with each other. But is it really writing?

For some reason, people seem to think that the traditional rules of writing do not apply to e-mails and other online forms of communication. It's not a simple relaxing of the rules, but rather a complete abandonment of them. Sometimes you're lucky to find a complete sentence, let alone proper grammar. The only punctuation you'll find is cute smiley faces, which are used by people too lazy to convey the emotional frame of reference through the written word. Imagine if Mark Twain put a :) at the end of a sentence any time he wanted the reader to know that he was kidding or being sarcastic? A sad thought indeed.

And forget spelling. Spell check is much easier than flipping through a dictionary, yet few people will take the nanosecond required to use it. I use spell check and grammar check on all my documents. Unfortunately, I only have spell-check available on my e-mail program.

Q: What about creativity, humor, and the art of public relations writing? How do you use those elements most effectively?

A: Building on the "100,000 Cable Modem Users Can't Be Wrong" example, humor and creativity can be used to not only communicate but also to distinguish your point. The catch is knowing your audience. Humor and creativity are useless unless you know how your audience will react to it. For the cable modems, we felt that our target audience was "Baby Boomers" and older. A younger audience would likely be more computer-savvy, and therefore already understand the value of high-speed cable modems. We were comfortable in making the subtle reference to the famous Elvis Presley album title because it is something to which an older audience would likely relate. The other key here is subtlety. An overt effort to be funny and creative simply for the sake of being funny and creative is rarely welcome. Humor and creativity should only be used for a purpose, and used sparingly. Otherwise, the writing may not be taken seriously.

Q: **Every writer gets "blocked" at times and finds it difficult to start a writing project. What do you do when that happens? How do you "jump start" the writing process?**

A: I am sure that people will need to find their own individual solution, for we all get "blocked" for different reasons. There are times when I just don't know where to start. I'm usually facing a deadline and have either too much information or not enough. Sometimes I'm blocked because I don't understand new information, such as when I had to write about computer servers. Other times it's because I just don't want to understand the information, as is the case when I'm writing about dreadfully boring subjects such as insurance policies or real estate programs.

To overcome these situations I employ a method that is effective for me. When I read the information I have, I highlight all the key points. I then formulate each of these points into sentences—sometimes even paragraphs, depending on the content. I review all of these key points—now put into my own words—and develop an outline or framework for the piece I'm writing. At this point, it can be as simple as pasting the sentences and paragraphs into the outline and literally building the story around them. If I have the time, I will come back to it the following day and edit for flow and clarity. Otherwise, I will do it on the spot.

Often I find myself shutting off the computer and getting a good night's rest before tackling a tough writing assignment. I find that I am a much better writer in the morning, so I will gladly get up at 4 a.m. to start a piece rather than have to completely rewrite at 7 a.m. what I stayed up trying to write the night before.

Q: **What are some of the most common problems you see in written materials produced by entry-level and junior staff? What advice can you offer to help young professionals sharpen their writing skills?**

A: The most obvious problems are poor sentence structure and grammatical errors. New writers simply don't seem willing to take the time to review their own writing and proof it. When I started out, I partnered with a co-worker and we proofed each other's work before showing it to our supervisor. Everything we wrote was written to the best of our ability. It wasn't easy and it meant that we worked a little longer and a little harder, but that's the way it should be done.

The other problem I typically see is clarity. For example, sometimes you will find the lead of a press release buried at the bottom of the first page. Other times you may not be sure exactly what stance the writer is trying to take. While grammar and spelling can be solved by learning the rules and practicing them regularly, clarity takes a lot more time. It requires good editors, and good mentors, who are willing to take the time to not only show writers the right path but also to help them find their own voice.

My best advice is to find someone who is a good editor and an accessible mentor. Then listen, but also try to find your own voice, and practice until it sings.

2

Basics of Public Relations Writing

In the classic motion picture "All About Eve," considered one of the greatest films of all time by the American Film Institute, Academy-Award winning screen actress Bette Davis delivers one of the most memorable lines in movie history: "Fasten your seat belts, it's going to be a bumpy night." Davis also has something to say about public relations in the film "Hush, Hush, Sweet Charlotte." When responding to an on-screen character who works in the public relations field, Davis says: "Public relations? That sounds like something dirty."

Public relations writers have to master the fundamentals or they, too, will be in for a "bumpy" career. Another reality is that some media professionals and others in the business world still view public relations as a "dirty" business. So, every piece of writing you create says something about your professionalism and gives you an opportunity to change negative perceptions of the field. The first news release you write and send as a public relations professional, and every piece of writing thereafter, will help define your competence. If that release contains inaccurate information, misspelled words, or typographical errors, your credibility will be damaged. Your writing, then, has to be correct—legally and ethically correct, as well as grammatically correct. You should choose language and content that is sensitive to the diverse audiences with whom you communicate. Certain rules of style must be followed.

This chapter focuses on some of the fundamentals important to the public relations writer. It is not possible to provide an exhaustive review of this subject in just a few pages; you might also take a look at the suggested reading list for more information. What follows are highlights—key principles relating to public relations writing including the rules of grammar, style guidelines, cultural sensitivity, and legal and ethical considerations. We conclude with a short section on the importance of rewriting and proofreading.

Grammar

Public relations writing must be grammatically correct and easy to read. "20 Secrets of Good Writing" (Exhibit 2.1) provides a good blueprint for the basics of writing. Public

Exhibit 2.1   "20 Secrets of Good Writing"

20 Secrets of Good Writing

Among the compendia of good writing principles one of the best and most useful is this list compiled by Ken Roman and Joel Raphaelson of the advertising agency Ogilvy & Mather Worldwide. "20 Secrets of Good Writing" sets forth sound, easy-to-follow suggestions for improving one's writing.

When you are speaking for Ogilvy & Mather, your writing must meet our standards. These allow ample room for individuality and freshness of expression. But "personal style" is not an excuse for sloppy, unprofessional writing.

Here are some suggestions on how to improve your writing—20 principles that all good writers follow.

1. Keep in mind that the reader doesn't have much time.
What you write must be clear on first reading. If you want your paper to be read by senior people, remember that they have punishing schedules, evening engagements, and bulging briefcases.

The shorter your paper, the better the chance it will be read at high levels. During World War II, no document of more than one page was allowed to reach Churchill's desk.

2. Know where you are going—and tell the reader. Start with an *outline* to organize your argument.
Begin important paragraphs with topic sentences that tell what follows. Conclude with a summary paragraph.

An outline not only helps the reader; it keeps you from getting lost en route. Compile a list of all your points before you start.

3. Make what you write easy to read.
For extra emphasis, underline entire sentences.
Number your points, as we do in this section.

Put main points into indented paragraphs like this.

4. Short sentences and short paragraphs are easier to read than long ones. Send telegrams, not essays.

5. Make your writing vigorous and direct.
Wherever possible use active verbs, and avoid the passive voice.

Passive	Active
We are concerned that if this recommendation is turned down, the brand's market share may be negatively affected.	We believe you must act on this recommendation to hold the brand's share.

6. Avoid clichés.
Find your own words.

Cliché	Direct
Turn over every rock for a solution	Try hard
Put it to the acid test	Test thoroughly
Few and far between	Few
Last but not least	Last
Iron out	Remove

7. Avoid vague modifiers such as "very" and "slightly." Search for the word or phrase that *precisely* states your meaning.

(continued)

Vague	Precise
Very overspent	Overspent by $1,000
Slightly behind schedule	One day late

8. Use specific concrete language.

Avoid technical jargon, what E. B. White calls "the language of mutilation."

There is always a simple, down-to-earth word that says the same thing as the show-off fad word or the abstraction.

Jargon	Plain English
Parameters	Limits, boundaries
Implement	Carry out
Viable	Practical, workable
Interface	To talk with
Optimum	Best
Meaningful	Real, actual
To impact	To affect
Resultful	Effective, to have results
Finalize	Complete
Judgmentally	I think
Input	Facts, information
Output	Results
It is believed that with the parameters that have been imposed by your management, a viable solution may be hard to find. If we are to impact the consumer to the optimum, further interface with your management may be the most meaningful step to take.	We believe that the limits your management gave us may rule out a practical solution. If we want our consumer program to succeed, maybe we ought to talk with your management again.

9. Find the right word. Know its precise meaning.

Use your dictionary, and your thesaurus.

Don't confuse words like these:

To "affect" something is to have an influence on it. (The new campaign affects few attitudes.)	"Effect" can mean to bring about (verb) or a result (noun). (It effected no change in attitudes, and had no effect.)
"It's" is the contraction of "it is." (It's the advertising of P&G.)	"Its" is the possessive form of "it" and does *not* take an apostrophe. (Check P&G and its advertising.)
"Principal" is the first in rank or performance. (The principal competition is P&G.)	"Principle" is a fundamental truth or rule. (The principle behind competing with P&G is to have a good product.)
"Imply" means to suggest indirectly. (The writer implies it won't work.)	"Infer" means to draw meaning out of something. (The reader infers it won't work.)
"i.e." means "that is."	"e.g." means "for example."

When you confuse words like these, your reader is justified in concluding that you don't know better. Illiteracy does not breed respect.

10. Don't make spelling mistakes.

When in doubt, check the dictionary. If you are congenitally a bad speller, make sure your final draft gets checked by someone who isn't thus crippled.

If your writing is careless, the reader may reasonably doubt the thoroughness of your thinking.

11. Don't overwrite or overstate.

Use no more words than necessary. Take the time to boil down your points.

Remember the story of the man who apologized for writing such a long letter, explaining that he just didn't have the time write a short one.

The Gettysburg Address used only 266 words.

12. Come to the point.

Churchill could have said, "The position in regard to France is very serious." What he did say was, "The news from France is bad."

Don't beat around the bush. Say what you think—in simple, declarative sentences. Write confidently.

13. State things as simply as you can.

Use familiar words and uncomplicated sentences.

(continued)

14. Handle numbers consistently.
Newspapers generally spell out numbers for ten and under, and use numerals for 11 and up.

Don't write M when you mean a thousand, or MM when you mean a million. The reader may not know this code. Write $5,000—not $5M. Write $7,000,000 (or $7 million)—not $7MM.

15. Avoid needless words.
The songwriter wrote, "Softly as in a morning sunrise"—and Ring Lardner explained that this was as opposed to a late afternoon or evening sunrise. Poetic license may be granted for a song, but not for phrases like these:

Don't write	Write
Advance plan	Plan
Take action	Act
Have a discussion	Discuss
Hold a meeting	Meet
Study in depth	Study
New innovations	Innovations
Consensus of opinion	Consensus
At the present time	Now
Until such time as	Until
In the majority of instances	Most
On a local basis	Locally
Basically unaware of	Did not know
In the area of	Approximately
At management level	By management
With regard to	About, concerning
In connection with	Of, in, on
In view of	Because
In the event of	If
For the purpose of	For
On the basis of	By, from
Despite the fact that	Although
In the majority of instances	Usually

Always go through your first draft once with the sole purpose of deleting all unnecessary words, phrases, and sentences. David Ogilvy has improved many pieces of writing by deleting entire paragraphs, and sometimes even whole pages.

16. Be concise, but readable.
Terseness is a virtue, if not carried to extremes. Don't leave out words. Write full sentences, and make them count.

17. Be brief, simple and natural.
Don't write, "The reasons are fourfold." Write, "There are four reasons."

Don't start sentences with "importantly." Write, "The important point is . . ."

Don't write "hopefully" when you mean "I hope that." "Hopefully" means "in a hopeful manner." Its common misuse annoys a great many literate people.

Never use the word "basically." It can always be deleted. It is a basically useless word.

Avoid the hostile term "against," as in "This campaign goes against teenagers." You are not *against* teenagers. On the contrary, you want them to buy your product. Write, "This campaign addresses teenagers," or "This campaign is aimed at teenagers."

18. Don't write like a lawyer or a bureaucrat.
"Re" is legalese meaning "in the matter of," and is never necessary.

The slash—as in and/or—is bureaucratese. Don't write, "We'll hold the meeting on Monday and/or Tuesday." Write, "We'll hold the meeting on Monday or Tuesday—or both days, if necessary."

19. Never be content with your first draft.
Rewrite, with an eye toward simplifying and clarifying. Rearrange. Revise. Above all, cut.

Mark Twain said that writers should strike out every third word on principle: "You have no idea what vigor it adds to your style."

For every major document, let time elapse between your first and second drafts—at least overnight. Then come at it with a questioning eye and a ruthless attitude.

The five examples that follow were taken from a single presentation. They show how editing shortened, sharpened, and clarified what the writer was trying to say.

(continued)

First Draft	Second Draft
Consumer perception of the brand changed very positively.	Consumer perception of the brand improved.
Generate promotion interest through high levels of advertising spending.	Use heavy advertising to stimulate interest in promotions.
Move from product advertising to an educational campaign, one that would instruct viewers on such things as . . .	Move from product advertising to an educational campaign on such subjects as . . .
Using the resources of Ogilvy & Mather in Europe, in addition to our Chicago office, we have been able to provide the company with media alternatives they had previously been unaware of.	Ogilvy & Mather offices in Europe and Chicago showed the company media alternatives it hadn't known about.
Based on their small budget, we have developed a media plan which is based on efficiency in reaching the target audience.	We developed a media plan that increases the efficiency of the small budget by focusing on prospects.

20. Have somebody else look over your draft. All O&M advertising copy is reviewed many times, even though it is written by professional writers. Before David Ogilvy makes a speech, he submits a draft to his partners for editing and comment.

What you write represents the agency as much as an advertisement by a creative director or a speech by a chairman. They solicit advice. Why not you?

■

(Reprinted from Ogilvy and Mather Worldwide.)

relations educators would attest that they have seen students year after year make many of the same mistakes in spelling, punctuation, and sentence structure. The following is an additional checklist to help improve your writing:

Spelling

- We learned it in grade school and it still applies most of the time: "i" before "e" (retrieve) except after "c" (receive). When adding a prefix that creates a double consonant (e.g., unnatural, misspell), do not drop a letter.
- If you add a prefix to a word that creates a double vowel, then you generally include a hyphen between the two vowels (e.g., re-establish).
- When you add a suffix to words ending in "e," you usually drop the "e" (e.g., true/truly). There are some exceptions (e.g., knowledgeable).

Punctuation

- Use a comma to separate a dependent clause (not as important as the main idea) from a main clause (the main idea); also include a comma before a conjunction (and, but, or) that separates two main clauses:

- ○ After she graduated from *college, Sue* accepted a job with a public relations firm.
- ○ Sue graduated from college in *May, and* she accepted a job with a public relations firm.
- Commas are used to separate descriptive phrases and supplemental or "add-on" thoughts that could be deleted without changing the meaning of the sentence.
  - ○ Sue, who served as senior class president, graduated from college in May.
- Semi-colons are used to connect two complete thoughts that form a single compound sentence, but without the use of "and" or some other conjunction:
  - ○ Sue graduated with a public relations degree in May; she plans to move to New York City and work for a public relations firm.
- If words such as "however" or "therefore" are used to connect thoughts, use a semi-colon before the word and a comma after:
  - ○ Sue graduated with a public relations degree in May; however, she will leave the area and begin her career in New York City.
- For a single full-sentence quote, use a comma and place the attribution before or after the quote:
  - ○ Sue said, "I'm excited about starting my job at the public relations firm."
  - ○ "I'm excited about starting my job at the public relations firm," said Sue.
- If the quote is more than one sentence, place the attribution before the quote and use a colon, or place the attribution in between sentences:
  - ○ Sue said: "I'm excited about starting my job at the public relations firm. The people there were impressed with my writing and editing skills so I'm glad I paid attention and worked hard in the public relations writing class."
  - ○ "I'm excited about starting my job at the public relations firm," said Sue. "The people there were impressed with my writing and editing skills so I'm glad I paid attention and worked hard in the public relations writing class."
- Always place the attribution in front of a partial quote:
  - ○ Sue said she was glad she "paid attention and worked hard in the public relations writing class."
- Use a hyphen to connect two words that describe something or someone; do not hyphenate if the first descriptive word ends in "y" (e.g., well-respected professional, highly respected writer). Know that certain words (e.g., firsthand, marketplace) are not hyphenated.

Sentence Structure

- Subjects and verbs must agree; identify the subject as singular or plural, and make sure the corresponding verb matches:
  - ○ *None* (singular subject) of the media *is* coming (singular verb) to the event.
  - ○ The *media* (plural subject) *are* not coming (plural verb) to the event.

- Nouns and pronouns must correspond; singular subjects/nouns require singular matching pronouns:
  - The *company* (singular) changed *its* policy after employees expressed concerns.
  - The *board* (singular) of directors made *its* decision at the annual meeting.
  - The board *members* (plural) voiced *their* opinions about the issue.
- Related thoughts or phrases included in a single sentence should have like form—ask yourself if you are using the same verb tenses:
  - Incorrect: Sue *enjoys attending* the PRSA conference and *likes to meet* other professionals.
  - Correct: Sue *enjoys attending* the PRSA conference and *likes meeting* other professionals.
- Use active rather than passive voice in your writing to make ideas direct and crisp; try keeping the "to be" tense to a minimum to make your writing more active:
  - Passive: *It was suggested by the client* that the firm do some research.
  - Active: *The client asked* the firm to do some research.
  - Passive: *The issue is being discussed* by staff members at the meeting.
  - Active: *Staff members are discussing* the issue at the meeting.

Word Usage

- Use "that" and "which" carefully. "That" is used to identify a specific, individual item and is not preceded by a comma; "which" introduces an extra fact about the item and is preceded by a comma. Use "who" when referring to a person, not "that" or "which." (Note: Using "that" makes writing smoother and more active; you can often avoid using "which.")
  - The Web site *that* Sue created is interactive and easy to read.
  - The Web site, *which* was created by Sue, is interactive and easy to read.
  - People *who* visit the Web site say it is interactive and easy to read.

- Make sure you are using the proper word form:
  - They're hoping to raise $10,000 at the event. ("They're" is short for "they are.")
  - Their goal is to raise $10,000 at the event. ("Their" shows possession; the goal belongs to them.)

Simplicity

In addition to using correct grammar, the public relations writer must write simply. To maintain simplicity in your writing:

- Keep sentences short. Experts recommend sentences that average 17 words or so, give or take a few words. That doesn't mean you should count the words in each sentence to see if you exceed the 17-word limit. If a sentence seems too long and thoughts get hard to follow, write two sentences instead of one. When writing more lengthy articles, you will want to use some longer sentences to avoid choppiness and monotony for the reader. Short introductory sentences will ease readers into the piece and encourage them to read further.

- Use words that the average person would know. You are not writing to impress people with your mastery of vocabulary. Always choose the more familiar word with the fewest letters and syllables. There are times when you will write for people who work in the medical field, the financial community, or some other specialized area. In those instances, it is acceptable to use a few technical words common to that industry. Most people in the insurance field know what a "deductible" is, for example. Overall, however, keep the complex words and jargon to a minimum.

- Avoid redundancy. Delete extra words that have the same meaning, or that present the same idea in a different way. For example, don't write "bad crisis" (have you ever heard of a good crisis?) or "positive asset" (assets are benefits so how can they be negative?). When describing something, don't overstate. Consider this sentence: "Smith is well educated and has a doctorate in political science and a master's in history." Smith's degrees indicate that he is well educated so that phrase should be removed from the sentence.

- Don't write more than you need to. Writing concisely takes more skill than being longwinded. Be brief. This is especially true for online communications. If you are sending an e-mail message, try to write it so the full message appears on a single screen or, at least, so the most important part of the message does. Articles for an electronic newsletter should be a few sentences to a few short paragraphs for optimum readability. In public relations writing, "less is more."

In addition, every writer should own a copy of *The Elements of Style* by William Strunk and E.B. White, and keep it close to the computer. Strunk and White say it is good writing style to avoid "qualifier" words like "very" and "rather," and to use the simpler versus the "fancy" word: "Do not be tempted by a twenty-dollar word when there is a ten-center handy, ready and able."

Style

Effective writing also has style. How is style defined? In the fashion industry, some believe that fashion designers and celebrities dictate style trends. Others see style as more personal—clothes that make the individual feel and look good and that help the person establish a unique identity, regardless of what the "cool people" are wearing. For public relations writers, writing style is influenced by several factors, including generally accepted rules for good writing, the writing policies of an organization and its public relations department, and the type of public relations piece you are writing. You also develop your own personal style, one that comes across in the words you choose and the way you present them.

Style is also defined by the media and your employer. When writing for the media, public relations practitioners should follow *The Associated Press (AP) Stylebook and Libel Manual*, which is also used by journalists. However, you may choose to use separate style guidelines for organizational publications such as newsletters and other promotional materials. For example, the AP stylebook states that job titles should not be capitalized when used after a person's name, so you wouldn't write a news release and capitalize job titles throughout. For internal publications, however, your organization may adopt its own style, one in which it is preferred to capitalize job titles whenever they are used. The key is consistency—make sure each piece you write for the media follows AP style, and each article for an internal publication follows your organization's style. Examples of the some of the most frequently used guidelines from the AP stylebook appear in Exhibit 2.2.

Exhibit 2.2   Tips from the Associated Press Stylebook

Numbers and Money

- One through nine: Numbers less than 10 are spelled out.
- 10 and above: Use Arabic numerals for 10 and greater.
- 1st Ward *vs.* first base: Follow the same rule for ordinal numbers, unless the number is part of a formal name.
- Sentences and casual uses: Numbers used at the beginning of a sentence should be spelled out, even if that number is 10 or above. *Exception*: calendar years. References to numbers as part of a casual expression should be spelled out.
- $1: When writing about money, always use a dollar sign and Arabic numerals, even if the monetary value is less than 10.
- 50 cents: Monetary values less than $1 should be expressed in Arabic numerals and the word "cents" (no hyphen).
- 3%: Use Arabic numerals, even if the monetary value is less than 10, and spell out the word "percent."

Ages and Dimensions

- He is 5 feet 6 inches tall *vs.* the 5-foot-6-inch man: Use Arabic numerals and spell out "inches," "feet," etc. Use hyphens if the dimension is being used as an adjective.
- She is 8 years old vs. the 8-year-old girl: Ages also are expressed in Arabic numerals, even if the age is less than 10. Use hyphens if the age is being used as an adjective.

(continued)

Directions and Addresses

- West *vs.* west: Capitalize compass directions when referring to a region only.
- St., Ave., Blvd. vs. Road, Drive, Circle: When referring to addresses, abbreviate "street," "avenue," and "boulevard." All other names should be written out.
- 50 North St. *vs.* North Street. The above rule applies only when numbers are used as part of the address. If no numbers are used, do not use the abbreviations for "street," "avenue," and "boulevard."

States, Cities and Abbreviations

- Martinsburg, W.Va. *vs.* Denver: Most cities should appear with their state; however, larger cities may stand alone. These exempted cities are listed under "Datelines" in the stylebook.
- NY vs. N.Y. *vs.* New York: State abbreviations according to AP style are not the same as postal codes. One difference is that AP style abbreviations always include periods. State abbreviations should always be used when accompanying a city; state names should be spelled out if standing alone.
- Alaska, Hawaii, Idaho, Iowa, Maine, Ohio, Texas, Utah: There are seven states that are never abbreviated regardless of the circumstance–the states with five or less letters and the last two admitted to the United States.
- U.S. Department of Treasury *vs.* the United States: Abbreviate "United States" when it is being used as an adjective; spell it out if it is being used as a proper noun.
- NASA *vs.* C.R.A.P.: Periods are not necessary when abbreviating organizational names, unless the letters spell out a word that would misrepresent the organization.

Titles

- Formal *vs.* functional: Formal titles, which indicate an authoritative position, are capitalized when used before a person's name. They are not capitalized if used after the person's name. A functional title, which indicates a person's occupation, is not capitalized.
- President George Bush *vs.* president of the United States: Follow the rule for formal titles. "President" is capitalized when used with a name, but not capitalized when the title stands alone.
- Dr. *vs.* Ph.D.: Use "Dr." as a formal title when used before a name of someone who holds a medical degree. "Dr." also may be used as a formal title before a name of someone who holds a doctorate in a nonmedical field; however, the person's academic specialization should be referenced to avoid confusion.
- Movies, TV programs, and books *vs.* reference materials: The titles of creative works should be enclosed in quotation marks; reference books, such as encyclopedias, almanacs and dictionaries, should not.

Dates and Times

- January 2002 *vs.* Jan. 31, 2002: Months are abbreviated when they accompany a day; spell them out when they are standing alone. Do not use a comma between the month and the year.

(continued)

- 11 a.m. *vs.* 11 o'clock *vs.* 11:00: The preferred style for expressing the time of day is to use "a.m." and "p.m." *Caution*: If using this format, be careful not to be redundant by using "this morning" or "this evening." If you want to use these phrases, indicate the time of day followed by "o'clock." Never express the top of the hour with ":00."

Capitalization
- English department *vs.* history department: Academic and organizational departments should not be capitalized, unless there is a proper noun or adjective within the title.

Another factor that defines style is the type of piece written. A news release announcing a company merger should be written in **news** or **inverted pyramid** style. This means that the release begins with the most important information in the first few paragraphs and concludes with background material that isn't as crucial to the story (more on this in chapter 6). An article for a hospital publication that focuses on the special contributions of a volunteer is written in **feature style**, with quotes and interesting details that create a vivid picture of the volunteer's personality and humanity.

How the reader is addressed differs between news and feature style writing. For the most part, materials sent to the media are written in third person and avoid personal terms; however, when writing for a specific public, such as readers of employee newsletters or customer brochures, it is good style to keep messages personal and "you-focused." Let your writing talk directly to the reader. For example, "this product will help you and your family live longer, healthier lives." The use of "I" and "you" also is common in memos and e-mail communication to keep messages direct and personal.

There is a broader sense of style that applies to writing, as well. It relates to the language and techniques a writer uses—those qualities that identify a piece of writing with the person who wrote it. Think about your favorite musical artists or groups. There's probably something that characterizes them—the special sound of the electric guitars, the beat of the drums, the pitch of the singer's voice and how that singer holds a note, how a group's songs often begin and end a certain way, or common themes that run through an artist's music. Look at the work of newspaper columnists, and you'll see how each has a characteristic style. Syndicated columnist Dave Barry uses humor to comment on everything from political races to airline food and his columns are generally written in first person. This approach has become his trademark writing style.

Your public relations writing style may not be quite as obvious as the vocal style of your favorite singer, or as evident as your favorite painter's style of using shape and colors. Your style will come through in the way your feature articles set a scene, describe people, and use quotes; in the headlines and subheads you write for brochures and promotional pieces; and in the leads you develop for news releases. It's not something you will try hard to create; it will come about naturally and feel comfortable to you. People who read your writing will say, "I could almost hear you saying those words." Your writing style will be an expression of who you are, as a writer and a person.

Diversity, Bias, and Cultural Sensitivity

Today's workplace is no longer dominated by college-educated White males. Organizations must design internal and external communications for diverse audiences and people with varied lifestyles—Black and White, male and female, single parents and married persons, gay and straight, part-time and full-time workers. Marketers are also recognizing the value of targeting diverse groups. Some companies develop specific marketing communications programs to target the lifestyle and interests of the gay and lesbian community. Others reach out to the Hispanic population, which is one of the fastest-growing ethnic groups in the United States.

Public relations professionals must reflect this diversity in their writing, both in the language they use and the creative approaches they take. It is more gender-sensitive to use "chairperson" rather than "chairman." Women are not referred to as "girls," "gals," or "ladies." Instead of writing, "A public relations professional should know his audience," it is better to make the statement more inclusive:

A public relations professional should know his or her audience.

OR

Public relations professionals should know their audiences.

Writers can use "his" or "him"—they do not have to delete these pronouns from their vocabulary entirely. If the subject is male, then using words like "chairman" or "spokesman" is fine. When a subject could be a man or a woman (e.g., public relations professional), using the plural form of the subject makes good sense. When using singular pronouns, make sure you write "her" in some instances and "his" in others to achieve balance.

Some additional sensitive language: refer to senior citizens as "seniors" or "elderly," not as "old folks" or "blue-haired ladies." "Gay" is the preferred term for a homosexual male and "lesbian" is preferred for a homosexual woman; homosexual can be used for both. Persons with disabilities and serious illnesses should not be described as "victims," "crippled" or "suffering from a disease" to avoid characterizing them as helpless. Feature writers should take care when describing skin color and other physical attributes that might stereotype or offend racial and ethnic groups such as Native Americans, African Americans, and Italian Americans, among others. As a guideline, always ask yourself whether the information is necessary for the piece you are writing.

On a broader level, public relations writers must understand the culture of diverse groups. For example, AIDS public information campaigns directed to teens and minority groups have to take into account distinct aspects of those cultures, including long-held perceptions of the immoral nature of homosexuality and beliefs that AIDS is a "White gay man's disease."

Knowing your target audience also affects your method of delivery. A 2001 study by the U.S. Commerce Department showed significant increases in the total number of Americans who owned computers and used the Internet—an important means of public relations communication. However, fewer Blacks (37%) and Hispanics (40%) owned computers than Whites (61%) and Asians (73%). Income was not necessarily a factor; in White families with incomes of $15,000 to $35,000, more than 46% owned computers compared to 32% of Black families. Though one study alone does not necessarily provide the whole picture, these statistics suggest that using online communication to reach Asian consumers, for example, would most likely be effective, but that perhaps more traditional methods may have a greater impact on Blacks and Hispanics.

These examples demonstrate the significance of culture and lifestyle to effective writing and communication. Public relations writers cannot just assume which messages and media will produce the best results, especially when communicating with a population whose traditions and mindset may be unfamiliar. Research, including interviews, focus groups and surveys, can help increase cultural awareness and strengthen the impact of written materials and their messages.

Legal Issues

Perhaps the most unflattering comment a person could make about something you've written is, "It sounds like a lawyer wrote this." Now, this is not an attack on lawyers. The fact is, however, many legal documents are complex and hard to understand. While public relations professionals should avoid writing like lawyers, they do need to think like lawyers when preparing publicity and other written materials. For example, consider the following situations:

- A news release announces that a new drug is the most effective for reducing high cholesterol.
- A not-for-profit organization creates a series of public service announcements featuring the songs of pop music stars.
- A corporate public relations professional places the full text of a positive product review published in a trade journal on the company's Web site.
- A school system kicks off a campaign titled "Just Do It," aimed at increasing academic achievement.
- A story on a new company vice president is published in the employee newsletter accompanied by a photograph of the vice president and her family.

Now, which, if any, of these scenarios pose legal problems? If you guessed "none," you could be right. But if you guessed "all of them," you could be right, too. The product news release may be okay, if there is substantial scientific data and many reputable sources to support the "most effective" claim. If not, you may be in trouble with the Federal Trade Commission (FTC), a government agency that regulates fair trade practices and monitors advertising and corporate communications for false and misleading information.

Any communication that includes *"puffing"*—nonobjective and exaggerated claims that are hard to verify (e.g., "the one and only product of its kind")—is subject to investigation by the FTC. The FTC takes a special interest in prescription drugs and products that position themselves as safer than others, as well as messages directed to children and the elderly. You should also familiarize yourself with FTC guidelines for labeling something "environmentally friendly" and the evidence needed to support that claim. A not-so-obvious problem involves use of the word "new." The FTC says any product more than six months old cannot be described as new, unless the product is being test marketed. In that case, you can promote it as new up to six months after the product is introduced in its final form. In general, it's best to stay away from glittering generalities.

The second and third situations bring up the issue of *copyright* infringement. Copyright protects the unauthorized duplication of original, published work. Original work that is written, designed, or performed is automatically protected by copyright; it does not have to be registered as such. An article published in the newspaper is owned by that publication and is therefore subject to copyright law. Comments made by someone in an online discussion group technically become the property of that person once they appear on the screen and are protected by copyright.

Generally, you have to get the copyright owner's permission, and sometimes pay a fee, to reproduce copyright-protected work. Popular songs and published media articles are among the items protected by copyright law. So, you can't produce that public service announcement, with even a few seconds of a song, until you've secured permission from the record company, the artist, or whoever the copyright holder is. If you want to publish a media article in its entirety on your Web site, you must contact the publisher for approval first. *Reprints*—copies of the article made for you by the publication for a fee—can be obtained for mass distribution as well. Online services such as Dow Jones WebReprints (www. djreprints.com) allow you to order and distribute reprints by e-mail or display them on your Web site the same day an article is published. And if you're thinking about using an illustration of Bugs Bunny, Mickey Mouse, or some other cute cartoon character on promotional materials, don't do it until you've cleared it with the copyright owner.

A word about *fair use*, an aspect of copyright law important to public relations writers: the fair use rule permits you to use short passages from copyrighted works, without the author's permission—if the purpose of your writing is educational—to report news or to comment on an issue. For example, if a noted consumer group endorses your product in a national magazine article, you could use a brief quote from that magazine piece in an employee newsletter article as long as you cite the source (the name of the magazine, the publication date, and the name of the author of the piece). You cannot, however, reprint several paragraphs or an entire page of the article without permission. Using that same product quote in a sales brochure sent to prospective customers without first getting permission will most likely violate copyright since your company stands to gain financially from the sales piece. If the quote is two short sentences and the entire article is 2,000 words, permission may not be necessary, but you still might want to talk to your company's attorney about it. It is probably wise to get permission to use any copyright material in marketing communications pieces that support sales and profit-making.

Similar to copyrights are *trademarks*—symbols or words that are identified with a particular product or company. Trademarks, like Nike's "Just Do It" slogan are usually identified by ™ or ®. Trademarks are registered with the Patent and Trademark Office to protect the relationship between a product and its parent company. Trademark law also includes the protection of brand names. When you write names such as Kleenex®, Xerox® or Coke®, make sure you are not treating them generically.

What about the photo of the new vice president and her family? Any time public communication includes personal information, you risk invading someone's *privacy*. In this instance, you should obtain the vice president's permission to publish the photo because it relates to her private life. If the photograph was just a "head and shoulders" shot of the vice president only, then getting approval to use it would not be necessary, although it might be the polite thing to do (let's face it, we all want to look our best, right?). Still, obtaining written consent is a wise move when dealing with pictures of people and their personal information. This is especially important for public relations practitioners working in health care. The Health Insurance Portability and Accountability Act (HIPAA) requires that strict guidelines be followed when obtaining authorization from patients to use their photos and personal information.

You also need to be aware of *appropriation*—using photos of employees, celebrities, or others, or their likenesses, in advertisements and other materials designed to promote profit. Never do this without first getting written permission. In addition, it's probably wise to have employees read over, initial, and approve news releases before they are sent to the media. This way, you protect yourself against sending out inaccurate, sensitive, or inappropriate information.

Regarding the Internet, any original work published on the Internet is protected by copyright. So, if you reproduce an article from an electronic publication or download and distribute copy from someone's Web site without permission, you are probably violating copyright. Access the Cyberspace Law Center (www.cybersquirrel.com) and the Electronic Frontier Foundation (www.eff.org) to learn more about online electronic rights and copyright.

Ethical Issues

All professionals—lawyers, doctors, teachers, accountants—confront ethical dilemmas on the job. This is not exclusive to public relations work, although some still define the function based solely on perceptions that public relations people deceive and "cover up." Consider this definition of public relations: "an effort to gull, diddle, and otherwise bamboozle people into thinking that something is different from what they believe it to be. The public relations man tilts reality to suit his taste."

As you can probably tell, this quote from Playboy magazine is a bit dated. The use of "public relations man" instead of a nongender-specific phrase is a sure tip-off. The fact is, good public relations professionals don't "diddle." They gain credibility by advising companies to always tell the truth and by being honest communicators themselves, even in times of crisis. A public relations professional puts the best interests of an organization and its public first. Those who pursue a public relations career because they want to go to fancy parties, maybe meet celebrities, and be on TV should consider another occupation. Besides, most practitioners will tell you, it's not that glamorous; public relations is hard work.

The Member Code of Ethics of the Public Relations Society of America (PRSA) provides some guidance for communicating with integrity (Exhibit 2.3). Much of the battle, however, often takes place before anything is written or officially communicated. Do further research to substantiate that something is "one of a kind," rather than simply sending out that message because the "the boss told you so." Convince others that communicating bad news quickly is better than saying "no comment." Public relations professionals are advocates for organizations, but they should also be advocates for "doing the right thing."

Exhibit 2.3   PRSA Member Code of Ethics 2000

PRSA Member Statement of Professional Values

This statement presents the core values of PRSA members and, more broadly, of the public relations profession. These values provide the foundation for the Member Code of Ethics and set the industry standard for the professional practice of public relations. These values are the fundamental beliefs that guide our behaviors and decision-making process. We believe our professional values are vital to the integrity of the profession as a whole.

ADVOCACY
- We serve the public interest by acting as responsible advocates for those we represent.
- We provide a voice in the marketplace of ideas, facts, and viewpoints to aid informed public debate.

HONESTY
- We adhere to the highest standards of accuracy and truth in advancing the interests of those we represent and in communicating with the public.

EXPERTISE
- We acquire and responsibly use specialized knowledge and experience.
- We advance the profession through continued professional development, research, and education.
- We build mutual understanding, creditibility, and relationships among a wide array of institutions and audiences.

INDEPENDENCE
- We provide objective counsel to those we represent.
- We are accountable for our actions.

LOYALTY
- We are faithful to those we represent, while honoring our obligation to serve the public interest.

(continued)

FAIRNESS

- We deal fairly with clients, employees, competitors, peers, vendors, the media, and the general public.
- We respect all opinions and support the right of free expression.

PRSA Code Provisions

FREE FLOW OF INFORMATION

Core Principle
Protecting and advancing the free flow of accurate and truthful information is essential to serving the public interest and contributing to informed decision making in a democratic society.

Intent
- To maintain the integrity of relationships with the media, government officials, and the public.
- To aid informed decision making.

Guidelines
A member shall:

- Preserve the integrity of the process of communication.
- Be honest and accurate in all communications.
- Act promptly to correct erroneous communications for which the practitioner is responsible.
- Preserve the free flow of unprejudiced information when giving or receiving gifts by ensuring that gifts are nominal, legal, and infrequent.

Examples of Improper Conduct Under the Provision:
- A member representing a ski manufacturer gives a pair of expensive racing skis to a sports magazine columnist to influence the columnist to write favorable articles about the product.
- A member entertains a government official beyond legal limits or in violation of government reporting requirements.

COMPETITION

Core Principle
Promoting healthy and fair competition among professionals preserves an ethical climate while fostering a robust business environment.

(continued)

Intent

- To promote respect and fair competition among public relations professionals.
- To serve the public interest by providing the widest choice of practitioner options.

Guidelines

A member shall:

- Follow ethical hiring practices designed to respect free and open competition without deliberately undermining a competitor.
- Preserve intellectual property rights in the marketplace.

Examples of Improper Conduct Under This Provision:

- A member employed by a "client organization" shares helpful information with a counseling firm that is competing with others for the organization's business.
- A member spreads malicious and unfounded rumors about a competitor in order to alienate the competitor's clients and employees in a ploy to recruit people and business.

DISCLOSURE OF INFORMATION

Core Principle

Open communication fosters informed decision making in a democratic society.

Intent

- To build trust with the public by revealing all information needed for responsible decision making.

Guidelines

A member shall:

- Be honest and accurate in all communications.
- Act promptly to correct erroneous communications for which the member is responsible.
- Investigate the truthfulness and accuracy of information released on behalf of those represented.
- Reveal the sponsors for causes and interests represented.
- Disclose financial interest (such as stock ownership) in a client's organization.
- Avoid deceptive practices.

Examples of Improper Conduct Under this Provision:

- Front groups: A member implements "grass roots" campaigns or letter-writing campaigns to legislators on behalf of undisclosed interest groups.

(continued)

- Lying by omission: A practitioner for a corporation knowingly fails to release financial information, giving a misleading impression of the corporation's performance.
- A member discovers inaccurate information disseminated via a Web site or media kit and does not correct the information.
- A member deceives the public by employing people to pose as volunteers to speak at public hearings and participate in "grass roots" campaigns.

SAFEGUARDING CONFIDENCES

Core Principle
Client trust requires appropriate protection of confidential and private information.

Intent
- To protect the privacy rights of clients, organizations, and individuals by safeguarding confidential information.

Guidelines
A member shall:

- Safeguard the confidences and privacy rights of present, former, and prospective clients and employees.
- Protect privileged, confidential, or insider information gained from a client or organization.
- Immediately advise an appropriate authority if a member discovers that confidential information is being divulged by an employee of a client company or organization.

Examples of Improper Conduct Under This Provision:
- A member changes jobs, takes confidential information, and uses that information in the new position to the detriment of the former employer.
- A member intentionally leaks proprietary information to the detriment of some other party.

CONFLICTS OF INTEREST

Core Principle
Avoiding real, potential, or perceived conflicts of interest builds the trust of clients, employers, and the publics.

Intent
- To earn trust and mutual respect with clients or employers.
- To build trust with the public by avoiding or ending situations that put one's personal or professional interests in conflict with society's interests.

(continued)

Guidelines

A member shall:

- Act in the best interests of the client or employer, even subordinating the member's personal interests.
- Avoid actions and circumstances that may appear to compromise good business judgment or create a conflict between personal and professional interests.
- Disclose promptly any existing or potential conflict or interest to affected clients or organizations.
- Encourage clients and customers to determine if a conflict exists after notifying all affected parties.

Examples of Improper Conduct Under This Provision

- The member fails to disclose that he or she has a strong financial interest in a client's chief competitor.
- The member represents a "competitor company" or a "conflicting interest" without informing a prospective client.

ENHANCING THE PROFESSION

Core Principle

Public relations professionals work constantly to strengthen the public's trust in the profession.

Intent

- To build respect and credibility with the public for the profession of public relations.
- To improve, adapt, and expand professional practices.

Guidelines

A member shall:

- Acknowledge that there is an obligation to protect and enhance the profession.
- Keep informed and educated about practices in the profession to ensure ethical conduct.
- Actively pursue personal professional development.
- Decline representation of clients or organizations that urge or require actions contrary to this Code.
- Accurately define what public relations activities can accomplish.
- Counsel subordinates in proper ethical decision making.
- Require that subordinates adhere to the ethical requirements of the Code.
- Report ethical violations, whether committed by PRSA members or not, to the appropriate authority.

(continued)

Examples of Improper Conduct Under This Provision:
- A PRSA member declares publicly that a product the client sells is safe, without disclosing evidence to the contrary.
- A member initially assigns some questionable client work to a non-member practitioner to avoid the ethical obligation of PRSA membership.

∎

Note. Reprinted with permission of the Public Relations Society of America.

As a public relations writer, you will find yourself in some interesting situations, especially when dealing with the media. Take a look at the situations that follow:

- A news release on a company expansion includes a quote from the CEO that you created since the CEO was not available for an interview.
- A story idea is presented as an "exclusive" to a trade publication and a business newspaper.
- Your company invites reporters to its corporate headquarters to preview a new product line, and agrees to cover the reporters' travel expenses.

See any ethical problems? You're probably thinking, "I would never make up a quote and put it in a news release. That's wrong." But counseling someone on how to best frame a message and then working with the person to write that message is acceptable in public relations practice. The president of the United States, for example, has communication staff members who help write the words we hear in presidential speeches. Following a plane crash, airline public relations staff will work closely with top management to write an initial statement for the CEO that conveys the right sympathetic tone while also sticking to the facts to avoid legal repercussions. You will find that senior executives sometimes have difficulty articulating their thoughts. They rely on the expertise of public relations staff to find just the right words to convey points succinctly and sensitively. The challenge for public relations writers is to prepare simple, hard-hitting quotes and statements that reflect the personality of the source, that sound like real words that person would actually say, and that reinforce important public relations and organizational messages. Before any such quotes become public communication, make sure the source has the chance to review, revise, and approve what you've written.

The second example requires that you know what an exclusive is. The definition of *exclusive* is "select" or "unshared." When you promise an exclusive to a publication, that means no one else is getting that story at that time. You are giving that publication something special. From an ethical standpoint, you cannot tell one publication that it has exclusive rights to a story, and then offer that same exclusive to a second publication, in hopes that at least one of them will publish it. If, based on the example above, the trade journal rejects the idea, then you can suggest it to the business newspaper. Used occasionally, but never for hard breaking news, an exclusive can strengthen a relationship with an editor who sees you considering her individual editorial needs. But once that editor finds out she's been deceived (and she will find out), your credibility will be damaged and you'll have a hard time placing publicity items in that publication in the future.

In the third situation, an organization has a major news announcement and wants the media to travel to some location to cover it. The sponsoring organization agrees to pay expenses, which can be attractive to smaller publications and freelancers who lack the funds to make the trip. But is it ethical to offer all-expense-paid trips and other "freebies" to the media? Does this amount to buying media coverage, and how does it affect media relations? Nowadays, of course, technology and the Internet make it possible for the media to have this kind of experience without leaving their desks. But when sponsoring this kind of media event, known as a *junket*, don't ever tell reporters that you expect a positive story in return for paying their way. You should rarely demand that the media cover your news, anyway; this could look like an attempt to buy coverage and would clearly be unethical. Don't offer travel monies without first knowing the policy of each news operation with which you deal. You can assume that most major newspapers and broadcast media have strict rules about paying their reporters' travel expenses. There's no need to force money on anyone, either. Simply let people know you can help them cover their travel and hotel expenses if necessary.

Bottom line—make sure the news that you are asking the media to cover is truly newsworthy and avoid even the perception that you are seeking positive coverage in return for "freebies." To do otherwise could result in the loss of respect, credibility, and reputation for both the organization and the public relations practitioner.

Rewriting and Proofreading

Good writers rewrite and proofread, and they know the first draft is seldom a final draft. In agency work, when you write a news release, it often has to be reviewed by your internal supervisor and the account executive for quality before it goes to the client. The copy may then come back to you and require some revision. Then, it is sent to the client, who usually sends it back with additional revisions. Finally, depending on the subject, a corporate attorney may need to read it to weed out any legally sensitive wording and to provide counsel on potential legal risks. One piece of advice in regard to rewrites—always consider the approval process when setting up a time line for writing copy. Build in an extra week or two, when you can, to allow for approvals and rewrites. Establish an absolute deadline for final copy, and attempt to complete and get approval of the final draft a few days before that deadline.

After the final rewrite comes the critical task of proofreading. You must become skilled at proofreading your own copy. There won't always be someone around to look over your work, so it's up to you to make sure your writing is clear and error-free. Imagine if a critical letter is dropped from the word "heroine" and the copy goes out to the media that way. Or, "tutoring" somehow becomes "torturing" in the literacy article you're writing. These are both true examples of errors that occurred on college application essays. Whoops! Here are some tips for better proofreading:

- Don't rely on spell check. It will not correct sound-alike words (your copy has the word "grate" but it should be "great"). If a word looks like it might be misspelled, or if you're not sure of the spelling, try to sound it out and then look it up in the dictionary. Get a copy of Webster's Speller or a similar reference book.

- Leave your work for a while and come back to it later. After you've scanned a piece of writing again and again, it's easy to overlook obvious errors. Set it aside for a while. When you begin reviewing it again, you'll not only catch mistakes you missed earlier, but you also may find a better, smoother way to write that sentence.

- Have someone else who knows nothing about the subject read it. He or she may find errors that you didn't spot and pinpoint passages that are hard to understand.

- Be on the lookout for typographical errors and spacing problems. Carefully review the document for letters that are dropped out of words, reversed letters within words, reversed or transposed words, missing or misplaced periods and punctuation, extra space between the letters of a word, and extra or no space between two words in a sentence.

References and Suggested Reading

Carden, A. (2002, August). A new era of patient confidentiality. *Public relations tactics.* New York: Public Relations Society of America.

Goldstein, N. (Ed.). (2002). *The Associated Press stylebook and briefing on media law* (Rev. and up.). Cambridge, MA: Perseus Publishing.

Moore, R. L., Farrar, R. T., & Collins, E. L. (1997). *Advertising and public relations law.* Mahwah, NJ: Lawrence Erlbaum Associates.

Newsom, D. & Carrell, B. (2001). *Public relations writing form and style* (6th ed.). Belmont, CA: Wadsworth.

Percent of U.S. households with a computer by income, by race/Hispanic origin. (2001). Retrieved December 5, 2002 from http://www.ntia.doc.gov/ntiahome/dn/hhs/ChartH4.htm

Percent of U.S. households with a computer by race/Hispanic origin, by U.S., rural, urban, and central cities. (2001). Retrieved December 5, 2002 from http://www.ntia.doc.gov/ntiahome/dn/hhs/ChartH3.htm

Percent of U.S. households with internet access, by race/Hispanic origin, by U.S., rural, urban, and central cities. (2001). Retrieved December 5, 2002 from http://www.ntia.doc.gov/ntiahome/dn/hhs/ChartH8.htm

PRSA member code of ethics 2000. (2000). Retrieved December 22, 2002 from http://www.prsa.org/_About/ethics/index.asp?ident=eth1

Smith, E. L. & Bernhardt, S. A. (1997). *Writing at work: Professional writing skills for people on the job.* New York: McGraw Hill/Contemporary Books.

Smith, R. F. (1999). *Groping for ethics in journalism* (4th ed.). Ames, IA: Iowa State University Press.

Smith, R. D. (2003). *Becoming a public relations writer* (2nd ed.). Mahwah, NJ: Lawrence Erlbaum Associates.

Strunk, W. & White, E. B. (1999). *The elements of style* (4th ed.). Boston: Allyn and Bacon.

CASES

Case 1: The Writing Test (Part A)

You have applied for a position at a public relations firm. During the first inter-view, you are asked to take a writing test. The first phase tests your knowledge of spelling and word usage. Your interviewer hands you the test that follows, and says you have 10 minutes to complete it.

Part One of Writing Exam: Spelling and Word Usage

I. In the space next to each word below, please provide the correct spelling of that word. If the word is correctly spelled, simply rewrite it as shown.

definately_____   liaison_____
ocassion_____   inovative_____
stratagy_____   concensus_____
tomorrow_____   tenative_____
comittee_____   knowledgable_____
superviser_____   pharmacutical_____

II. Circle the *correct word* in parentheses in the sentences below:
   a. Corporate executives are concerned about the (affect/effect) the product recall will have on future sales.
   b. The vice president (complimented/complemented) her for doing excel-lent work on the publicity campaign.
   c. Melissa accepted the position as the governor's press (aid/aide).
   d. Cory said he was not (averse/adverse) to working in New York City.
   e. He is one of the company's (principle/principal) stockholders.
   f. The client said she would go no (further/farther) with the discussion until she had more information.
   g. The editor said the magazine would not publish the news release be-cause he was (disinterested/uninterested) in the subject.
   h. She told the interviewer that she (all ready, already) knew something about the company.
   i. The spokesperson (alluded/eluded) to a change in management.

j. Jim ordered more (stationary/stationery) from the printer.

k. The CEO sought the (advice/advise) of public relations (council/counsel) about handling the upcoming layoffs.

l. Public relations professionals must be skilled writers who can quickly (compose/comprise) copy at the computer as well as alert advisors who keep management (appraised/apprised) of changing public sentiment.

III. Select a simpler, more familiar word for:

equitable_____

stringent_____

endeavor_____

proficient_____

segregate_____

deficiency_____

acknowledge_____

predominant_____

disseminate_____

immense_____

foster_____

surpass_____

IV. Revise the following sentences to eliminate bias or insensitive language:

1. Humphrey Bogart, Cary Grant, and Ms. Hepburn are some of the greatest motion picture stars of all time.

2. AIDS patients often have difficulty paying for medical care.

3. Each employee will be asked for his opinion about the need for an on-site day care program.

4. She was amazed at how easily he moved through the crowd, especially since he was confined to a wheelchair.

5. In nominating the secretaries for the award, he said: "These girls do a great job for me. I don't know how I could do my job without them."

6. The student needs extra help because he is a slow learner.

7. He is one of the most successful businessmen in the city.

8. His research focused on the work ethic of the Oriental community.

Case 2: The Writing Test (Part B)

For the next phase of the writing test (see Case 1), you are asked to edit the following news release for distribution to the national business and financial media. You are instructed to correct grammatical and Associated Press style errors, simplify phrasing, and reduce wordiness to improve readability. You have 10 minutes to edit the release.

LEADING U.S. FINANCIAL FIRM NAMES NEW PRESIDENT

The Board of Directors of Connors-Walsh, Incorporated, one of the world's premiere financial planning companies, voted to elect a new president and cheif operating officer today.

Frances A. Kennedy was chosen to replace Allan Edwards, who has announced his retirement and will leave his current post after having served as president for a total of twenty years. Kennedy will assume her many responsibilities as president in a few weeks, on March 1.

Kennedy brings a vast amount of business and financial planning knowledge to her new post due to the fact that she has worked in the field for a number of years. Prior to joining Connors-Walsh, she was the Executive Vice President of Equity, Inc., a major life insurance company, for eight years, and she also served as a Top Executive for many other notable firms including Nathan-Thomas Inc., an investment firm that has offices across the nation and throughout the U.S.

With a Bachelor's of Arts degree in history from Syracuse Univeristy and a Master's in Business Administration from Cornell U., Kennedy belongs to a great number of professional groups and organizations whose members work in the financial planning arena. These groups are the National Financial Planners Association, of which she is a former president and is still a member, the Boston Business Executives. The New England Insurance Association, a group she also served on the board for and the International Association of Investment Bankers.

Connors-Walsh is one of the top financial firms in the country, with more than thrity million dollars in assets, and they are a leading provider of life insurance and business pension plans in the United States. The firm's services encompas a wide range of areas including mutual fund management, real estate investment, and financial brokerage services.

Case 3: The Writing Test (Part C)

After completing parts A and B of the writing exam (see Cases 1 and 2), your interviewer introduces the next part of the test.

"We want to see if you can write strong transitions. This is a creative writing test, too, since you have to come up with a transition sentence that connects two different subjects."

You are handed the following copy—six lead paragraphs taken from six different news stories—and asked to write a one-sentence transition statement that connects each paragraph below to the preceding paragraph. You have 15 minutes to complete this part of the test.

1. Fortune magazine's top 200 "Most Admired" companies spend twice as much on public relations and corporate communications than companies with weaker reputations, according to the results of a recent study.

2. A scientist who helps communities fight polluters and a history professor who researches and writes about the Holocaust are among this year's winners of the MacArthur Foundation "genius grants" awarded annually to "exceptionally talented and promising individuals."

3. First there was "Take Your Daughter to Work Day," followed soon after by "Take Your Child to Work." Now, Pet Sitters International is hoping that people will catch on to the first "Take Your Dog to Work Day."

4. A Kansas State microbiologist says outdoor grills and bug zappers don't mix. Cooking food on a grill that is too close to a bug zapper can be unsafe since zappers can spread bacteria or viruses up to 6 feet away.

5. The Gluco–Watch, a breakthrough device that would eliminate the need for diabetics to draw blood in order to test their glucose levels, has cleared another significant hurdle in the Food and Drug Administration's pre-market approval process.

6. If tailgaters and road construction delays are driving you crazy, then you may need to see a counselor—a "road-rage" counselor, that is. A 31-year-old teacher and hypnotherapist has started a counseling practice devoted exclusively to helping motorists deal with their anger behind the wheel.

Case 4: An Editing Exercise

As a senior intern in your college's public relations office, you are responsible for coordinating the production of a program for the upcoming inauguration of the college's new president. You are now gathering all the copy for the program. The first page of the program—an historical overview of the college—is submitted for your review by another intern in the office. Below is the copy you received. Edit the copy for errors in spelling, punctuation, and grammar.

Upton Colleges (UC) origins can be traced back to the 1930s, when Collier University (CU) first offered extension courses in the Upton, NY area. Seeing a need for a college in the Upton area business and community leaders urged Collier University to open such a college. As a result, CU established Upton College of Collier University in 1945 as a private two year undergraduate instituion.

Upton Colleges opening convocation was held on September 30, 1945 at the original downtown Upton campus. In spring 1946, the College added upper level courses to their two year academic structure.

In 1952 the Upton College Foundation was established as a seperate entity to support the College, and four years later they began their first official fundraising drive to finance the development of a new campus. The College moved from their downtown location to the current campus on Ballantine Road in 1961.

Upton College and Collier University maintain an academic relationship, however, Upton became financially and legally independant from CU in 1994. At this time, UC established their own board of trustees and began using Upton

College as their corporate name. UC also uses the name Upton College of Collier University which reflects their CU ties.

The newly-established UC board of trustees, insted of Collier Univerity then became responsible for selecting the president of the College. This happened for the first time in the 1996-97 academic year and this is Upton Colleges first presidential inauguration.

Regardless of there undergraduate major, students who graduate from Upton Colleges bachelors degree programs receive the Collier University bacalaureate degree, as they have since the Colleges first convocation in 1945. In January 1998, the College began it's first graduate program. Graduates of Upton Colleges master's degree programs receive the Upton College degree.

3

The Public Relations Process and Research

Before they step onto the playing field, football players and other athletes must carefully consider who and what they will be up against, and then come up with a plan of attack for reaching a predetermined goal—to win the game. Joe Paterno, the legendary head coach of the Penn State college football team, explains it by saying, "The will to win is important, but the will to prepare is vital" (Boone, 1999, p. 31).

Public relations professionals should heed coach Paterno's advice and prepare before they "take the field." They must first research a situation, and then establish goals and a sensible "plan of attack" based on their findings. Winning public relations programs, publicity efforts, and written materials always start with an effective game plan. This chapter introduces the four-step public relations process and focuses on the first step—research.

The Public Relations Process

Every public relations piece you write is usually part of a larger program. That product news release you prepare fits into a broader plan for creating consumer interest and advancing sales goals. Employee newsletters support an ongoing internal communications program aimed at keeping employees informed and building trust and morale. Good program development involves these key elements: ***Research*** (conducting a *situation analysis*); ***Planning*** (identifying the *target publics*, setting *goals* and *objectives*, determining *strategies* and *tactics*, and establishing a *budget* and *timetable*); ***Execution*** (implementing the plan); and ***Evaluation*** (measuring its success).

Research

The goal of this start-up phase is to try to gain a thorough understanding of a problem or some other situation your organization is facing. The introductory section of a written program plan that summarizes research results is called the *situation analysis*. The following is a condensed version of a situation analysis included in a winning entry submitted to the 2002 PRSA Silver Anvil Awards competition:

> Carpet One, the nation's largest floor covering retail group, wanted to offer its member store owners an original philanthropic program that would enable them to support their local communities. Carpet One and its public relations firm, Clarke and Company, believed that a successful program needed to address an issue of genuine importance to the 700 independent Carpet One store owners and their customers. A poll showed Carpet One members wanted a grassroots community relations program that would have strong local impact and could be customized to their community. Children and schools topped the list as the most important issues, and development of a program that connected Carpet One members with their local schools began.

This summary gives you an idea of the kind of information a situation analysis produces: relevant background information on the organization and its mission; a statement of the public relations problem in relation to that mission; and research findings that clarify public perceptions and provide a greater understanding of the problem and its effects. The situation analysis also points out special planning challenges (e.g., need for "an original philanthropic program" that could be customized to the communities of 700 member stores). The situation analysis is critical to your planning success because it justifies the need for your program and lays the foundation for the ideas that follow.

Research Methods

When facing a research problem, first consider *secondary sources*, those created by someone else but still useful to you. Secondary sources provide background information that increases your general understanding of a problem or subject. They also can offer some initial insight into public concerns or opinions about the subject. The Internet has made access to secondary sources much easier and more efficient. What used to take a day or two at the public library can now be done in an hour or two at your desktop. However, don't rule out the resources available through public and university libraries. Libraries contain numerous reference books, major newspaper indexes, statistical abstracts, and census reports valuable to the public relations writer. To save time, contact a reference librarian and enlist his or her support in identifying the best sources for your search. Some other background research sources useful to public relations writers include:

- *Files and archives*. Letters, proposals, and other business documents stored in personal and company files can provide a good research starting point. Maintain a *"clippings file"* of media articles published about your organization and on issues that impact your organization. For example, if you are a public relations director for a pharmaceutical company, you should be clipping articles regularly from mass media and trade publications relating to the industry, competitor news and product stories, and consumer health trends. Such articles may

provide excellent points of reference when you begin campaigns, prepare proposals, or update written materials. Many organizations also have in-house
archives where they maintain historical data and copies of previously published
brochures, annual reports, newsletters, and other useful background pieces.

- *Existing survey data*. Universities, professional associations, government
agencies, polling organizations, and some consulting firms regularly conduct
regional and national public opinion studies. It is likely that someone has conducted a survey and gathered data on a subject you want to investigate (see
Exhibit 3.1).

Exhibit 3.1   Online Research Sources for Public Relations Writers

Dow Jones Interactive (www.dowjones.com)

This site is a great source for current news and business stories with links to the *Wall Street
Journal*, *Barron's*, and *Business Newswire*. Corporate news releases also are featured.

Gallup (www.gallup.com)

This well-known polling organization's site makes it possible to monitor current national public opinion on business, economic, lifestyle, and political issues. The site features concise summaries of opinion studies including questions asked, findings, and
graphics.

LEXIS-NEXIS (www.lexis-nexis.com)

An excellent online resource with more than 31,000 sources and 2 billion documents including news and business stories, legal articles and court cases, government documents, public records, tax, and regulatory information. Subscription or pay-as-you go.

National Opinion Research Center (NORC) at the University of Chicago (www.norc.uchicago.edu)

This site maintains an extensive library of public attitude surveys conducted on health,
education, and social issues. A single copy of any NORC paper is available at no charge;
fees are charged for additional information, but will probably be lower than the cost of
original surveys. Also check out the **Roper Center for Public Opinion Research at
the University of Connecticut (www.ropercenter.uconn.edu),** which houses a large
archive of current research including survey data from Gallup and many other polling
organizations. This subscription service features iPoll, a comprehensive, up-to-date
source for U.S. nationwide public opinion that provides access to responses to more
than 380,000 questions.

Online Public Relations (www.online-pr.com)

This easy-to-use, extensive catalog of public relations, media, and marketing resources
features links to hundreds of online media sites, product and industry information, reference books, statistics, and e-mail directories.

(continued)

PR Newswire (www.prnewswire.com)
One of the leading wire services specializing in the electronic distribution of news to the media and financial community. An archived database features corporate and other news releases from the past three days to the past three years.

ProfNet (www.profnet.com)
This Internet service links public relations professionals with journalists looking for expert sources. The service, which is free to reporters, has a database that includes professors at more than 1,000 colleges and universities in North America and Europe.

PR Place (www.prplace.com)
This site is an excellent resource for public relations professionals with addresses for and links to public relations organizations and publications, news sources and services on the Web, and online and other commercial databases. The site features a comprehensive and free U.S. media guide.

PR Web (www.prweb.com)
A good general source of free information for public relations professionals, this site features news, articles written by public relations counselors, and lots of news releases distributed by Fortune 500 and other companies.

U.S. Census Bureau (www.census.gov)
Demographic data based on the most recent census includes detailed information about the U.S. population, income and education levels, housing, occupations, ancestry, and many other subjects. Data is available for specific states, counties, and regions of the country.

- *Case histories*. Professional associations, like PRSA, and many public relations books and textbooks available in college and public libraries detail public relations campaigns undertaken by various organizations. Often, these case studies outline research techniques and findings, strategic planning, communications efforts, and evaluation methods from successful campaigns and can give you ideas for your public relations programming.
- *Media directories*. Researching the media and creating and updating media lists is routine in public relations work. Directories published by Bacon's and other companies offer comprehensive state-by-state listings of newspapers, magazines, broadcast media and business publications. Local chapters of the PRSA and other professional communications groups may produce a media directory for a specific city or area, as well. Most directories can be purchased in printed form and on CD-ROM. Many public and university libraries carry current editions of media directories. Details on media directories are provided in chapter 6.

- *Online databases and networks*. Databases and online retrieval services like Lexis-Nexis make it possible for you to access thousands of publications and millions of news articles and other documents. Commercial online services like America Online and Compuserve not only offer their own exclusive databases but features such as e-mail, Internet access and chat rooms for interactive discussions of various topics in "real-time," meaning people respond to your comments instantly, as if you were having a face-to-face conversation.

- *Listservs*. A listserv is an electronic mailing list distribution system. When you join a specific listserv group, you receive e-mail communication from others who subscribe to that mailing list, and you can send e-mail messages to them as well. Listserv messages are sent to the e-mail addresses of everyone within that listserv group. Some mailing lists, however, are designed to deliver e-mail only. You can find a directory of mailing lists at www.liszt.com.

- *World Wide Web*. Many organizations now have their own Web sites, and many publications have online versions for the Web. So, if you're looking for news stories, or for facts about a competitor, a prospective client, or a major issue, it's likely you'll be able to find it on the Web. Unlike commercial services such as America Online that charge monthly fees, Web access is free. You do need to purchase and install Netscape or some other Web browser software in order to search the Web. Search engines, such as Lycos and Yahoo, can help you locate specific information on the Web. If you're looking for information on medical advances in cancer treatment, for example, you could access a search engine and enter the key words "cancer treatment." The search engine will then do the work for you, identifying various Web sources on the subject that you can then readily access. You might also start by reviewing the search engine's list of subjects (in this case, the subheading might be "Health" or "Medicine") and click on one of those first to narrow your search. A word of caution about gathering information through the Web—consider the credibility of the source. It doesn't take a lot of time, effort, or money to construct a Web site and many of them contain false or misleading information. Exhibit 3.1 lists some credible and useful Web sites and online resources for public relations professionals.

Secondary sources are a great place to start when conducting research and, sometimes, they can produce much of the background information you need. It is usually necessary, however, to do some *primary research*. The simplest form of primary research is *interviewing* people who are knowledgeable about the subject to get additional facts. If you are asked to write publicity materials for a new consumer product, you might ask the company's marketing manager some questions to learn more about the product's development, what distinguishes it from other products on the market, and how it has been designed to meet a specific and timely consumer need.

Once background research and one-on-one interviews are completed, you need to assess if more feedback is required from the public being targeted. Maybe you are launching an employee publication or creating a program to educate people about sexual harassment in the workplace. Making assumptions about employee reading habits or about their knowledge of what constitutes sexual harassment is not enough. If you don't know with certainty what their attitudes are, then you risk producing a publication employees won't read, or designing informational materials that overlook important and misunderstood messages about harassment in the workplace.

For example, once Carpet One store owners identified children and schools as the most important issues in their communities, members of the American Library Association were interviewed to find what kind of programs would be beneficial to schools. It turned out that donating books or permanent floor covering directly to local schools posed problems because of varying institutional requirements; however, the school librarians said an in-school reading program could be valuable. Specialists in children's theatre and elementary reading were then interviewed to create a program that would have educational value and hold children's interest.

Public opinion research, such as *focus groups* and *surveys*, is beneficial to the writing process in situations like these. However, because it can be time-consuming and costly, it is often not possible to do the amount of research necessary to get a complete reading of public opinion in a given situation. Let's take a closer look at interviews, and at the application of focus groups and surveys to campaigns and writing projects.

Interviews

What an interviewer does is comparable to the labors of a painter and a psychologist. A talented interviewer, like a painter, can create a mood and, like a psychologist, can get people to open up in ways they never thought possible. Some interviewing tips:

Before the Interview

- Make an appointment and let the person know how long you expect the interview to run. Prior to the interview, send a note or an e-mail message to confirm the time, place, and expected length of the interview. Remind the person of your goal and include some of the questions you plan to ask to help him prepare.

- Find out what you can about the person being interviewed—is this a talkative person, or someone who shares less freely? Talk to others who have interviewed or met this person, and get some suggestions from them on establishing rapport with the individual.

- If you plan to use a tape recorder, ask the person in advance if he or she is comfortable with that. Check the recorder's batteries and make sure you have enough tape. Bring a notepad and an extra pen or two in case the first pen you use runs dry.

Conducting the Interview

- Start by finding some general topic to talk about that is unrelated to the interview. A relevant item from the day's news is a safe choice. This can increase comfort levels and indicate how the person will interact with you as the interview progresses. Don't drag this out, though, and be alert to signals that say, "I don't want to make small talk; let's get down to business."

- Begin the interview by restating the goal. Tell the person what you are writing, why you are writing it, and how it will be used. Even though this ground may have been covered in a previous conversation or e-mail message, the people you interview are often busy and juggle multiple responsibilities, and they may need reminding.

- Come prepared with a written list of questions. Ask general, easy-to-answer questions first. Have the individual discuss his current job description or talk about his education and professional background to ease into the interview. Questions should be phrased to prevent "yes" or "no" answers. Don't ask, "Are you happy to be working as an executive for this company?" Do ask, "What do you think will be the most rewarding aspects of this job?" Follow up on short, nonrevealing answers to get more descriptive, detailed responses. If the person says, "I took this job because the company has a good reputation," follow up by asking, "What specific aspects of the company's reputation appealed to you?"

- Listen. Try not to interrupt people when they are talking. And don't feel like someone always has to be saying something. Brief pauses here and there are okay. Acknowledge the person's responses with genuine interest, good eye contact, a nod of the head and a smile, but don't overdo.

- Don't think you have to stick to the script. When you ask people to share their knowledge or talk about themselves, they can easily get sidetracked. If what's being said has merit, go with the flow, but make sure the interview doesn't lose focus. Offer a smooth transition to get things back on track: "That must have been quite an experience for you. I can tell you're proud of that accomplishment. I don't want to take up too much more of your time, however, I would like to ask you a few more questions before we finish, if that's all right."

- Look over the questions you came in with before wrapping up the interview. Make sure you've asked all the important questions. Ask a final question that will produce a strong concluding thought or quote for your article. This could be a follow-up question that reinforces a main point or theme discussed during the interview: "You said earlier that you are going to help the company explore new ways to be more competitive in the global marketplace. Maybe you could offer a final thought on why this is so important at this point in the company's history." Say "thank you" and, as a courtesy, let the person know your time frame for completing the piece.

After the Interview

- Review your interview notes right away. Find a chair in a hallway or do it in your car (you shouldn't be driving, of course) before you get back to the office. When writing fast, it sometimes is difficult to read your own handwriting. Reviewing your notes immediately after the interview, while the conversation is fresh in your mind, will make deciphering your notes a bit easier when you return to look at them later.

- Send a copy of the published article with a brief thank you note. Some organizations may require that you clear all quotes with the source before public relations materials are published or distributed, so make sure you're following policy.

E-mail can be used effectively to conduct interviews; however, it's important to understand its limitations as well as its advantages:

Advantages

- If someone is on the other side of the country, or the other side of the world, you can correspond by e-mail. This will save on travel and phone costs, and you can complete the interview rather quickly.
- Having the interviewee respond via e-mail ensures accuracy of quotes and other information.

Disadvantages

- E-mail interviews are static. You send the questions and wait for a response, without the opportunity to observe gestures or nonverbal reactions that add color to feature articles and other pieces. Personal interviews are more fluid; you ask a question and the person responds at that moment. There's more give-and-take between interviewer and interviewee.
- If someone receives your e-mail questions and finds a few of the questions vague, that person will have to send an e-mail back to you asking for clarification. In personal or phone interviews, that clarification occurs within seconds after the question is asked. E-mail clarification could take a while, depending on how soon the receiver accesses and reads messages that day.
- E-mail does not allow you to follow up the moment the question is asked (unless you're in a chat room) and to ask someone to elaborate on a response. You have to wait until the answers to questions are e-mailed back, and then follow up if more detail is needed. At that point, another e-mail or a phone call may be necessary to flesh out responses.

Focus Groups

Focus groups are small group interviews that allow public relations and marketing professionals to probe the attitudes of an audience. Each focus group consists of 8 to 12 participants who share some common characteristic. A moderator asks open-ended questions and participants have the chance to discuss in-depth their reactions to a situation, product, or program. Focus groups attempt to find out why people feel or think the way they do. Often, focus group findings are used to identify key concerns that shape the questions for a larger-scale survey.

Focus groups are economical and relatively easy to organize. They can help you to get a quick reading of public opinion on an issue, or to receive helpful feedback on the quality of communication tools. However, the opinions shared in focus groups do not represent the majority view and you should not present findings in that way. On their own, focus groups can help public relations writers shape messages with greater impact. They can also provide insight into a public's views on how to best deliver a message so people will read it, understand it, and believe it.

Fleishman-Hillard public relations firm conducted focus groups with women in California's Hispanic community in response to increasing illnesses and deaths caused by consumption of homemade or "bathtub" cheese made by unlicensed Hispanic vendors. The focus groups showed that while Hispanic consumers were aware of the risks of eating unlicensed cheese, they felt that the benefits of better taste and lower cost outweighed those risks. They also indicated that they could tell by tasting the cheese if it was safe to eat; however, salmonella and other bacteria in the unlicensed cheese cannot be detected by taste, sight, or smell.

Based on the focus group research, the California Milk Advisory Board, with Fleishman-Hillard, launched a campaign to educate Hispanic consumers about the health risks of unlicensed cheese and to correct some of the misconceptions they had about detecting unsafe cheese. Focus groups showed that Hispanics had a long-held cultural practice of purchasing unlicensed cheese, so participants stressed that a campaign to impact those buying habits and change behavior had to feature strong messages about the potential for serious illness or death.

Focus group members indicated that Edward James Olmos, a well-known Hispanic actor, would have credibility as a media spokesperson on this issue; the campaign eventually featured Olmos in a series of Spanish-language public service announcements. Brochures had a soap opera format and presented the problem as a "real-life drama," an approach that focus group members said would encourage readership by Hispanic consumers. Materials also stressed that it is not possible to simply taste cheese and know whether it is tainted. They also presented tips for storing and handling homemade cheese to prevent contamination. The campaign generated extensive media exposure and favorable response in the Hispanic community. Focus group findings served as the foundation for this successful campaign.

In addition, focus groups can help ensure that organizations sponsor publicity activities that target audiences will support. Reynolds Metals Company, to celebrate the 50th anniversary of Reynolds Wrap aluminum foil, considered sponsoring a publicity stunt to draw attention to the product. One idea was to unfurl a huge roll of Reynolds Wrap over San Francisco's Golden Gate Bridge. Focus group participants, however, reacted negatively to this idea and stated they would be more receptive to purchasing products from companies that help worthy causes.

As a result, Reynolds teamed up with the National Association of Meal Programs to lead a major volunteer recruitment drive for the "Meals on Wheels" program. This partnership made sense since Reynolds Wrap is a staple of the program, which delivers hot and cold meals to homebound people. The recruitment became the key message of the anniversary campaign, appearing on Reynolds Wrap cartons, grocery bags, the Reynolds Web site and all other promotional materials. The goal was to recruit 50,000 volunteers during the 50th anniversary year. The campaign recruited more than 70,000 volunteers, far surpassing the 50,000 goal, and helped

Reynolds gain much attention and respect for its charitable efforts. Focus groups made the difference.

Surveys

If you want to assess public opinion of a large or geographically widespread group of people, then a survey may be the best research tool. Different methods can be used in survey research. Telephone polls are used to survey community members about election issues and voting preferences. Mail surveys are sent by automobile manufacturers, immediately after a new car purchase, to find out how the new car owner rates the quality of service provided by the dealer and the salesperson. Registration cards are included with new products to analyze buyers' demographics and preferences. E-mail surveys are sent by product manufacturers to people who have visited a Web site to gauge reactions to the site and to the products.

Whatever the method, results are most exact when the individuals surveyed have been chosen in such a way that each person in a group has an equal chance of being selected. So, you might begin with a list of 1,000 names and select every 20th name; that will produce a random sample of 200 people. This scientific method ensures that the findings will better represent how everyone in that group feels about an issue. Whenever possible, it's best to survey all members of a group.

Surveys can help public relations professionals clearly see what large numbers of people know or don't know about a subject. Messages can then be formed and sent that reinforce what people know and, more importantly, explain what they don't know and how this lack of knowledge affects them. The American Medical Women's Association (AMWA) relied on survey findings to plan and implement a campaign aimed at increasing awareness of thyroid disease and how to detect it. The survey of adults 40+ showed that 90% of those polled did not know about the central role of the thyroid gland in overall body functioning; two-thirds of women had never been tested for thyroid disease, despite the fact that women are much more likely to suffer from thyroid disease than men; and 75% of those women who experienced thyroid disease symptoms did not see a doctor and seek testing for the disease. Left undetected, thyroid disease can lead to serious health problems, such as infertility and high cholesterol.

Using the survey research as its guide, the AMWA launched a public relations program to educate women about the thyroid gland and thyroid disease, and to increase the total number of women tested for the disease. The campaign's creative theme, "Gland Central," conveyed in itself the key message about the thyroid gland's critical role in the body. All educational and written materials, including brochures and the AMWA's Web site, emphasized the "Gland Central" message. The "Gland Central" campaign kicked off with a major media event, along with free thyroid disease testing at Grand Central Station in New York City. The program resulted in a 40% increase in the number of women tested for thyroid disease. Extensive primary research and surveys guided message development for the campaign.

Sometimes, it's what people know and like that become the focus of public relations efforts. Nabisco Foods wanted to do something special to mark the 85th anniversary of Oreo® cookies. Nabisco used an 800 number to survey 100,000 consumers about their views of the Oreo®. The company learned that most everyone, regardless of how they preferred to eat an Oreo®, liked to "play" with the cookie and had "fun" eating it. Adults said eating Oreos brought back fond childhood memories. In response to consumer feedback the anniversary campaign focused its key messages on the nostalgia and fun associated with eating Oreos. This included an "Only Oreo® Moments" contest that asked people of all ages to share special Oreo® moments through photographs, essays, or tapes. The winner received $10,000, and the winner's story became an Oreo® commercial. In the end, Nabisco scored a "slam dunk" (you can't talk about Oreos without using the word "dunk") with sales up 40% and consumer excitement about the cookie greater than ever—proof that success can be sweet for public relations professionals who make survey research integral to their efforts.

Additional Primary Research

- *Mail and telephone analysis*. Analyzing an organization's incoming mail and telephone calls is a simple, yet often overlooked, method of tracking public opinion. In this type of research, mail and telephone calls are tracked for positive and negative comments on a daily basis. The tracking sheets are then periodically analyzed to detect emerging issues.

- *Call-in lines*. Another way to track public opinion is through toll-free telephone numbers for customer service, information, or complaints. Such "call-in" lines provide immediate feedback to an organization so it can keep on top of emerging issues. It also offers two-way interpersonal communication and the positive image of a concerned organization that goes with it.

- *Field reports*. Employees working on the "front line" are some of the best resources an organization has. Whether an employee works at a reception desk or as a salesperson, he or she has direct access to the customer and can provide important feedback and observations. Some organizations offer these employees special training so they can provide even more insight from their dealings with customers.

- *Audits*. Audits come in many shapes and sizes, but all take an in-depth look at an organization's target publics and communication efforts. An organization might want to audit its publics occasionally to make sure they haven't changed. A publications audit reviews an organization's collateral materials to make sure they support the corporate identity and deliver a consistent message. A communication audit focuses on messages the organization sends, the media used, and the results of the messages to help identify missing linkages or blockages in the communication process. Communication audits can be time consuming, but are essential if an organization wants to make sure it is communicating successfully with both internal and external publics.

Exhibit 3-2 lists specific research methods that can be used when planning specific public relations projects. Additional evaluation techniques can be found in chapter 15.

Exhibit 3.2   Which Research Is Best for Your Project?

Strategic Planning

If you need to . . .	then try these methods to collect data:
Identify and/or segment your target publics	Field reports, communication audits, content analysis, phone/mail analysis, call-in lines
Measure your target publics' perceptions	Focus groups, phone/mail analysis, content analysis, surveys
Obtain demographics of your target publics	Online databases/networks, reference books, Web sites, library references
Identify lifestyle trends of your target publics	Surveys, focus groups, online databases/networks, library references, Web sites
Identify media preferences of your target publics	Surveys, focus groups, online databases/networks, media directories, Web sites, library references
Identify purchasing patterns of your target publics	Surveys, focus groups, online databases/networks, library references, Web sites
Identify readership preferences of your target publics	Surveys, online databases/networks, media directories, Web sites
Identify readership habits of your target publics	Focus groups, interviews, online databases/networks, Web sites
Identify motivators for your target publics	Focus groups, surveys, online databases/networks
Monitor issues important to your publics and/or organization	Focus groups, surveys, content analysis, Web sites
Monitor trends within your publics and/or organization	Focus groups, surveys, content analysis, Web sites, organizational files/archives
Monitor trends within your industry	Web sites, online databases/networks, content analysis, organizational files/archives
Measure public opinion on a large scale	Surveys, online databases/networks, listservs, Web sites, library references
Measure public opinion on a smaller, in-depth scale	Focus groups, online databases/networks
Identify potential problems	Communication audits, content analysis, phone/mail analysis, call-in lines, Web sites, online databases/networks, listservs
Identify strengths and weaknesses of the organization	Communication audit
Determine the effectiveness of current communication strategies and tactics	Communication audit

(continued)

Formulate strategy	Surveys, case studies, organizational files/archives, Web sites
Get ideas for a campaign or special event	Case studies, organizational files/archives, Web sites
Get ideas for news articles	Online databases/networks, Web sites
Generate publicity	Surveys
Shape questions for a survey	Focus groups
Test new messages	Focus groups
Test a new logo and/or slogan	Focus groups, organizational files/archives, Web sites
Obtain facts and figures to support a proposal	Databases/networks, library references, Web sites
Identify and/or monitor your competition	Web sites, content analysis, organizational files/archives, surveys, online databases/networks, field reports
Identify prospective clients	Web sites, content analysis, online databases/networks
Prevent a crisis	Communication audits, content analysis, phone/mail analysis, call-in lines, Web sites, online databases/networks, listservs
Get a reality check	Field reports, communication audits, content analysis, phone/mail analysis, call-in lines, Web sites, listservs
Tactics	
Create a brochure	Organizational files/archives, Web sites, focus groups
Develop a backgrounder	Interviews, organizational files/archives, Web sites
Write a news release, media alert, or pitch letter	Interviews, organizational files/archives, online databases/networks, media directories
Write and/or test a fund-raising letter	Organizational files/archives, focus groups
Write a speech	Interviews, organizational files/archives, online databases/networks, Web sites
Write a "how to" article	Interviews, organizational files/archives, Web sites
Write an organizational history	Interviews, organizational files/archives
Write a letter to the editor or op-ed	Organizational files/archives, content analysis, online databases/archives, Web sites, media directories
Write newsletter articles	Interviews, online databases/networks, Web sites

(continued)

Evaluation

Measure change in awareness	Benchmark surveys, content analysis, distribution numbers, media impressions, Web site hits
Measure change in attitude and/or interest	Benchmark surveys, phone/mail analysis
Measure change in behavior	Benchmark surveys, attendance numbers, money raised
Measure change in public opinion	Benchmark surveys, focus groups
Measure publicity	Content analysis, media impressions, advertising equivalency

■

References and Suggested Reading

Ault, P., Agee, W., Cameron, G., & Wilcox, D. (2002). *Public relations strategies and tactics* (7th ed.). Boston: Allyn & Bacon.

Baskin, O., Aronoff, C. E., & Lattimore, D. L. (1996). *Public relations: The profession and the practice* (4th ed.). New York: McGraw Hill.

Boone, L. E. (1999). *Quotable Business, 2nd edition.* New York: Random House.

Brody, E. W. & Stone, G. C. (1989). *Public relations research.* Westport, CT: Praeger Publishers.

Broom, G. M. & Dozier, D. M. (1996). *Using research in public relations: Applications to program management* (2nd ed.). Upper Saddle River, NJ: Prentice Hall.

Cutlip, S., Center, A., & Broom, G. (1999). *Effective public relations* (8th ed.). Upper Saddle River, NJ: Prentice Hall.

The Carpet One magic carpet time tour (2002). Program nomination submitted to PRSA Silver Anvil Awards. New York.

Wilson, L. (2000). *Strategic program planning for effective public relations campaigns* (3rd ed.). Dubuque, IA: Kendall/Hunt.

CASES

Case 5: Alcohol Awareness Month (Part A)

As public information specialist for the Council on Alcohol and Drug Dependence, your job involves using a variety of communication methods to help better educate area residents of all ages about the use, misuse, and abuse of alcohol and other drugs. The council is a nonprofit health agency and receives funding primarily from the United Way, the state health department, foundation grants, and corporate and private donations. It provides the community with a variety of free services such as short-term counseling for individuals affected by alcohol and drug abuse, education and prevention programs directed to schools, and referrals to other substance treatment programs, to name a few. These services are administered by paid staff, most of whom are trained social workers, counselors, and educators.

You report to LaToya Glover, the council's executive director, who oversees all agency operations—this includes managing the budget, handling fund raising and development, and working with the board of directors on policy matters. Before you joined the staff just a few weeks ago, the executive director also handled marketing and public relations in conjunction with a board sub-committee. The public information position was recently added to relieve the executive director of day-to-day marketing and public relations tasks and to make it possible for one individual to put all of his or her focus on these important activities.

It is now early December and at a Monday staff meeting, a discussion begins about plans for Alcohol Awareness Month in April. Typically, the council sponsors special events and attempts to gain more extensive media coverage during that month; it often does this by focusing on a current alcohol- or drug-related issue that has been receiving much attention both in the community and in the local and national press. By emphasizing a newsworthy issue, one that has generated much social concern, the council positions itself and its staff as experts on the issue, leading to greater visibility for the agency and its services.

After some deliberation, it is decided that the focus of next year's Alcohol Awareness Month campaign should be binge drinking, something that is especially prevalent among high school and college students. A binge drinker, by definition, consumes five or more drinks in one sitting. National surveys have shown that one-third of high school seniors and more than 40% of college students had at least one occasion of binge drinking in a previous two-week period. Because there are several colleges and universities in your community there is a great deal of local interest in this subject. Area educators and education administrators have been trying to tackle this dangerous problem, which has been the cause of an increasing number of accidental deaths due to alcohol overdose on college campuses nationwide.

At the staff meeting, the executive director asks you to take a major role in planning and coordinating Alcohol Awareness Month activities, to include the preparation of various publicity and written materials. As binge drinking is a subject you have heard about, but are not overly familiar with, you take the logical first step—asking more questions and conducting additional research.

Assignments

1. Assume you are still at the staff meeting with your executive director and others from the council's staff. What are the five most important questions you might ask at this time? Write each question *exactly* as it should be asked; be specific when stating each question. In a short paragraph for each, explain why you would ask that question and what you would hope to learn that would help you plan the upcoming campaign.

2. Identify five secondary sources (include Internet sources in this list) and five primary sources that you would consult to further research this subject. In a short paper, list each source by name (be as specific as you can). Then, briefly explain the relevance of the source and what you would hope to learn from that source that would help you plan the campaign and public relations materials.

Case 6: The Web Site Research Project

Shortly after graduation, you begin your first job at a small public relations firm. The firm services a variety of clients, mostly local and regional companies and a few national clients as well. One of your major projects is to help revamp the firm's Web site; your primary task is to revise the site's written material.

You are now preparing for a meeting with the firm's senior vice president, who is supervising the Web site project. She plans to discuss in more detail the site's history and to share her ideas for reworking the site. Before the meeting, you talk to a few employees to get some background on the site, fully review the agency's client roster, and do some reading on Web site development and on-line writing.

At the meeting, the senior vice president says the firm realized the importance of creating the Web site two years ago, and that staff has been trying to update it somewhat regularly since then, but mostly by doing "little things," such as adding information on new staff and clients. She believes the site provides the necessary information about the firm, its staff and its services, but the overall content could "have more spark" and be more interesting.

"The site needs to be informative and tell people who we are, but it also needs to say something about what we do for clients and how we do it. What I mean is, we stress to clients and prospective clients that we are creative problem solvers and copywriters, but our Web site doesn't reflect that claim all that well. Frankly, it's a bit dull and the copy is dry. It's a functional site, but we'd like it to be more than that. Anyone who visits our site should see right away how we approach a writing assignment. If the site does a great job of creatively and persuasively positioning us with our important constituencies, then it would say something to prospective clients about how we could do the same for them."

She suggests that at this point it might be useful to conduct a competitive analysis and look at other agency Web sites, not only to get some tips for rewriting your firm's site, but also to get some ideas on how to distinguish your site's content from the others.

Assignment

Locate and review two Web sites produced by public relations firms. Sources such as PR Web (*www.prweb.com*), PRSA (*www.prsa.org*) and BusinessWire (*www.businesswire.com*) are good starting points for information on firms and their Web sites. Examine each site and its content. Then prepare a written analysis to include the following:

- *Two-paragraph overview of each site*. State the name of the firm and give a brief description of the firm, its major clients, and services. Summarize what you believe are the key goals and audiences of the site.
- *Content*. Identify content areas that are common to each site. Note and describe distinguishing copy features of each site as well as copy you think is creatively presented and well written. Cite an example of good writing from each site, and briefly explain why you think this is good writing.
- *Conclusions*. Discuss the implications of this competitive analysis as they relate to copywriting for your firm's new Web site. Recommend specific content that should be included within your site and the audiences that the content should target. Suggest content or Web site features that would help distinguish your firm's site from the others.

Case 7: Small Business Person of the Year (Part A)

Torolla, Jerome & McCarthy, Inc. is a small public relations and marketing firm located in upstate New York (or, you can make this the city where your college or university is located). One morning, Len Torolla, the agency's president, calls Jim Middleton into his office to talk about a new client project. Middleton is a public relations account executive with the firm.

"I just got back from a meeting with Vanda White of Grogan's, and she had some really good news to share," Torolla says. Middleton was acquainted with White and knew that she was the president of Grogan's, a rather unusual, family-owned variety store in that city. "Vanda found out this morning that she won the state's 'Small Business Person of the Year' award, and she'd like us to put together a publicity and public relations campaign to promote that. I think you would be the best person to handle that project."

"That sounds interesting. What else do you know about the award?" Middleton asks.

"Well, she didn't give me too many details. I told her you would get in touch with her to set up a meeting, hopefully for later today or tomorrow. I know she mentioned that 200 other businesses in the state were nominated, so she had some pretty stiff competition. She's familiar with some of the other public relations work you've done for our clients, so she's comfortable with you working on this project."

"OK, I'll give her a call and set up the first meeting. Grogan's has a Web site, right? And I know we've done a few brochures and printed pieces for them. I'll look over those materials before I meet with her," Middleton says.

"Good. Oh, and she hasn't really given us a budget to work with, but I'm pretty sure she'll go along with our recommendation on that, if the plan looks good. I'll leave it in your hands, then. Touch base with me after your meeting to let me know how things went," Torolla says, as he leaves Middleton's office to take another phone call.

Middleton returns to his office, accesses the Grogan's Web site, and jots down the following key points:

- Grogan's began 30 years ago as a small, "five-and-dime" store, selling arts, crafts, cards, candy, and other small items.
- The store has expanded its product line in the past 10 years, and now specializes in selling a wide variety of seasonal (e.g., Christmas, Valentine's Day) merchandise, including the biggest selection of Halloween masks and costumes in the state.
- Grogan's has become well-known for its innovative holiday displays manufactured by a European animation company. Among its best-known displays is a 15-foot, mechanized ogre named Claude. People from throughout the state, and even neighboring states, often travel to the area and visit the store in the fall to see this Halloween attraction.

After reviewing the Web site and some previous store brochures housed in agency files, Middleton realizes that he still needs more specific information about the store, about White, and about her recent award. With that in mind, he picks up the phone and calls White to set up their first meeting, and begins thinking about all the additional questions that have to be asked.

Assignment

Write 10 important questions that need to be asked during the meeting with Vanda White. Present these questions in the exact words Middleton should use when asking them. In a short paragraph for each question, explain the significance of that question and how the information produced might be used in written materials prepared for the campaign.

Case 8: The New Hospital Service (Part A)

You work as a public relations assistant for St. Francis Hospital, located in a city of 100,000 people. St. Francis is one of three hospitals in the area serving a population that is increasingly older; almost 40% of the area's residents are 50+. One morning you arrive at the office and find a handwritten note on your desk from Scott Nakagawa, the director of public relations and development. It says:

> I need you to get more information about a new service we'll start phasing in next week. We're going to allow patients to have their pets come in for visits. Great idea, don't you think? I'd like you to get more info on the program—you can start by talking to Deb Hughes in the physical therapy program, since she came up with the idea, and then go from there. Probably want to send out a news release, good feature story idea. Out of the office most of the day—do as much as you can with this. Touch base after 4 p.m.

After reading the note, you make your "To Do" list for the day, and then take a few minutes to proofread brochure copy that has to be delivered to the printer later that morning. You then tackle the assignment outlined in your boss's note.

Assignments

1. Assume you begin researching this subject by speaking to Deb Hughes of the physical therapy program. Prepare a list of questions you want to ask when interviewing her. In one sentence, state the specific question you would ask. In a second sentence, justify the importance of that question.

2. In a brief report, describe additional methods you would use to research this subject, and gather necessary information for public relations materials. For

this report:

(a) Identify and examine two or three specific secondary sources. Cite each source, summarize its content, and highlight key facts taken from the sources that you might use in written materials.

(b) Identify three people, other than Hughes and your boss, whom you would want to interview and, possibly, quote in publicity materials. List and briefly describe each source (be as specific as you can; identify the source by title/organization or affiliation), explain the source's relevance, and prepare a few questions to ask each source.

4

Planning and Execution

A famous man once said: "Just the facts, ma'am." Your first guess might be that this person was a journalist or a scientist. But the man who said this was detective Joe Friday on the television series "Dragnet." Each week, police detectives on contemporary television dramas also make this statement, or something like it, as they listen to people share facts about robberies, murders, and other crimes in an effort to solve a case.

Like a detective, a public relations writer many times faces an assignment that involves the unknown. You may be asked to write about an animal health product used to control worm and fly infestation of beef cattle or to prepare an article on estate planning for people nearing retirement age. Chances are good that you're not familiar with these subjects and you won't have prior knowledge of many subjects you write about. But if you're asked to write about something unknown to you, you do it, and you learn fast.

It's a simple but important concept: You have to investigate and understand a subject before you can write about it. You must develop expertise by quickly identifying and accessing appropriate primary and secondary sources of information, coming up with the right questions and asking them of the right people in the right way, and being a good listener and note taker. The ability to transform complex material into simple reading is one reason why public relations practitioners are so valuable to an organization. To be a good public relations writer, you need to take a lesson from Joe Friday, who did his job best when he had all the facts. Once you have gotten "the facts" in the research phase of the public relations process (as discussed in chapter 3), it's time to move on to the planning phase. During this phase, you will identify the *publics* that your program must reach and influence, set *goals* and *objectives*, develop *strategies* and *tactics*, establish a *budget* and *timetable*, and create appropriate public relations *messages*.

Target Publics

Target publics are chosen for a public relations program based on the issue of the campaign and the publics' interest in that issue. They are the groups of people that must be reached and influenced in order for the program to be successful. In the Carpet One case in chapter 3, the primary publics were Carpet One members; the elementary schools selected by Carpet One members; and, the kindergarten, first grade, and second grade students in those schools. The campaign also identified secondary publics who could be influencers and support Carpet One's program messages: the students' parents, the news media, and public officials in the local communities.

Goals and Objectives

Goals are the core of any public relations program. They establish the program's direction and purpose. The Carpet One program had three goals:

1. To increase positive community visibility while avoiding overcommercialization.
2. To create a unique philanthropic effort that would create goodwill for Carpet One members in their local communities while benefiting schools and children.
3. To increase store owner support and satisfaction with the parent company.

This program, like many public relations programs, has goals that are ***information-based***. Such goals focus on informing, educating, or increasing awareness; in this case, building awareness of the Carpet One stores in their communities was an information-based goal. Goals may also be ***acceptance-based***, aimed at changing the target public's interest level, or ***action-based***, which are concerned with changing behavior or motivating people to do something. Increasing store owner support and satisfaction is an action-based goal.

Some key points regarding "awareness" goals. While they are often the easiest to execute, their success is much harder to measure. You can't just assume that extensive media coverage of an issue made your target public more aware. To truly measure awareness change, you must first find out what awareness levels are before a program is launched, and then do a post-program survey to gauge shifts in awareness levels after the program is completed. What is usually more significant, however, is what people do as a result of that awareness. A smart planner ties information-based goals to action-based goals that contribute to the "bottom line." Heinz North America did just that in a 2002 Silver Anvil award-winning campaign. When the company was ready to announce a new color of Heinz EZ Squirt ketchup, the company worked with Jack Horner Communications Inc. (JHC) to develop a public relations plan that would create a media "buzz" (awareness). The ultimate goal of the plan, however, was to increase Heinz's market share through sales of the new product (action).

The terms "goal" and "objective" are often used interchangeably; however, objectives are much more specific than goals. Goals set the general course; objectives spell out the returns more exactly. Objectives commonly state specific expectations for change within a given time frame (e.g., increase donations by 10% this year); they become yardsticks by which the success of a program is measured. The launch of Heinz Funky Purple EZ Squirt had four objectives that would need to be met in order to increase market share to 60%:

1. Accumulate at least 150 million media impressions and a minimum of 500 media stories for at least one month.
2. Secure at least 100 television stories (including five national hits).

3. Obtain an advertising equivalency (see chapter 15) of more than $2 million.
4. Drive consumer interest in the new product to help Heinz sell more than 1 million bottles.

While *evaluation* is the last step of the public relations process (chapter 15 is devoted exclusively to this topic), you need to think about measuring program effectiveness early in the planning process. Setting goals and objectives is closely linked with evaluation since the most basic measure of program success is to ask yourself, "Did we reach our goals?" Heinz used the following methods to measure its campaign goals:

- *Tracking sales*. Heinz sold 2.5 million bottles of its new product and reached its objective of increasing market share to 60%. In addition, the launch of Funky Purple EZ Squirt helped spur a 7.6% growth in Heinz's core ketchup business.
- *Assessing media coverage*. More than 300,000 media impressions were accumulated, nearly 2,000 media stories were placed, more than 1,000 television stories were aired, and an overall advertising equivalency of more than $2 million was reached.

Compare the above figures to those stated in the objectives and you'll find this campaign was hugely successful. If the objectives had not been clearly stated and measurable, however, how would Heinz have defined "success"?

Strategies and Tactics

Goals and objectives state *what* you want to accomplish. Strategies and tactics outline *how* you will accomplish them. Strategies are the general approaches you devise to reach goals and objectives. Tactics are the tools used or a series of activities carried out to execute the strategy. Public relations program strategies often fall into three categories:

- *Relationship-building* strategies, which involve cultivating support through one-on-one discussions and establishing partnerships with credible individuals and influencer groups who support, endorse, and promote your program.
- *Communication* strategies, which involve providing information to publics through face-to-face tactics (i.e., meetings, seminars, presentations), mass media/publicity tactics (i.e., news and feature stories in magazines and newspapers, radio public service announcements, television and satellite interviews), and directed media tactics (i.e., brochures, e-mail, newsletters, videos), which are personalized to a specific audience.
- *Event-oriented* strategies, which use organized activities to influence groups of people and create publicity.

Carpet One used all three strategies in "The Carpet One Magic Carpet Time Tour" program, which involved a traveling program that would bring schools an "adventure in reading featuring live actors and creative storytelling." "Magic carpet" samples for each performance were donated by Carpet One member stores; the samples would otherwise have been discarded. More than 600 performances were given in all 50 states during the 2001–2002 school year.

Relationship building with local store owners and schools was a core component of The Carpet One Magic Carpet Time Tour. Each participating Carpet One store owner nominated a local school to receive a free tour performance. A step-by-step guidebook explaining every aspect of the program was developed for members. It also included activities that members could implement to extend "the magic" after the tour performance. A Carpet One tour coordinator handled performance arrangements with the schools and regularly updated Carpet One members on plans in their communities. Carpet One also forged strategic relationships with Radio Disney, which helped develop the tour concept, and Disney Publishing, which provided discounted storybooks for the tour.

Collateral materials for the tour included development of a logo for use on posters, book stickers, carpet labels, and stationery. Localized news releases and news advisories were sent to media in each community. The tour itself was an event. The performers arrived in each community in vans wrapped in The Carpet One Magic Carpet Time Tour graphics. The tour was recognized by official proclamations in several states, and public officials, a secondary target public, attended numerous performances, which were extensively covered by the media.

Budget

Before implementing program strategies and tactics, people will want to know their cost. Actually, it is helpful to know budget limitations at the start of the planning process. That way, you can decide on research, strategic direction, and tactics that are realistically based on available monies. Can you do original surveys and focus groups, or will you have to rely on less costly informal research methods? Will it be possible to sponsor an elaborate event, or is a simpler and more cost effective activity all you can afford? Don't miss the point here, though. Always plan programs to include activities that will best target your publics and get results. Remember that a simple and inexpensive idea can be just as effective as a big one costing "megabucks."

Budget procedures vary depending on the type of organization for which you work. Corporations allocate annual operating budgets to public relations departments. These cover staff salaries and costs incurred for publications, and special events and other public relations projects coordinated by the department during the year. Not-for-profit groups often supplement their public relations program budgets with monies from corporate sponsors and foundation grants. Public relations firms establish budgets, to a large degree, based on time. They may charge fees based on individual projects or charge monthly fees or *retainers* to cover the number of hours agency staff spends counseling, writing, planning, and coordinating projects. In addition to retainers, they bill clients for "out-of-pocket" expenses such as printing costs and travel.

Carpet One utilized a budget of $1,000,000 for the extensive Carpet One Magic Carpet Time Tour, which included nine actors, costumes, props, three tour vans, storybooks, and collateral materials. The Heinz Funky Purple EZ Squirt campaign budgeted $100,000 for its media blitz, which included news releases, photographs, customized press kits, blind-taste-test baskets, and video.

Timetable

Besides establishing a budget that specifies all program costs, you must also create a timetable to guide you in executing the program. This document includes a listing of weekly tasks to be completed, deadlines for each task, and the individual(s) responsible for completing each task. It identifies dates when significant events will occur, such as major meetings and campaign launch events; it indicates when any written materials should be prepared, approved, printed, distributed, and followed up; and it designates when other critical planning and promotional activities should occur. Organize separate timetables for major events since they involve numerous and detailed planning steps such as securing a site, confirming speakers, and making media contacts.

The Heinz Funky Purple EZ Squirt case illustrates how to think strategically when timing programs to produce greater impact (see Exhibit 4.1). During the first phase of the campaign, Heinz distributed a creative news release and "mystery" photo announcing that a new color would soon join the ranks of Blastin' Green Heinz EZ Squirt. Although simple, these creative tactics caused such a media buzz that PR Week Magazine acknowledged the announcement as a "Play of the Week." Follow-up media calls were made and interviews were arranged. The announcement that purple was the new ketchup color was made 42 days later on July 31. On that day, media kits and blind-taste-test baskets arrived at top U.S. media outlets, video b-roll was made available via satellite on that day only, and follow-up calls were made to arrange interviews.

Developing the Message

The planning process is not just used for public relations programs; it also is applied to each piece of writing you create—starting with research (see Exhibit 4.2). Just as research is used to help identify the problem or situation an organization is facing, it also is used to identify the best way to write your message. A writing project might begin with some scribbled notes left on your desk by a supervisor who asks you to "look into this and write something up by tomorrow." Most of the time, you have to figure out on your own how to get started. The people you need to talk to are out of town for a week or don't return your e-mails or phone calls. You'd like to survey public perception about an issue as the basis for a campaign, but the client doesn't want to spend the money on that kind of research. So, you gather information in the most efficient, economical, and creative manner possible, often with little time to spare. Whatever the project, there are five key questions you should always ask to guide the research effort:

1. Why am I writing this piece?
2. Who is my audience, and what do they know or think?

Exhibit 4.1   Timetable: Heinz Funky Purple EZ Squirt

HEINZ EZ SQUIRT PROJECT TIMELINE
As of April 27, 2001

May 7, 2001	First release is drafted and provided for approval	JHC
May 8 & 9, 2001*	Photo shoot of product	JHC/Heinz/ Michael Ray
May 11, 2001*	Photo proofs back to Heinz for selection	JHC/Heinz/ Michael Ray
May 14, 2001	Edits and changes to first release are provided to JHC	Heinz
May 14, 2001	Kids' "guess the next color" Web page design provided to Heinz for approval	JHC
May 14, 2001	Photo selection determined and ordered	JHC/Heinz
May 16, 2001	Begin photo retouching with fingerprints, etc.	JHC
May 16, 2001	First release provided for final approval	Heinz/JHC
May 17, 2001	Photo is sent for duplication	JHC
May 18, 2001	Approved first release duplicated for mailing	JHC
May 21, 2001	Edits and changes to Kids' "guess the next color" Web page design are provided to JHC	Heinz
May 23, 2001	Kids' "guess the next color" Web page design provided to Heinz for final approval	JHC
May 23, 2001	Photos in house	JHC
May 23, 2001	Begin first press kit assembly	JHC
May 29, 2001	Kids' "guess the next color" Web page design provided to Heinz Web site provider	JHC
June 4, 2001	First press kit is mailed out. Mailing includes: Lead release and "crime scene" photo in an orange envelope.	JHC
June 4, 2001	First release and photo are distributed on wire	JHC

(continued)

June 4, 2001	Kids' "Guess" contest information is posted on Heinz Ketchup Web site	Heinz Web site Provider
June 7, 2001	Media follow-up on first press kit begins	JHC
June 11, 2001	Second release and map are drafted and provided for approval	JHC
June 15, 2001	Edits and changes to second release and map are provided to JHC	Heinz
June 19, 2001	Second release and map provided for final approval	JHC
June 20, 2001*	B-roll footage taped in Iowa	Heinz/ New Perspectives
June 21, 2001	Approved lead release duplicated for mailing	JHC
June 21, 2001	Map provided to Web site provider for posting on July 9	JHC
June 25, 2001	Begin second press kit assembly	JHC
June 27, 2001*	B-roll footage taped in Pittsburgh, if not already taped in May	JHC/Heinz/ New Perspectives
June 28, 2001*	Review of all b-roll taped—bits selected and provided to New Perspectives for editing and creation	JHC
July 9, 2001	Second press kit is mailed out. Mailing includes: second release and map in a blue envelope	JHC
July 9, 2001*	B-roll footage tape provided for approval	JHC/ New Perspectives
July 12, 2001	Media follow-up on second press kit begins	JHC
July 13, 2001*	Edits and or approval of b-roll footage	Heinz
July 18, 2001*	B-roll footage provided to Heinz for final approval	JHC
July 18, 2001	E-mail blast copy for both correct and incorrect guesses, and announcement release are provided for approval	JHC
July 20, 2001*	B-roll dubs are duplicated	New Perspectives

(continued)

July 23, 2001	Edits and or approval for e-mail blast copy, and announcement release to JHC	Heinz
July 25, 2001	Announcement release & e-mail blast copy provided for final approval	JHC
July 25, 2001	EZ Squirt supply delivered to JHC	Heinz
July 26, 2001	Begin assembly of packages to top media	JHC
July 27, 2001*	B-roll provided to Medialink for Aug. 1 distribution	JHC
July 31, 2001	Third initiative is sent via Fed Ex, mailing includes announcement release and a bottle of new EZ Squirt to top 100	JHC
August 1, 2001	B-roll is distributed on satellite	Medialink
August 1, 2001	Announcement release is distributed on wire	JHC
August 1, 2001	Media follow-up to top 100 sent product	JHC
August 1, 2001	E-mail blasts are sent to kids who guessed both correct and incorrect colors. Random winners of the iMac computers are announced in this e-mail blast	JHC
August 8, 2001	Text and design of teachers' post card mailing are provided for approval	JHC
August 8, 2001	Press release announcing art class opportunity provided for approval	JHC
August 13, 2001	Edits and/or approval for post card copy and layout to JHC	Heinz
August 13, 2001	Edit and/or approval for press release to JHC	Heinz
August 15, 2001	Post card copy & layout provided for final approval	JHC
August 15, 2001	Press release provided for final approval	JHC
August 17, 2001	Post cards are printed	Printer
August 17, 2001	Press release duplicated	JHC
August 22, 2001	Post cards are prepared for mailing	JHC

(continued)

September 4, 2001	Post card mailing to art teachers is mailed out	JHC
September 4, 2001	Art lesson plans and information are posted on Heinz Ketchup Web site	JHC/Heinz Web site provider
September 4, 2001	Press release distributed to teacher/art publications and via Business Wire	JHC
September 11, 2001	Form press release for announcing winning schools provided for approval	JHC
September 18, 2001	Edits and/or approval for form release to JHC	Heinz
September 21, 2001	Form release provided for final approval	JHC
October 19, 2001	Deadline for art contest entries	
October 24, 2001	Approved release finalized for distribution	JHC
October 29, 2001	Winning schools are notified and photos are posted on Heinz Ketchup Web site	JHC/Heinz Web site provider
October 29, 2001	Regional press releases faxed to media in towns with winning schools	JHC

*Indicates tentative dates. These dates are suggestions only and have not been confirmed with any vendor as of this time.

--■

Note. Courtesy of Heinz North America.

3. How will the piece be used and/or distributed?
4. What facts do I have, and what additional information do I need?
5. Which research methods should I use, and what specific sources should I consult?

Why am I writing this piece? Always begin by asking the question, "Is there a good reason for writing this?" If you are writing a news release, first make sure that you have legitimate information to share and that you're not doing this simply to make your organization look good or to satisfy the personal whim of a staff member. A company news release about hiring two new managers is newsworthy; a release announcing that the company softball team won its game over the weekend is not.

You must confirm the purpose of the piece and its value to the organization. News provided by public relations professionals about major staff changes is published regularly in local newspapers' business sections, in business publications, and in trade journals. Staff releases create goodwill by publicly recognizing employees and making them feel like they are officially "on board." They also help organizations to stay continually visible to important audiences. Potential customers or clients who know and respect someone your company has hired might take notice, which could lead to new business opportunities. On the other hand, the media will simply not care about the company softball team's record and will view such a release as a blatant attempt to get exposure. If, however, that softball game took place as part of a community fund raiser and the team raised significant money for a local charitable cause, then an editor might see news value in the story.

Exhibit 4.2   An Example of Public Relations Writing and the Planning Process

---

Management Graphics, Inc. (MGI), a manufacturer of equipment for quality color printing, used strategic thinking in the development of written materials for its major product, JetStream:

Situation/research. The JetStream product allows print shops to take files produced by artists and writers and turn them into premium color graphics through a special imaging process. MGI's research showed, however, that its primary public, quick print shops such as Kinko's, did not fully understand the technology behind JetStream.

Goals. MGI designed a public relations effort to (1) increase understanding of the technology and clear up end-user misconceptions, which would (2) help them make more informed decisions about equipment purchases, and (3) better position MGI as a leader in the use of this technology.

Strategy and Tactics. MGI and its public relations firm, Padilla Speer Beardsley Inc. (PSB), Minneapolis, designed an educational campaign that involved explaining this technology to the audience in targeted trade publications. Two articles were developed that featured MGI technical experts responding to frequently asked questions about the technology and other issues important to the end user. After talking with printing professionals about trade media preferences, PSB targeted two key publications and successfully placed those articles.

Budget. Total budget was $3,500, which included the agency's time to interview end users, complete the articles, and handle media submission and placement.

Evaluation. The published articles reached 100,000 readers and prompted many end users to contact MGI about this technology and its products. A major quick print shop distributed article reprints to its 500 franchises, which generated sales leads.

You need to know about deadlines up front, as well. Find out if a deadline has already been established by someone, whether that be an editor who's expecting the material or a designer who needs the copy to prepare artwork for the printer. If no deadline is in place, then look realistically at the project and set a deadline on which all involved parties can agree. Establishing deadlines at the start helps you determine how much time can be devoted to research and how extensive that research can be.

Who is the target public, and what do its members know or think? Everything you write is written for somebody and to influence people in some way. Before you start collecting facts, make sure you understand who the intended public is. Is a fund-raising piece directed to long-time donors in hopes they will donate again, or is it targeted to potential first-time donors? If the latter, your writing will need to provide more background information, since these people may not know much about the organization and its goals. In addition, it should be more persuasive in its approach than a letter sent to those who already support the cause.

Research is especially critical when you are writing for unfamiliar publics. Before you write, find out what the public knows about you and if it is even interested in what you have to say. For example, suppose you are preparing to write that letter to first-time donors. Research might show that potential donors question how much of the money raised is really used to help the neediest people in their area. In that case, a fund-raising letter can be more persuasive if it indicates details such as the percentage of dollars allocated to help those in need, explains how funds are distributed and to whom, and includes personal stories to show how donations have benefited specific local individuals with great need.

How will the piece be used and/or distributed? Once you know who you want to reach and what you want to tell them, it's time to focus on *how* to deliver the message. The way a message is used and distributed depends on the target public and the message itself. If the message requires detailed information, as in the above example of the fundraising appeal, a letter is more appropriate than a postcard. However, if the goal of a message is to simply attract attention for a fund-raising event, a postcard may be more appropriate. Chapters 5 to 13 outline the many different writing formats and activities from which to choose when selecting the best way to reach your target public.

You will also need to consider the media preferences of your target public when deciding the best way to deliver your message. In addition to newspapers, TV and radio, the growth of specialized media, such as trade publications and cable channels, offer opportunities to deliver messages to a society that is becoming increasingly segmented. Continuing advancements in technology also have given us the Internet, fax, and e-mail to quickly reach large numbers of people.

What information do I have, and what facts do I need? Jot down anything you already know about a subject. Include any details provided by the person who assigned the writing project. Then, draw up a list of questions that will produce additional information you need, keeping in mind the purpose of your written piece and the public(s) for which you are writing.

Let's say you are an intern in a corporate communications department. You are asked to write an article about a new vice president. Your supervisor tells you the piece

will be published in the next issue of the company newsletter. At that moment, upon receiving the assignment, there are some key questions you should ask:

- How long should the piece be, in total words or pages (e.g., 500 words or two
  pages double-spaced)?
- What is the preferred tone of the piece—a straightforward news approach announcing this vice president has joined the staff or a human interest piece focusing more on the person?
- Do you have any materials that would help me get started, such as a resumé?
- What is my deadline?

Once you get the answers to these questions, you can begin the research process
by making some preliminary notes. You know the vice president's name and title, his
phone number, and e-mail address. You know he started two weeks ago and which
division of the company he will head. Your boss told you that the new vice president
came to your company from another Fortune 500 firm. That's about all you know.

Now, you make a list of questions to get additional facts for your story. You need
more specifics about the vice president's background and experience. A resume will
provide some information, but you will need to talk directly with the vice president
to get interesting quotes and more detail to fill out the article. You want to get a sense
of the vice president's strengths, expertise, and business philosophies. This information will help build employee confidence in his managerial abilities. Some specific
questions to ask:

- How has the managerial experience gained in previous jobs prepared you for
  your position with this company?
- Why did you decide to make the move to this firm? What attracted you to this
  company and to the division head post?
- What are your goals as division head, and how do you plan to achieve them?
- What personal and professional qualities do you bring to this position that will
  help you do an effective job?

You could also get personal information about the vice president's family and hobbies, if this kind of material is appropriate for the "new executive" articles published in
the newsletter.

Which research methods should I use, and what specific sources do I consult? There
are times when much of the information you need is supplied primarily by talking with
one source, like in the previous example involving the new company vice president. But
in other instances, you need to use different methods and consult a variety of sources,
such as those reviewed in chapter 3, to get all the facts. The trick, many times, is to use
those methods and sources that will produce the greatest results in the shortest period of
time, and do so cost-effectively.

References and Suggested Reading

Heinz EZ Squirt Funky Purple launch. (2002). Program nomination submitted to PRSA Silver Anvil Awards. New York.

Rea, P. J. & Kerzner, H. (1997). *Strategic planning: A practical guide.* Hoboken, NJ: John Wiley & Sons.

Smith, R. (2002). *Strategic planning for public relations.* Mahwah, NJ: Lawrence Erlbaum Associates.

The Carpet One Magic Carpet Time Tour. (2002). Program nomination submitted to PRSA Silver Anvil Awards. New York.

Wilson, L. (2000). *Strategic program planning for effective public relations campaigns* (3rd ed.). Dubuque, IA: Kendall/Hunt Publishing Company.

CASES

Case 9: Holiday Web Site

You are a freelance public relations professional with a specialty in Web site development and electronic communications. One of your clients is Small-Towns USA, a manufacturer of miniature lighted village collectibles. The company has built a solid base of customers who have become avid collectors. They are primarily women, 35 to 64, with household incomes of $45,000+. The village products can be purchased in major department stores and gift shops, and from thousands of other dealers. In the last two years, an increasing number of consumers have accessed the company's Web site and ordered the products on line. You helped SmallTowns develop the Web site, and now assist the company periodically with upgrades to the site.

Elise Gonzalez, SmallTowns' marketing communications director, calls a meeting with you to discuss changes to the Web site in preparation for the up-coming Christmas season, a time when many consumers purchase the products for holiday decorating. Research also shows many people start and sustain an interest in collecting during the holidays.

"We're a little concerned about reaching our sales goals this year," Elise says. "It seems that many of our dealers have high inventories and are worried that they won't have enough customer traffic to move the products. So, we're looking for some creative promotional ideas to give the products a boost. We want current collectors to maintain their level of purchasing, but we also want to bring new buyers into the fold, in big numbers if possible. We think the Web site might be one way for us to build awareness and help motivate people to visit a dealer."

"I know you said you were going to survey Web site visitors, and get their reactions to the site," you say. "What kind of feedback did you get from them?"

"Well, most everybody had positive comments about the design of the site. They like the color photos of the products; they like being able to order online; and they like the fact that we don't overload the site with copy. But we also heard a lot of people saying that the site could be more interesting, content-wise. Besides product information, they said there's not a lot going on at the site. They'd like more interactive features, maybe even some games. Something else that came up a lot was including more general information and advice on decorating and collecting."

"Hmm, some interesting thoughts. So, I guess you want to make some changes to the site. Are you thinking we should do something special for the holidays?"

"Exactly," Elise says. "Let's come up with some new content ideas, and we'll do it all under some kind of holiday theme. Oh, we've also been giving some thought to getting more involved in charitable causes, and the Web site survey confirmed that our primary customers would be supportive of that. Maybe you could come up with a suggestion for some kind of charitable tie-in? I'd be interested in your recommendations on charities that might fit nicely with our goals, and some kind of special program we could undertake with them that would help them to raise some money or further their goals in some way."

"That's a great idea, and kicking something like that off around the holidays is smart. I'll probably give some thought to charities you could establish a long-term relationship with, because I think it's important that people see this as something you're truly committed to, not just a one-time stunt to get some publicity."

"Absolutely. That's the way we want to think about it," Elise says. "So, just to recap here, we're looking to revamp the Web site and come up with a charity partnership that would support public relations and marketing efforts during the fourth quarter of the year. If you've got any specific ideas about other consumer audiences we might be better targeting, I'd love to hear them."

"Sounds good. So, I'll pull together a preliminary plan and we'll get together in a week or so? How does that sound?" Elise concurs and you ask a few more questions before concluding the meeting.

Assignments

1. Describe five additional research activities you would undertake before preparing the plan for Elise Gonzalez. In two or three sentences, clearly identify the research activity and examples of specific sources you would consult as part of that activity. Then, in a sentence or two explain the significance of each research activity and identify key information you would hope to gain that would be useful to the preparation of your plan.
2. Prepare a three- to four-page plan for revamping SmallTowns USA's Web site that includes the following:
   - Introduction/Situation Analysis
   - Goals
   - Publics (be as specific as you can when identifying and describing each audience, and briefly explain your reasons for targeting each group.)
   - Recommendations for content additions to the Web site and for a possible charity tie-in. Make sure your ideas are specific and clearly explained.
   - Evaluation methods

Case 10: The PRSSA Project (Part A)

Founded in 1968, the Public Relations Student Society of America (PRSSA) is the pre-professional, student counterpart of the Public Relations Society of America (PRSA); PRSA is the world's largest association for public relations professionals. PRSSA helps prepare students for membership in the professional society and, more generally, for successful public relations careers by providing career development activities as well as networking opportunities with practicing public relations professionals. PRSSA members pay annual dues, which entitle them to receive PRSA and PRSSA publications, reduced conference rates, and a reduced PRSA associate member rate upon graduation. (For more information on PRSSA, go to *www.prssa.org*.)

Your college's PRSSA chapter has been active for many years. The chapter sponsors several guest speakers and panel discussions on public relations and career topics throughout the year, and operates a public relations firm that provides services to various campus groups. For example, the firm handles publicity of concerts, films, and other student entertainment sponsored by the college's Student Activities Office and programming board. On occasion, the chapter assists nonprofit groups in the community with the planning of fundraising events and public service campaigns.

In the past two years, however, chapter membership and member participation has declined. There is much excitement each year surrounding the national conference, and this annual event is well attended by chapter members. Following the national conference, attendance at chapter meetings and overall member involvement drops off considerably. Your chapter's board is concerned that almost two-thirds of students enrolled in the public relations program have shown no interest in joining the PRSSA, and that most of the current members are juniors and seniors. The board conducts a survey to gauge perceptions of current PRSSA members, and perceptions of non-PRSSA members who are studying in the public relations program. The survey reveals that:

- A majority of current members said the main reasons they are involved in the chapter are "to attend the national conference" and "to build up their resumé."
- Most of the nonactive members said they are unable to attend weekly meetings, due to part-time jobs, classes and other commitments, so they find it hard to get too involved. Some commented that because they miss meetings, they don't know what the chapter is doing, especially since they are not kept informed in any way about decisions made at meetings and about chapter activities.
- Most of the newer chapter members—freshmen and sophomores—said they attended a few meetings, but got discouraged because they "weren't given anything to do." They also said they often felt like "outsiders" at

meetings because most of the juniors and seniors knew each other and usually talked among themselves.

- Seventy-five percent of the nonmembers said they hadn't joined because of the "cost/dues." They feel dues are high and don't see how the money spent on dues will benefit them. Half of the nonmembers said they "didn't know much about PRSSA" and some (mainly transfers and commuters) said they had "never heard of PRSSA," but that it sounded like something in which they might be interested.

Based on the survey results, which confirmed many assumptions made by board members about member and nonmember attitudes, the board sets out to develop and execute a public relations campaign to revitalize the PRSSA chapter. The board allocates $200 from the budget to be used for the campaign.

Assignment

Working in teams, prepare a four- to five-page plan for the PRSSA chapter that includes the following:

- Introduction/Situation Analysis
- Objectives
- Publics (be specific, and briefly explain your reasons for targeting each group).
- Strategies (for each strategy, include one or two key tactics to support that strategy; note special timing considerations as they relate to strategies/tactics)
- Budget (indicate how the $200 budget would be used, based on proposed strategies)
- Evaluation methods

Case 11: Theater Company's 25th Anniversary

Established more than two decades ago, The Star Theater is a professional theater company. It has gained a reputation as one of the top 20 regional theater companies in the country. Star's season runs from September to May and features six productions, mainly dramas and comedies, although it often features a musical during the Christmas season.

The company's producing director is Richard West, a former New York City-based actor and director with many stage credits, including some Broadway hits. He oversees the company's operations and $3 million annual budget, and works closely with the artistic director on the selection of the seasons' shows. He also serves as liaison to the board of directors; the board is made up of corporate and community leaders and is primarily responsible for fund raising and development. Under West's direction, Star's ticket sales in the last year increased 30%.

The company offers an interesting variety of plays, from classics written by well-known playwrights such as Tennessee Williams, Neil Simon and Noel Coward, to newer productions that had recent runs on- and off-Broadway. It will occasionally stage a lesser-known work by an up-and-coming playwright, and often likes to feature works of great social significance. Most of the actors are professionals from across the United States who belong to the Actors Equity Association; local talent is used on occasion to fill smaller roles. The company has a tradition of using area children in its Christmas show, for example. All actors are paid for their work.

You have recently been hired as a public relations and marketing assistant for Star. You report to Emily Bonaventura, the director of public relations and marketing, who, in turn, reports directly to West. One morning, Bonaventura visits your office to talk about a meeting she had that morning with West.

"You know that next year is our 25th anniversary, and Richard and I were talking about that this morning. He really wants to make a 'big splash' with this anniversary, not just with the media, but in the community as well. As we were talking, he suggested that we might want to think about some programming next year that really helps us reach out into the community in some new ways. Maybe start building some new relationships with groups that don't fit the basic Star theatergoer mold."

"From what I can gather," you say, "people who buy season subscriptions fit a certain profile, don't they? They're usually 50+, professional, tend to be higher income, right?"

"That's pretty much the type, yes. We do bring in the occasional school groups, and get some younger professionals, but we haven't really tapped into those audiences as well as we could. The last survey we did showed those groups weren't too aware of what we do here—some even mentioned that they viewed theater as 'boring entertainment'—but those students and 20- and 30-somethings who had come to a show or two really enjoyed the experience."

"I thought you said that we do some programs in the local schools? Aren't they having much of an impact?"

"We do, but usually that involves Richard or actors from some of the shows speaking to a class here and there about theater and acting careers. We do have an excellent relationship with the local colleges and universities and their theater programs, and we offer internships and other special programs for those students. It's really the junior and senior high school students—even the elementary school kids—whom we want to focus on. Richard sees a real opportunity to get more young people excited about and interested in theater—'the patrons of tomorrow,' as he puts it."

"So, how did you leave it with him? It sounds like we're starting to develop a focus for this anniversary campaign."

"He wants to see a plan from us, and I'd like your help putting it together. You've already given some thought to media activities, so I really don't want to bring that into this plan. Let's focus on public relations and community outreach efforts that can help us start building relationships with younger people. If we could generate media interest in some of these programs, that's great, but it shouldn't be the primary concern."

Bonaventura continues: "Of course, we don't want to forget our loyal patron base in all this, either. We'll want to look at ways for this 25th anniversary campaign to impact them in some way, too. Don't worry about budget too much at this point. Just keep in mind, we don't have a fortune to spend. Why don't you start giving this some thought, maybe even jot down some ideas that we could talk more about next week?"

Assignment

Working alone or in teams of two, prepare a four-page preliminary public relations plan for the 25th anniversary of The Star Theater that includes the following elements:

- Introduction/Situation Analysis
- Objectives
- Publics (be specific, and briefly explain your reasons for targeting each group).
- Strategies (for each strategy, include two or three key tactics that support that strategy; emphasize any special timing considerations as they relate to specific strategies/tactics.)
- Evaluation methods

Case 12: The New Hospital Service (Part B)

You have been gathering information on the new pet visitation program at St. Francis Hospital. The program will allow patients brief visits with their family pets while they are in the hospital. After interviewing key hospital personnel and consulting several other sources, you learn that:

- St. Francis is the only hospital in your area offering such a pet visitation program. Hospital officials believe that giving patients the chance to see their pets will help speed recovery. The program takes effect 3 weeks from today.
- Patients will be allowed half-hour visits with their pets between 6 and 8 p.m. daily, but only if their physicians approve. A special visitation area will be set up; pets will not be allowed in patient rooms.
- At this time, only cats and dogs will be admitted. A current health certificate must be presented in advance of the first visit to prove that pets have had the appropriate shots and are in good health.
- To control the risk of infection, patients who visit with pets must wear disposable gowns to limit the transfer of pet hair or fur. The separate

visitation area is a safe distance from areas where other patients may be receiving treatment. Hospital staff will supervise the visitation room, make sure gowns are properly disposed of, and monitor patients and their roommates closely after pet visits to see that there are no adverse effects.

- Hospital officials hope to eventually establish an animal-assisted therapy program, where animals will be an integral part of patient care and rehabilitation. They see the pet visitation program as a good first step in that direction. Presently, the state health department has approved such therapy programs for nursing homes and other long-term care facilities.

When Scott Nakagawa, the director of public relations and development, returns to the office later that same day, you tell him what you've learned about the pet visitation program and that you will begin thinking about how you might get the media interested in this program and get the word out to area residents.

Assignment

Prepare a three-page plan that outlines ideas for publicizing the pet visitation program. Include the following in your plan:

- Goals of the publicity campaign
- Publics—identify specific groups and briefly explain why each group should be targeted.
- Messages—state the key messages that you want to convey; highlight any specific messages that you want specific publics to receive about the program.
- Media/Strategies—list and explain techniques you would recommend to get exposure in the media and the community for the pet visitation program.
- Timing—note special timing considerations (when should the campaign kick off, should certain techniques be implemented at specific times, etc.).
- Evaluation methods

Tips from the Top

"Writing, Planning and Freelance Work"
Linda Schmidt, freelance public relations writer, Atlanta, GA

Linda Schmidt has worked in the public relations field for more than 30 years. Prior to her freelance career, she did corporate communications and marketing communications work for companies including Turner Broadcasting, Canada Life Assurance and Cox Communications. She talks about the role of planning in freelance writing projects, as well as the challenges of being a freelance writer.

Q: How does a project begin for you? Does someone just call you up and say, "we need you to do this for us?"

A: First, I should tell you I'm fortunate to have a long-time client list. I have monthly jobs with two regular clients. Then, of course, there are the occasional jobs. Usually, I'll get a phone call and the client will say, " We've got a project and we need it done in three days. How soon can you get over here?" Or, I may get a referral. Either way, timing is usually an issue.

Q: That doesn't give you a lot of time to plan, does it? Is that typical?

A: Several years ago, when I first started, there was more of a planning process. Someone would say, "We're thinking of doing something and how much time do you think we need to do this," and we'd set up a timetable. Today, people seem to need it done right away. Everything has become accelerated with e-mail and faxing. It all trickles down to the writing end.

Q: So, let's take a specific job you've done recently and talk about the first meeting with the client. What are the important questions you like to ask?

A: I was hired by an agency to work on a project for one of its clients, a forest management company. The owners of the company were looking to grow their business and focus more on timberland investment. They needed an investor presentation, a booklet for investors. I went in for the meeting and my agency contact talked about the type of presentation that was needed. The agency's client was there, too, and talked more about the business and its goals, and why the company wanted to move forward in this area.

I asked the usual questions: Who are the publics? They were the investor community, financial analysts, and wealthy individual investors. I wanted to know as much as I could about the business and timberland investment. The meeting was not even an hour, but it was not enough of a framework to ask meaty questions. Before I left, I got a big stack of information and was told to "go home, read this, and call if you have questions." The last thing I ask before I leave a meeting is when they have to have this done. Do they want me to e-mail a first page when it's done so they can start looking it over? Can I e-mail the finished copy or do they want it on a disk? Are there specific formatting requirements?

Q: Your research continues at this point, right?

A: Yes. Most of the broader research and planning was already done by the client. [The project] is generally well thought out by the time it gets to me. My research for this project involved delving into what the company and industry were all about. I had research from the timberland field and I was loaded up with examples of other investor presentations. A good freelance writer has to be a quick study and grasp something really fast. I had to learn the subject and get more familiar with the type of piece I was writing. Although I had done annual reports, I had not done an investor presentation before.

Q: How did you decide to approach this piece? Was there a strategy?

A: This had to be written more like an annual report, in that kind of factual language and talk, not like a promotional piece. One thing they stressed was investors won't read it unless it's brief. That's a challenge, trying to make it brief yet compelling. Almost everything you write, you're trying to sell something, though. In this case, they wanted to sell ideas and try to get investors to put money into them.

Q: Now it's time to write. How do you get started? Do you follow a certain system?

A: I never do a detailed outline, but that is just my personal style. I look at the project as a whole. I knew I wanted specific sections so I listed those. Then I went through my sources and noted where each source fit into each section.

In any case, it's a challenge to work around family and volunteer activities since I work part-time, so I usually work when the kids are in school. I need three or four hours in a block to write. I have to start with the introduction to get the voice of the piece. I labor over that part until I get it just right. It might take me 45 minutes to write the first paragraph, and a half hour to write the rest of a section. I finished this piece over the course of five days.

Q: Do you ever know what kind of impact your writing had?

A: Sometimes you get zero feedback. The client occasionally says that she loved it, or it was what she wanted, or that it was the basis for what was needed.

Q: In summary, then, how critical is planning to what you write?

A: Somebody has to have done the planning. If it hasn't been done, and you aren't given the opportunity to do it, what you produce probably won't be used or it will be way off the mark. You're not always in control of the planning process, which can put you at a disadvantage. If what you do is off the mark, it can be difficult to get back and reclaim your credibility. That's always a risk.

Q: Could we talk briefly about freelancing in general? What are some of the key advantages and disadvantages, from your perspective?

A: There's flexibility, but it's not as liberating as some think it is. You're at the beck and call of clients and you can't really say "no." There are a lot of nights and weekends. I got called on a Friday to do a project and it was needed by Tuesday. And it was Labor Day weekend. However, if you love to write, it's ideal, and it's fun to learn about new things.

On the downside, it's somewhat task-oriented. You don't usually get involved, like you might expect, in strategy sessions. There are times when you get to use more of your [public relations] skills. I was working with an HR (human resources) person on the Labor Day piece and I helped her to focus on what she was trying to say, and how she was trying to say it. You can help your clients to see the bigger picture if they are open to your opinions.

Q: You've been freelancing for more than 15 years. Based on your experience, what are the most important qualities of a successful freelance writer?

A: You have to be self-disciplined, a self-starter, and have natural curiosity. You also have to be politically oriented in a corporate sense. You're not always called upon to give your input. As a freelance writer, you're not a counselor. I know my regular clients and I can say, "You really don't want to do it that way" to them, if I feel strongly about a piece or tactic.

Also, when I'm with new clients, I buy into their organization as soon as possible. Right away, I start saying "we" and "our"—how are "we" going to do this? A client that makes widgets is passionate about it, and you will be expected to be just as passionate about those widgets. The interest and commitment you demonstrate go a long way in creating good client relationships.

I would say to someone right out of college, don't go into freelance work right away. You'll be a better writer by getting experience in the corporate or non-profit world, and you'll know more about how companies and offices operate.

5

Memos, Letters, Reports, and Proposals

It's been said that death and taxes are the only certainties in life. Public relations practitioners can add a third item to that list: writing business documents. Statements such as "Send me a memo on that" or "Great idea, why don't you come up with a proposal?" are part of everyday conversations between public relations professionals and the people with whom they work.

To meet the challenge of good business writing, keep in mind the colorful comments about business writing made by American motion picture producer Samuel Goldwyn of Metro Goldwyn Mayer (MGM): "I read part of it all the way through," and "A verbal agreement isn't worth the paper it's written on" (Boone, 1999, pp. 63, 289). Those who receive your memos, letters, reports, and proposals should be able to read these documents quickly and with ease all the way through to absorb your meaning clearly. Also, without written documents in place, decisions made at meetings or great ideas shared in hallway conversations may be forgotten. Putting them in writing is the professional, smart, and safe thing to do.

Memoranda

Memos are documents that pass along information inside an organization. The most basic memos are brief—a few paragraphs to a page long. Memos are used for the following:

Purpose	Example
Inform about new developments.	Some important changes have been made to the company profit-sharing plan that you need to know about.
Inform about upcoming events.	Next Tuesday is "Take Your Son or Daughter to Work Day," and we want to encourage you to take part in that special day.

Confirm verbal decisions and agreements.	As we discussed this morning, I will begin planning the June 10 news conference.
Provide program and activity progress reports.	The annual meeting is one month away, so I thought I should update you on our progress in planning this event.

Every memo is written (1) to someone; (2) by someone else; (3) at some point in time, (4) about some subject. These are the four items that should be included in the standard memo heading:

Memorandum

To:	Deborah Pearson
From:	James Curry
Date:	November 15, 2002
Subject:	Annual Meeting Progress Report

There are variations of the heading. Some organizations begin the memo heading with the date or always include job titles. It's a good idea to include job titles when the sender and recipient are not well acquainted.

When writing memos, use proper spacing. Single space between sentences within a paragraph, and double space between paragraphs. Leave some white space between the last line of the heading and the first paragraph of the memo. Paragraphs may be indented, depending on the style your organization prefers. Regarding the content of memos:

- Clearly state the memo's purpose in the first sentence. Don't waste time on details that prevent the reader from quickly seeing your reason for writing, as the following paragraph does:

  A few days ago, I called and left a voice mail message for you about a project I am working on. I need to speak with you and get some information that will help me write an article for the employee newsletter on the employee diversity training workshops.

A better opening paragraph gets right to the point with fewer words:

  I would like to arrange an interview with you to talk about the upcoming employee diversity training workshops. The information will be used to write an employee newsletter article.

- Emphasize the most important points in the body of the memo. Write short sentences and paragraphs. Use "I," "you," and "we" to keep it direct and personal:

First, I would like to get a quote from you on the value of these workshops to employees and what the company hopes to achieve by running these workshops. I also need some additional facts:

○ The days, times and locations of the workshops.

○ The content and format of the workshops—what will employees learn and in what activities will they take part?

○ Measures you will use to evaluate the success of the workshops.

- In the closing, say what you will do next or what you want the receiver to do. Avoid using general statements such as, "I look forward to hearing from you." Make your call-to-action specific:

  I need this information by Friday, June 9. Please e-mail your responses to me by that date. Thank you.

  OR

  I would like to meet or talk with you by phone for 20 to 30 minutes some-time during the week of June 5-9. I will call you this Friday, June 2, to arrange a convenient day and time for the interview.

There are times when a longer memo is justified. Many public relations profession-als create *planning memos*, which present program plans in memo format to others within the organization. The same memo heading is used but the document runs several pages in length. Each program planning element is detailed, from the situation analysis to evaluation methods. A short paragraph at the beginning of the memo introduces the content that follows, and a brief conclusion reinforces the strengths and benefits of the plan. Subheads are used to separate each section. Planning memos also make greater use of numbered items, graphics, and bullet points to make the content easy to read and cer-tain items jump off the page. For example, use numbers when listing program goals, highlight strategies in italics, and list key tactics under each strategy with bullets.

Voice Mail

Most of us have had the following experience: You're checking your voice mail and sud-denly you hear the name or voice of a person famous for long-winded messages. Be-cause you're busy, and you suspect this is another unessential message, you instantly press the delete button. Unfortunately, there may have been vital information in that message but because the person rambled on, you never listened long enough to hear it. If used properly, telephone answering systems like voice mail are an excellent substitute for the written memo, and a good way to get important information to large groups quickly and simultaneously. How can you make the best use of voice mail?

- State your message in 30 seconds or less. Write down what you want to say be-fore you send voice mail. Identify yourself, briefly explain why you are calling, and quickly mention the information most relevant to the receiver. Leave your name and phone number if you are the contact person, or let people know how they can find out more about the subject.

- Leave out all the details. Focus on main points and refer people to written documents, Web sites, or other sources that can provide more specifics. If your intention is to get a return phone call, there's no need to say everything. Share the main reason for your call and express your interest in talking further about the matter. Suggest the best time to call back within the next day or two.

- Return calls promptly. When you are the receiver, be courteous and get back to someone as soon as you can. Your quick response ensures that others will give your voice mail the same consideration. Revise your voice mail answering message to let people know that you are out of the office for an extended period, when you will return, and who they can speak with in case of an emergency.

Letters

Blaise Pascal, a French philosopher, once said, "I have made this letter longer than usual, only because I have not had the time to make it shorter" (Boone, 1999, p. 57). This is not the way to go for business letters you write. Well-written letters are clear in their purpose, to the point, and generally follow the content guidelines for good memo writing. They provide information and verify arrangements, but are directed primarily to external audiences. Public relations letters, for example, confirm price quotes and production timetables with printing companies, or respond to dissatisfied customers and offer apologies for a negative experience. Letters follow a specified format:

- *Heading*. This includes the date, followed by a single-spaced block that includes the name, title, company, and address of the receiver. Leave a single space between the date and the person's name. Your company and address are unnecessary in the heading since most letters are distributed on letterhead, with the company name and address clearly visible.

- *Salutation*. Use "Dear Mr. or Ms." or accepted formal titles such as "Dr." or "Professor," never "Dear Sir or Madam." It has become more common to use the person's full name, as well (e.g., "Dear P. Jones," "Dear Pat Jones"). First names are fine for letters being sent to familiar business associates.

- *Body*. State your reason for sending the letter in a brief first paragraph. Other paragraphs are short and present key ideas. It is okay to use bold type or underscoring to highlight a point or two, but don't overdo. Like memos, single space between sentences in a paragraph, double space between paragraphs.

- *Closing and signature*. Use "Sincerely" for most letters; "Regards" or "Best Regards" are used more often in letters to people you know well.

In addition to basic business letters, public relations people write specialized letters that are more persuasive in tone. These include **appeal letters**, typically written by not-for-profit organizations to solicit donations and support (see Exhibit 5.1); **pitch letters** to

Exhibit 5.1   Reprint from PR Professional Daily: "Effective Fundraising Letters"

While public relations professionals are usually the people in their organizations responsible for generating charitable contributions, standard public relations techniques don't always apply when creating effective fund-raising campaigns. Here are a few tips for creating fundraising mailings that get attention (and contributions):

- Clearly identify your organization and what your organization does.
- Clearly identify the purpose of your fund-raising campaign, whether it be for your operation costs (if you are a nonprofit organization), for a specific charitable cause, or for a charitable organization. Be sure to express the importance and urgency of the cause.
- Be specific, if appropriate, about how much you intend to raise, how much you've raised for the same purpose in the past, and how much you hope the mailing recipient will contribute.
- Emphasize any affiliation with a well-known, well respected nonprofit organization, and include the organization's logo if possible.
- Create a theme that can be expressed visually and verbally. Use this theme to create a catchy tag phrase and opening paragraph to the letter. For example, you could use a fishing theme and say something like, "We're angling for your contribution."
- Appeal to the heart—and the head. Use quotes, anecdotes, and descriptions that appeal to the emotions. Then reinforce the emotions with facts and statistics.
- Be positive—no "gloom and doom." Although charitable causes usually involve sad circumstances, don't overdramatize or dwell on the negative aspects. This will only depress the reader. Instead, focus on how the charity has helped the cause in the past and how further contributions can help it even more.
- Don't use pressure. In the long run, making people feel guilty is not an effective fund-raising technique. Contributors who feel good about their efforts are more likely to repeat the gesture year after year.
- Tell readers what benefits they will receive for their contributions (e.g., tax deductions, charity membership, or sponsorship recognition). Keep in mind that businesses will need practical reasons to make a donation. Give them specific information as to how a donation will help them promote a positive public image and achieve visibility within the community (e.g., you will announce their name at your event or print their logo on your program, newspaper ads, banners, etc.)
- Make it as simple as possible for contributors to make a donation. Include all the information and tools a contributor will need, such as payment information, a self-addressed stamped envelope, a toll-free number, and a contact name. ∎

Note: Reprinted with permission of PR Professional Daily (R. Whitlock, May 27, 1999).

present story ideas to media contacts (these are discussed in chapter 7); and *new business* or *prospecting letters*, which are used by public relations firms to introduce themselves to potential clients. Prospecting letters introduce the firm and the writer, include background information about the potential client and reasons why public relations services are needed, suggest a few ways in which public relations can benefit the prospect, and request a face-to-face meeting.

You may also write letters in response to legitimate customer complaints or other criticisms of your organization. In their book *Writing that Works: How to Communicate Effectively in Business* Kenneth Roman and Joel Raphaelson suggest that it is best to be courteous rather than defensive when responding to all complaints. When writing these letters:

- In the first paragraph, acknowledge the person's complaint. Don't accuse someone of overreacting. Show that you are aware of the person's concerns and be respectful of his or her feelings.
- In the body of the letter, tell the person how you plan to respond to the complaint. Indicate specific steps to be taken and when those steps will be taken as well as other decision makers who will be consulted. In addition, offer apologies for any inconvenience or upset the situation may have caused. If there's a chance a situation may prompt a lawsuit, you should consult with the organization's legal staff before publicly acknowledging any fault.
- In a closing paragraph, point out that you welcome future suggestions and feedback and that you value that person's continued business and support.

There are situations where a concern or complaint is unjustified or is based on inaccurate information about company policy or procedure. In those cases, state your company's position in a polite and straightforward manner and make an effort to clarify any misconceptions.

E-mail

Many people have abandoned the traditional letter for electronic mail (e-mail). E-mail gets information to employees, the media, clients, and others in minutes as opposed to hours or days. But e-mail generally is sent to those who welcome that kind of communication. A sure way to alienate media contacts is to keep sending e-mails for which they didn't ask. In response, they may activate a mechanism to automatically block any messages coming from your e-mail address. E-mail works best when you:

- First decide if e-mail is the best choice. Some messages are better sent by other methods. If, for example, you are extending an invitation to a conference speaker or attempting to get a local company to sponsor your community event, a more formal letter printed and mailed on your organization's letterhead is advised. Once contact is made, e-mail becomes a good follow-up tool.

- Include a strong subject line that connects with the receiver's interests. The media and others you deal with receive loads of e-mail each day. A well-conceived subject line can make your message stand out. If you are trying to get a business reporter to take an interest in something your company has done, write a subject line that uses business-type words or clearly states the benefit to readers: "ABC, 123 companies announce merger."

- Keep your message brief. Get to the point quickly in the first paragraph. Limit your message to a few short paragraphs, except in those instances when someone has requested more depth. It is recommended that you include a formal closing with your name, title, company, phone, and fax numbers.

- Follow the rules of good writing. One of e-mail's benefits is its speed of delivery, but that doesn't give you the license to be hasty and sloppy when preparing messages. Write in complete sentences, use spell check, and take time to proofread. Hold back on the use of cute online symbols (e.g., :-) to relay humor. They are fine for personal e-mail, but inappropriate for professional communications. Guidelines for e-mail etiquette are featured in Exhibit 5.2.

- Think twice about sending attachments. There is nothing more frustrating than receiving an attachment file that you cannot open. Always ask first if it's all right to send an attachment, and before sending it, find out if you are using compatible word processing programs.

Exhibit 5.2   E-mail Etiquette

Words actually make up less than 10 percent of the messages we send. The rest of the message is communicated through things like body posture, gestures, eye contact, facial expressions, and how we use our voice. With e-mail messages, or any written message, we don't have nonverbal and vocal support. So we must rely on words alone.

Although e-mail is quick, convenient, and fun, don't make the assumption that writing e-mail messages is any different than writing a letter you would send through the mail. When drafting an e-mail message for someone other than close friends, be professional and follow these guidelines:

- Include a salutation. Refer to the person to whom you are writing the e-mail the same as you would in person. If you normally use the person's first name, then start your message with "Dear Michael." Otherwise, use the appropriate courtesy title with the person's last name.

- Use correct spelling and grammar. Yes, it's easy to click on that reply button and beat out a quick message. That doesn't mean you can be sloppy. Write in complete sentences and use correct grammar. Use spell check and the dictionary. Also, stay away from the many abbreviations that have cropped up in e-mail use; for example, using "BTW" for "by the way" or "TTYL" for "talk to you later."

- Use capitalization correctly. Follow the same rules for capitalization that you would in any other written communication. If you type your e-mail using all capital letters, it will make the receiver feel like he or she is getting yelled at. On

(continued)

the other hand, if you don't use any capital letters, even at the start of sentences, you may be sending a message that you have low self-confidence.

- Use normal punctuation. Again, follow the standard rules. Because we don't have the support of nonverbal and vocal cues in e-mail, we tend to make up for that with excessive exclamation marks, dashes, or series of dots that seem to go on forever. Messages that are well thought out and constructed shouldn't need any extra help.

- Avoid using smiley faces. Another way we have attempted to make up for the lack of nonverbal and vocal cues in e-mail is through the development of a series of cute online symbols used for emphasis and emotion, such as using :-) for happy, :-(for sad, ;-) for sarcasm, or :-O for surprise or yelling. Do you really want to include one of these in a business e-mail? Enough said.

- Always add a signature. Your e-mail address may not always accurately indicate who is sending the e-mail, so always include a "signature." Your signature may consist of just your name or your name, title, company, address, phone, Web site, and e-mail (the information that would typically be on the company's printed letterhead). Many e-mail senders have begun adding quotes or images at the end of their signatures. These have no place in business e-mail.

- Proofread carefully. Once your message has been drafted, take a solid, critical look at it. Be objective and try to read it through the eyes of the receiver. Is there any confusing language? Is there any content that could be misinterpreted?

- Make the message easy to read. Using the above guidelines will help improve the clarity of your message. To improve the readability format of the message, indent paragraphs or double space between them. Also, while most computers now automatically will "wrap" words from one line to the next, some may have to be wrapped manually. The standard sentence length for e-mail is 80 characters, at which point you would hit the return button to go to the next line. If you're not sure whether your computer handles wrapping automatically, send a message to yourself.

- Protect the thread. The thread is the series of messages that has been exchanged since the original message. When replying to a message, continue the thread by clicking on "reply" rather than starting a new message. The thread contains important background information that will help put the new message in context for the receiver.

- Don't be hasty. Because e-mail is so quick and convenient, we are tempted to reply to messages right away. Not only will this affect how well written your message is, but it also may cause regrets later on. If you're upset over an e-mail message you receive, don't react immediately. Take some time to think over the response, or consider if a response is even necessary. Once you hit the send button, there's no getting that message back.

- Keep private things private. Never think of e-mails as personal and confidential. Companies have the right to monitor their employees' e-mail practices; messages can remain on your computer system (yes, even after you delete them), and they can be forwarded to other people. When composing an e-mail message, make sure you are comfortable with the information being shared with others.

Reports

When you have considerable information to share, write a report. These multi-page documents are used to inform clients and senior managers about the results of public opinion studies and other research efforts, or to provide in-depth assessment of a campaign or project. Many of the same guidelines for writing memos and letters apply to reports. Brevity, clarity, simple language, and graphics enhance reports. A model for report writing is the *research report*, which includes the following sections:

- Cover page with a title that summarizes the focus of the report and includes the name(s) of those submitting the report and the date of submission.
- Table of contents outlining the report sections and their page numbers.
- Executive summary that highlights significant findings, conclusions, and recommendations in one or two pages.
- Introduction that explains the purpose of the report, the history of the research problem, research methods used, and limitations of the study.
- Body of the report, which presents detailed findings. If survey results are shared, findings are best presented in percentages rather than numbers (e.g., 30% said "yes," 50% said "no," 20% said "no opinion"). Charts and graphs make the data easy to read and understand.
- Analysis and conclusions. The report writer must interpret the data, pull out the most significant findings, and discuss their implications.
- Recommendations on how the organization should proceed based on the research findings.
- Supporting materials. These can include copies of questionnaires or related media articles that add perspective to the subject.
- Bibliography that lists the sources used in compiling the report.

Annual Reports

Another type of report written by public relations professionals is the annual report. Annual reports review the financial performance and accomplishments of an organization in a given year, and define strategic direction for the future. For-profit companies that trade stock publicly are required by law to produce specific financial information for their shareholders, investors, and the financial community. This information often is included in an annual report, which can double as a promotional tool written with stockholders, employees, and other key publics in mind. Not-for-profit agencies are not obligated to produce annual reports. Many do, however, because of increasing public scrutiny of charitable groups and how they spend fund-raising dollars. The annual report is a way to build donor confidence in their cause and their financial management.

Formats for annual reports vary. A large corporation may create a lengthy, magazine-style report with four-color photographs and high-tech graphics. Not-for-profit groups, sensitive to the way administrative dollars are spent, create less slick reports printed in black and white. Online versions of annual reports are included on many organizations' Web sites. Annual reports, as with any other printed piece, should reflect the character of the organization.

Most annual reports contain common elements: 1) a theme, for example, Tandy Corporation/Radio Shack used the annual report theme line "We've Got Goals" in conjunction with its "You've Got Questions, We've Got Answers" advertising campaign theme; 2) a letter to shareholders from the CEO addressing the company's performance in the past year, key challenges, and future goals (Exhibit 5.3 is a good example taken from a Gap, Inc. annual report); 3) detailed financial facts, figures, and statements; 4) information on the company, its people, and its products or services, with an emphasis on the past year's innovations; and 5) an examination of critical issues the company faces and how it plans to tackle those issues in the future. Other than the financial data, public relations writers, or the firms they hire to work on these time-consuming pieces, write most sections of the report, including the letter from the CEO. When producing annual reports:

Exhibit 5.3   CEO Letter to Shareholders: The Gap Annual Report

Dear Shareholders:

"Less is more." We take these three words to heart at Gap Inc. They mean focus and simplicity—in the way we sell our products, serve our customers, run our company.

These three words also constantly challenge us: Is our marketing as clear, our merchandising as focused as possible? Are our operations as efficient and streamlined as they can be? And, most important, are we consistently offering our customers the convenient, easy and enjoyable shopping experience they expect?

In 1998, we met these challenges more often than not, and our customers rewarded us with the best overall year in our company's history. The financial results speak for themselves: net sales, net earnings, return on equity and earnings per share all increased significantly.

Our performance also speaks to the culture and spirit of this company, to the passion our more than 110,000 employees worldwide bring each day to our offices, our stores, our customers. In 1998, that passion propelled each of our brands—Gap, Banana Republic and Old Navy—to new levels of success, to greater challenges and to fresh opportunities.

Quality growth continues to be a priority for Gap Inc. To make our products easily available to more people in more places, Gap, Banana Republic and Old Navy opened a total of 318 new stores in 1998—nearly one a day—on our way to adding 22 percent in square feet to our

(continued)

retail footprint around the world. In the United States, we expanded our presence to all 50 states by opening a Gap store in Anchorage, Alaska. Gap Inc. now operates more than 2,400 stores throughout the United States, the United Kingdom, Canada, France, Japan and Germany—and there are still tremendous growth opportunities for our brands around the world.

Creative energy and strategic operating discipline. The balance between these enabled us to improve our operations in 1998 while realizing high-impact paybacks on several new and ongoing initiatives. At the beginning of the year, for instance, we challenged our Gap brand to become the world's headquarters for khakis. Toward that end, we created and unleashed an integrated merchandising, media and in-store marketing campaign that increased our market share and drove sales throughout the year. Such efforts companywide in 1998 increased Gap Inc.'s overall return on investment and boosted our sales per square foot—while growing topline revenues 39 percent. Those are key indicators that we are achieving quality growth.

At Gap, we continued our pursuit of a single global identity by making several brand-wide improvements. First, we integrated the merchandising and field management functions of our Gap, GapKids and Gap Outlet divisions. Then, to ensure that our customers experience brand consistency everywhere we do business—from Tupelo to Tokyo—we adopted a global approach to marketing the Gap brand, coordinating the tone, text and timing of our messages worldwide. Gap's Online Store also completed its first full year of business on the Internet in 1998, adding GapKids and babyGap Web sites. Our expanded online presence makes us more available to and convenient for our customers.

Banana Republic sharpened its brand image and extended its reach with tightly focused merchandising and seamlessly integrated marketing. The brand's first-ever television ads conveyed the romance and sophistication of the Banana Republic lifestyle, and inspired many new customers to experience the casual luxury of collections like Fall's "Suede" and Holiday's "Cashmere." And the debut of the Banana Republic Catalog extended the brand's reach directly into customers' homes, enabling them to conveniently place orders with knowledgeable style consultants around the clock. Supported by a call and fulfillment center in Ohio, Catalog proved that the brand's behind-the-scenes infrastructure was every bit as strong as its up-front creativity.

Gap Inc.'s youngest brand, Old Navy, continued its five-year-old mission to make "fun, family, fashion and value" part of every American's shopping vocabulary. On its way to opening more than 100 new stores in 1998, Old Navy strengthened its distinctive voice in the retail apparel

(continued)

market with delightfully irreverent marketing, including crowd-pleasing grand opening celebrations, merchandise promotions and community-service events—not to mention the advertising power of our own Magic the Dog. As a result, Old Navy became a brand of choice in schools, offices and playgrounds all over the United States.

Gap. Banana Republic. Old Navy. We believe these three distinctive brands combine in a Gap Inc. portfolio that is uniquely positioned not just to expand in the near term, but to generate sustained, high-quality growth well into the 21st century. We'll face tough challenges along the way, of course, but we think we'll be ready for them. Driven by a passion to make everything we do the best it can be, to make "less is more" a reality, we're looking to the future every day. And the truth is, we like what we see.

Millard S. Drexler   Donald G. Fisher
President and Chief Executive Officer   *Chairman and Founder*

Note. Reprinted with the permission of Gap, Inc.

- Be honest. This is less a "tip" than it is a necessity. Annual reports are factual, straightforward documents. Maintain a positive tone, but never hide negative news or distort financial information in the company's favor.
- Be creative and interesting. Break the mold and try something new. Foodmaker, the parent company of Jack in the Box restaurants, presented an annual report in comic-book form, which was well received by stockholders and financial analysts. Wichita Children's Home won praise by presenting its report through the eyes of a child living at the home, with type that looked like a child's handwriting.
- Be easy to read. Avoid overloading people with highly technical terms and facts. Focus on main points and use simple, easy-to-understand language. Write in active voice and use photos, charts, and other visuals.

- Be mission-driven. Annual reports connect with the company's goals. The Wichita Children's Home saw its report as a tool for educating people about the home's importance to abused children, and as a vehicle to recruit new donors. The report is credited with a 5 to 10% increase in funding.

Proposals

Proposals are designed much like standard reports, but they do more than provide facts, findings, and suggestions; they aim to convince the reader to take a specific course of action. Public relations firms develop new business proposals to present their credentials to prospective clients and demonstrate how their services can help the clients' businesses. Corporate public relations practitioners draft proposals for senior management to sell them on the benefits of making charitable donations, sponsoring a new event, or initiating some other program.

Not-for-profit professionals seeking outside funding for projects design *grant proposals* and submit those to corporations and foundations. Some funding sources provide forms and exact criteria for completion of grant proposals, while others simply tell you to submit a proposal. In general, well-written grant proposals make their case with concise and persuasive language, and incorporate statistics and other hard evidence to justify the funding request.

The Corporation for Public Broadcasting, which reviews hundreds of annual grant requests and provides major funding to public television and radio stations, provides tips for grant proposal writing on its Web site (www.cpb.org/grants/grantwriting.html). It lists four components of a grant proposal: 1) the narrative, or body of the proposal; 2) the budget, with specific cost projections; 3) supporting materials as requested by the funding source such as case studies and letters of support for your request; and 4) authorized signatures from appropriate, high-ranking officials within your organization. The narrative, structured much like a public relations program plan, should answer the following questions:

- What do we want? (A clear statement of the funding need.)
- What public concern or issue will be addressed and why? (Background on the problem and reasons the proposal should be supported.)
- Who will benefit and why?
- What goals and measurable objectives can be accomplished?
- What methods or activities will be used to achieve those goals and objectives? (Includes a detailed timetable to show project flow from start to finish.)
- How will results be evaluated or measured?
- Who are we and why are we qualified to meet this need? (Includes credentials of key staff involved in the project as well as the organization's resume.)

Arthur Asa Berger, in his book *Improving Writing Skills: Memos, Letters, Reports and Proposals*, states that, in general, proposals are most persuasive when they:

- Appeal to the self-interest of, and have clear benefits for, all the involved parties.

- Use your reader's ideas and beliefs to your advantage, by knowing what the reader is looking for before you develop and submit the proposal.

- Deal with short-term or long-term benefits, or both if appropriate; focus on long-term benefits if short-term costs are great or vice versa.

- Emphasize cost efficiency by showing that the proposal leads to a payoff or to increased savings.

- Have a writing style that expresses confidence in the value of your ideas without being too arrogant.

- Show how your proposed actions or solutions are better than all others suggested.

References and Suggested Reading

Alred, G. J., Brusau, C. T., & Oliu, W. E. (2000). *The business writer's handbook* (6th ed.). Boston: St. Martin's.

The AMA style guide for business writing. (1996). New York: AMACOM.

Argenti, P. A. & Forman, J. (2002). *The power of corporate communication: Crafting the voice and image of your business.* New York: McGraw Hill.

Basic elements of grant writing. (2000). Retrieved December 22, 2002 from http://www.cpb.org/grants/grantwriting.html

Berger, A. A. (1993). *Improving writing skills: Memos, letters, reports and proposals.* Thousand Oaks, CA: Sage Publications.

Boone, L. E. (1999). *Quotable Business, 2nd edition.* New York: Random House.

Davidson, W. (2001). *Business writing: What works, what won't* (Rev. ed.). New York: St. Martin's Press.

Dobrian, J. (1997). *Business writing skills.* New York: AMACOM.

E-Mail etiquette. (1998). Retrieved February 5, 2003 from http://www.iwill follow.com/email/htm

Gap, Inc. 1998 Annual Report. Retrieved December 22, 2002 from www.gapinc.com

Roman, K. & Raphaelson, J. (2000). *Writing that works: How to communicate effectively in business* (3rd ed.). New York: HarperResource.

Seglin, J. L. & Coleman, E. (2002). *The AMA handbook of business letters* (3rd ed.). New York: AMACOM.

CASES

Case 13: Law Firm Launches PR Program (Part A)

Fleischman, Craig, Gurdak, and Heasley is the second largest law firm in a city of 400,000 people. The 75-year-old firm employs 50 attorneys and has an executive committee comprised of eight senior partners. Among its specialties are corporate and tax law, wills and estate planning, and real estate law. Two of the firm's partners have extensive experience with legal cases relating to medical malpractice, right-to-die and other health care issues, and another has developed a national reputation for her expertise in environmental law. The firm's clients include large and small businesses, hospitals, banks, school districts, engineering firms, as well as individuals. Recently, in response to the aging Baby Boomer population, the firm has been trying to build its client base of professional men and women nearing retirement age who have special legal and estate planning needs.

Many of the firm's attorneys are graduates of Harvard, Georgetown, Columbia, Duke, and other leading law schools. Firm partners and associates are active in *pro bono* work; a major focus is providing free legal advice to local persons with AIDS. A few of the attorneys have taken leadership roles on the boards of directors of civic, cultural, and nonprofit groups such as the local symphony and the United Way.

One year ago, the firm hired Margaret Bogan as its first-ever marketing and client relations director. Bogan worked previously for a large advertising agency in the area as a copywriter and marketing specialist. Most of her first year with the firm has been spent doing market research, developing brochures and informational materials, and getting to know the firm and its clients. She also created a Web site for the firm and an online newsletter for internal audiences. As her responsibilities expanded, Bogan realized she needed additional staff, and the firm agreed to provide budget monies to hire a marketing assistant. Bogan hired Lisa Chen, a recent college graduate with a degree in public relations. Chen meets with Bogan the second day on the job to discuss an important project.

"Up to this point, I've been focusing most of my efforts on marketing, but I think we could be doing a lot more in the public relations area," Bogan says. "That's one of the main reasons I brought you on board, Lisa, since you have that kind of background. I think the time has come for us to develop an ongoing public relations program for the firm, and I'm going to ask you to take the lead on this. I'm more of a marketing person than a public relations person so I'm looking to you to provide some strategic direction."

"I'm glad you have that kind of confidence in me," Chen replies. "From what I can tell, the firm hasn't done too much public relations programming. I'm curious, how do you think the senior partners view public relations?"

"Many of them don't understand what public relations is and how it can be used effectively. I think there are a few who still don't see why we even need a marketing program. They think the firm sells itself. On some level, they're right, since much of the business and corporate work they do comes from client referrals. But the market is much more competitive now, which they are slowly starting to appreciate. As you know, lawyers now have the constitutional right to promote their services, but the partners here have been cautious about the kinds of promotion we do. We don't advertise; we rarely send out news releases, and we've got little presence in the local media. I should add that our key competitors seem to pop up in the press quite often."

"It's interesting that you say that. I notice that the client study the firm just completed reinforces this 'lack of presence' you're talking about."

"Yes. We surveyed our clients and asked them what they thought about the firm and how it is perceived. What we found is that our clients think the work we do for them is top-notch and that the firm is well-respected in legal circles, but they don't hear or read about the firm all that much and they'd like to see us having a higher profile in the community. That's why I think public relations can be valuable since it directly addresses those kinds of concerns."

"I'm hearing, then, that you'd like me to come up with some public relations ideas for the firm. Do you want me to focus strictly on publicity activities or do you want some suggestions on how to build our profile in the community?"

"A mix of both would be good. Any ideas you have that will help us be more visible to our clients, to prospective clients, and to other key publics. But I'd like you to limit your recommendations to five or six public relations activities that provide a good starting point for the firm. If we could only get involved in six public relations activities or projects right now, what would they be? Don't worry about going into a lot of detail—just give me a general description of the activity, what it involves, and why we should do it. The partners will be interested in knowing how public relations will help the firm grow and contribute to the bottom line, so each activity you suggest needs to be explained and justified with those interests in mind. Since this is more of a preliminary proposal to help give me a better idea of how to begin, why not put your suggestions in memo form—four pages or so should do it—and get those to me in one week."

Assignment

Work in teams of two or three to discuss start-up public relations activities for the law firm and to write the four-page memorandum for Bogan. Structure your memo's content based on the public relations program outline presented in chapters 3 and 4. Also include a brief introduction and conclusion. When explaining recommended start-up activities, be sure to indicate the publics targeted for each activity.

Case 14: The Samaritan House Appeal

As a new public relations and development assistant for The Samaritan House, your duties include planning special events, handling publicity and media relations, and writing most of the fund-raising campaign materials. The Samaritan House, a social service agency established in the early 1900s, has more than 300 operations in cities nationwide. The International Association of Good Samaritans is the parent organization that coordinates all The Samaritan Houses. The Samaritan House in your city is one of the largest in the country, with 350 employees, 25 social service programs, and an annual budget of $11 million. In addition to running several homeless shelters and soup kitchens in your area, The Samaritan House offers alcohol and drug rehabilitation programs and a learning center where disadvantaged individuals can learn computer and other job skills.

While many of those who use the services are low-income elderly and single-parent families, a growing number are middle-class adults who recently lost a job due to major company downsizing in your area. Some of these individuals have found new jobs, but at much lower salaries, which is making it difficult to keep up with their bills. Others have failed to find work in a market where the unemployment rate has steadily increased in the past two years. As a result, The Samaritan House has seen a 10% jump in the number of people using its services in the past year.

One of your main tasks at this time is to create solicitation materials to raise money for the annual Thanksgiving dinner, one of The Samaritan House's major events. People with nowhere to go or who can't afford to prepare a holiday meal for themselves and their families are treated to a delicious turkey dinner with all the trimmings. The major source of funding for the dinner is financial donations from individuals and local businesses. A donation of $2 will feed one hungry person; $20 will feed 10 people; $28 will feed 15 people; $38 will feed 45 people; and $120 will feed 60 people. Your research of previous dinners produces some additional facts:

- Last year, 2,000 people enjoyed The Samaritan House's Thanksgiving dinner in your city. Many of those in attendance were single mothers with children under 10 and senior citizens without spouses or whose children live a great distance away. This year, The Samaritan House in your city plans to serve more people on Thanksgiving Day. In addition to serving those who come to The Samaritan House, it will also be delivering a hot holiday meal to more than 1,000 men and women who can't leave their homes due to age, illness, or disability.

- During its existence, The Samaritan House has fed tens of thousands of people on Thanksgiving. The Samaritan House serves three hot, nutritious meals every day of the year in its dining room to hungry people in your area. This year, in total, The Samaritan House in your city has served more than 300,000 meals to hungry people.
- Community donations are vital for this event and provide more than 75% of the total funding needed. Individual contributions are important this year because of cutbacks in government funding and reductions in the area's business work force.
- This year, like every year, many volunteers from throughout the community will share part of their Thanksgiving Day to help prepare and serve the meals.

Assignments

1. Write a one-page, direct mail fund-raising letter to prospective, first-time donors who have not supported the Thanksgiving dinner in the past.
2. Write a one-page, direct mail fund-raising letter to individuals who made a donation to support the Thanksgiving dinner last year, encouraging them to support the event again this year.

Case 15: The Shopping Bag Complaint

You work in the public relations department of Tees & Flannels, a national retail clothing chain. Tees & Flannels sells casual and outdoor clothing that appeals mainly to teens and college students. One day, Jacob Zellers, the company's public relations director, shares with you an angry letter from a parent whose daughters recently purchased clothing at one of your stores. The letter reads:

> Yesterday, my 12- and 14-year-old daughters bought some T-shirts at your store. I was shocked by the high prices they paid for the shirts, but I was even more disturbed by the images on the shopping bag—a young man stripped naked to the waist with two young girls on each side of him. The three of them are rolling around on a couch in a very suggestive manner.

> This picture, in my opinion, is completely inappropriate, considering that 12- and 14-year-olds like my daughters are your typical customers. What messages do my girls get when they go to your store and get bags like this? Clearly, the young people on this bag are up to no good; from the dirty grin on the young man's face, it's clear he has other things on his mind besides clothes. Is it really necessary to show half naked people on your shopping bags and to promote sexual behavior among adolescents in this way? Not only is it unnecessary, it's irresponsible.

I did talk about this with my daughters and I explained that this kind of advertising is not acceptable because it treats girls as sexual objects. Honestly, they are puzzled by it all and don't really understand why your store would use this kind of picture on its bags. Frankly, I have a hard time grasping that myself. I ask you to stop using these bags and to please reconsider the kind of sexual images you are conveying. My feeling is, this letter will probably end up in a trash can in some office in your corporate headquarters, but I needed to express my concerns nonetheless. Please, please be more sensitive to your impressionable young customers, and be more sensitive to the concerns of parents like me who, I should add, supply the money that teenagers use to buy your overpriced clothes.

Sincerely,
Michael Chalmers

After you read the letter, Zellers replies: "We need to respond to Mr. Chalmers' concerns. I would like to send a letter to him clarifying our corporate position on the bag's design. Let's also be sure that we're sensitive to his feelings and that we give him a personal response. I don't want this to look like a form letter."

"Have other customers been complaining about the bags?" you ask.

"Some have, but they are definitely in the minority," explains Zellers. The bags have been in the stores for about three months and we've only had a few complaints. This is the first letter we've received. Most people don't seem to care one way or the other and if they do, they're not telling us about it."

"So, what is our position on this?" you ask. "Obviously, these images target our young audience so there is value from a marketing perspective, but I don't think that argument will carry much weight with Mr. Chalmers. I mean, the people shown on these bags aren't doing anything that's clearly sexual, really. How old are the models, anyway?"

"All of them are at least 18. The young man is actually 22, and the two young ladies are both 21. They just look young, that's all," answers Zellers. "There has been talk of hiring older-looking models in some of the recent marketing meetings. I'm not sure where those discussions will lead, but we are talking about the issue. Basically, our position is that the bags show a bunch of kids having a good time. It's some friends getting together and goofing around, period. Yes, the images are fun and wild and even a bit sexy, but the idea is to show the fun and excitement of youth, not to promote teen-age sex. That's the wrong interpretation of what we're aiming for with the bags."

"It will be a challenge to write this letter, but I'll take my best shot," you say.

Assignment

Write a public relations letter in response to Mr. Chalmers concerns about Tees & Flannels' shopping bags.

Case 16: A Report on Lactose Intolerance (Part A)

Many people have difficulty drinking milk and eating dairy products due to a condition called lactose intolerance. Some people don't have enough of the lactase enzyme in their bodies; lactase helps break down milk sugar, or lactose, so it is more easily digested. People who are lactose intolerant experience a variety of symptoms within several minutes to a few hours after eating dairy foods including cramps, nausea, gas, and diarrhea. Lactose intolerance is not a life-threatening condition and its symptoms can be controlled with dietary changes. There is no treatment available to help individuals produce more lactase in their systems, but there are some lactose-reduced products available in grocery stores for people who want to enjoy the taste of milk and dairy foods without all the distress and discomfort.

A company that will soon be launching a lactose-reduced milk called Dairy-Good is looking to hire a public relations agency to assist with this effort. The company's marketing director approached your firm knowing that it has much experience in the food and beverage industry. Aaron Weinstein, a senior account executive who is leading the Dairy-Good pitch, enlists your help.

"We're starting to gear up for the Dairy-Good pitch, but there's still so much I don't know about lactose intolerance," Weinstein says. "I did read an article in a medical journal that talked about how a lot of people don't even know they are lactose intolerant, so we may want to think about doing a public education campaign to support the marketing efforts. That could really help draw consumers to the product."

"I think I read that somewhere, too," you respond. "I've been doing a little reading on the subject myself."

"Great, so you've already got a head start. I'd like you to do more research so we can plan our new business presentation with as much knowledge about lactose intolerance as possible. I'd like to find out more about the medical aspects of the condition, what it is and how it's treated, but I'd also like to know more about the competition that Dairy-Good will be up against and get some information on how those products are publicized and marketed."

You add: "As part of that, I'll also look into who the primary consumers of lactose-reduced products are, and I'll check out which groups of people are most affected by lactose intolerance so we can begin thinking about the audiences we might want to target."

"That sounds good. Get me as much detail as you can. I'd like to see statistics on the number of people who are lactose intolerant. Does it affect certain age groups and ethnic populations more than others? That would be very useful data."

"I'll get started on this right away, since I know the presentation is not too far off. Once I finish my research, I'll compile my findings in a report. Could I have about a week to do this?"

"That seems reasonable," Weinstein says. "I'd be interested in your reactions to the research, as well. Include a section at the end of the report where you draw some conclusions about the information you've gathered, and how it might guide us in developing the Dairy-Good campaign."

Assignment

Work in teams of two or three to do research on lactose intolerance and to prepare a report of your findings. In addition to a title page, your report should include the following:

- Executive Summary
- Statement of Problem/Introduction specifying the purpose of the report and explaining the research methods used to investigate the subject
- Findings, including pertinent statistics
- Analysis and Conclusions
- Recommendations for the Dairy-Good campaign
- Bibliography of sources consulted

6

News Releases

When author Mark Twain was 74, newspapers published rumors that he had died. Advising the Associated Press that the stories of his death were false, Twain said, "The report of my death was an exaggeration . . . I would not do such a thing at my time of life." The news release hasn't died either, even though you might occasionally hear or read about how this tool has outlived its usefulness. Bennett & Company's 13th annual media survey in 2002 found that nearly 83% of the print, broadcast, and freelance journalists who responded said public relations professionals supply anywhere from 1% to as much as 30% of their story information (see www.bennettandco.com). The majority of journalists—47%—said the best way for outside news sources to grab their attention is to send a news release via e-mail.

It is true that some news releases deserve a swift burial because they fail to report legitimate news, they don't get to the news until the fifth paragraph on a second page, or they are loaded with grand statements that hype an organization. You have to think like a journalist when identifying news subjects and preparing news releases, but that thinking has to be balanced with your responsibilities as a public relations professional to position your organization in the most positive way and to support business objectives.

Public relations professionals succeed at placing news releases when they write about newsworthy subjects, create headlines and leads that get the media's attention and content that meets journalistic standards, consider timing issues and emphasize local angles, and select the best means of distribution.

Types of News Releases

Take a look at the following headlines:

- Coors Elects Two New Board Members, Announces Quarterly Dividend
- Mattel Completes Merger with The Learning Company
- The Big New Yorker Pizza Makes Nationwide Debut Today as Pizza Hut's Largest New Product Introduction in History
- Kellogg Company Donates Food to Kosovo Refugees
- Volkswagen Announces Voluntary Recall

These headlines are taken from actual news releases sent out by each of the companies identified. They illustrate the variety of news announcements that organizations make through news releases. These announcements can be grouped into three main categories:

- *Routine news events* such as staff hirings and promotions, staff appointments to boards of community and professional organizations, meetings and seminars held by clubs and organizations, and reports of quarterly company earnings.
- *Significant, one-time news events* such as the launch of new products or services, expansions or mergers, company and employee awards and distinctions, and charitable activities such as community fund-raising events and monetary donations to the arts, education, or other worthy causes (see Exhibits 6.1–6.3).
- *"Bad news" events* such as product recalls, work force reductions and plant closings, environmental spills and other accidents, and responses to activists.

Format

News releases are straightforward and should be printed on company letterhead. Stay away from decorative paper and fancy typefaces. Indent paragraphs, use 1½- to double-line spacing, and make margins at least 1 inch to allow editors to make notes on the release.

News releases have an identifiable format. They include the name, organization, and phone number of a contact person, usually the public relations person, who can be reached for more information. *Contact information* is often included at the top of the release, although e-mail news releases and releases posted on Web sites usually include contacts at the bottom so that the reader can get to the news right away.

Releases should also include *release information* to let the media know when the material may be published. Many releases carry the line "For Immediate Release" near the top of the page and above the headline. In addition to the release date, include the date that the release is being distributed to the media.

As the previous examples show, always begin your news release with a concise and informative *headline* that summarizes the story in a way that will get an editor's attention. Understand that many of the headlines you write will not appear in print as you've written them. Their primary purpose is to help media quickly determine the news value of your story. The Pizza Hut headline—The Big New Yorker Pizza Makes Nationwide Debut Today as Pizza Hut's Largest New Product Introduction in History—effectively conveys the main news point. In addition, the headline gives extra weight to the story by noting that this is a national event and the "largest new product introduction" in the company's history. (For more on good headline writing, see Exhibit 6.4.)

A point-of-origin *dateline* appears at the start of the first sentence of releases sent out regionally and nationally. The dateline notes the city, and in most cases the state,

Exhibit 6.1   News Release: Ivory Soap

One Procter & Gamble Plaza
Cincinnati, OH 45202

Contacts: Heather Bandura
PainePR
949-809-6716
hbandura@painepr.com

115 YEARS AFTER ITS BIRTH, THE IVORY BABY WILL RETURN IN 2003 AFTER AN EXHAUSTIVE NATIONWIDE SEARCH

Search will be Conducted From October 2002 Through May 2003, with Ivory Soap Asking American Families: Do you Know an Ivory Baby?

CINCINNATI, OHIO – August 16, 2002 – Ivory Soap is embarking on a nationwide search to the find the next Ivory Baby. It's been 30 years since Americans saw the last Ivory Baby, but the advertising icon is returning to celebrate its 115th birthday after being introduced to the public in 1887. The selected Ivory Baby will be featured in an upcoming 2003 Ivory Soap advertisement.

"Despite the many changes that the Ivory Baby has undergone since 1887 – from the early designs by such renowned artists as Jessie Wilcox Smith and Edward Steichen, to the much-remembered 'That Ivory Look' ads of the 1950s – the Ivory Baby has always stood as a symbol of purity and mildness," said Ed Rider, chief archivist from Procter & Gamble, the makers of Ivory Soap. "In celebration of the Ivory Baby's 115th birthday, we are excited to select another Ivory Baby that will hold a place in the long-standing history of one of America's most-treasured brands."

From October 2002 through May 12, 2003, consumers will be eligible to enter their children into the national model search. Beginning in the fall, Ivory Soap will host Ivory Baby model search events throughout the country.

Additionally, with the help of *Parents* magazine, regional Ivory Baby search events will be held at Gymboree retail locations, a leader in child developmental play

– more –

(continued)

Ivory Baby Release
Page 2 of 2

programs and infant/children clothing. Exact locations, as well as dates and times will be announced at a later date to consumers and the media.

If consumers cannot attend a regional event, they are invited to submit photos of their children by visiting the Ivory Web site (www.ivory.com) or by mailing an entry to the address indicated on Ivory Soap packaging or in-store displays. The Ivory Baby will be selected in May by a national panel consisting of modeling professionals.

In addition to the search for the next Ivory Baby, consumers also have the chance to win college scholarships and cash prizes totaling $200,000. More than 500 specially marked bars of Ivory Soap will contain the following:

- One $50,000 scholarship
- Ten $10,000 scholarships
- Five-Hundred $100 cash prizes

"Since 1879, Ivory Soap has been a natural choice for parents when selecting a product to clean their baby's soft and delicate skin," said Alexandra Lipinski, marketing director, Procter & Gamble. "By re-introducing the Ivory Baby to America, we are reminding parents that Ivory Soap's pure and natural clean is ideal not only for their babies, but for their whole family."

About Ivory Soap and Procter & Gamble (P&G)

Ivory Soap recently celebrated more than 120 years of mild, natural cleaning. From October 2002 through May 15, 2003, consumers will be eligible to participate in the "Search for the Next Ivory Baby" contest.

P&G markets approximately 250 brands and employs nearly 106,000 people in more than 80 countries worldwide. P&G's beauty business had approximately $7.3 billion in global sales in fiscal year 2000/01, making it one of the world's largest beauty companies. Its beauty brands include Pantene®, Olay®, SK-II®, Max Factor®, Cover Girl®, Joy®, Hugo Boss® and the recently acquired Clairol brands, including Herbal Essence® and Nice 'n Easy®.

###

Note. Courtesy of Procter & Gamble.

Exhibit 6.2   News Release: Fisher-Price

Fisher-Price, Inc.
675 Avenue of the Americas, 2nd Floor New York, NY 10010
Telephone: 212.620.8200 Fax: 212.620.8380

FOR IMMEDIATE RELEASE   CONTACT: Stephanie Bennett/Ellie Bagli
Freeman Public Relations
(973) 470-0400
sbennett@freemanpr.com
ebagli@freemanpr.com

FISHER-PRICE'S CHICKEN DANCE ELMO
HEATS UP THE HOLIDAY SHOPPING SEASON

(NEW YORK, NY) November 19, 2002 – The turkey hasn't even been dressed, but there's one "bird" that's already heating up this holiday season. Chicken Dance Elmo, the newest Sesame Street sensation from Fisher-Price, is flying off store shelves at a rate that is surpassing the excitement of Tickle Me Elmo, according to company executives.

Just as the Chicken Dance song has topped dance party music lists, Chicken Dance Elmo "rules the roost" of this year's hot holiday toy lists.

- The editors of *Toy Wishes Magazine*, the celebrated resource guide designed to put the fun back in toy shopping, have announced that Chicken Dance Elmo is one of its coveted 'Hot Dozen,' the list of twelve toys it predicts to be the top sellers of holiday 2002.

  "Elmo is going to do for the Chicken Dance what Chubby Checker did for the twist," says Jim Silver, publisher of *Toy Wishes Magazine*. "You can't help but start flapping your arms and wiggling your behind. Not only did we predict that Chicken Dance Elmo is going to be one of the big sellers of holiday 2002, but we also think the new dance craze is going to be the Chicken Dance, courtesy of Elmo."

- The highly-regarded <u>Oppenheim Toy Portfolio 2003: The Best Toys, Books, Videos, Music & Software for Kids</u> awarded Chicken Dance Elmo its highest honor, a Platinum Award.

- Editors of *Parents* Magazine named the toy as one of the "Best Toys of 2002."

- more -

(continued)

2 / Fisher-Price's Chicken Dance Elmo Heats Up the Holiday Season

- Chicken Dance Elmo is featured on the Toys "R" Us list of hot holiday toys.

- Reports from eBay are showing that more than 600 people have posted the product for auction.

- This fall, the toy was recognized as Ambassador to Cincinnati, as Chicken Dance Elmo "assisted" Verne Troyer, Mini Me of "Austin Powers" fame, in leading 25,000+ Oktoberfest-Zinzinnati attendees in the Chicken Dance.

- Wayne Brady was a hit with his studio audience when he danced along with Chicken Dance Elmo and, with the help of Fisher-Price, gave Chicken Dance Elmo to everyone there.

- With all the hype about opposing pitchers walking Barry Bonds of the San Francisco Giants at Pacific Bell Park, Chicken Dance Elmo made a brief TV appearance during this year's World Series. As the Chicken Dance song blared through the park's loud speakers, cameras zoomed in on a fan who was waving his own Chicken Dance Elmo.

- Parents and kids recently lined up for blocks in New York's famed Times Square to see Sesame Street's Elmo and his friend Gordon kick off the holiday dance party season at Toys "R" Us Times Square, where they taught the standing room only crowd of toddlers the ever-popular Chicken Dance.

"Elmo makes magic wherever he goes, even in a yellow chicken suit," notes Neil Friedman, president of Fisher-Price. "Of course, it's impossible to predict just how popular a toy may be, but we've done our best to prepare for the demand."

Dressed in a yellow chicken suit, Elmo is ready to take on the dance party favorite. Kids just press Elmo's foot and he sings the popular Chicken Dance song and as he sings, Elmo moves up and down and flaps his "chicken" wings back and forth, just like the real Chicken Dance! Recommended for children 1 ½ years and up, Chicken Dance Elmo retails for approximately $19.99 and is available now at major toy stores nationwide.

Clear some room in the barnyard this holiday season. Chicken Dance Elmo is probably coming home to roost.

- more -

(continued)

3 / Fisher-Price's Chicken Dance Elmo Heats Up the Holiday Season

Fisher-Price, Inc., a wholly-owned subsidiary of Mattel, Inc. (NYSE:MAT) and located in East Aurora, New York, is the leading brand of infant and preschool toys in the world. Celebrating over 70 years of excellence in children's products, some of the Company's best known "classic" brands include Little People®, Power Wheels® and View-Master®. The Fisher-Price brand includes some of the most popular and widely recognized character brands – from Barney™ and Blue's Clues™ to Disney, Dora the Explorer™, Sesame Street® and Winnie the Pooh. The Company also develops and markets juvenile products called babygear (nursery monitors, infant swings, high chairs and more) that are designed to help families get the best possible start in life. The Company's web site can be found at www.fisher-price.com, providing valuable articles and resources to new and expectant parents.

# # #

---

from which the news originates. The AP Stylebook includes a detailed list of how datelines should appear. The date that the release is being distributed may appear beside the dateline or above the headline.

If your release is two pages, make sure the word "more" appears at the bottom of the first page (do try, however, to keep news releases as short as possible). In the top left corner of the second page, include a *slug*—a few words that summarize the story along with the page number. End the release with "30" or "###" so editors know there are no additional pages.

Body of the Release

The body of the news release should be structured using the ***inverted pyramid style***, with the most important facts presented in the first few paragraphs (the news summary) and supporting details in later paragraphs. Write the release so the first two or three paragraphs can stand alone and tell the story. The first paragraph, known as the ***news lead***, describes the news focus of the release and why the information is important. The next one or two paragraphs include details—who, what, where, how, and when. Subsequent information is then included to complement and expand on the facts already provided. Conclude the release by describing the organization. Statements at the end of the release that attempt to wrap up the story come off looking like the writer's opinions. Instead, include a summary paragraph or "***boilerplate***" that provides further background on the organization's history, mission, product line, and standing in the industry. Boilerplates should be used consistently and should not change from release to release.

Here are some additional pointers for writing body copy:

Exhibit 6.3   News Release: USGA

United States Golf Association
Golf House PO Box 708 Far Hills NJ 07931-0708
908 781-1040 Fax 908 234-2179
http://www.usga.org

News
Contact: Craig Smith

#87, 10/31/02
For Release: Upon Receipt
(http://www.usga.org)
E–mail address: mediarelations@usga.org

USGA MUSEUM RECEIVES NEW ARTIFACT
FOUND AT WORLD TRADE CENTER SITE

Far Hills, N.J. – The United States Golf Association Museum has received

a new item for its display, honoring those who lost their lives in the terrorist

attacks on the World Trade Center on Sept. 11, 2001.

Robert Kiernan, a New York City firefighter from Engine 273, found a

TaylorMade Firesole Driver in the rubble of the World Trade Center toward the

end of the recovery efforts, in May. Kiernan sent the artifact to TaylorMade

officials, who decided to donate it to the USGA Museum.

Kiernan was at Golf House Thursday (Oct. 31) along with three colleagues

from the New York City Fire Department, Tom Wood of Engine 273 and Benny

Rebecca and Lou Minutoli, both of Ladder 129. The four firefighters were joined

by TaylorMade President Mark King and Senior Director of Corporate

Communication John Steinbach to make the presentation of the clubhead to

USGA officials.

"Certain items would really hit home for people during the recovery

process," Kiernan said. "For me, as a golfer, it was this club."

-more-

U.S. Open • U.S. Women's Open • U.S. Senior Open • U.S. Junior Amateur • U.S. Amateur Public Links • U.S. Amateur • U.S. Mid-Amateur
USGA Senior Amateur • U.S. Girls' Junior • U.S. Women's Amateur Public Links • U.S. Women's Amateur • U.S. Women's Mid-Amateur
USGA Senior Women's Amateur • U.S. Men's State Team • U.S. Women's State Team • Walker Cup • Curtis Cup • World Amateur Team •
Women's World Amateur Team

Museum Addition – page 2

The clubhead will be added to the USGA Museum's display of items recovered from the World Trade Center site, including a ball found in the rubble that was presented to the USGA during the 2002 U.S. Open at Bethpage State Park in Farmingdale, N.Y.

"Visitors to the museum frequently comment on the impact of the items recovered from the World Trade Center," said Rand Jerris, USGA director of museum and archives. "The artifacts serve as a reminder that the victims of September 11th were people with true passions and interests."

For more information about the USGA Museum and the Sept. 11th display, contact Rand Jerris at (908) 234-2300.

∎

Note. Courtesy of USGA.

- Write short paragraphs, especially the first few paragraphs, and simple sentences. Limit paragraphs to a few sentences; three is okay for paragraphs that come later in the release, but keep the sentences short. Sentences should convey one thought at a time. Use commas sparingly.
- Avoid using adjectives (e.g., exciting, great, ground breaking). News releases should be written objectively; if the product or event is newsworthy, it will sell itself. If the focus of the news release truly is "ground breaking," write such subjective information as a quote.
- Make sure quotes are strong. In addition to being wonderful vehicles for including subjective information and opinions in a news release, quotes can increase the release's value. Many reporters like to get firsthand quotes from your sources, but a quote within your release can let reporters know a credible source is available for comment. Quotes should neither rephrase facts that have already been presented, nor should they state the obvious. Strong quotes expand on those facts by offering something new and by advancing the story. If a news release states that a company expansion will add 100 new jobs and help the area's economy, follow that statement with a quote from a company official that talks about the kinds of jobs being added and the company's opinions on what this growth means for the community and its future. Don't waste valuable space by quoting the company official as being "excited," "pleased," or "happy" about the company expansion.

Exhibit 6.4   What's the Story? Tips for Writing News Release Headlines

- Keep your headline to eight to 12 words. Use bold type or underscore the headline to make it stand out.
- Always include an active verb (i.e., "announces," "launches," "introduces," "names," "awards," "presents").
- If something is "first," "new," or unusual in another way (and you can prove it), say so in the headline.
- Emphasize the local angle. Stories about a "local businessperson," a "community" event, or "area residents" should use those words and phrases in the headline. Remember to be specific about the area you are talking about, however. "Local" means different things to different people.
- Appeal to the special interests of editors and your target audience. A news release on a new weight loss product sent to health/fitness publications could be introduced by a headline including words and phrases such as "healthy," "dieters," and "fewer calories."
- Consider using a subhead that expands on the main headline by singling out a key aspect of the story. This is especially useful when writing and sending e-mail news releases that have to quickly convey the significant news aspects of a story.

Leads

The *lead*, more than any other element of the release, is the key to the success of your news release. Editors and news directors at major media receive hundreds of news releases each week, so there isn't always time to read the complete release before deciding to keep it or dump it (another reason why releases are written in inverted pyramid style with the most important information at the top). A scan of the lead tells an editor right away if your news is relevant and worth publishing. In the Bennett & Company survey, one journalist responded, "If I can't figure out what the news is within two sentences, it's 'delete' or in the trash can" (see www.bennettandco.com). It is essential, then, that the main news point is stated clearly in the lead paragraph.

The public relations writer's lead has subtle differences from that of the journalist's lead. Journalists are trained to write news leads that give the reader a sense of "who, what, when, where, why and how." While that information should be included in the top half of a news release, such details seldom appear in the lead. Instead, the lead focuses on the most significant aspects of the story and carefully brings in a detail or two that has public relations value:

> Leading online retailer Amazon.com, Inc. today announced that it is joining with The Starbright Foundation to help raise money for seriously ill children. The Internet's No. 1 book and No. 1 music store has created a special feature for "The Emperor's New Clothes: An All-Star Illustrated Retelling of the Classic Fairy Tale" to spur sales of the book, which will raise funds for the foundation.

In this lead, Amazon.com notes its status in the industry, which is a common technique used by publicity writers. The journalist might leave out such a description in a first paragraph and choose to stress the charitable organization over the company (e.g., "A foundation that helps seriously ill children has found a new partner on the Internet"). In addition, the book title or "product" might not be mentioned in the journalist's lead. Still, the public relations techniques used in this lead never overpower the key news point.

Other tips for writing good leads are:

- Keep it to one or two sentences, maybe a bit longer, if sentences are short and copy is lively and interesting to read. Leads that are too long risk burying the news in unnecessary detail.

- Use active voice. Writing "XYZ Company named a new chief financial officer this afternoon" sounds more current than writing "A new chief financial officer was named today by XYZ Company." You can't always avoid the less-active verb form, especially if your release announces something that happened a few days ago. In those cases, use the present perfect tense and avoid mentioning the "day" the event took place: "The XYZ Company announces that Kim Behrens has been named chief financial officer." Or, even more active, "Kim Behrens is the new chief financial officer for The XYZ Company, a leading U.S. manufacturer of..."

- Tailor the style of your lead to the story subject. A *straight* or *hard lead* works best for announcements of staff appointments and other hard news:

  Mattel, Inc. today announced that it has completed its merger with The Learning Company. The Learning Company is now a division of Mattel.

  For other subjects, write *interest* or *feature leads* that are softer, less straightforward and more creative in their approach. An example:

  Teenagers touring New York City with playwright Tony Kushner. Young immigrants writing with author Junot Diaz. The elderly sharing tales of growing up in New Mexico with novelist Denise Chavez. These are only some of the community enriching activities that noted writers will be leading as recipients of the Lila Wallace-Reader's Digest Fund Writers' Awards 2000.

Instead of starting the release with "The Lila Wallace-Reader's Digest Fund announces this year's winners of its writers' awards," a rather dry lead approach, the writer focuses first on some of the notable people involved and their community projects. This angle encourages the editor to read on and helps to build interest in the story.

The following feature lead demonstrates how a company can design a news release around consumer research and a major holiday to gain publicity:

If kids have their way this Mother's Day, it looks as if moms' lives will get a bit easier. Two limos, robot maids that never run out of energy, and $11,000,000.57 are just a few of the gift ideas kids shared during a recent survey sponsored by Sears.

- Avoid starting with a preposition or a quote. Prepositional phrases such as "At a ceremony held at city hall" or "After a meeting to discuss board policy" delay the news. Instead of beginning your release with a direct quote, paraphrase for better style. Consider the following:

> "Present market conditions are continuing to erode prices and it is not likely that OPEC will be able to change the current trend. There is, therefore, a good chance that the price of gasoline and heating oil may drop by 5 to 10 cents a gallon by the end of the year." This statement was made by Mr. John G. Buckley, vice president, Northeast Petroleum Corporation, during a speech today at the spring convention of the Empire State Petroleum Association in Ellenville, N.Y.

This lead has some good qualities. It shares a main idea from the speech rather than stating, "John G. Buckley gave a speech today. . .", and it summarizes the key facts of the story in a few sentences. It is long, however, and the most newsworthy element is mentioned in the second sentence of the quote. A stronger lead is:

> A New York state petroleum executive said today that gasoline and heating oil prices may drop 5 to 10 cents a gallon by next year. John G. Buckley, vice president of Northeast Petroleum Corporation, made this prediction at the spring convention of. . .

The revised lead deletes details that are better mentioned in a second and third paragraph. Notice how moving the speaker's name and title to the second paragraph simplifies the lead without reducing its news value, and that the lead is now active, not passive. Exhibit 6.5 offers additional lead-writing guidelines.

Localizing

Each release you write should have "local" interest. One reporter responding to the Bennett & Company survey stated that he only looks at news releases that pertain to his newspaper's coverage area. Simply put, newspaper editors want to know how your story affects people who live in their city or area. Trade magazines want news that is relevant to people who work in a certain industry. *Localizing* is a technique that allows you to increase the number of media placements for a single news announcement. You do this by creating multiple versions of a news release, with each version emphasizing local points of interest for media serving specific geographic areas or populations. This may entail simply rewording the lead. An illustration:

> Cobb Medical Center, one of the largest health care facilities in the Midwest, today named Roberta Brown as its chief executive officer.

This is a lead for the version of this news release sent to media in the city where Cobb is located and hospital trade media. But the creative public relations writer knows that localizing this release makes it possible to extend coverage significantly. By raising

Exhibit 6.5   Lead with Your Best Stuff: Adding Value to News Release Leads

The lead of a news release should do more than simply summarize the story. Before writing the lead, you need to begin by sizing up the *news value* of the story. Ask yourself, why is this newsworthy?

For example, a grocery store chain in a northeastern city decides to launch a unique program with local police in an effort to get handguns off the street. Each person who turns in a handgun during a designated two-week period will get $50 worth of free groceries from the store. This story has news value for several reasons: it involves two major *local* organizations; it is *unusual* in that the chain has never taken part in a program like this and because it is not a typical community outreach program for a grocery store; it is *significant* because it has the potential to greatly *impact* the community by reducing crime; and it is *timely* because the program responds to a sharp increase in drive-by shootings in that city in recent months.

Once news value has been determined, decide on the best *news angle*. What will the focus or slant of the story be? What information needs to be played up to hook the media and convince them that the story has value? Consider the "local" and "unusual" aspects of the story:

● Two local organizations—starting an innovative new crime prevention program— that involves giving free groceries to area residents who turn in handguns.

The news angle then lays the groundwork for your news lead. But try to write your lead so that it gets the main news point across in an interesting and creative way:

● A major supermarket chain is joining with local police to launch an unusual program aimed at taking a bite out of crime—exchanging guns for groceries.

---

a few questions about Brown's background, the writer creates several local angles. One localized version is the *hometown release* sent to the media in the town or city where Brown grew up:

Former Cleveland Resident Assumes Top Hospital Post
Roberta Brown, a native of Cleveland, has been named chief executive officer of Cobb Medical Center, one of the largest health care facilities in the Midwest.

This new version of the release, written exclusively for Cleveland media, highlights Brown's connection to that area in the headline and the lead. If Brown held previous positions in Cleveland, has parents still living in that area, or has achieved some distinction while living there, those facts can be included in the release as well. Publications produced by colleges that Brown attended and by professional associations she holds membership in are other targets for localized releases.

Keep in mind that all localized versions of news releases include much of the same information. Local information is always stated at the beginning of the release. After the lead, sprinkle other local facts throughout the rest of the release, where appropriate. Any release on Brown's new position would give more details about her duties, her previous positions within the hospital and other related jobs, background on the center, and possibly a quote from her or the head of the hospital board on her appointment.

National companies get better media coverage when they localize. If a company is introducing a product nationwide, it can localize the news for media in a specific city by having a dealer in that area make the announcement. Organizations can get local coverage by connecting themselves and their executives to national trends:

> Statistics released by Temp Services of America (TSA), a leading industry association, show nearly 30 percent of America's temporary workforce find full-time employment as a result of temporary work. Helen Smith, president of Temps, Inc. in Buffalo, confirms that people in her area have also found that temporary employment is a good path to a full-time job.

Timing

"It's all in the timing" is an expression that definitely applies to news releases. Your challenge is to stay on top of your organization's news and to share it with the media when it happens. Daily newspapers are interested in "today" and "yesterday," broadcast media think about "this morning" and "this afternoon," and online media can report news minutes after it happens. You have a little more flexibility with trade publications and magazines that circulate less frequently. Whatever the case, the more recent or timely your development is, the more interest the media will have in it.

Many releases indicate they are "For Immediate Release" but in reality, most releases should be written for immediate publication. There are occasions when an organization embargoes distribution of material. An *embargo* is a restriction that asks the media to hold information for release until a designated date. For example, companies officially launching a new product at a media event on a specific day establish embargoes with trade publications interested in writing about the product. Because many trade publications come out only once a month, providing information in advance helps them develop in-depth stories that can be published at the same time as those in daily or weekly newspapers. This gives everyone with an interest in the story an even news break.

Publicists sending out information about new CDs and upcoming films embargo with the media to time the release of information so that it coincides with the first day the CD goes on sale or with the motion picture's premiere. Embargoes are reserved for special situations like these, and should not be abused. Once media agree to an embargo, it is unethical for you to give a publication permission to publish before the embargo date. This does serious damage to media relationships.

Finally, know your media's deadlines. With the exception of hard news, daily newspapers usually want news releases on community events at least two weeks in advance.

Special sections and Sunday editions have distinct deadlines, too. You need to get news releases to monthly trade and consumer publications at least a month or two in advance of the desired publication date. Depending on the publication, it could be several months in advance. Call the media you deal with and ask about deadlines before sending your releases.

Distribution

It's not just what your release says, but how you get it into the media's hands, that can make all the difference. Before sending a news release, become familiar with the existing media outlets that reach your target audiences and that cover your industry and the communities your organization serves. Prepare and regularly update a list of print, broadcast, and online media and include the names of key reporters and editors working for those media (see Exhibits 6.6 and 6.7). Know the news release subjects they are interested in, and stay aware of the kinds of in-depth stories they like to publish and air that might spin off from a news release you send.

Exhibit 6.6   Types of Media
_____

Daily Newspapers

Dailies in small- to medium-sized cities that primarily serve one local area; dailies in major metropolitan areas (e.g., *The New York Times*) that serve a local market but also have regional editions and national distribution; and national newspapers such as *USA Today*. Dailies publish Sunday editions, columns, event calendar listings, and weekly feature sections on business/money, food, health, technology and other subjects that can be good publicity outlets.

Weekly Newspapers

Community and hometown newspapers read by residents in specific towns, villages, or suburban areas. In addition to hard news of interest to people in that community, content typically focuses on community events; news about local residents and businesses; and articles/columns on health, family, home and quality of life. Also, business, arts and entertainment, and other special interest newspapers circulate in many cities and regions.

Magazines

National magazines include general interest (e.g., *TV Guide*, *People*), news and business (e.g., *Time*, *Business Week*) and special interest (e.g., *Good Housekeeping*, *Vogue*, *Men's Health*). Some regional and local magazines are published for readers in a certain city or geographic region (e.g., *Rochester Business Journal*, *Colorado Parent*, *Arizona Senior World*). Special interest magazines are good outlets for personality profiles and feature articles on lifestyle, consumer, and business trends. Magazines plan and prepare editorial content several weeks to several months before publishing an issue.

(continued)

Trade and Business-to-Business Publications

Newspapers and magazines designed for people who work in a specific industry and who want to stay current with happenings in their industry (e.g., *Real Estate Executive, Modern Healthcare, Florida Farmer*). Trade media also target business professionals whose companies use products and services produced by a specific industry and are affected by changes in that industry (e.g., *Electronic Buyers' News, Pollution Equipment News*). Content includes articles on industry trends, information on new products and services, and employee and business news relating to specific companies serving that industry. Generally circulate on a weekly, biweekly, and monthly basis.

Radio and Television

Includes stations in local markets that broadcast local newscasts and talk/public service programming as well as national networks such as NBC, CBS, ABC, Fox, PBS, ESPN, and National Public Radio. In addition to national cable TV networks, local cable networks broadcast news, public affairs, and other interview-type programs on issues affecting a particular community and look to area organizations for sources and guests.

Online Publications

Many daily newspapers, magazines, and other publications have online versions. E-commerce businesses, consumer product companies, health and trade associations, and other organizations produce online newsletters targeting a variety of special interests. Online newsletters are included as a link within Web sites and are e-mailed directly to interested consumers upon request.

Exhibit 6.7   Helpful Media Directories and Web Sites

A specific public relations research activity involves identifying appropriate media outlets to reach target publics. Media generally fall into one of two categories: mass media (i.e., daily newspapers, television) that reach a wide consumer audience, and specialized media that focus on the interests of more narrowly defined consumer and industry groups (see Exhibit 6.6 for detail). Some publications and Web sites that can help you research the media are:

Bacon's (www.baconsinfo.com)
Bacon's publishes a wide variety of directories for newspapers, magazines, radio, and TV/cable, as well as subject-specific media directories for business, computer/high-tech, and medical/health. A Media Calendar Directory includes information on special issues and sections planned by major magazines and newspapers. Indexes categorize media by market, circulation, and editorial content. (*Note:* This is a general information site. It does not include online media listings.)

(continued)

Burrelle's (www.burrelles.com)

Billed as having the "largest and most comprehensive print and broadcast media directories" in the country, Burrelle's has more than 300,000 media contacts and 60,000 media. Directories for daily newspapers, non-daily newspapers, magazines and newsletters, radio, television, and cable are available. Media listings include addresses, telephone and fax numbers, e-mail addresses, and Web sites. (*Note:* This site includes general information on Burrelle's services and only includes samples of media listings.)

Editor and Publisher Interactive (www.mediainfo.com)

The online version of the International Yearbook, with links to newspapers, is available for purchase at this site. Search by media category, publication name, or location. Also available are print versions of the Market Guide and Directory of Syndicated Services. Lots of news on the media industry.

Gebbie Press (www.gebbiepress.com)

Gebbie Press is best known for its All-In-One-Directory, which includes extensive listings of U.S. daily and weekly newspapers, consumer and trade magazines, Black and Hispanic media, and news syndicates and networks. More than 22,000 listings include addresses, phone and fax numbers, and URL and e-mail address. The Web site also has links to print and electronic media on the Internet and provides e-mail addresses for more than 3,000 print and broadcast media.

MediaFinder (www.mediafinder.com)

This useful site for researching media and preparing media lists of newspapers, magazines, trade journals, newsletters, catalogues and other periodicals includes information on more than 100,000 publications. Data includes content information, circulation, advertising rates, production schedules, list rentals, contact names, phone numbers, and e-mail addresses. Search an extensive list of media subject categories from "accounting" to "zoology."

Newslink (www.newslink.org)

This site lists and links to the online versions of national and international newspapers including dailies, weeklies, business, specialty and alternative press, and college newspapers. Links to broadcast media, magazines, and journals also are available.

Check with your media contacts and honor their preferences for receiving news releases. Sometimes, the situation can dictate the method of delivery. A local company with news regarding a serious or emergency situation may use the fax, a Web site, e-mail, and maybe a news conference to get the word out. If a situation has an immediate effect on many people in a large geographic area, or if a story has national interest, electronic distribution by a newswire and satellite delivery are efficient methods.

Although the preference of receiving information via e-mail has steadily increased in recent years, give careful consideration to e-mail news release distribution. Your goal here is to present just enough information to interest a media contact in your story and then direct the receiver to a Web site that has the full text of the release and more background information on the subject. You may choose to write the information as a news summary (the beginning of a news release that contains the essential information) or as a fact sheet (who, what, where, etc.). As mentioned before, never send information to media contacts by e-mail without first getting their approval. Include a strong subject line and headline, and make sure all the necessary contact information is provided. Avoid mass mailing your e-mail releases. Editors may not even look at your release if the heading shows that the same copy went to 20 other editors at the same time, or if it is accompanied by a large attachment that wasn't requested.

References and Suggested Reading

13th annual media survey results. (2002). Retrieved December 5, 2002 from http://www.bennettandco.com/mediacenter.php3?Main=MediaCenter&firstSub= MediaSurvey13

Amazon.com joins with the Starbright Foundation to help kids. (1998). Retrieved December 5, 2002 from Amazon.com

Andrews, R., Biggs, M., & Seidel, M. (Eds.). (1990). *The Columbia world book of quotations*. New York: Columbia University Press.

Aronson, M. & Spetner, D. (1998). *The public relations writer's handbook*. San Francisco: Jossey-Bass.

Borden, K. (2002). *Bulletproof news releases: Help at last for the publicity deficient* (2nd ed.). Marietta, GA: Franklin-Sarrett Publishers.

Brody, E. W. & Lattimore, D. L. (1990). *Public relations writing*. Westport, CT: Praeger Publishers.

Goldstein, N. (Ed.). (2002). *The Associated Press stylebook and briefing on media law* (Rev. ed.). Cambridge, MA: Perseus Publishing.

McIntyre, C. V. (1992). *Writing effective news releases: How to get free publicity for yourself, your business, or your organization*. Colorado Springs, CO: Piccadilly Books.

Ries, A. & Ries, L. (2002). *The fall of advertising and the rise of PR*. New York: HarperBusiness.

CASES

Case 17: The New Coach

Three months ago Felice Shofar, head women's basketball coach at Metro College, resigned her position in a brief written statement without citing a reason for leaving. Luke Hammer, 48, a former quarterback with the Chicago Bears and currently the athletic director at Metro, immediately started a search for a new coach at the undergraduate, coed, four-year college located in Metropolis, IL., a city of 175,000.

The Metro search committee, chaired by Hammer, received and screened a total of 110 applications. Metropolis invited five of the applicants to the college for interviews and offered the position to Lucinda Smart earlier this week. Smart accepted the coaching position.

You are the sports information director at Metro. For the past 10 years, the college's Division III women's basketball team has been nationally ranked and participated in four national tournaments, reaching the semifinals twice and winning the national title last year. The *Metropolis Evening Sun* has given extensive coverage to the women's team—far better coverage that it has given to the men's team, which has had a losing record for eight of the past 10 years. So, you know the local media will be interested in this story, and you begin work on a news release announcing that Smart has been hired. After receiving Smart's resumé from Hammer, you pull out the following details about her background:

- *Education*: Joplin High School, Joplin, MO; B. A. Anthropology, Loyola, Chicago; M. S. sports management, College of the Hills, Forest Ridge, Pennsylvania.
- *Experience*: Two years, assistant store manager, J. C. Penney's department store, Joplin, MO; three years, center, Women's All-Star Hoopsters touring team; two years, assistant basketball coach, College of the Hills.

In addition, you find out the following personal information: Age, 30; parents: Mr. and Mrs. Charles Smart, 2 Cedar Lane, Joplin; born and grew up in Joplin; single; one child, Peter, age 3.

You call Hammer to make a last minute check of details. He tells you that Smart's salary is $50,000. You also learn in that conversation that Felice Shofar is now head basketball coach at a Division I university.

"I think I have most of the information I need, but I'd like to include a quote from you in the release."

"Sure," Hammer says. "Use this: 'We feel fortunate to be able to secure a person who is so highly qualified to lead our outstanding girls' basketball team. We expect great things from Cindy Smart, and we know she'll deliver the goods.'"

Assignments

1. Write a news release to be faxed to the *Metropolis Evening Sun*. Indicate that it is "For Immediate Release."
2. Write a news release for distribution to the Joplin media.
3. Write news releases for alumni publications produced by College of the Hills and Loyola.

Case 18: A Packaging Innovation

Jamaal Morris is public relations director for the Portland, Maine-based CreamySmooth Ice Cream, Inc., a leading producer of super premium ice cream and low-fat frozen yogurt made with all natural ingredients. Creamy Smooth, established in 1982, has gained a reputation for its humanitarian efforts; the company gives 7% of its pretax profits to philanthropic and social causes including pro-environment groups and activities.

One afternoon, Stephen Michaels, CreamySmooth's director of packaging development, calls Jamaal to his office to discuss a publicity opportunity:

"You know that we've been working on a new environmentally-friendly container for our ice cream, and we're finally ready to send out a news release about it. I think the media will be interested in this, especially since we are the first U.S. ice cream company to use this kind of pint container," Michaels says.

"Yes, I think we can get some coverage with this. Now, let me make sure I'm clear on some of the facts. These new containers are made of unbleached, brown paperboard, right? But how is that safer for the environment?" Jamaal asks.

"The way I understand it, they don't use any bleaching agents in the manufacturing process. Apparently, some of these chemicals are harmful to the environment. You should probably call Amy Ford at earthWatch. You know her, right? We've been consulting with her on this project. She can tell you more about this from an environmental perspective. I'm afraid my explanation would just confuse you. I do know that no one has ever adapted this technology to ice cream containers before, so we're doing something pretty special here. It's our hope that our 'Nature-Safe pint' will become the new industry standard."

Before leaving Michaels' office, Jamaal learns that the company plans to begin switching to the new containers in the next month. The goal is to convert a substantial number of its containers in another six months. "The other great part of this is, we're not going to keep the packaging idea to ourselves. We plan to share it with our competitors and other manufacturers. The bottom line here is that this new packaging can really have an impact on protecting our environment, and that's what we really care about most."

After leaving Michaels' office, Morris calls Amy Ford at earthWatch, a non-profit advocacy group known worldwide for its efforts to protect the environment and to get corporations to establish environmentally friendly policies. He jots down the following notes on the environmental aspects of this new packaging, based on his conversation with Ford:

> Standard papermaking, like used w/many food packages, uses chlorine as a bleaching agent. Bleaching process discharges millions of gallons of organochlorine-laced wastewater every day. Chemicals used in process are extremely toxic, considered human health hazards. EPA identified some of these chemicals (i.e. dioxins) as carcinogens. New packaging process doesn't use bleach, significantly reduces damage to environment. Unbleached packaging material meets environmental, commercial, and FDA requirements.

A review of company fact sheets and other internal documents reveals that a St. Louis company, Brookwood International, helped develop the "Nature-Safe" packaging material. DrinkTime Cup Company will print and produce the packaging at its Atlanta facility.

Assignments

1. Write a news release for distribution to the food sections of national daily newspapers.
2. Write a news release for distribution to "Ice Cream Reporter," a newsletter targeted to the interests of executives working in the ice cream industry.

Case 19: PRSA Honors Three Members

This year, as it has in the past, the New York City-based Public Relations Society of America (PRSA), the world's leading professional organization of public relations practitioners, is honoring three of its members by selecting them to be the recipients of the society's highest individual awards.

Today is Nov. 14, the day of the society's annual awards luncheon. The event is taking place during the PRSA's international conference at the Anaheim Hilton and Towers Convention Center in Anaheim, CA. Presentations of the individual awards will be made to the three winners at the noon luncheon. The PRSA Individual Awards Committee decided on the selection of this year's winners three months ago in mid-August. As public relations director of PRSA, you have on hand the following rough notes about the three honorees and their awards:

Deborah Hosts, senior vp, Hosts and Boyd, Denver, largest pr counseling firm in CO, received Gold Anvil Award for "significant contribution to pr profession" . . . . . Syracuse, NY native & Phi Beta Kappa grad West Virginia U majoring in pr . . . 1st job, asst dir news bureau, Syracuse U . . . then joined Daniel Edelman Inc, Chicago, as acct exec, stayed 10 yrs . . . Opened own firm 15 yrs ago with Patricia Boyd in Denver . . . Has won PRSA Silver awards in areas of community relations, public service, multicultural pr. Former president of national Women in Communications group . . . Long recognized as leading advocate for licensing system for pr people . . . Selected last year as a "Public Relations All Star" by *Inside PR* magazine.

Michael Owen, Ph.D., chair, pr dept, Boston U School of Public Communication, got PRSA Outstanding Educator Award for "advancing pr education" . . . authored one of 1st pr theory and research texts . . . presented many papers at annual conferences of PRSA and Assoc. for Educ in Journalism & Mass Commun. (AEJMC) . . . Twice elected chair of PRSA Educators Section . . . past Boston PRSA chapter president . . . BA, MA psych, U of Mass, Ph.D in sociology, Princeton . . . friends call him "O" . . .

Thomas Munster, vp of pr, Brooke Electronics, Melbourne, FL, got Paul M. Lund public service award for "contribution to the common good through public service activities" . . . he donates 400 hrs/yr to Melbourne fire dept, counsels fire chief on public policy issues, creates fire prevention materials to help curb accidental & deliberate fires . . . Last year produced series of VNRs credited by Amer Heart Assn as major factor in alerting nation to dangers of high cholesterol levels . . . Last March 12 Melbourne mayor proclaimed Munster's birthday as "Tom Munster Day" to recognize his public service, presented Tom w/6-ft high bday card signed by 20,000 . . . he has served on PRSA board of directors, past chair of PRSA Universal Accreditation Board . . . Graduate Duke U (poli sci), member of school's board of trustees.

In presenting the awards, Maria Lopez, president of The Lopez Group public relations firm, Miami, FL., and chair of the Individual Awards Committee, said: "The practitioners we honor with these awards exemplify the highest standards of our profession. Their actions demonstrate the positive contributions of public relations to American society and bring credit to our calling through public service."

Assignments

1. Write a news release for distribution on PR Newswire immediately following the Nov. 14 awards luncheon. Use an Anaheim dateline.
2. Write the following releases using an Anaheim dateline. Indicate that each is "For Immediate Release:"
   (a) A release on Hosts and her award to be sent to the *Denver Post*.
   (b) A release on Owen and his award to be sent to the *Boston Globe*.

(c) A release on Munster and his award to be sent to the *Melbourne Florida Today*, a morning daily.

(d) A release for publication in *PR Week*, a weekly newspaper for the public relations industry.

Case 20: Announcing a Product Recall

Founded in 1940, the Play-Well Company has established a reputation as one of the leading manufacturers of quality toys and games for toddlers and children. Its product line includes items such as musical and crib toys for newborns as well as a variety of preschool games and educational toys for children age 5 and older. One of Play-Well's most popular toys is Zoomers, a brand of battery-operated cars and vehicles that is designed for children to ride on sidewalks, grass, and hard surfaces. There are dozens of models, from motorcycles to trucks, for use by children 2 to 7 years old. Vehicle speeds range from 1 to 5 miles per hour.

Recently, Play-Well and the U.S. Consumer Product Safety Commission (CPSC) received complaints from parents and consumers about Zoomers. There have been 800 reports that the vehicles' electrical components have malfunctioned and overheated, not only when cars are being ridden, but also when they are simply parked or stored in the garage or home. A dozen children have suffered minor burns to the hands, legs, and feet and 100 fires have been reported. Some homeowners have experienced property damage to houses and garages due to the fires, totaling $250,000.

After careful and quick deliberation, and with public safety as the top priority, Play-Well decides to conduct a voluntary recall of Zoomers products. You are asked to write the news release announcing the recall and schedule a meeting with Michael Hayes, vice president of consumer relations, to get more details.

"We need to move quickly on this recall and let people know right away which vehicles are affected and what they should be doing now to protect themselves and their kids," Hayes says. "We're working closely with the CPSC on this, as well."

"So, are we talking about recalling all Zoomers or just certain models?"

"The recall does not include any sold after November 1999, only those sold before that time. Still, that's about 10 million Zoomers that are part of the recall, and you know that there are about 100 model names, so this could get confusing. We're setting up an 800 number for people to call or they can log on to our company Web site and find out if their model is being recalled. The company will make every effort to help consumers identify if their model needs repairs," Hayes says.

"Now, one of the reports I read did say that all models with two batteries are being recalled, so we need to make that point. We can also tell people to look for model names on each vehicle. I'm assuming that we also want to tell parents that they should disable the cars immediately and not let their kids use the vehicles until any repairs have been made."

"To go back to your first point, we are recalling all the models with two batteries, but some one-battery models are affected, too, so we need to make sure people know that," Hayes says. "And yes, stress that batteries should be removed immediately and that consumers should contact a service center to schedule repairs. The service centers will install new electrical parts free of charge and do free safety checkups. Repairs can be scheduled by calling the 800-ZOOMERS number, or someone can go to the Web site, www.zoomers.com, and get a list of service centers in their area."

"That sounds good. I think I have enough information to draft the release. I know that legal and other senior people will need to look this over before it goes out, so I'll get started on this right away and have something to you in an hour or so."

Assignment

Write a news release to announce the Zoomers product recall for national distribution on PR Newswire.

Tips from the Top

"Using Newswires and Electronic Methods to Deliver Your Message"
David B. Armon

David Armon is president of PR Newswire America. He talks about trends in newswire and electronic distribution, and shares his thoughts on the Internet and how it has altered the way media and consumers get information.

Q: What is PR Newswire and how does it work?

A: PR Newswire is the leading provider of electronic distribution, targeting and measurement services on behalf of companies, organizations, and agencies worldwide that seek to reach the news media, the investment community, and the general public with their up-to-the-minute, full-text news developments.

In order to send a news release over PR Newswire, a company must become a member of PR Newswire. Membership allows us to verify the company's authenticity and integrity and make sure that it adheres to our stringent policies. Once approved, the client can send in a news release in a number of ways including through our password-protected client extranet, PRN Direct.

Once received by PR Newswire, a member of our editorial team will call the client to verify the release and contact information and to alert the client to any errors found in the release. The release will be sent out to the client's desired circuit through PR Newswire's private distribution network at the time indicated by the client. Releases can be sent in English to the U.S. media or translated in multiple languages and sent internationally.

Once the release has been issued, the client will receive a call and an e-mail with the time the release crossed the wires. Within the hour, the client will also receive a complimentary e-mail notification reporting the posting of the release on up to 20 of the top news Web sites. Besides sending news releases over the wire, we also use satellite, fax, and e-mail.

Q. Why would a company use a newswire to send out its news release?

A. There are many reasons to use a newswire to send out your news release. The newswire is a private network that allows for the precise delivery of your message. In order to comply with the SEC's disclosure regulations, public companies use a newswire to issue financial news, such as earnings announcements, to the media and financial community because it is delivered simultaneously to all parties.

Our vast distribution network allows a company to reach key audiences worldwide. We reach all major newsrooms across the country including print, radio, and television. We also provide our clients' news to the media through our media-only Web site, PR Newswire for Journalists, where more than 60,000 journalists are registered to receive news on the companies and industries they follow, directly to their desktop. Consumers can access our clients' news releases on more than 3,600 Web sites and online databases, and institutional investors receive PR Newswire's content through Thomson's First Call Network, Bloomberg, and Reuters terminals.

Q. You mentioned the consumer as one of your key audiences. So, I gather that news releases aren't just for the media anymore?

A. The Web has lowered the barriers to entering "newswireville." Now, consumers and individual investors can easily access news releases and other information through online databases and news sites, online services, search engines, and other Web sites. The news release has changed from information given only to reporters to a document now seen by everyone on the Internet.

Q. Regarding the Internet, what impact has it had on news release writing and distribution, from the public relations professional's standpoint?

A. The immediacy of the Internet poses some real challenges for the public relations professional, but it also provides some real opportunity. The writing of news releases has changed as a result of the Internet because releases are no longer written solely to interest the media in a broader story. Now anyone can read a news release on the Internet and it is picked up verbatim; public relations people need to write to communicate their message directly to the consumer reader.

In the past year, we have seen the news release evolve from a text document to an interactive multimedia platform that includes, in addition to text, video and audio, photos and logos, interactive capabilities and links to additional information, deliverable over the Internet, directly to key audiences everywhere. And, you can get better placement in a newspaper and e-zines if your online story includes a logo, photo, or some other artwork.

Lastly, because of the Internet, PR professionals need to do a better job of communicating news inside [the organization] because employees have to get the information before the rest of the world. You don't want angry employees saying "Why did I read about our company on Yahoo! before you sent it to us?"

Q. Can you highlight any notable technological advancements having an impact on the way public relations professionals handle the media and publicity efforts now, as compared to the previous decade?

A. As we discussed earlier, the Internet has had a huge impact on the way PR professionals handle the media and publicity efforts. For example, technology exists now to track how many reporters have accessed a release online and provide information back to the client on the reporter (adhering to privacy laws). This analysis allows you to begin tracking usage immediately after an announcement is made. Also, there are new technologies that allow a company to attach a survey to a news release and poll its online audience; this allows a company to get immediate feedback on its news, gauge general interest over time, and perhaps tweak its messages. You can even sell products directly from a news release through new interactive technology.

Also, PR Newswire has introduced two new products: the Tbutton News Meter™, a custom survey offering qualitative feedback on corporate news, and Tbutton Consumer Features™, an e-commerce application that provides instant consumer commerce opportunities.

Q. Shifting to the media, how is the Internet and the Web changing the way they do their jobs?

A. Reporters and editors can get information as it happens, right at their desks. They can participate in conference calls and press conferences on the Web. We now make it possible for reporters to watch video news releases at their desks, which can help print reporters add more color to their stories. Many companies have password-protected, media-only Web sites where reporters and editors can access and instantly download photos, news releases, and other background materials.

Q. Let's talk for a minute about ProfNet and how reporters and public relations professionals use that service.

A. Reporters looking for expert news sources use the ProfNet service to make online requests for interviews. These requests are provided to public relations practitioners who use the service through online feeds three times a day to match their company experts with the media's needs. ProfNet also offers a good way for PR people to monitor trends and see what kinds of stories the media are writing. The ProfNet Experts Database allows a public relations person to submit a profile on an 'expert' that is searchable by the media.

Q. Every year, there always seems to be someone or some trade article proclaiming the "news release is dead." What's your opinion?

A. Companies and organizations will always have to issue information. The news release will evolve over time to meet the needs of a company's core audiences, much like the multimedia news release we discussed earlier helps a company directly reach its consumers, employees, individual investors, business partners, suppliers, vendors, etc....audiences way beyond the media. The news release is no longer just a one-way communication device; it is an interactive platform. The news release will definitely not become obsolete!

Q. Clearly, the technology has prompted a lot of changes in how we get information to the media. But what about the fundamentals of good publicity and media relations? Have they changed all that much?

A. With all the changes in distribution, one thing has not changed. Relationships with reporters and editors remain key. Reporters still say, "If you're looking to get coverage, and you don't know my publication or my beat, don't call me." You still need to be a good writer, and you need to have subject knowledge and to be able to put your story in perspective.

You must customize your news to target media outlets, and that includes [customizing] distribution. We ask media what information they wish to see and how they wish to receive it, and then we deliver it in the preferred manner, so they don't get deluged with useless information. The content is still driving the message. You can't rely on the technology to do the job for you.

7

Media Alerts, Pitch Letters, and Public Relations Photos

In 1969, as the Rolling Stones prepared for a major U.S. concert tour, publicist David Horowitz remarked: "I wouldn't say we have a publicity strategy for this tour. The Stones, we believe, make their own news" (Malloy, 1995). That might have been true for the Stones more than 30 years ago. To some degree, that still might be true of the legendary band. But today, with so many organizations, people, and events competing day-to-day for headlines, you can't rely on a name or status alone to guarantee media coverage.

The fact is, the media are not watching every move the average organization makes. Reporters don't just sit around waiting for your company or client to do something worth reporting, except, maybe during times of crisis. In general, the media won't know about goings-on in your company unless you tell them. Most of the publicity you get for your organization will result from ideas you come up with and proactively present as potential story subjects (Exhibit 7.1).

As chapter 6 pointed out, news releases are generally used to announce company developments to the media. Besides writing and sending announcements, public relations professionals should also host events, suggest story ideas, make spokespersons available for interviews, and provide photo opportunities. Media alerts and pitch letters are important tools in this strategic publicity process. This chapter provides information on the proper use of media alerts and pitch letters, how to write media alerts and pitch letters to get a positive response, and what to think about when creating publicity photos and writing photo captions.

Media Alerts

While news releases can provide a starting point for more in-depth stories, many times they give an editor enough information to be published as written, or in some slightly edited or expanded form. In essence, you have already prepared the story for them.

Exhibit 7.1   What's the Story: A Nose for News

Public relations professionals must size up the news value of potential stories before suggesting ideas to editors. One important question is, how *significant* is the story? Does it have a dramatic effect on people? If a company plans to expand and create hundreds of new jobs, or if it plans to lay off people, those stories are significant and newsworthy. The media likes *conflict*. So, if your organization gets into trouble, there will be reporters at your door, even if you don't want them there. The media will cover strikes, activist group protests, union disagreements, and other such stories without much prodding from you. But most of the time, public relations professionals find themselves trying to interest editors and reporters in subjects that aren't as hard-hitting or controversial. In those cases, consider the following factors to get your organization "in the news":

- *Localizing*. There is a saying that "news isn't news unless it's local." One of the best ways to get your company in the news is to tie-in to the day's national events. Invite the media to interview one of your organization's "experts" who can comment on a national story that is unfolding.
- *Prominence*. If you are planning a campaign or a special event, involve a famous person, if you can. Actors, politicians, and well-known athletes connect themselves to charitable causes, which helps increase media interest. Every community has its own local celebrities, too, from the mayor to the beloved quarterback of the college football team, who can enhance the media appeal of your public relations program.
- *Timeliness*. Try to get news out when it happens. Getting the media to cover something that happened a week or two ago is difficult. Major company anniversaries (10th, 20th, 25th, etc.) are an excellent time to talk about the company's history, its notable successes, and its vision for the future. Consult *Chase's Annual Events* (many libraries carry this book) to find out if there is a national day, week, or month celebrated that you can use to promote your organization. Also, connect with trends. If more people are choosing to work part time in order to spend more time with their children, let the media know about your company's efforts to accommodate part-time employees, the benefits of flexible work schedules, and how that flexibility is supporting corporate productivity.
- *Human interest*. People like to read and hear about other interesting people, and the media likes to write about those people and their personal stories. For example, many not-for-profit health agencies sponsor annual road races or walk-a-thons to raise money for medical research and programming. To keep the media interested, they suggest new feature stories each year about noteworthy people participating in the event. Maybe one year it's a story about a young person running the race whose parent is afflicted with the disease. During the 10th year of the fund raiser, the focus might be on a runner or volunteer who has been involved every year since the event began.
- *The strange and extraordinary*. Remarkable achievements and quirky situations hold interest for the media. A person who beats the odds, breaks a record, or does something exceptional is a good subject for an article. At graduation time, high schools and colleges get media exposure by focusing on a high school senior who

(continued)

had perfect attendance or a college student who overcame major obstacles to receive her degree. To introduce Dawn Princess, the twin sister ship of Sun Princess, Princess Cruises reunited the cast members of the popular 1970s television show "The Love Boat." Princess sponsored a national search for look-alikes to the show's original cast members, reinforcing the "twins" theme of the campaign. A bit off the wall? Sure, but the unusual contest generated extensive media coverage and contributed to the most successful launch in the cruise line's history.

Media alerts have a different purpose. Their content is not intended for publication. Instead, media alerts introduce the media to a potential story and invite them to cover it. Also known as media advisories, media alerts are written to entice the media to cover your news conference, special event, or company announcement. If editors and news directors consider your event or development worthwhile, they assign reporters to cover and write stories about it. For example, organizations send media alerts to get coverage of news conferences that focus on company expansions and other hard news announcements, and to get coverage of special events and ceremonies where a new product is unveiled, a person is honored for achievement, or a building is opened or dedicated.

Media alerts and news releases do share some common features. Both are printed on your organization's letterhead and include contact information. Both should be brief; media alerts are never more than one page. Content must be clear, well written, error-free and presented in AP style. And, like news releases, media alerts are distributed by mail, by fax, by satellite, and by e-mail, depending on individual media preferences and the urgency of the news.

The major difference between media alerts and news releases is that media alerts should not "tell all." They should give just enough detail to indicate that a newsworthy event is scheduled, what and who it involves, and where and when it is taking place. If your media alert contains too much detail, news staffs may find it unnecessary to send reporters since you've already given them enough information to write the story. As a result, what could have been a longer story ends up as a news brief.

Exhibit 7.2 is an example of a well-crafted media alert:

- Notice that it is clearly labeled "Media Advisory" and that it includes a strong headline in bold to catch the editor's attention.
- The first paragraph offers a concise summary of the news event. The remainder of the advisory is presented in a simple, easy-to-read "Who, What, When, and Where" format.
- The "Facts" section includes notable points that establish the event's success, history, and credibility. The last item highlights a good photo opportunity— children being treated at the Jimmy Fund Clinic who will be participating in the event and when that will happen.

  A few final points about media alerts:

Exhibit 7.2 Media Alert: John Hancock

CONTACT: Pam Kruh
617-572-0558

Media Advisory

John Hancock, the Boston Red Sox and the Jimmy Fund Take Another Big Swing at Cancer.

More than 120 New Englanders will step up to the plate October 2nd at Fenway Park for a chance to hit one off the Green Monster and raise money for the Jimmy Fund at the eighth annual John Hancock Fantasy Day at Fenway Park. Thirty-two teams of four each signed up raising an initial $192,000 for the fight against cancer. They will have a chance to contribute more money to the cause through their batting efforts.

WHO: John Hancock, the Boston Red Sox and the Jimmy Fund / Dana-Farber Cancer Institute

WHAT: John Hancock Fantasy Day at Fenway Park

WHERE: Fenway Park, Yawkey Way

WHEN: Saturday, October 2, 1999, from 8 a.m. to 5 p.m.

FACTS: Over the past seven years, the event has raised $1,409,307 for the Jimmy Fund's fight against cancer.

Last year, Fantasy Day participants raised $252,156, including a total of 40 Green Monster hits and 8 home runs.

John Hancock donates an extra $1,000 for every ball that hits the Green Monster and $2,000 for every ball that is hit out of the park.

Two teams of children being treated at the Jimmy Fund Clinic will participate in the event. The children will be hitting at 10:30 a.m. and 11:00 a.m.

WORLDWIDE SPONSOR

JOHN HANCOCK MUTUAL LIFE INSURANCE COMPANY
JOHN HANCOCK PLACE, P.O. BOX 111, BOSTON, MASSACHUSETTS 02117

Note: Reprinted with permission of John Hancock Financial Services.

- Proofread media alerts carefully before they are distributed. You don't want to embarrass yourself by leaving out a critical piece of information, such as the time or date of the event, or by misspelling the name of a company executive.

- Send media alerts a few days in advance of the news event; more lead time may be needed if travel is required, or if the media you work with prefer more advance notice. Most editors maintain a file for future stories. Even though a decision to cover your event usually will not be made until the day before or the day of your event, sending a media alert in advance can create some initial awareness and help media personnel in their efforts to stay organized.

There are mixed feelings among practitioners about the need for follow-up after media alerts are distributed. Many believe that you need to follow up to remind busy media contacts about the event, to make sure they received the material, and to further "sell" the event and its news value. Follow-up can also give event planners an idea of how many reporters to expect, which helps when determining room set-up and when responding to pointed questions from bosses and clients about the expected media turnout. But some professionals say follow-up calls are a waste of time because the best response you can expect is "maybe we'll send someone, depending on what else happens that day." Another reason is many media contacts find follow-up calls and e-mails annoying.

The best advice is to know your media contacts and how each will react to follow ups. When you do follow up, be polite and call at convenient times. A TV news director will not appreciate your call at 4:30 in the afternoon when the first newscast of the evening is just minutes away. If using the telephone, state your case quickly and clearly. Introduce yourself, ask if your media alert was received, and if there are any questions about it. Be prepared to briefly explain your event and its news value for journalists who say they don't recall receiving the material, and arrange to fax or e-mail another copy of the alert. The typical follow-up call should last no more than a minute, maybe two, unless the person you are speaking with asks for specific information, or invites you to "sell" the story further. Speak to the individual needs of each media person and ask what you can do to help that person get the story he or she needs.

Pitch Letters

Read any newspaper or magazine, or watch any television news or talk show, and you will see articles, interviews, and news subjects most likely suggested or "pitched" by a public relations source. Here are three examples:

- A wire story on the food page of a daily newspaper about the entertaining chef of three food and cooking programs on a cable network
- An article about the launch of the "first of a new generation" of video game systems in the science and technology section of a major news magazine

- An interview on a national morning talk show with an author whose current book focuses on the need for better educated teachers in our schools

In each of these cases, it's likely that the organizations and individuals involved pitched their stories. Each has a specific, "bottom-line" goal in trying to cultivate media interest. The cable network is trying to promote its food programs and boost viewership. The video company is looking to build consumer interest in its product and strengthen its reputation as a leader and innovator in that industry. The author is hoping to position himself as an expert on education and to stimulate book sales. But the media has no interest in what the organizations want; their goal is to provide news and information in which readers and viewers are interested.

In the case of the video game story, then, the astute public relations professional recommends an angle focusing on the impact this new video game will have on consumers and how it will revolutionize the industry. The company gets exposure indirectly by being identified as the product's manufacturer and through quotes from corporate marketing and product development executives. Emphasis is on the consumer product and the issues and trends surrounding it, not on the company and how wonderful it is for introducing this product.

That's the key to successful media pitching. You need to put your own interests aside, and concentrate on finding a news "hook" or angle that appeals to the media. Many times, that involves making your company and its product part of a "bigger-picture story." In the case of the video game company, that "bigger picture" is the growth of the video game industry and notable trends in video game technology. The company is really secondary to the story. Timeliness also strengthens your pitch. The talk show interview on teaching standards took place days before the start of a new school year, and the video story ran one week before the product hit the market.

Public relations professionals can pitch story ideas over the telephone, and some editors prefer that approach. It is challenging, however, to reach busy editors by phone, and even if you do, you will want to send something in writing after the call to recap your phone conversation. Many practitioners begin the process by writing and sending a persuasive *pitch letter*. A pitch letter is a one-page proposal designed to sell a story idea. Some professionals write longer pitch letters, but one page—three to five paragraphs—is usually enough to present your idea and get your main points across. Most of the time, after they accept your pitch, editors will run with it and assign a staff person to the story. Some trade publications with small staffs may ask the public relations person to prepare and submit the article.

The best results come from individualized pitches. Target a specific idea to a specific editor or reporter at a specific publication. The media likes exclusivity—getting a story idea that no other publication is getting at that time and being the first to publish such a story. Consider your goals and target audience first and select a publication that greatly influences or is widely read by that group. Before sending the pitch letter, read the publication and become familiar with the type of stories it likes to publish, preferred story angles, and the most appropriate editor or section to pitch. Do not send the same pitch letter to different editors at the same publication. If you have questions about which editor to pitch to, contact the publication (you might start with the editor you think is most appropriate) and ask for some guidance.

Pitch letters, like the one shown in Exhibit 7.3 sent to a trade publication, have three key parts: a creative and attention-getting first paragraph; a body containing key facts that build interest in the story; and a brief closing paragraph with a clear "call to action."

Exhibit 7.3   E-mail Pitch Letter: Taylor Devices
_____

From: Ann Carden
Sent: Thursday, May 16, 2002 12:26 PM
To: melnick@modernsteel.com
Subject: The Wobbly Bridge

Dear Mr. Melnick—I'm writing on behalf of Taylor Devices with a feature idea that I'm sure would interest your readers. Taylor recently helped to take the wobble out of London's so-called "Wobbly Bridge." Originally known as the Millennium Bridge, the $36 million slender sliver of steel spanning the Thames was opened on June 10, 2000 and closed two days later. The 330m lateral suspension pedestrian bridge, which features a 4m-wide suspension deck with no support towers and a 700-ton steel/aluminum deck with two concrete piers, developed an excessive swaying when used by more than 1,000 pedestrians.

The Problem
The problem was traced to the synchronized footfall of pedestrians stepping or shifting their body weights in unison. The movement was described as "similar to a ship rolling in a storm." Testing revealed that as few as 500 people stepping in unison were the critical mass to provide an uncontrollable deck response with accelerations of up to .25g and displacements of up to plus or minus 3 inches at .5 to 1.1Hz.

The Solution
After considering several options, passive damping was chosen as the best solution. Thirty-seven viscous dampers were integrated into the bridge deck architecture or hidden under the deck to reduce the sway. Fifty tuned mass oscillators were added to limit vertical deck deflection under footfalls. Taylor Devices' patented Frictionless Hermetic Dampers were selected for the retrofit of the bridge.

The Result
After several tests with more than 2,000 people, the bridge was declared "rock solid" and reopened in Feburary 2002. Dynamic response amplitudes were reduced by at least 40 to one for all modes. Peak measured accelerations were reduced from .25g undamped to .006g damped—an improvement of 42 to one.

I hope you will consider pursuing this idea for Modern Steel. I would be happy to arrange an interview for you with a representative from Taylor Devices. Please contact me at

(continued)

acarden@gelia.com or 716-759-0930. A number of pictures from the retrofit project are available to accompany a story. In addition, you might find it interesting to visit the BBC's Web site at http://news.bbc.co.uk/hi/english/static/in_depth/uk/2000/millennium_bridge/ to see before and after pictures of the bridge, as well as a video showing the swaying shortly after it opened.

Taylor Devices, Inc., is the leading manufacturer of shock absorbers, liquid springs, shock isolation systems, seismic isolators, vibration dampers, power plant snubbers, and other types of hydro-mechanical energy management products.

$\blacksquare$

Note: Courtesy of Taylor Devices, Inc., North Tonawanda, N.Y.

- In the first paragraph, share a startling statistic, or present a hard-hitting fact that introduces your idea in an interesting way and makes an immediate connection with the editor and the publication. If you are framing your pitch around a lifestyle issue or a trend, start your letter by discussing the recent popularity of that issue or some significant aspect of that trend. Try to avoid being too self-serving in the lead paragraph. Your initial focus must be on the benefit of this story to the publication and its readers. Don't say that you know what a publication's readers want or need. There's nothing wrong with indicating your knowledge of who the readers are and why this story may be of interest to them at some point in the letter, but avoid general statements that seem pushy or presume you know more about the publication than an editor does.

- In the body of the letter, expand the story angle and suggest credible sources. Share statistics, anecdotes, and details that build interest and legitimize the story. In a pitch letter on the new video games system, you could mention that the video game industry is a $6.3 billion business, and that analysts expect video game revenues to soon surpass motion picture revenues for the first time in history. These facts better position the new video game system as a more substantial news story. Pitches about people and human interest stories include interesting facts in the body of the letter about a person's background that show how that person is unusual or different from others like him. For issue and trends stories, offer the name and key credentials of knowledgeable sources and spokespersons who are available for interviews.

- There's no need to say too much in a last sentence or paragraph. State the goal of your pitch letter (arranging an interview with a spokesperson, setting up a meeting to discuss the idea further, etc.). Indicate your plans for following up and reinforce your willingness to help arrange interviews, supply photographs, or provide any additional information.

You can use e-mail to pitch ideas, but play by the rules. Check with editors first to see if they welcome e-mail pitches. Never send unsolicited e-mail. If you do pitch this way, keep your e-mail brief. Write two or three short (one or two sentences each) strong paragraphs and an informative and catchy message subject line and headline. Also, don't keep sending follow-up e-mail messages to see how they liked your idea. Wait several days to a week and then call or send a brief e-mail message to check on the status of your pitch, and to discuss the merit of the idea further, if afforded that opportunity. When getting permission from editors up front to contact them by e-mail, ask them about how follow-up should be handled.

Public Relations Photos

Rock music singer and songwriter Rod Stewart said it in a 1970s album title: "Every Picture Tells a Story." Ansel Adams, one of the 20th century's most beloved and renowned photographers, once said, "A true photograph need not be explained, nor can it be contained in words." Like these artists, public relations professionals should understand the impact of a good photograph. A visually interesting photo sent with a news release can make your story stand out to editors and help your chances of getting published. Publicity photographs used by public relations professionals generally fall into one of three categories:

- *Head shots*. These accompany news releases about people working for your organization. When an executive is promoted at your company, for example, it is common to send a news release and a head-and-shoulders or "mug shot" of that person to the "People in Motion" or "Company Matters" column published in the business section of the daily newspaper. Hometown newspapers, trade magazines, college publications, and association newsletters also use head shots.
- *Product photos*. Consumer magazines and trade publications often have sections on product news. If your company is launching a new product, updating an old product, or making changes to product packaging, send a product shot with your news release to add visual appeal.
- *Event and feature photos*. These include photographs taken before an event to attract attention and promote participation in the event, those taken during an event that can be published after the fact, and "people" or "action" photos that complement feature and human interest stories. Theater companies send out photos of actors rehearsing scenes to publicize plays before they open and generate advance ticket sales. Organizations promote new construction projects by distributing photos taken of company executives shoveling dirt or surveying the site during a ground-breaking ceremony. A feature about the hands-on approach of a new corporate CEO might include a photograph of him or her in the factory examining a specific assembly line procedure with line workers.

Head shots and product photos are usually straightforward and static, although some product photos show someone using the product in its natural environment. In product photos, make sure the product name and company logo are visible. Most publicity photos, though, should be full of action. Avoid the "grip and grin" photo that

Exhibit 7.4   Working with Local Media: Bigger Is Not Always Better

You've been asked to publicize something in a local market. Your first instinct might be to send publicity materials to the daily newspapers or local television stations in that city or area. While the major media in a local market reach thousands of people and promise widespread message exposure, they may not provide the most effective channels for reaching specific populations in that community. Consider some of the specialized media in a local market that can help you get messages more directly to niche groups and result in publicity efforts that have greater impact:

Newsletters

Professional and business organizations, social clubs, civic groups, churches, and other community groups typically produce newsletters or bulletins for their members, and may be receptive to publishing your publicity material if it is tailored to their readers' interests.

Local television and radio talk shows

Some markets have locally-produced talk and public affairs programs that air on cable access and local public television stations (PBS). Some local radio stations, especially public radio and stations with all-news-and-talk formats, feature local programming or call-in shows on issues affecting the community.

Community, business and special interest newspapers

Most cities have weekly or hometown newspapers that publish news geared to residents of specific towns and suburbs. In addition to business newspapers and arts and entertainment publications, you may also find specialized newspapers targeted to parents, African Americans, and other ethnic groups. Many of these smaller publications may even reprint your news release or publish your photo "as is."

High school and college media

Many publish daily or weekly newspapers and some operate radio stations that have a loyal listener base in that community. These media provide an excellent way to reach students and a younger audience, but don't forget that teachers, administrators, and staff get information from media as well.

shows people shaking hands and smiling at the camera. While these posed photos do occasionally end up in print, you will make a more positive impression on the media if your photos look natural and capture people while they are involved in an activity as it is happening. For instance, a keynote speaker at a fund-raising dinner should be photographed while delivering the speech and talking with guests informally before and after the speech. Besides getting action into your photos, there are other rules to follow when producing photos for media publication:

- <u>Know the media's photo needs and guidelines</u>. Find out if the media with which you deal accept photographs from outside sources. If they don't, ask if they assign staff photographers to take photos at newsworthy events, and what the procedure is for alerting them to photo opportunities. It is best to talk directly with editors about their individual needs and policies; most media directory listings also make note of a publication's interest in receiving photos. If you do send photographs, make sure you review publications first to see what kind of action shots they like to use. Whenever possible, offer exclusive photos to encourage publication.

- <u>Create and reproduce high-quality photos</u>. Prints that are washed out, have poor contrast, or some other technical flaw are unacceptable to the media. Unless you are well-trained in photography, hire a professional photographer for major events and photo opportunities. Brief photographers before a shoot on the kinds of photos you and your target media are looking for, and how the photos will be used. Regardless of whether photos are taken by a professional or staff member, remember to include a photo credit with the picture.

- <u>Avoid clutter and excessive promotion</u>. Don't overcrowd your photos. The more people you try to cram into a shot, the less likely it is that your photo will have any action. Focus on two or three people who are relevant to the story and who can provide action in the photo to tell the story in a lively and creative way. The exception might be if the people shown are well-known and involved in a major news event, but you still want those people talking with each other as opposed to staring straight ahead at the camera. It is acceptable to work your organization's name or logo into a photo, but do it subtly. You might set up the photo of a store grand opening so that the company sign is visible in the shot, but you would not want to have all the corporate executives in the photo wearing T-shirts and holding shopping bags imprinted with large company logos. Editors are interested in publishing news, not in promoting your company.

- <u>Write descriptive captions, or **cutlines**</u>. Send photos with two- to three-sentence cutlines that explain the action. Include contact information and a headline as you would at the start of a news release. When writing cutlines, use the present tense in the first sentence and any other sentences that describe what is happening in the photo. Don't waste this valuable space by stating the obvious. Background sentences providing additional detail and key facts about the news event can be written in past tense. Make only one reference to the company or client.

Try to identify people based on the action taking place rather than on their location (i.e., pictured left to right are...) in the shot, except in those situations where there are several people pictured and it would be awkward to do otherwise. The following is an example of a publicity photo cutline:

LIONS CLUB FUND RAISER IS JUST "DUCK-Y"

Kerry Ann Gleason, 4, points at hundreds of cute rubber ducks drifting by as she sits with her father, Robert, during the Camden Lions Club's 10th annual Labor Day Duck Derby fund raiser. Kerry's mother, Anita, and her brother, James, look on. The event, held on the Fulton River in Camden, raised $12,000 to benefit the club's many community activities such as youth sports and the Adopt-a-Park program.

- <u>Select the most appropriate format</u>. Ask about preferred format for photo submissions. Some media like 5" × 7" or 8" × 10" prints, while others would rather receive a color slide or transparency. You can also post photos on your Web site and let media know they can download photos there, which is something more companies are doing to accommodate media deadlines.

References and Suggested Reading

Ansel Adams (n.d.). Retrieved on December 6, 2002, from http://www.jokemonster.com/quotes/a/q141169.html

Howard, C. M. & Mathews, W. K. (2000). *On deadline: Managing media relations* (3rd ed.). Prospect Heights, IL: Waveland Press.

Hunt, T. & Grunig, J.E. (1997). *Public relations techniques*. Stamford, CT: International Thomson Publishing, 1997.

Malloy, M. (Ed.) (1995). *The Great Rock 'N' Roll Quote Book*. New York: St. Martin's Griffin.

Marsh, C. (1996). *A quick and not dirty guide to business writing: 25 business and public relations documents every business writer should know*. Upper Saddle River, NJ: Pearson PTP.

Matthis, M. E. (2002). *Feeding the media beast: An easy recipe for great publicity*. West Lafayette, IN: Purdue University Press, 2002.

Parkhurst, W. (2000). *How to get publicity: Revised and updated for the Internet age*. New York: HarperBusiness.

Stewart, R. (1971). Every picture tells a story. [record]. Location: Mercury.

CASES

Case 21: Small Business Person of the Year (Part B)

In chapter 3, case 7, Jim Middleton, public relations director for Torolla, Jerome & McCarthy, started research for a public relations campaign for an agency client, Grogan's retail store. The focus of the campaign is the announcement that Vanda White, president of Grogan's, is this year's winner of the Small Business Person of the Year Award in New York state. Middleton's research efforts produced some additional facts important to the campaign:

- White is one of 200 small business persons and owners from her state nominated for the award this year. The award is given annually to an entrepreneur in each of the 50 states by the Small Business Administration (SBA). State winners now compete for the U.S. Small Business Person of the Year Award. That award will be presented at a dinner in Washington, D.C. in two months.
- White's late father, Alvin Grogan, founded Grogan's 30 years ago. Grogan earned a reputation as one of the area's most respected businessmen. White's oldest son, Doug, is currently one of the store's management trainees and is preparing to take over as president in the future.
- For the past 15 years, under White's leadership, Grogan's gross sales have tripled. Its staff has doubled in size in the last two years. In addition, Grogan's moved from its original location a year ago to a larger facility one mile away.

As part of the campaign to promote White's award, Middleton creates a media packet including a news release about the award; feature stories about White and Grogan's; a head-and-shoulders photograph of White; and a photo of Claude, a 15-foot mechanized ogre and one of Grogan's best-known Halloween displays. He plans to distribute these to area and statewide daily, weekly, and business newspapers. He also proposes organizing several special events, including an awards presentation in Durham, where Grogan's is located.

His idea is to hold the event on May 1, the start of National Small Business Month. The event would feature two presentations, one by Mayor Jeffrey Young proclaiming May 1 "Vanda White Day" in Durham, and the other by Durham

County Executive Malcolm King to honor White with a special citation for her contributions to small business growth in the county. The 10 a.m. event will be held at the Durham Chamber of Commerce Briefing Center, 500 Main St. Coffee, juice, bagels, and pastries will be served. Middleton discusses the idea with White, who endorses it wholeheartedly, and then begins making the arrangements.

Assignments

1. The media kit includes a photograph of Vanda White and her son Doug talking in front of the Claude display. Write a two-sentence cutline for this photo. Include a headline.
2. It is now two weeks before the May 1 awards presentation. Middleton needs to inform the local media about the event in hopes they will attend and cover it. Using information from this case and case 7 in chapter 3, write a one-page media alert for distribution to the local media.
3. Middleton begins arranging media interviews and feature article opportunities for White during the month of May. He targets WDHM-FM, an all-news-and-talk radio station in Durham, that frequently features interviews with notable local and national people on a wide variety of issues. He also plans to pitch *Business First*, the major weekly business newspaper in the state.
   (a) Write a one-page pitch letter to interest WDHM in doing an on-air interview with White.
   (b) Write a one-page pitch letter to *Business First* to interest the newspaper in writing a feature story about White.

Case 22: Promoting the "Road Rage" Expert

Your firm, Cary & Associates, located in the San Francisco area, does much of its public relations work for individuals. Clients include authors promoting new books and physicians looking to share their expertise about specific medical treatments or conditions.

As an account executive with Cary & Associates, one of your primary duties involves planning and executing publicity campaigns for several high-profile medical experts. One morning, you are called to a meeting with Lois Weeks, your boss and an account supervisor for the agency.

"We have a new client coming in shortly, and I would like you to work with her. I thought I should brief you about her before she gets here. Her name is Mariah Conrad and believe it or not, she's a 'road rage' expert. Apparently, lots of people have trouble handling their anger on the highway and they need someone to talk to about it. She's building part of her practice around this specialty."

"Road rage, huh? I experience a little of that from time to time myself. This morning on my way to work, as a matter of fact. What else do we know about her?"

Weeks continues: "I've got her resumé here. Let's see, Dr. Conrad is 39, a licensed psychiatrist, and a hypnotherapist. She advocates using meditation and hypnotherapy to help drivers deal with their road rage. She's written a book, too. It's got a catchy title—*Don't Drive Yourself Crazy: Controlling Your Road Rage*. It's due out in a month or so. She's also started traveling around the country doing seminars on road rage at companies and at American Automobile Association offices. Oh, when I was talking with her on the phone, she said that one of the things she does with her clients is to first 'size up' their personality types. You know, like drivers who speed up when someone else tries to pass them. She diagnoses those drivers as having a 'competitive personality.' Interesting stuff, don't you think?"

"She's got some good credentials, that's for sure," you say. "What does she want us to do for her, do you have a sense of that?"

"I know she hopes to build up her practice, but she's also really interested in positioning herself as the leading authority on this subject. It's a pretty timely topic, and lots of people seem to be interested in it. Like you said, we all probably act like raging drivers at times. I know she's definitely interested in getting on some of the morning talk shows like 'TODAY' and 'Good Morning America.' I bet we could get her on 'Oprah,' too. We also talked about possibly working with her on a Web site. She'll be here in about a half an hour. It might be good for us to come up with some questions we'll want to ask, and then we can go from there."

Assignments

1. Write an e-mail pitch letter to interest a producer of NBC's "TODAY" show in scheduling an interview with Dr. Conrad. Your letter should be no longer than three short paragraphs and include a strong message subject line to attract the producer's attention.
2. Write a one-page pitch letter to be sent to either *USA Today* or an automotive magazine such as *Car and Driver*. The goal of the letter is to interest the publication in writing a feature story on Dr. Conrad.
3. Working in teams of two, prepare a media list of other national consumer magazines and television programs that might be interested in doing an interview with or writing a story about Dr. Conrad. Include the name of the publication or program, a mailing address and Web site address, frequency of distribution and circulation (or for TV, how often the program airs and how many people watch the show); a brief description of its content and target audience; a key contact name, title, phone number, and e-mail address; and deadline information.

Case 23: The Kickoff Dinner (Part A)

The Smithville Blue Sox is a Triple A baseball team. Triple A is the highest minor league classification; each Triple A team is an affiliate of a major league team.

For the past 10 years, the team has invited local residents to meet the players at a business-style luncheon. The luncheon, sponsored by the Smithville Downtown Business Association (SDBA), is held the day before the first game of the season. This year, the team is trying something new—a buffet style dinner to attract more families. The dinner is free (the SDBA will again cover all the costs) and features hamburgers, hot dogs, french fries, pizza, salads, and ice cream. The dinner is scheduled for April 15 from 5 to 8 p.m. at the Smithville Convention Center.

As a public relations intern for the team, you are helping to plan and publicize the upcoming event. You meet briefly with Carol Kaiser, Blue Sox public relations and marketing director, to discuss this new approach.

"Basically, we want to put more focus this year on families and get more kids involved with the team and more families at the games. We talked about the new format with the SDBA and they think it's a great idea. I'm going to have you help me with some of the event setup, but I really want you to focus on getting the word out to the community and the media. Reporters usually show up because it's right before opening day and they know they'll be able to interview many of the players in one place. So, what questions can I answer for you? I'm sure you've got a few."

"I looked over the media clippings from the past few lunches and those answered some of my questions. I assume that most of the players will be at the dinner. And do we hold some kind of formal gathering for the media, or do we just invite them and let them roam around during the dinner and interview people that way?"

"We try to get as many of the players there as possible, and usually most of them show up," Kaiser responds. "Before the dinner starts, we like to have Tommy DeSoto, our general manager, and some of the players say a few words about the upcoming season. That's really set up for the media more than anyone else. We'll do that in the main lobby of the convention center around 5 o'clock. It's the kickoff to the dinner, really. We pick 5 p.m. because we can get TV coverage during the 5 and 6 p.m. news and additional coverage at 11."

"What about after that?" you ask. "I assume it's okay for the media to stay for the dinner so they can get some quotes from some of the children and parents."

"Most of the reporters will probably stay around for the early part of the dinner for that very reason. We may get some media requests in advance of the dinner for individual interviews with some of the players, and we do our best to accommodate those requests, too," Kaiser says.

"So, have we decided who will speak at 5 o'clock? You said the general manager makes some comments."

"We're definitely planning to have Mike McGinty there at 5. He's the new pitcher from California, and many people are saying he could help lead the Sox to a league championship this year. His dad, John, pitched in the majors for a while. Our first baseman, Carlos Pena, will be there, too. He was a popular player last year with the press and the fans, and he's an excellent spokesper-son for the team."

"Okay, that's about everything I need to know at this point. Oh, one more thing. I've been reading about the Kids Club we started last year for the 12 and under crowd. Do we want to tie that in with the dinner somehow? It certainly fits with the new family theme."

"Definitely," Kaiser replies. "The club is really starting to take off. Parents seem to like it because it costs nothing to join, and children get free admission to six games during the season as members. The children love it because we hold some special autograph-signing sessions just for Kids Club members and they get discounts on caps and some of the other team clothing. The dinner would be a good place to get more children to sign up or to at least let them and their moms and dads know more about the club."

"I know you're on your way out to a meeting so why don't I get started on some of the media materials we'll need, and I'll have some copy ready when you get back."

"Sounds good. I like a person who takes initiative. I should be back in two hours. I can look at your copy then."

Assignments

1. Write a one-page media alert inviting the local media to the April 15 Blue Sox community dinner.

2. Write an announcement for use in print media "Events Calendars." Event listings usually begin with the name, date, and location of the event (feel free to come up with a creative name for the Blue Sox dinner) followed by a two- or three-sentence description of the event. They also include information on the cost of admission, and a phone number to call for more information.

3. At the dinner, you take several photographs, including one with the new pitcher, Mike McGinty. In the photo, McGinty is seated at a table (right side of photo) holding an ice cream cone in one hand and signing auto-graphs for two happy Smithville youth and Kids Club members: Jennifer Bermudez, 10, seated next to McGinty on the left side of the photo, and her brother Ricky, 12, standing between the two with his baseball cap and glove on. Write a two-sentence cutline for this photograph to be pub-lished in the Blue Sox fan newsletter, and to be distributed to area weekly newspapers.

Case 24: The Illuminec Corporation

In 1979, at the age of 28, Helmut Bergmann came to the United States from his homeland in Vienna to establish the U.S. manufacturing division of Wuensche International, an Austrian fiber optics company. At the time, Bergmann and his wife had a 1-year-old daughter and they had concerns about uprooting her and leaving their families behind. After much discussion, they decided this opportunity was too good to pass up, so they packed up and came to America. Bergmann headed Wuensche's U.S. division successfully for 10 years before deciding to start his own fiber optics company, Illuminec, Inc. Illuminec makes custom and standard fiber optic lighting systems that illuminate microscopes, industrial products, and medical equipment such as blood analyzers.

Bergmann built the company from an eight-person, $800,000 business with a few custom-made products to one today that has more than 120 employees, a standard product line of 250 items, and current sales of $13 million. At Illuminec, there is an emphasis on employee communication to keep workers informed about new product and company developments. Illuminec has further distinguished itself from the competition by recently implementing an "on time or free" product shipment policy. The policy guarantees that products are delivered within 48 hours of placing the order. During the program's first year, Illuminec shipped more than 6,000 products and had to pay for only 10 shipments that did not arrive in 48 hours.

In the past year, Illuminec has seen a sharp increase in the number of manufacturers using its illumination systems for online product inspections. These companies include No-Leak Diapers, a leading manufacturer of disposable diapers. Illuminec's fiber-optic illumination helps No-Leak carefully inspect its products to ensure that diapers are properly sealed, which prevents leakage. Another company, Sweetland Farms, measures the thickness of its cookies using Illuminec's products. Food and consumer product companies say a major reason for using Illuminec's lighting devices is to protect themselves from liability and lawsuits resulting from defective products or products that consumers say "don't live up to their advertising claims." Bergmann believes that service to food companies is becoming a significant segment of Illuminec's business.

A machinist by trade, Bergmann came to Wuensche in that capacity in 1971. A few years later, he took over as head of Wuensche's fiber-optic assembly department and got more involved in the design and marketing of fiber-optic illumination products. He says that much of his success can be attributed to "learning and knowing the fiber-optic business, from the ground up."

Assignments

1. Assume you are the marketing communications director for Illuminec Inc. You have a contact at *Business Week* magazine—a reporter/writer whose main focus is business and high technology. Write an e-mail pitch letter to interest that reporter in doing a story on Illuminec.
2. Working alone or in teams of two, prepare a media list of 10 to 15 trade publications that would be interested in receiving news about Illuminec.

List the name of each publication, its mailing address and Web site address, and frequency of distribution and total circulation; provide a brief description of the publication's content and target audiences including key contact names, titles, phone numbers and e-mail addresses along with deadline information.

3. Select one trade publication from the list in #2. Write a one-page pitch letter to interest a specific editor at that publication in writing a major feature article on Illuminec.

Tips from the Top

"Effective Media Pitching"
Linda Finnell

As a former senior producer for "TODAY," Linda Finnell handled live bookings for the show and story pitches. Based on her experiences, she offers some "dos and don'ts" for public relations professionals when pitching story ideas to the media.

Q: **Your job involves a lot of contact with public relations professionals. I'm curious—what's your impression of public relations people?**

A: My impression of PR people is the same as my impression of people in general. There are folks who "get it" and folks who don't.

Q: **In a typical week of "TODAY" programming, how much of the story content is based on ideas pitched by public relations professionals?**

A: I'm not sure there is such a thing as a typical week of programming at "TODAY." But to try and answer the question, if you take away news stories, entertainment spots, book spots and the spots from our own contributors, probably a handful.

Q: **Of those pitches you get, which ones interest you the most?**

A: The pitches that interest us the most are the stories WE find interesting. If it's a story that people are talking about . . . or a story we can use to springboard off the headlines . . . or there's a "gee-whiz" factor to the story or something so compelling it touches us in a unique way.

Q: **Here's a scenario. I'm a public relations person who works for a major company, and we've just launched a new consumer food product. How could I position a pitch to get exposure for the product on "TODAY?"**

A: To be honest, it's going to be a tough sell. Generally—not always—but generally we don't do spots that have a commercial plug because we're very aware of not making a spot a commercial. And when I say "pass," companies end up outside the [studio] window trying to get their product on air regardless. These folks would fall into the "don't get it" category. But if it's brand new, the only one, unbelievable or unique, we still might do it. Again, it all depends on what it is.

Q: **Give me an example of a recent successful pitch that is a model for public relations professionals to follow.**

A: A recent successful pitch...I'll have to get back to you on that one.

Q: **Pitches are done by telephone, by snail mail, by fax and, by e-mail. Which method do you prefer and why?**

A: I prefer e-mails or snail mail, or you can overnight or send the material via messenger. We don't take faxes, as the machines tend to stay so busy we can't get our material out or get a fax we need. Using the telephone is a big waste of time for me. If I spoke to every PR person with a pitch, I wouldn't have time to do my job. Or eat. Or go home. It's way too time-consuming to speak with folks on the phone. It's much easier if I have hard copy. Then I can go through the ideas on my time when it's convenient for me.

Q: **More people seem to be using e-mail these days to pitch story ideas. What's your view of e-mail pitches?**

A: E-mail is great for me. I keep that system up in my computer at all times. I know as soon as I get new e-mail. I can open an e-mail and determine if it's something I can wait on a day...or two...or 10 or 20. Sometimes I get way behind on getting answers back to folks but I always, always try to get folks an answer. Eventually.

Q: **I would imagine you've heard your share of not-so-good pitches. What are some of the most common mistakes people make when they pitch ideas to you?**

A: Don't call to tell me you are faxing, overnighting, or mailing me material. It's a huge waste of time. Also, address the pitch to me. On the cover letter. If you send a letter to "general assignment producer," you won't get a response unless we're interested. If you send a letter to Linda Finnell, you'll (generally) get a response to let you know if we're interested or not.

　　If you do call and get me on the phone, ask me if it's a good time to talk. I've had folks call me and launch into a pitch where the only time I've been able to speak is when they come up for air. If you've sent me material, there's no reason to send material to another producer. It's double work. In the same vein, if you've e-mailed material, don't overnight me the same thing. Again, it's double work.

Q: **Is there any one thing that really bothers you about some of the pitches you receive?**

A: This is my pet peeve—a huge pet peeve. Always, always, always disclose who your client is to me in the letter. Please don't make me ask. I don't want to have to find out that you really aren't pitching a segment about healthy eating for healthy hearts, but that you're really pitching your client who makes cereal. Or, you don't want to talk about how folks can cope with osteoporosis, but you're offering a doctor from the drug company you represent that makes a new drug for osteoporosis. You get the picture. Just let me know who the client is up front. It makes my job easier.

Q: Any other advice you can offer about proper pitching?

A: I get a lot of pitches for chefs or a lifestyle issue where people want to demonstrate something on the show. I'll ask for a tape of the person doing live television, but what I get is a tape of the person that's edited—not live. Also, if you're sending me your client's appearance on "Oprah," please make sure the tape is cued to your client's appearance, not the theme song.

Q: What about follow-up? Do you want public relations people to call you back after they've pitched an idea, or should they wait for you to call?

A: I prefer people to wait to hear from me as I'm pretty good about getting answers back to folks. If it's an e-mail, I answer it. If it's a pitch through the mail, my assistant will call.

    However, I know there are times when a booking might be competitive or last minute, or I might be busy with a breaking news story and someone needs an answer sooner than later. In those cases, a call is totally appropriate. I think it comes down to the publicist using common sense.

Q: Good media pitches are based on many factors, but if you had to pick two or three that really make the difference, what would they be?

A: Be concise. Make sure I can read the first paragraph and know exactly the "what" and "when" of what you're pitching. While I can only speak for myself, I would bet that most people have busy days. Keep that in mind when you're pitching someone. Remember, not only am I getting a pitch from you, but I'm hearing from your competitors and the woman who starts her morning every day with Katie and Matt who's got a great idea for a spot.

    The bottom line is, know the person you're pitching. Find out what's the best time to call. Watch the show if you're pitching to a television program— know the kind of spots we do. Go through all of the above questions. Should I call you? Fax you? E-mail you? Get to know the people you're pitching and all their quirks and habits, and what works best for them. The publicists I have the best relationships with know all the above about me. They "get it." And I even take their calls.

8

Backgrounders, Features, and Advocacy Writing

In a May 2001 *Newsweek* article, Beyonce Knowles, a member of the popular music group Destiny's Child, attributes some of the group's success to controversy surrounding the "comings and goings" of group members. Some of the original group members quit over disputes with Matthew Knowles, Beyonce's dad and the group's manager, and this helped generate more media attention. She adds, "I think in order for your group to be successful, your story has to be interesting."

The controversy aside, Knowles makes a good point. If you want more extensive media coverage, you need to position your story in an interesting way. Public relations materials such as backgrounders, feature articles, and opinion pieces can help you do that. These tools include facts, stories, and points of view relating to your organization and its people, and help you illustrate in an interesting way the impact your organization has on the community, an industry, or society in general.

There are many instances, as well, when media contacts need more detailed information than what is provided in a news release or a media alert. Once the media respond to your "new product launch" media alert, for example, they will need more background information on your company and the product to complete their stories. Or, your news release could prompt an invitation from a trade media editor to submit a longer article that shares one of your executive's thoughts on a timely industry subject.

But what kind of information should be included in backgrounders? How would you write an "experts" article for a trade journal, or craft a lively letter to the editor worthy of publication on the newspaper's opinion page? This chapter will familiarize you with the types of backgrounders, articles, and opinion pieces written by public relations people, discuss how and why these tools are used in practice, and provide you with guidelines for properly structuring and writing these pieces.

Background Materials

Background materials come in many shapes and sizes, from one-page fact sheets to multiple-page corporate profiles. Background pieces are not written for publication; they are primarily intended to assist media writers when they are preparing their own stories. Updated versions should be kept "on the shelf" at all times in order to respond quickly to media inquiries, especially during a crisis. All background materials should include contact information at the top of a first page, just like a news release, followed by a heading that clearly identifies the piece (e.g., "Company Fact Sheet," "Corporate Profile"). They should be written in a factual tone and not offer any opinions or conclusions. Background materials are:

- Distributed at media events and news conferences to help reporters quickly grasp a subject and frame questions for spokespeople, and to provide them with statistics and other historical information for use in the stories they write.
- Sent to reporters after a story is pitched to further explain the idea and convince an editor of the story's value.
- Included in information packets about a company, a product, or a service given to prospective clients and customers.
- Provided to new employees to acquaint them with the organization, or to inform employees about critical issues or new policies being considered.
- Used as secondary sources for the preparation of brochures, reports, and other public relations materials.

Fact Sheets

One of the most basic public relations pieces is the fact sheet. Fact sheets are brief documents that summarize key facts about a company, a product, an issue, or an event (see Exhibit 8.1). They can help consumers, employees, media personnel, and other audiences get a quick, basic understanding of a subject. Fact sheets can be presented in narrative or news-story form; list a series of notable facts using bullet points; or follow a longer Q & A format and raise frequently-asked questions about a subject followed by concise answers.

A company fact sheet often presents material under subject headings such as "Company Description," "Corporate Structure," "Key Personnel," "Products and Services," and "Corporate Mission and Philosophies." There are variations on these headings, as seen in the Lands' End clothing company fact sheet on its corporate Web site, which features information on its catalogs, outlet and inlet stores, clothing quality and service, and contact information.

Fact sheets are designed to inform. They briefly summarize the scope of an organization's services and influence, the features and benefits of a new product, the extent of a problem, or the significance of a social issue. They also highlight interesting and provocative facts that further someone's interest in the subject. A reporter might see an unusual item in a fact sheet that provides an interesting story angle that's worth pursuing and use some of the fact sheet content to add more color to an article.

For example, fact sheets on Burger King® posted on the company's Web site (www.burgerking.com) lists statistics on the total number of Burger King restaurants worldwide and company sales figures, as well as items such as "Approximately 55.3%

Exhibit 8.1   Fact Sheet: Pillsbury BAKE-OFF Contest

CONTACT:
MARLENE JOHNSON
Pillsbury Bake-Off® PR
XXX-XXX-XXXX

FACT SHEET
THE 40ᵗʰ PILLSBURY BAKE-OFF® CONTEST

Contest Highlights
- $1 Million Grand Prize
- Quick and Easy Preparation
- Awards Program Host – Marie Osmond
- New Recipe Category – Luscious & Lighter Main & Side Dishes
- Complete Contest information at www.bakeoff.com
- Co-sponsor: GE Appliances – supplies 100 GE Spectra™ Ranges for finalists to prepare their recipes at the Contest plus Contest prizes

Date/ Location
One hundred finalists will compete in Orlando, Fla., Feb. 24-27, 2002, at the Pillsbury Bake-Off® Contest. The competition will take place at the Portofino Bay Hotel at Universal Orlando, a Loews Hotel.

Finalist Prizes
Cash, Prizes and Trips totaling more than $1.5 million:
- Grand Prize Winner earns $1 million and GE Profile™ Kitchen, which consists of a range, refrigerator, microwave, dishwasher and compactor. (Total estimated retail value $5,000.)
- Three other Recipe Category Winners each receive $10,000.
- Twelve more winners each receive $2,000.
- One non-cash-winning finalist receives the GE Innovation Award for the most innovative recipe and wins a GE Profile™ Kitchen.
- Each of the 100 finalists wins an expense-paid trip to Orlando with a three-night stay at the Portofino Bay Hotel at Universal Orlando, a Loews Hotel, $100 expense money and a GE Profile™ Advantium™ 120 Oven.
- From the company that created the speedcook category, the GE Advantium™ 120 oven is a new versatile appliance that cooks up to four times faster than a traditional oven with halogen lights, microwave energy and radiant heat. For more information on the new oven, consumers may call the GE Answer Center® directly at 800-626-2000 or visit www.GEAppliances.com.
- Cutco Cutlery awards a knife gift set to all 100 finalists plus complete sets of knives to the grand prize and category winners.

Awards Host Marie Osmond
An international celebrity, Marie Osmond is known for a number of accomplishments in the world of entertainment, including the original "Donny & Marie Show" in the late '70s, numerous hit records, authoring a *New York Times* top ten best-selling book, starring roles in musical theater productions on Broadway and in national touring companies, the daytime "Donny & Marie" entertainment/talk show, her top-selling line of Marie Osmond Collector Dolls and her role as co-founder and co-host of Children's Miracle Network.

(continued)

- 2 -

Recipe Categories	**Contestants entered their best original recipes for the following:** • Easy Weeknight Meals • Luscious & Lighter Main & Side Dishes • Fast & Fabulous Desserts & Treats • Casual Snacks & Appetizers
Qualifying Products	**Contestants used one or more of these products in their recipes:** • Green Giant® – Selected frozen and canned vegetables and frozen meal starters • Old El Paso® – Selected Mexican products • Pillsbury® – Selected refrigerated doughs and dessert baking mixes • Progresso® – Bread crumbs
Recipe Judging	All entries were required to be quick and easy and meet the requirements of the category entered. Recipes are judged for 1) taste and appearance, 2) consumer appeal, 3) creativity, and 4) appropriate use of eligible products. From June through Oct. 15, 2001, Bake-Off® entries were submitted via mail or online to an independent judging agency that screened all recipes to make sure rules were followed. The agency's home economists reviewed the eligible recipes, selecting the ones that best met judging criteria. Each recipe was assigned a code number, and the contestant's name was removed. The coded recipes then were sent to the Pillsbury Bake-Off® test kitchens. After a further screening, selected recipes were prepared for taste panels of home economists. The recipes that passed this test were given additional kitchen testing. A search was conducted to insure that the recipes had not been nationally published or winners in national contests. The 100 winning Bake-Off® recipes then were chosen. At this time, the names of the finalists were provided by the judging agency. By Dec. 15, 2001, the 100 winners were notified that they had been selected for the finals of the Pillsbury Bake-Off® Contest. Final judging will be done by consumer research and a panel of food experts. The judges work in jury-room secrecy.
The Event	On Feb. 26, 2002, the 100 finalists prepare their recipes for final judging in 100 GE Appliances mini kitchens set up in the Portofino Bay Hotel at Universal Orlando, a Loews Hotel. The winners will be announced during an awards ceremony hosted by Marie Osmond that airs live on CBS at 11 a.m. EST on Feb. 27.
The Location	The Portofino Bay Hotel is a stunning re-creation of the Mediterranean seaside village of the same name and is a part of the Universal Orlando resort. The Universal Orlando resort destination (www.universalorlando.com) includes two dramatically distinct adjacent theme parks, the Universal Studios motion picture and television theme park and Islands of Adventure, Orlando's next generation theme park, the Hard Rock Hotel, also a Loews Hotel, and CityWalk, a 30-acre dining, shopping, club and live-entertainment venue.
Contest History	Originally launched in 1949, the Pillsbury Bake-Off® Contest has been recognizing America's most creative cooks for more than 50 years. The contest has awarded a $1 million grand prize for the last three competitions. Celebrity hosts have included Arthur Godfrey, Art Linkletter, Bob Barker, Willard Scott, Alex Trebek and Phylicia Rashad.
Bake-Off® Trademark	Bake-Off® has been a registered trademark since 1971. Therefore, it should not be used in a generic sense to refer to any cooking contest other than the Pillsbury Bake-Off® Contest.

◼

Note. Reprinted with the permission of the Pillsbury Company. BAKE-OFF is a registered trademark of the Pillsbury Company.

of Burger King business is drive-thru" and "There are 1,537 possible ways for a customer to order a WHOPPER® sandwich."

Backgrounders

Like fact sheets, backgrounders are informational pieces. Backgrounders, however, explain a subject in more detail than a fact sheet and are generally two or more pages long. Many are written like articles in paragraph form or use a "Q & A" approach. One of the most common and useful backgrounders is the ***historical backgrounder*** or ***organizational history***. This piece gives a chronological account of the history of an organization, the birth and evolution of a product, or the origins of a program or issue.

The "History of The Quilt" backgrounder, shown in Exhibit 8.2, has good backgrounder form. The piece begins with a paragraph establishing the beginnings of The Quilt, and moves on to a second paragraph that further explains The Quilt and its purpose. Remaining paragraphs offer a detailed history of The Quilt from its roots to the present, concluding with information on The Quilt's impact today. Instead of paragraphs, some historical backgrounders use a timeline approach. They begin with an introductory paragraph or two about how the company got started, and then list significant years from the founding of the company to present day, along with notable achievements during each of those years.

Biographical Sketches

The biographical sketch, also known as a biography or a "bio," is a background piece about a person. Public relations people should develop a file of biographies of senior managers and other key executives in the firm. This can be done by conducting staff interviews or by distributing a form that asks for written biographical information. Update biographies every six months or once a year.

Biographies (Exhibit 8.3) acquaint reporters and editors with the expertise of company personnel and establish them as potential media sources. Public relations writers preparing publicity materials and newsletter articles on staff awards, promotions, and other employee news readily access bios to get needed background information for those pieces. Biographical sketches generally include:

- Name, current job title, and a brief job description in the first paragraph.
- More specifics on job duties and activities, with an emphasis on special knowledge or practice areas.
- Career history, including an overview of related positions with past employers, and other relevant work experiences.
- Professional activities and education, such as memberships and leadership positions held in professional and trade organizations, certifications or accreditations (e.g., APR—Accredited in Public Relations), professional awards and honors, colleges attended, and degrees earned.
- Community and public service work including board positions held with not-for-profit agencies, charitable causes, schools, and other community organizations.

Exhibit 8.2   Historical Backgrounder: The NAMES Project

www.aidsquilt.org

VIEW THE QUILT

ABOUT THE QUILT

- Background & FAQ's
- Contacts & Staff
- Chapters & Affiliates
- Programs
- Sponsors
- Make a Quilt Panel

NEWS

GET INVOLVED

COMMUNITY

QUILT STORE

History of the Quilt

In June of 1987, a small group of strangers gathered in a San Francisco storefront to document the lives they feared history would neglect. Their goal was to create a memorial for those who had died of AIDS, and to thereby help people understand the devastating impact of the disease. This meeting of devoted friends and lovers served as the foundation of the NAMES Project AIDS Memorial Quilt.

Today the Quilt is a powerful visual reminder of the AIDS pandemic. More than 43,000 individual 3-by-6-foot memorial panels -- each one commemorating the life of someone who has died of AIDS -- have been sewn together by friends, lovers and family members. This is the story of how the Quilt began...

Activist Beginnings

The Quilt was conceived in November of 1985 by long-time San Francisco gay rights activist Cleve Jones. Since the 1978 assassinations of gay San Francisco Supervisor Harvey Milk and Mayor George Moscone, Jones had helped organize the annual candlelight march honoring these men. While planning the 1985 march, he learned that over 1,000 San Franciscans had been lost to AIDS. He asked each of his fellow marchers to write on placards the names of friends and loved ones who had died of AIDS. At the end of the march, Jones and others stood on ladders taping these placards to the walls of the San Francisco Federal Building. The wall of names looked like a patchwork quilt.

Inspired by this sight, Jones and friends made plans for a larger memorial. A little over a year later, he created the first panel for the AIDS Memorial Quilt in memory of his friend Marvin Feldman. In June of 1987, Jones teamed up with Mike Smith and several others to formally organize the NAMES Project Foundation.

Public response to the Quilt was immediate. People in the U.S. cities most affected by AIDS -- New York, Los Angeles and San Francisco -- sent panels to the San Francisco workshop. Generous donors rapidly supplied sewing machines, equipment and volunteers.

(continued)

The Inaugural Display

On October 11, 1987, the Quilt was displayed for the first time on the National Mall in Washington, D.C., during the National March on Washington for Lesbian and Gay Rights. It covered a space larger than a football field and included 1,920 panels. Half a million people visited the Quilt that weekend.

The overwhelming response to the Quilt's inaugural display led to a four-month, 20-city, national tour for the Quilt in the spring of 1988. The tour raised nearly $500,000 for hundreds of AIDS service organizations. More than 9,000 volunteers across the country helped the seven-person traveling crew move and display the Quilt. Local panels were added in each city, tripling the Quilt's size to more than 6,000 panels by the end of the tour.

The Quilt Grows

The Quilt returned to Washington, D.C. in October of 1988, when 8,288 panels were displayed on the Ellipse in front of the White House. Celebrities, politicians, families, lovers and friends read aloud the names of the people represented by the Quilt panels. The reading of names is now a tradition followed at nearly every Quilt display.

In 1989 a second tour of North America brought the Quilt to 19 additional cities in the United States and Canada. That tour and other 1989 displays raised nearly a quarter of a million dollars for AIDS service organizations. In October of that year, the Quilt was again displayed on the Ellipse in Washington, D.C.

By 1992, the AIDS Memorial Quilt included panels from every state and 28 countries. In October 1992, the entire Quilt returned to Washington, D.C. And in January 1993, the NAMES Project was invited to march in President Clinton's inaugural parade.

The last display of the entire AIDS Memorial Quilt was in October of 1996. The Quilt covered the entire National Mall in Washington, D.C.

The Quilt Today

Today there are around 50 NAMES Project chapters in the United States and 36 independent Quilt affiliates around the world. Since 1987, over 13 million people have visited the Quilt at thousands of displays worldwide. Through such displays, the NAMES Project Foundation has raised over $3 million for AIDS service organizations throughout North America.

Note. Reprinted with the permission of The Names Project Foundation.

Exhibit 8.3 Biographical Sketch: Kodak

GEORGE M. C. FISHER
Chairman and Chief Executive Officer
Eastman Kodak Company

George M. C. Fisher was named chairman, president, and chief executive officer of Eastman Kodak Company effective December 1, 1993. He retained the titles of chairman and CEO in December 1996, when he created a separate office of president and chief operating officer.

Before joining Kodak, George Fisher was chairman and chief executive officer of Motorola, Incorporated. Fisher joined Motorola in 1976 after ten years in research and development at Bell Telephone Laboratories. In April 1984, he was appointed senior vice president and assistant general manager of the Communications Sector. Mr. Fisher was elected senior executive vice president and deputy to the chief executive officer in July 1986, and a director of Motorola in August 1986. He became president and chief executive officer in 1988, and was elected chairman of the board and chief executive officer in 1990.

Fisher is a member of The Business Roundtable and The Business Council. He is a member of the boards of the University of Illinois Foundation and the U.S.-China Business Council, having served as chairman of both of these organizations from 1997-1999. He is a member of the Council on Competitiveness, having served as chairman from 1991 to 1993. He is an elected fellow of the American Academy of Arts & Sciences and the Foreign Policy Association and an elected member of the National Academy of Engineering.

He is a past member of the boards of American Express Company, Minnesota Mining & Manufacturing, Brown University and The National Urban League, Inc.

He has been active in U.S./International trade issues through advisory groups to the U.S. Trade Representative and the U.S. Secretary of Commerce. Currently he participates on the Advisory Council for Trade Policy and Negotiations (ACTPN). Formerly, he was chairman of the Industry Policy Advisory Committee (IPAC).

Born in Anna, Illinois, he received a Bachelor of Science (B.S.) degree in Engineering at the University of Illinois, and both a Master of Science (M.S.) degree in Engineering (1964) and a Ph.D. in Applied Mathematics (1966) from Brown University.

ISSUED BY:

COMMUNICATIONS AND PUBLIC AFFAIRS
EASTMAN KODAK COMPANY
343 STATE STREET
ROCHESTER, NY 14650

10/99

Note. Reprinted with the permission of the Eastman Kodak Company.

Personal information related to family and hobbies might be included, if that material is relevant and according to the wishes of the person. Quotes are sometimes featured in bios to make the individual's personality come alive and to convey his or her perspectives on important issues.

Features

Features appear every day in the media, and editors look to public relations professionals for good feature story ideas. A feature story focuses on an interesting aspect of an organization and has much greater depth and color than a shorter news story.

With some thought, you can take what seems like a basic news announcement and successfully pitch it as a feature. A school district wants to inform the local media about an award it received from the county for its classes and programs directed to senior citizens in the community. Instead of simply making that announcement and focusing on the award—which could have resulted in a three- or four-paragraph story—the district stresses a specific class in which high school students from the district help seniors learn computer skills. The result was a longer feature with the headline: "Lessons for young and old: Students help seniors learn computer skills." This feature angle puts less focus on the award, and more emphasis on a particular class that shows the positive results of teens and seniors working together.

A popular media feature is the *personality* or *company profile*. The personality profile provides an in-depth look at a noteworthy person connected to your organization. A good time to pitch the media on doing a personality piece is when an individual gains recognition or reaches a milestone—your CEO wins an industry award for excellence in business management, or a volunteer begins 25 years of service to your not-for-profit agency. Company profiles are often done by the media during a significant stage in the company's history such as the announcement of a major expansion, celebration of a 50th anniversary, or the launch of an innovative product or service.

Media features are usually arranged in one of two ways. The most common approach involves successfully pitching a story idea, providing additional background information, and suggesting sources for interviews. The reporter then writes the finished piece. There are times when you write a feature from scratch, after discussing the idea with an editor and getting her approval to submit it. This is often the case when you are working with consumer and trade publications that have small staffs. As stated in chapter 7, it is best to pitch one specific idea to one publication at a time. Before you spend the time and energy to write a feature, confirm that the editor is receptive to receiving and publishing it.

Types of Features

Good feature ideas come from many sources. Read daily newspapers and magazines and monitor broadcast news programs to see how other organizations and your competitors get feature coverage. Some of the best features on people are found on newspaper sports pages, in men's magazines (such as *GQ*), and in entertainment publications. Look through consumer and trade media to stay on top of lifestyle and business trends that you can tie to your organization's products and people. PR Newswire's Feature News section offers insight on popular feature topics:

- *Human interest*—stories about organizations or people making special efforts to help improve the quality of life for others, or about people overcoming challenges and obstacles. Example: a story from the American Greyhound Council about a special program that matches greyhounds, best known as racing dogs, with disabled people who need companions to help them open doors, turn on light switches, and manage day-to-day activities.
- *Advice*—"how-to" stories that provide insight on better health, parenting, and other lifestyle issues. Example: in response to a trend showing sharp increases in childhood obesity, a personal trainer and successful author offers tips on how to help children establish better dietary habits.
- *The unusual*—stories about interesting trends and fads. Example: more people are replacing red meat with exotic ostrich and buffalo burgers to cut down on fat, according to SPINS, a natural products market research company.

Writing the Feature

Features offer greater freedom for creative writing. Most traditional features should have a beginning, a middle and an end, in contrast to news releases and news stories that follow inverted pyramid style. One of the more distinguishing elements of the feature is the lead. Whereas news release leads make a rather straightforward announcement, feature leads are designed to get the reader's attention and bring them into the story in an imaginative way. Some feature leads are quite effective by using just a few words. Take this lead from a Newhouse News Service feature about the marketing, consumer popularity, and expense of official major league baseball caps:

> "So many caps. So little money."

In contrast, a *descriptive lead* is longer and more effectively paints a picture of someone or sets a scene, like this lead taken from a personality profile in *Sports Illustrated*:

> The unofficial town hall in Alvin, S.C., the home of Georgia Tech senior quarterback Joe Hamilton, is Kinlaw's Barber Shop, also known as Football Headquarters. Last Thursday night, 50 men, 40 of them related to Hamilton, gathered at Kinlaw's to watch the Yellow Jackets play Maryland. When Hamilton made a big play, the place erupted into a party of dancing, hugging and screaming. "After an interception or a big touchdown run," Hamilton said last Friday in Alvin, where he had gone for the weekend, "I sometimes think to myself, man, what are they saying about that back at the barber shop?" (Oct. 11, 1999)

A paragraph or two after the lead, the feature writer states the focus of the story more clearly, and then goes on to complete the piece using background information, descriptive language, revealing quotes, and lots of detail. In personality profiles, like the Hamilton piece, stories told by the person and by others close to him add color. His coaches, for example, reminisce about Hamilton's early days as a player and his memorable experiences on and off the field. A strong concluding paragraph will bring the reader full circle and reconnect with the opening paragraph, using either a statement or quote:

> . . . but the fact that Hamilton dominated the Seminoles defense may help him convince NFL scouts that he's for real. It comes as no surprise that Hamilton's favorite quarterback is Doug Flutie, even if he doesn't come from Alvin.

Technical Articles

The technical article is a feature targeted mostly to trade and business media. Its goal is to position your organization and its people as experts on industry issues and business challenges. Technical articles are also known as *by-lined articles* because they usually carry the by-line of someone in your company with particular technical expertise. They are often written, however, by public relations professionals after conducting research and an extensive interview with the expert.

The head of a credit counseling organization could develop a by-lined article for the local newspaper's "Business" or "Money" section on how to interpret credit card offers and choose the one best suited to a person's financial situation. *Public Relations Tactics*, a trade publication produced by the Public Relations Society of America, includes many by-lined, *"how-to" articles* by public relations professionals. These focus on everything from writing good news releases to choosing the best Web search engines for your research needs. Technical articles are developed with these guidelines in mind:

- <u>Pitch the story before you write it</u>. Identify a newsworthy subject and a credible expert before you pitch an idea. Outline the subject briefly for the editor by telephone or in a letter. Stress the timeliness and relevance of the subject, how the target audience will benefit from reading the piece, and why the writer is qualified to comment on the subject. If appropriate, suggest an issue or special section to which the article could be targeted. Once interest in the story has been confirmed, send a follow-up letter to recap your discussion and the time frame for completing the piece. Also, ask for the editor's ideas on specific points the article should cover.
- <u>Conduct interviews</u>. In addition to an interview with the expert, talk with others, such as trade association leaders and customers, to expand your knowledge of the subject and to get facts and reactions that strengthen your piece. This is especially important when writing *market impact technical articles* that detail how a new product or service will benefit an industry.
- <u>Resist promotional writing</u>. In a market impact piece, you might mention the product once or twice, but how-to articles should give general advice and information without making mention of the company or product. Attribute statistics

to industry sources, and support strong claims or predictions. Be concise and avoid criticizing the competition. The strength of this type of article is that the reader is likely to perceive the writer of the piece as the expert, which in turn will reflect positively on the organization.

Advocacy Writing

It can be argued that all public relations writing advocates something. Technical articles advocate an organization's knowledge of an industry and the expertise of its people. There are, however, specific tools—letters to the editor, op-ed articles, and advocacy advertising—you can use to more strongly establish a public position or express a point of view. Print media offer such opportunities for public relations professionals mainly on their opinion-editorial (op-ed) pages, which are typically among the most popular and highly read pages in the newspaper.

Letters to the Editor

When a negative or inaccurate story about your organization appears in the press, a well-written letter to the editor can help your organization lessen the bad publicity or correct false information. Letters are used to respond positively to media coverage, as well. A hospital public relations person, for example, could send a letter to commend a reporter's series on health care or a health issue, and then use that platform to create further awareness of the hospital's services and to present the hospital as an information resource. In addition, not-for-profit organizations write "thank you" letters to an editor after major fund-raising events to thank the community for its support. Your chances of seeing a letter in print versus the news release you send can be higher since some newspapers print 50% or more of the letters they receive. Some suggestions for writing letters to the editor:

- Keep the letter short, about 250 to 300 words. Most newspapers publish letter guidelines on the op-ed page, so follow their rules.
- Each letter should begin with "Dear Editor" or "To the Editor," and conclude with the name, title, and organization of the sender. Sometimes, writing letters on behalf of senior managers and CEOs (with their knowledge and approval, of course) and signing their names can carry more weight and help you get published.
- The first paragraph of the letter should reference the specific article or issue to which you are responding. Mention the headline and date of the article. Other letters should quickly identify the subject and indicate why this subject is timely.
- The remaining few paragraphs of the letter should give more background on the subject, making reference to hard facts and statistics when possible. Then, express your opinion or reaction, and conclude by summarizing your main point. Exhibit 8.4, a published letter to the editor, illustrates good form and content.

Exhibit 8.4   Letter to the Editor: Edison Electric Institute

701 Pennsylvania Avenue, N.W.
Washington, D.C. 20004-2696
Telephone 202-508-5555

 **EDISON ELECTRIC
INSTITUTE**

THOMAS R. KUHN
President

November 30, 2001

Letters to the Editor
The Wall Street Journal
200 Liberty Street
New York, New York 10281

To the Editor:

The sudden and dramatic meltdown of Enron's energy trading empire has unquestionably shocked everyone in the energy world. Significantly, however, the energy markets *are* working despite Enron's collapse – contracts are being written, there have been no price spikes or supply interruptions. In other words, competitive energy markets are a good bit sturdier than the report in today's paper implies ("Shock Waves: Enron's Swoon Leaves a Grand Experiment in a State of Disarray," November 30).

For starters, there already are perhaps a dozen other wholesale electricity trading platforms up and running in the U.S., some of them easily rivals to Enron at the height of its reign. Those entities already are filling any breach left by Enron.

And while few would dispute the major impact left by the implosion of California's flawed electricity deregulation plan, it is also far too early to write the obituary for competitive electric markets. Electricity competition is a reality, despite the not unexpected speed bumps that accompany any major regulatory shift in an industry as large and complex as electric power. In the long run, customers will be the beneficiaries of competitive electric markets that work.

Sincerely,

Thomas R. Kuhn

- Maintain a positive tone in the letter. Avoid name calling and harsh criticism. When responding to a critical or inaccurate story, focus your energy on "setting the record straight" and creating a positive impression about your organization. Consider the consequences of "burning your bridges" with the reporter and publication.

Op-Ed Articles

Op-ed articles are longer versions of letters to the editor that allow you to comment on a subject in more depth. There are times when your response to an article or your opinions about an issue will be welcomed in a longer opinion piece, especially when the subject is timely or controversial. Op-ed pieces are set up much like technical articles in that they include the by-line of the company expert qualified to talk about the issue. Like technical articles, op-ed pieces should identify key message points or arguments and then use facts, statistics, and supporting evidence to back up those views. The end of the article, besides summarizing main points, should leave the reader with a clear solution to a problem, or state the best reasons for the organization and the public to show continued concern about an issue.

Organizations also distribute op-ed pieces to coincide with timely events such as a national day, week, or month. A university professor of social work, for instance, wrote an op-ed piece published during Hispanic Heritage Month to comment on the growing influence of the Hispanic/Latino community in the United States.

Keep in mind—most newspapers reserve the right to edit letters to the editor and op-ed commentaries. This policy is usually included in the paper's guidelines.

Public Relations Advertising

Organizations wishing to take a public stand on an issue or express a point of view in the media can also create public relations or institutional advertising. Editors can choose to print your op-ed letters and articles, or they can reject them completely. The advantage of running an ad is that you pay for the space, which means your message will appear in print exactly as you want it to. Ads produced by Anheuser-Busch and other beer companies asking you to drink responsibly and to use designated drivers are public relations ads. They advocate a corporate point of view, not the product. When creating copy for public relations ads:

- Put some thought into the headline. Raise a provocative question or recommend that the reader think a certain way or do something specific about an issue. Some ad headlines have impact when written more like news headlines. Whatever the case, make the headline strong and catchy. A public relations ad placed by Verizon, a telecommunications company, carried the headline: "When One Million People Get Together, A Million Good Things Happen." The ad promoted Verizon's $1 million donation to five major charities in celebration of the company's one millionth long-distance phone service customer.
- Make the first paragraph an extension of the headline. That first sentence in the body of the ad needs to build off of the idea presented in the headline.

- Write simple body copy, use active voice, and keep sentences and paragraphs short. It is acceptable to use incomplete sentences in ad copy for emphasis.

- Recap the main point at the end. Effective ads do that creatively, and bring the reader back to the key idea raised in the headline and first paragraph. Some ads include a final statement that asks the reader to take a desired action. The Verizon ad concluded by informing customers about a letter being sent to them about the company's $1 million charitable donations and encouraging visits to its Web site to learn more about the campaign.

References and Suggested Reading

Aamidor, A. (1999). *Real feature writing*. Mahwah, NJ: Lawrence Erlbaum Associates.

About Lands' End (2003). Retrieved December 5, 2002 from http://www.landsend.com/cd/fp/help/0,,1_36877_36883_37027,00.html?sid=0431003556596190160

Ali, L. (2001, May 21). A date with destiny. *Newsweek*.

Bivins, T. H. (1999). *Public relations writing: The essentials of style and format* (4th ed.). New York: McGraw Hill.

Corporate facts. (2002). Retrieved December 5, 2002 from http://www.burgerking.com/CompanyInfo/onlinepressroom/corp_facts.asp

Feature news. (2003). Retrieved March 2, 2003 from http://www.prnewswire.com/news/.

Fink, C. C. (1998). *Writing opinion for impact*. Ames, IA: Iowa State University Press.

Sports Illustrated. (1999, October 11).

CASES

Case 25: Alcohol Awareness Month (Part B)

As discussed in chapter 3, case 5, you are a public information specialist with the Council on Alcohol and Drug Dependence. The council is a not-for-profit agency whose mission is to educate people on the dangers of substance abuse and to prevent individuals, especially young people, from abusing alcohol and other drugs.

You have been asked to plan and implement public relations activities during Alcohol Awareness Month in April to increase knowledge of the risks associated with binge drinking. A binge drinker consumes five or more drinks in a sitting one or more times within a two-week period. The primary target audience is college students, who are among the largest populations involved in binge drinking. Research shows that college students who are binge drinkers tend to miss classes and have poor academic performance; many leave college before finishing their studies. Binge drinkers are more likely to engage in unprotected sex, damage property, and get in trouble with the law.

One of your strategies for Alcohol Awareness Month is to provide information on binge drinking to campus media in your area, in hopes that they will cover the issue in some depth. A key tactic is preparation of written background materials for information kits and the council's Web site.

Assignments

Using information compiled from research completed for case 5, as well as any additional information you choose to seek out at this time, prepare the following pieces for the media packet described above:

- A three-page backgrounder on the history and impact of the binge drinking problem on U.S. college campuses from the 1980s to today.
- A 500-word op-ed piece on the dangers of binge drinking. This piece should carry the by-line of LaToya Glover, the council's executive director.

Case 26: Primo Pizza Advocates Safer Driving (Part A)

Your state, like many states across the country, is facing an alarming trend: a sharp increase in the number of automobile accidents involving young drivers. Every 17 minutes in the United States, a novice driver dies in an automobile crash. Nationally, one-third of teen deaths are caused by motor vehicle accidents; this is more than any other cause such as cancer, heart disease, homicide, suicide, or AIDS. Teens are four times more likely to be involved in an auto accident than all other age groups combined, except for adults 75 and older, and 16-year-olds are three times more likely to be in a crash than 18- and 19-year-olds. Teen car crashes cost $32 billion annually, kill 6,300 teenagers and 9,000 other motorists, and injure more than 600,000 others in this country.

In a few months, your state legislature will vote on a bill to enact a new driver licensing system. Under the new system, full driving privileges for young drivers are "phased in over an appropriate period of time." After earning their learner's permit, young drivers would have to wait six months before applying for a license. If they commit any serious traffic violations during that six-month period, they could not apply for the license for a full year from the time the permit was issued. The bill also requires that permit holders applying for a license would have to submit a written statement from a parent, guardian, or driving instructor that affirms the young driver has had at least 30 hours of on-the-road driving experience. The bill has steadily gained support from political leaders, automobile associations, and consumer safety groups.

Primo Pizza, a chain of more than 50 pizza shops operated exclusively in your state, also has decided to endorse the bill since so much of its business involves pizza delivery. In the past, another major pizza chain received negative publicity and experienced legal problems when a number of its delivery people were involved in serious car crashes involving high-speed, reckless driving. Anthony Roe, the president of Primo Pizza, believes this is an important issue for his company. He has asked you, Primo Pizza's director of public affairs and community relations, to meet with him to talk about ways in which the company could publicly express its support of the new driver licensing bill.

"This bill is something I really believe in. It has the potential to help young drivers develop better and safer driving habits because they'll have more sufficient time to learn the rules of the road under an adult's supervision. Having more time to learn how to drive can also mean better risk management skills, since they'll probably be exposed to a wider variety of situations that will test their ability to think fast and make good decisions behind the wheel. We hire many younger drivers and if they come to us with well-developed driving habits, that would certainly benefit our business."

"What's also really great about this is the fact that we have become known for our concerns about safe driving," you say. "Most people will probably not see this as a blatant attempt by Pizza Primo to jump on a bandwagon and get some positive press. But, of course, it does bring with it some public relations and marketing benefits, there's no question about that. Can you refresh my memory about some of the steps we take to promote safe driving?"

"Sure. We start by looking closely at people's driving records before we hire them, and new drivers never start driving right away," Roe explains. "We usually have them go out with another, more experienced driver for the first week or so. Then after that, a manager or a senior driver goes out on a delivery with a newer driver every few weeks for a two-month period to monitor how well that person is doing behind the wheel."

"Don't the drivers have to attend some courses, as well?" you ask.

"Yes, but we don't call them courses; we call them safe-driving workshops. We sponsor a few of those during the year and all of our drivers are required to attend. Those are kind of interesting because they expose our drivers to real-life driving problems they might encounter on the road, and ask them to act out how they would respond to certain hazardous situations. Local police and auto club personnel run those for us in each town or city where we have shops," Roe says.

"I bet we could interest the media in writing some feature stories about those workshops, especially since we can talk about them in relation to the licensing bill, which is a timely topic right now. I also see us using the op-ed page quite effectively for this campaign to get some media exposure. Those are a few thoughts off the top of my head, but I'd like to give some more thought to this campaign and draw up a more formal proposal with specific recommendations."

Assignments

1. Write a letter to the editor for distribution to statewide print media endorsing the driver licensing bill. The letter should be 300 to 400 words and be signed by Anthony Roe, president of Primo Pizza.

2. Write copy for a Primo Pizza public relations advertisement that establishes the company's position on young drivers and advocates passage of the new driver licensing bill. Your ad copy should begin with a creative headline and a brief description of any appropriate visuals. Limit the copy to no more than three or four short paragraphs.

Case 27: United Way Feature Stories

The United Way of America (UWA), based in Alexandria, VA is a national system of volunteers, contributors, and local charities that helps meet the health and human-care needs of millions of people. Its mission is to "increase the organized capacity of people to care for one another."

The UWA provides research, training, advertising, and other support services to the 1,400 locally-based United Ways in cities across the country. The main focus of the local United Ways is to raise money, which is then distributed to United Way member agencies in those areas. These member agencies include a variety of organizations, from those that fight hunger or work to strengthen families, to others that assist older adults or help youth at risk. Many member agencies that receive United Way funds are the local chapters of nationally-known social and human service organizations such as the Salvation Army and American Red Cross.

You have recently started an internship with the United Way (UW) in the city or area where your college is located. Langston Hill, the UW's director of communications, tells you about a meeting he has just come from with the editors of a local weekly newspaper.

"As you know, we recently did a survey that showed many people in the area don't have a complete picture of the United Way's role, where our fund-raising dollars go, and how the money we raise is used to help all kinds of people in the community," Hill says. "So, I shared those findings and suggested that the paper start running a series of articles on the different member agencies the United Way supports. They liked that idea, and said they would have no problem with us writing the articles, as long as they could edit them as they saw fit. They also want us to send them some United Way background materials."

"Do they want the articles to give an overview of the agencies and what they do, or would they prefer some other kind of focus?" you ask.

"The articles need to talk about the mission of each agency, but it will probably be more interesting if we identify a more distinct angle. For some of the agencies, UW funds are used to support one particular program, so we'd want to focus on that. In other cases, we might make it more of a human interest piece. You know, talk about people who benefit from the agency's programs, or even a story from the perspective of local agency volunteers who are making a difference. Of course, we need to make sure that the agency's connection to the United Way is mentioned in the article, but these can't be promotional pieces for us. The focus should be on the member agency and how it helps the community, and then we can weave in somewhere how the services they provide are made possible by UW funding," Hill says.

"I gather that these articles should have feature-type leads, lots of good quotes. These are feature articles, really. How about length?"

"Yes, they definitely want us to write in feature style. They said to shoot for about 500 words. No more than two pages, double-spaced. As you've probably figured out by now, I'd like you to take on this project. I think it would be a good experience for you, and help you learn more about us and the agencies we serve. And, it will give you some excellent interviewing and feature writing practice, too."

"I would definitely agree with that," you respond. "I'll get started on it today."

Assignments

1. Write a three-page backgrounder focusing on the key accomplishments and community impact of the local United Way chapter in your area.

2. Select a United Way agency in your area, and write:

- A two-page feature story on that agency for publication in the UW article series explained in the case.
- A one-page biographical sketch of the agency's executive director.

Case 28: Defending Home Health Care

Cathryn Constantine handles public relations for PersonalCare, the oldest home health care agency in a medium-sized city. PersonalCare offers three levels of service: companions, who assist the elderly and disabled with dressing and personal hygiene and handle household activities such as light housecleaning, meal preparation, and shopping; home health aides, who perform household activities, but who also have the training to take vital signs and assist with patient exercise routines; and registered and licensed practical nurses, who can provide more involved medical care for those recuperating from major surgery or others with chronic illnesses such as cancer and Alzheimer's disease. All of PersonalCare's companions and aides are supervised and trained by registered nurses.

Home health care has experienced a tremendous upsurge in popularity. It costs much less to hire a home health aide than it does to provide care for someone in a hospital or nursing home. The person receiving home health care enjoys the comfort and security of his or her own home, which can have emotional benefits and speed the healing process.

Recently, the morning daily newspaper ran a story on the front page of its local section with the headline, "Home health care aide convicted of stealing from elderly woman." This led to a few more stories on the risks of hiring home health aides to care for the elderly and disabled in their private homes. After reading these negative stories, Constantine approaches Theresa English, the agency's executive director, to discuss the impact of this media coverage.

"Even though this incident didn't involve us, I feel like we have a responsibility to respond to all the negative press," Constantine says. "If people start perceiving that it's dangerous to bring a home health aide into their homes, and that all people who work as home health aides are criminals and can't be trusted, it could hurt our business. Unfortunately, that's the picture that the local media has been painting, and it's an undeserved stereotype that we need to correct since most home health aides are responsible citizens."

"So far, we haven't had any problems with aides committing thefts. But I see what you mean. The average person will not necessarily separate one home health agency from another. It gives all of us a bad name. What do you suggest we do about it?" English asks.

"Theresa, I'd like us to organize a public relations program that informs people in our community about the value of home health care and helps them to become smart consumers when it comes to selecting a home health care agency.

People might not know, for instance, that many agencies, like ours, are licensed by the state, which means all employees are required to go through an intensive screening, and their references are carefully checked. We screen employees to see if there is any criminal activity in their background before anyone is placed in a person's home. It's also pretty easy to get information on an agency's reputation by checking with the Better Business Bureau or a chamber of commerce. Consumers should find out if the agency is insured for general and professional liability and how that protects them. Those are some of the tips we could offer."

"I like this idea, Cathryn, and I like the fact you're suggesting we be proactive and take a leadership role on this issue. We can provide an important service to the community and strengthen the agency's reputation in the community and in the home health care industry at the same time. It might even bring us some new clients."

"True. I think we have an excellent opportunity to show people just how critical home health care has become, and how it will be even more critical in the next decade as the elderly population increases significantly in size. We do a lot of good for people. Many sons and daughters tell us that they don't know what they would have done without this service and the companionship it provides day-to-day for their elderly parents. That's a story we need to tell," Constantine says.

Assignments

1. Prepare the following pieces for the PersonalCare public information program:
    (a). A bulleted fact sheet that outlines 10 tips for selecting a reputable home health care agency. Do research to gather information for the fact sheet.
    (b). A three-page feature/human interest story on the important role of home health care and the benefits it provides to home health care users and their families.
2. Assume you are Cathryn Constantine and you have decided to respond to the negative media stories that have recently been published in the local newspaper about home health care. Write a 500-word op-ed article to be sent to the local media that explains the positive aspects of home health care and dispels negative images of home health care workers.

9

Newsletters

"What we have here is a failure to communicate." That line from 1967's "Cool Hand Luke" with Paul Newman has gone down in movie history. Organizations that fail to communicate with their employees and other target publics could become history themselves. Public relations professionals who create newsletters must make every effort to keep communication flowing between the organization and the people it depends on for survival. In the case of employees, an informed workforce is more productive and can be the best salespeople an organization can have. For customers, regular communication establishes and maintains critical relationships.

Some public relations historians trace the origins of the newsletter back to the days of Julius Caesar. Today, it serves much the same purpose as it did centuries ago—to communicate news and useful information to a well-defined group of people. Good newsletters are like good newspapers in that their main purpose is to report important happenings to their target publics. Newsletters publish news; they are not promotional vehicles for senior managers to brag about the great job they do or how wonderful their company is.

In addition, newsletters target readers who have special interests rather than a mass audience. News releases sent to the mass media can be rewritten, whereas you, the public relations person, control the content of newsletter articles. A newsletter also has the qualities of a personal letter; it talks directly to individual readers and their unique interests. Because readers receive newsletters at regular, planned intervals—weekly, monthly, or quarterly—they come to rely on them as news sources, if they are well written and executed. Newsletters share the traits of other well-developed public relations tools in that they need a sense of purpose, publics, and strategy; their success depends upon many other factors such as good timing, targeted content, crisp writing, and reader-friendly design.

Newsletter Goals, Publics, and Strategy

Newsletters are used for many reasons and target both internal and external publics. Organizations publish internal newsletters to keep employees updated on company developments and management decisions. Professional associations, such as the American Medical Association, send newsletters to their members to help them stay in touch with association and industry news. Companies develop external newsletters to attract and retain customers, and inform them about new products and services.

Robert F. Abbott, in the 2001 edition of his book, *A Manager's Guide to Newsletters: Communicating for Results*, says that effective newsletters are strategic publications that must be planned with four critical questions in mind:

- Should we use a newsletter?
- What do we want (organization's goals) from the newsletter?
- What do our readers or members (target publics) want?
- What is our strategy statement?

To begin, ask yourself if a newsletter is a worthwhile investment. The public you are targeting may have grown so large or become so spread out geographically that it is hard for members to maintain personal communication, and difficult for senior management to have frequent and direct contact with them. Or, maybe the public needs detailed information on an ongoing basis. Know going in, however, that producing a newsletter can require a major commitment of time, staff resources, and money. Examine the costs and potential impact of other methods for communicating with the designated audience before committing to a newsletter.

After you decide to do a newsletter, be clear about its goals. The purpose of an internal corporate newsletter could be to support top management's desire to have open communication with employees and acknowledge their value to the company, which can help strengthen morale and build employee trust. It would make sense to include straightforward information about the company's profits and performance as well as stories that recognize the positive contributions of employees (actually, employee newsletters should usually include those kinds of stories). A product manufacturer's customer newsletter might aim to strengthen relationships with readers and strive to keep them loyal to the company and its products. Content could include new product stories, with a focus on the customer benefits of those products. See Exhibit 9.1 for more on writing effective customer newsletters.

These examples illustrate the third point, that newsletters must be written with the public's interests and information needs firmly in mind. Newsletters are most effective with publics that already have a relationship with an organization. Talk to potential readers, conduct focus groups, and do surveys to find out what they want to know, and to uncover issues and subjects that are important to them before you start writing. Balance their needs with your goals. Once you have addressed these first three questions, create a *mission statement*, like this one for *pr reporter,* which markets to public relations practitioners (target audience):

> *pr reporter* is a weekly publication dedicated to the behavioral aspects of public relations, public affairs, and communication strategies. Its quick read format keeps you up-to-date on the latest theories, research, public opinions, case studies, and successful public relations techniques (readers' needs).

pr reporter, which is published by Lawrence Ragan Communications, is available by subscription only (organization's goals).

Exhibit 9.1   Writing an Effective Customer Newsletter

Good customer newsletters do more than focus on the benefits of your company's products and services. The Southeast-based Publix Super Markets, one of the largest grocery store chains in the United States, produces the acclaimed *Family Style* quarterly newsletter for its customers. It includes store-specific articles, recipes, and coupons, but puts much of its focus on helpful features for a family audience such as how to survive a hurricane and how to prepare kids to go back to school. This approach has strengthened loyalty to Publix and its store brand. Product manufacturers should avoid the hard sell in customer newsletters and include informative articles that have value to customers and their businesses such as:

- A regular column by your CEO that focuses on significant business and industry trends and shares the CEO's insights about where customer industries are heading.
- By-lined articles written by other experts in your company that provide customers with information on manufacturing processes, emerging technologies, market development, and other subjects related to workplace productivity and profitability.
- Case studies and application features that show how a customer used one of your products or services to successfully solve a business problem.
- Profiles that humanize executives and highlight their expertise, which builds credibility and reinforces customer confidence in your company and its people.

Developing the Newsletter and Its Content

With goals, target readers, and strategy in place, the next step is to begin developing the newsletter and its content. Before any writing is done:

- Select an editor. No matter how many people are involved in the process, you need one person to oversee the newsletter and keep it on track. The editor may assemble a group of contributors—staff members from each department who submit news from their area. Some companies pay busy staffers for stories or story ideas to encourage involvement in the newsletter and depending on their workloads and individual job demands.
- Decide on the frequency of distribution. High involvement audiences, those more willing to respond to your messages, such as college alumni, can receive the newsletter quarterly in the winter, spring, summer, and fall. Low involvement audiences, like potential customers, should be targeted on a monthly basis, if there is enough legitimate information to share and adequate staff and money to do the job. Employee newsletters generally circulate weekly, biweekly or monthly, depending on the size of the organization, the amount of information that needs to get to them on a regular basis, and reader interest.

- Establish a budget. Printing and mailing costs are the main budget items. Small quantities (a few hundred) can be photocopied in-house or for a reasonable price using high-quality photocopy machines like those at a quick copy center. For large quantities with color and complex designs, it's more cost effective to hire an offset printing company. Or do both–print large quantitites of paper using accent colors, and then use that paper to photocopy your newsletter in-house. Additional funds may be needed for freelance writers and design, although desktop publishing systems make it possible to do all the typesetting and layout in-house at no cost.

- Determine the length and format. Many newsletters are four pages—one 11" × 17" sheet of paper folded to four 8½" × 11" pages—or eight pages (two folded 11" × 17" sheets) in length. You might be tempted to publish longer newsletters if you circulate them less frequently. But the average reader spends just a few minutes reading a newsletter and may not read a long newsletter as thoroughly as a shorter one. Therefore, a better option to consider is distributing shorter versions more often. You may need a bigger budget to do this, but it could produce greater returns from the newsletter in the long run.

- Develop the content. Many employee newsletters include stories on subjects like the organization's future plans, company policies and procedures, and financial performance. Include other stories on topics such as:
  - Employee benefits and human resources matters
  - Staff additions and promotions
  - Advice on improving job performance (e.g., "10 tips for dealing with criticism on the job") and on dealing with family and life outside of work (e.g., "A checklist for choosing a child daycare center")
  - New products and services, promotions, and campaigns
  - Profiles of employees and how their jobs benefit the organization
  - Regular and guest columns from the CEO and other executives who comment on important new advancements, industry trends affecting the organization, the organization's competitive position, etc.
  - Company/employee involvement in the community and charitable activities

You might consider creating a ***content formula*** to follow for each issue to ensure a balanced publication. This entails outlining the percentage of space that should be devoted to each type of article. For example, a content formula based on the above examples might look like this:

- Company news: 30%
- CEO column: 10%
- Program or product feature: 20%
- Human resource issues: 15%
- New staff and promotions: 10%
- Employee or customer profile: 15%

Exhibit 9.2 is an example of the types of stories Children's Hospital Boston features on the cover of its newsletter for staff, employees, patient families, and friends of the hospital.

Writing Newsletter Articles

Newsletter writers need something specific to write about. Where do you find good story ideas? Attend board of directors' meetings. Review internal documents such as reports and proposals, summaries of company-sponsored research studies, executive speeches, and news releases. Talk to department heads and other internal decision makers. Professional and trade associations involved in your industry, government agencies that establish regulations affecting your business, and stories published in other print and electronic media are also sources of news. Be sensitive to copyright law when using published materials. Always make an effort to write in a way that will foster two-way communication between employees and administration by providing a mechanism for feedback. So, if you are writing an article about a new employee program or a controversial issue, include a name and phone number of someone who can provide more information or to whom readers can direct opinions and comments.

When crafting effective newsletter content and articles:

- Write strong headlines, subheads, and captions. These draw readers into stories, and sometimes, they are all the reader sees. Headlines should use active verbs and emphasize reader benefits or state problems to which readers want solutions:
New MIS Classroom Simplifies Computer Training
Reorganization to Benefit Chapter Members
Focus on Skin Cancer: Tanning Beds Have Darker Consequences

- Keep in mind that the higher a headline is placed on a page, the more important the story will be perceived by the reader.

- Use the appropriate writing style based on the article. Hard news stories (e.g., XYZ Company Reports Record Earnings) use straight news leads and inverted pyramid style, and should always explain the subject in simple language. Features are less rigid. They can take a chronological approach, like a profile of a long-time employee. The story could lead with an interesting fact about how she joined the company and then trace her time with the company from the early years to the present. Exhibit 9.3 shows a feature taken from Partners, a national newsletter to which middle schools subscribe and use in their efforts to build good parent relations. Notice how the piece uses a bold headline and subheads that could stand alone and tell the basic story. The writer personalizes it by using words like "our" and "you," and by using conversational phrasing throughout.

- Write with busy people in mind. Concise stories with short sentences and paragraphs are best. Rewrite and edit carefully so that each story is complete and appears in full on one page. If you continue a story on a following page, the reader may not finish it. In that case, make sure the most crucial information is presented within the first page of the article.

Exhibit 9.2   Newsletter: Children's Hospital of Boston

www.childrenshospital.org/chnews

Children's News

Children's Hospital Boston
The *first* place for children

July 18, 2003

Games boost kids' confidence, asthma knowledge

Earlier this month, Children's teamed up with the Boston Public Health Commission to host the second annual Boston Asthma Games, an event that educates children with asthma about their chronic condition while showing them that they can enjoy physical activity just like other kids.

For half of the day, more than 50 participants between 5 and 12 years old played games such as flag football and soccer on the fields of the Roxbury branch of the YMCA. Later, the games moved to the indoor pool—a setting that is often considered off-limits for asthmatic children. "One of my favorite parts of the event is to see kids in a pool," says **Amy Burack, RN**, Community Asthma Program manager, who coordinated the event. "This kind of activity tells the kids, 'you have asthma and you can do anything.'"

A participant learns to use a peak flow meter.

One of the biggest changes from last year's event was better incorporation of kids' families into the activities. Children with asthma participated in the same games as their siblings without asthma, and parents found a wealth of information about the chronic illness. Organizers explained appropriate classification of asthma, daily control methods, proper management plans and how to deal with asthma during the hot months of summer.

"We hope the education will trickle down to kids through the parents," says Burack. "Even more important, by promoting the link between asthma health and physical activity, we showed the children that their asthma can be controlled—it doesn't have to control them."

Margaret Reid, RN, director of the city's Asthma Prevention and Control program, praised the event for its successful approach. "These games provide an opportunity for children with asthma to participate in physical activity in a safe, supportive environment. It also helps their caretakers relax and see what these kids are capable of."-*zB*

Walking the walk

Over 1,600 staff, employees, patient families and friends of Children's converged on the Charles River on June 21 to raise money and awareness of the hospital's mission. Many departments got into the spirit of summer by forming teams for the first annual Miles for Miracles Walk, which was organized by the Children's Hospital Trust. The Blue Smocks represented Volunteer Services, the Blade Runners turned out from the Department of Surgery, For Eyes walked for Ophthalmology, and the Walk-a-Reetas of Wolbach topped off their walk attire with sombreros. Above, James Mandell, MD, president and CEO, is joined by the Big Apple Clown Care Unit and the Walk's mascots at the finish line.

Children's offers special thanks to event sponsors: Aquafina, WBZ-TV 4, WBZ NewsRadio 1030, CambridgeSide Galleria, Dunkin Donuts and the 150 volunteers who made the walk possible.

New center looks to kids' needs in disaster planning

This month, Children's announced the creation of a new Center for Biopreparedness that will plan for biological, chemical or radiation disasters affecting children and their caregivers. The center was created after several federal agencies identified Children's as a national resource for public health protection.

Michael Shannon, MD, MPH, explains Children's efforts to prepare for dealing with a disaster.

Michael Shannon, MD, MPH, chief of Emergency Medicine, says that pediatrics is an important component of the nation's disaster planning. "As a nation we must be prepared to protect our kids," he said. "As pediatricians, it is incumbent upon us to develop the protocols and practices to do so."

The new center, drawing on experts from Emergency Medicine, Informatics, Infectious Diseases and other departments, will determine best practices for treating children who are exposed to hazardous materials.

1

Note: Reprinted with permission of Children's Hospital Boston, Copyright © 2003.

Exhibit 9.3   Newsletter Article: Partners

Survival Guide—

Shopping with Your Teen

"I don't have *any* jeans I can wear."
"I have swimming *tomorrow* and I can't fit in my suit!"
"I can't wear *that*, I'd look like a *nerd!*"
"It's gotta have *Michael Jordan* on it."
"It's gotta be *Nike*."
"It's gotta be *Fila*."
"It's gotta . . ."

Help!

These pleas for new clothes–more clothes–can drive a parent crazy. Shopping can be torture for parents while at the same time being a joyride for our kids. Our resources are limited; our children's desires are not. What can we do to keep our sanity, stay within the budget, and still help our youngsters get clothes they like? (And let's not forget the all-important factor—clothes that *we* won't be embarrassed for them to wear!)

Set a monetary limit and stick to it.

Whether you have $20 or $200 to spend on your child's wardrobe, let him know that you won't spend more. Not even for that last great bargain that's so hard to resist. This will help teach your child the self-discipline that's vital for staying within a budget.

Let your child make some decisions.

If she insists on name-brand jeans that cost twice as much as the ones you have picked out, let her get them (*if* the cost is within the amount you have budgeted). But make her aware that for the same amount of money, she could have *two* pairs instead of one.

Middle-grade students often need the security of wearing "what everybody else wears." If you force her to buy no-name jeans, they'll end up in a drawer, never to see the light of day; your child's clothing problem isn't solved, and your money is wasted.

Give your child the responsibility of handling the money.

If you feel comfortable handing him the cash to hold, do so. Having to give up real money in exchange for his purchases is a valuable lesson in itself. Credit cards and checks are a step or two removed from the reality of spending cash. It's a more concrete experience to hand over real money than to have your mom or dad write a check. It's also much easier to see how much money is left. If your offspring does not hold onto the cash, be sure that he keeps a running total so that he knows *exactly* how much money he has spent.

Allow your child to choose, but retain veto power—and use it sparingly.

The truth is, we're not always thrilled by the styles our kids think are great. But for the most part, they aren't really objectionable in any serious way. If your child likes baggy jeans, and you prefer the more fitted variety, hold your tongue. (Remember the styles *your* parents hated?) However, if she wants to wear something that you think is too suggestive or otherwise inappropriate, stand your ground firmly–but not combatively.

If you've done your job, your child already knows what you think is acceptable. If she tries to test the limits, don't make a big scene, but do stick to your principles. If you've given her the freedom to make the majority of her clothing decisions, she'll probably accept your limits without much of a battle. ▲

Note: Reprinted with permission of Trackside Publishing, Iowa City, IA, 2000.

- Write articles in different formats. Complex subjects are easy to explain in a Q & A format. How-to articles written with subheads and bulleted items present advice in a clear, easy-to-follow manner. Another article from the Partners publication focuses on how parents should prepare for a meeting with their child's teacher. The article has a few introductory paragraphs and then uses key subheads that lay out the steps involved: "Getting ready," "At the meeting," "Before you leave," and "At home." The text under each subhead is a series of bulleted suggestions. For example, under "At the meeting," parents are advised to "Take notes" and "Keep in mind that the teacher also cares about your child's best interests."

Other Newsletter Considerations

One of the first items that the newsletter reader sees is the title, or *nameplate*, of the newsletter at the top of the first page. The Ragan Report, a weekly newsletter that publishes news and research of interest to corporate communications and public relations professionals, recommends a simple nameplate that includes the company name followed by one or two words (e.g., AT&T Now, Philip Morris Globe, SATURNews). Some organizations take a more personal approach, such as "NIPSCOfolks" or "Rodale Press's What's Going on Here," and that's okay, too, if it suits the nature and content of the publication. A cute or clever name is not absolutely necessary, although the name should be one that readers remember and with which they can identify. It's the content and substance that get people to read your newsletter and motivate them to keep reading. Other design and writing tips:

- Make sure the overall "look and feel" of the newsletter is consistent with how you want the organization perceived. As stated earlier in this chapter, there are many newsletter styles and formats from which to choose. Select one that is reflective of your organization's character. For example, a not-for-profit organization should use a simple, low-cost design for a fund-raising piece rather than an expensive one using full color. Otherwise, the recipient may question whether the organization really needs a donation if it can afford to produce such elaborate materials.

- Create an attractive cover page that draws the reader into each issue. Feature a cover story of major interest to readers and include a photo or some other visual element. Include a table of contents on the first page or at least a partial listing of notable stories inside.

- Use "pull quotes" and sidebars. A *pull quote* is a comment taken or pulled from a story and highlighted in large, bold, or italic type. Pull quotes are placed in boxes or surrounded by extra white space within the text of the story; they break up the text of longer stories and add visual appeal. Look for interesting or provocative pull quotes that will get the readers' attention, give them a sense of the story's subject matter, and entice them to read further. *Sidebars* are short pieces that expand on an aspect of a larger story. They are presented as a boxed item on the same page as the main story with their own short headline. An article about employee charitable activities during the holidays could have a sidebar focusing on one employee helping people in need in a special way. By including a sidebar, you can cut down on the amount of detail presented in a single story. The result is two shorter, easier-to-read pieces.

- Use 10- or 12-point text type and a clean, highly readable typeface like Times Roman or Courier. It's best to select separate typefaces for the body and headlines. Too much type printed in bold, italics, and all capital letters is hard to read, so use these techniques for emphasis and to single out names or key ideas. Try to include a photo or illustration on each page, and make sure your newsletter has the same graphic look for each issue.

- Include a masthead. *Mastheads* are small boxed items that include the name of the publication; the volume and/or issue number and date; the names of the newsletter editor, staff, and contributors; information on how to contact the editor; and the newsletter's mission or editorial statement (based on the strategy statement). Some mastheads also include the names of the organization's president/CEO and board of directors.

E-zines

The growth of the Internet has prompted many organizations to publish online newsletters, or e-zines, that are posted on their Web sites or e-mailed on request to targeted readers. With e-mail becoming a popular form of communication, electronic newsletters offer an opportunity to stay in touch with target publics. The main advantages of an electronic newsletter, or e-zine, are immediacy and convenience:

- People can read about new developments shortly after they happen, instead of having to wait a month to get the printed, hard-copy newsletter. Timely, consistent information helps builds customer trust and loyalty, increases brand recognition, and positions the organization as "the" source of information.

- E-zines can be designed to drive traffic to an organization's Web site by including articles with Web site links that make it possible for readers to quickly log on to find out what's happening. While visiting, readers may be exposed to other information on the Web site, including any special promotions or discount offers.

- E-zines save organizations money on printing and postage costs and are easily distributed.

These benefits create challenges, as well. Online newsletters require continual updates to keep news fresh. Stories must be written with even greater attention to brevity and to the special needs of online readers.

Habitat for Humanity International distributes its free e-zine, Habitat Extra!, to subscribers twice a month. The purpose of the e-zine is to keep readers informed of upcoming events, the latest news, and updates to the organization's Web site. It complements the organization's other online publication, Habitat World, which is posted bimonthly. Habitat Extra! features several one-paragraph stories, each with a headline, news lead and a link to the full text of that story on another page. Because e-zine articles should be brief, the news leads get right to the point, like this one written for an article titled "World Leaders Build celebrates housebuilding around the globe":

> This summer, 45 heads of state and government from around the world are volunteering to build some 1,000 Habitat houses with affiliates in their respective countries.

Karl Walinskas, owner of The Speaking Connection, offers these additional tips for developing a productive and informative e-zine:

- Lead with substance, not promotion. The e-zine should be a relationship building tool, not an advertisement for an organization's products and services. Include material that will be valuable to the reader, such as:
  - How-to articles
  - Industry news
  - Useful Web sites and links

  Walinskas suggests limiting the promotional aspect of your e-zine to 20% of its content.
- Keep it short. People who use the Internet are usually looking for specific information, which they want fast. Write five or six brief articles (each consisting of a few lines to one or two short paragraphs), include helpful tips, and use bulleted lists. You might also consider placing a table of contents at the beginning that outlines what information is included in each issue and link the titles to longer articles. That way, readers don't need to scroll through information in which they are not interested.
- Respect your subscribers. Whether people want to receive your e-zine is completely voluntary. E-zines should never be distributed unsolicited. The easiest way to start building a subscriber list is by including a "subscription submit" button on your home page. Every issue of the newsletter should include an "opt out" statement near the top that tells the reader how to unsubscribe to the e-zine.
- When distributing the e-zine, make sure to protect the privacy of your subscribers. Suppress the distribution list so that individual e-mail addresses do not appear. This will also alleviate the need for readers to scroll through a list of addresses before they reach the articles and prevent other people (including the e-zine's readers) from looking for names with which to build their own e-mail list.

References and Suggested Reading

Abbott, R. F. (2001). *A manager's guide to newsletters: Communicating for results.* Airdrie, Alberta, Canada: Word Engines Press.

Habitat for Humanity (2003). Retrieved January 23, 2003 from http://www.habitat.org/example.html.

Hudson, H. P. (1998). *Publishing newsletters* (Rev. ed.). Rhinebeck, NY: H & M Publishing.

pr reporter (2003). Retrieved January 23, 2003 from http://www2.ragan.com/html/main.isx?sub=32.

U.S. Chamber of Commerce recognizes IDFA among founders. (2002). Retrieved on December 15, 2002, from http://www.idfa.org/news/stories/2002/02/commerce.cfm

Walinskas, K. (2000, April). *The art of the e-zine*. Retrieved January 19, 2003 from http://www.speakingconnection.com/Communication_Articles/E-zines_4-00-B.html. The text starts

CASES

Case 29: The "That's Good Business" Article Series

In 1912, President William Howard Taft founded the United States Chamber of Commerce (www.uschamber.com) because he saw a need for a "single voice to speak for the nation's business community." Today, the Chamber of Commerce, based in Washington, D. C., works aggressively to further the interests of business and free enterprise by developing pro-business legislation, promoting economic reform, and preventing regulatory actions that negatively affect business. The U. S. chamber is the parent organization of 3,000 state and local chambers.

You are a public relations assistant with the chamber in your city or area. Its mission is to improve the local business climate, attract new businesses and stimulate economic growth, and enhance the quality of life for those who live and work in your area. Local companies pay annual dues to become chamber members. The chamber offers a variety of programs and services for its members including health and life insurance plans, business counseling, loans and financial assistance, and workshops and business networking opportunities. Your chamber's travel and tourism division aims to bring visitors and tourists to the area by promoting events, outdoor activities, historic sites, and other entertainment.

You call a meeting with Daniel Conzola, the chamber's director of communications, to discuss the chamber's monthly member newsletter and the findings of a recent readership survey. "Overall, the survey results are good. Most of our members think the newsletter has strong content and that it's easy to read. They especially like the stories on business trends and how the Internet can help your business."

"That's encouraging," Conzola says. "So, where are we falling short? Are there certain stories they'd like to see more of in the newsletter?"

"There is one subject that came up a lot. Many of our members said they'd like to read more articles about other business success stories and the benefits of running a business in this area. A large number of community and political leaders who received the newsletter and responded to the survey expressed an interest in reading more business profiles, too."

"That doesn't really surprise me," Conzola replies. "I think I've told you about Pulse, this new coalition of community leaders that's trying to bring more business into the area. I've been representing the chamber at Pulse meetings. Anyway, one of Pulse's goals is to better position our community as a place where people can build a career, settle down, and be successful. As you know, we've had some major industry layoffs in the area recently and we're all concerned that this bad news is all people have been hearing about. The group agrees that we need to do a better job of telling the business success stories so that people in the area start feeling more optimistic and sharing that optimism with others."

"Pulse's mission seems to tie in with what our newsletter readers are asking for," you respond. "Let me make a suggestion. Why don't we start a regular feature in the newsletter where each month we profile a different chamber business? We could call it something like, "That's Good Business." Each article would showcase the business and what it does, talk about its secrets to success, why this area is good for business, that sort of thing."

"I like it. And let's mix it up. Write about large and small companies that have been in business for a long time but also about newer, up-and-coming firms. Let's not make these pieces read like fact sheets, either. Look for interesting angles and use quotes. The articles should have some personality, don't you think?" Conzola asks.

"That was the approach I had in mind. Plus, I would think that the chamber members we write about will appreciate the exposure and see even more value in their membership," you say. "I'll start putting together a list of businesses that might be good subjects for the first few pieces in the series. You know, this might also be a good time to revisit my idea for stories about young professionals making a name for themselves in the local business community."

"Actually, the timing may be right for that. Pulse is also hoping to come up with some strategies for attracting more young professionals to the area who want to work and settle down here. The chamber might be able to contribute to that effort by including positive stories about successful young professionals in our newsletter. It sends the kind of message we want people to hear, that our community is a great place for young people to establish a career, start a family, and have a nice quality of life. We have a growing number of 20-something chamber members, and they would probably be interested in reading about their business peers," Conzola says.

Assignments

1. Identify a business that is a member of the chamber of commerce in your city or area. Most chambers produce a membership directory that could provide a starting point for you; you may be able to access the directory online, as well. (If there is no chamber in your area, select any business.) Write a 500- to 700-word newsletter article for the "That's Good Business" series. Your piece should include quotes from appropriate sources.

2. Identify and interview a young professional (22- to 30-years-old) working and living in your city or area. Write a 500- to 700-word profile of that individual for publication in the chamber newsletter. Include quotes and information that will support the chamber's goals of promoting the community as a place where young people can establish a career, start a family, and have a nice quality of life.

Case 30: The HMO Publication

Health maintenance organizations (HMOs) have become a cost effective alternative to traditional health insurance policies. HMOs are a form of managed care in which a specific group of doctors and health care providers sign a contract and agree to be part of the HMO. HMO members or subscribers pay a monthly premium or fee in exchange for comprehensive medical care provided by this group of doctors including doctor visits, hospital stays, X-rays and lab tests, emergency care, and other services. They choose a primary care doctor from the HMO group, or one is assigned to them.

HMO members sometimes make a small co-payment for services such as $5 for a prescription or $25 for an emergency room visit. Those enrolled in an HMO are limited to those doctors and hospitals that have agreements with the HMO. Use of non-HMO doctors is generally not covered. Total costs to subscribers are usually lower than those associated with other health care programs.

In the traditional health insurance or fee-for-service model, individuals pay a monthly premium to an insurance company, as well as an annual deductible. A deductible is a sum of money paid by the insured person before the insurance payments begin. Then, after medical care is provided, the insurer shares costs incurred above the deductible amount with the patient. For a hospital stay, for example, the insurance company may cover 80% of the bill and the patient pays the remaining 20%. With this kind of insurance policy, the insured may choose any doctor or hospital. Out-of-pocket costs are usually higher than those of HMO subscribers, and there is more paperwork involved since insurance claims often have to be filed. HMO members don't have to deal with claim forms. (For more information, go to www.thriveonline.com/health/powerful/best plan).

Jakeema Bennett is a corporate communications specialist with MediSure, a health maintenance organization. In addition to the medical care they receive, MediSure members get discounts on purchases at selected retail stores, on fitness center memberships, on eyewear and other optical services, and on entertainment such as reduced-price admission to museums.

At the weekly department staff meeting, Bennett and Robert Ladowski, the corporate communications director, talk over a new project. "I've got an idea for a new custom publication that we might develop for our members," Ladowski says. "Many of our competitors have been successfully using these pieces to provide useful health information to their subscribers. I've been looking at their publications and there's a major focus on preventive care, with many stories on how to prevent illness and tips for people on how to live healthier lives. The reality is, as an HMO we get a fixed fee for the services we provide, unlike fee-for-service programs. So, giving our subscribers a better handle on preventive care is smart from a business standpoint."

"I've seen some of those publications," Bennett says. "Many of them are printed in color, and some have a magazine-style design. Are we thinking of doing something similar?"

"My thought was an 8½" x 11" format, maybe eight pages or so for each issue. I have the budget to publish in color and to use photos and artwork, so I think we should do that. These will be mailed to peoples' homes so we want them to stand out. I think we could do this quarterly to start, with an issue in the spring, summer, fall, and winter. You've been doing our employee newsletter so it struck me that this would be a good project for you."

"How about content?" Bennett asks. "Some ideas come to mind right away, based on what I've seen in competitor publications. Do you have some suggestions?"

Ladowski replies: "Well, I'd really like you to come up with the content, but I do think the piece should have a standard format—a strong cover story for each issue, and regular sections inside the publication that pretty much stay the same from issue to issue. For instance, I've seen a regular feature in another HMO publication on diet and weight loss. Each issue carries a story on that subject. I'd be interested in taking that kind of approach, but I'll leave it to you to come up with some recommendations. Obviously, we may want to include MediSure-specific articles in the publication, but most of the content should offer general health information. I'd like to get the first issue out in three or four months. Does that seem reasonable?"

"I think so. I'd like to do some more research first, if I could. Then, I'll get back to you with some specific thoughts on content and an outline for the first issue."

Assignments

1. Assume you are Jakeema Bennett. List four research activities you would undertake before producing the first issue of the MediSure subscriber publication. Summarize the research activity in a sentence or two, and briefly explain what you would hope to learn from the activity that would help you plan this publication.

2. Working alone or with a partner, write a memo to Robert Ladowski that states the goals of the new subscriber publication and presents suggested content for the first issue. Your memo should conclude with a four-month timeline for writing and producing the publication. List timeline activities in the order they should occur, along with an estimated number of days

(or weeks) for completing that activity. Content recommendations should include:

- A creative name for the new publication.
- Three cover story ideas. Briefly explain each idea and why it would be a suitable cover story.
- Suggestions on six regular features/sections. Assume that "diet and weight loss" is one of those regular features. Justify each of your choices.
- A specific story idea or two under each general section identified above.
- Any other content you deem appropriate.

3. Select one of the story ideas presented in #2. Research and write a 500-word article on that subject for publication in the first issue of MediSure's subscriber publication.

Case 31: Creating the PRSA Chapter Newsletter

Brad McCully recently graduated from college with a degree in public relations. McCully was an active member of the Public Relations Student Society of America (PRSSA) chapter at his college. Soon after graduation, he joined the Public Relations Society of America (PRSA) as an associate member. Graduating PRSSA members may join the professional society at a lower rate than full members.

PRSA, the largest professional association for public relations practitioners in the world, provides its members with professional development support, regional and national conferences, publications, networking opportunities, and other benefits. PRSA members can also take an exam and earn accreditation, or APR, which is a designation that indicates a member has achieved a high level of experience and competence. Each PRSA member also becomes a member of one of the society's local chapters; there are 100 PRSA chapters in major cities and communities throughout the United States. Local chapters have their own boards of directors and sponsor professional development activities and other programs for the benefit of local members.

At a monthly program sponsored by his local PRSA chapter, McCully strikes up a conversation with Michelle LeBlanc, one of the chapter's officers. "This is my third PRSA program, so I haven't been connected to the chapter all that long," McCully says. "I wondered if the chapter communicates with members on a regular basis, outside of the fliers we get that announce the monthly programs."

"We had a monthly newsletter and we used that to keep members up-to-date on chapter developments," LeBlanc says. "Our members also told us they wanted to see information in the newsletter that would help them in their careers, or help them to do their jobs better, so we started including those kinds of stories as well. But we haven't put out a regular newsletter for about two years now. It takes some effort to get a newsletter together, as you probably well know, and you really need to have someone who can take the lead on it and keep it going month to month."

McCully responds: "I know I'm new to the chapter, but I do have some pretty good newsletter experience. In one of my internships, I wrote most of the stories for three or four issues of an employee newsletter, and did most of the layout using desktop publishing. I'd be willing to take this project on, if I can get the support of a few other members to help do the writing. Maybe the chapter secretary could help with proofreading and distribution."

"I bet the board would jump at the idea," LeBlanc replies. "Actually, we've been thinking we might eventually have an electronic newsletter, since many of our members are using e-mail every day. For now, we'll get it started as a hard-copy version, until we can figure out the best way to get this to people electronically. Here's what I would suggest. Start giving more thought to content. I can get you copies of some past issues, if that would help. We'll plan to have you come to the next board meeting, so you can meet the other board members and share your ideas for the newsletter. I'm sure they'll have thoughts, too. Since many of them may not know you, be prepared to sell yourself and emphasize your ability to carry through on this project."

Assignment

1. Working with a partner, prepare a memorandum for LeBlanc and the board that presents your approach to the PRSA chapter newsletter. Include:

   - An introduction that clearly explains the goals of the newsletter.
   - Key content areas. Suggest some of the general types of stories that could be published in the newsletter as well as any ideas for regular monthly features.
   - Ten story ideas for the first issue. List, briefly explain and justify each idea.

2. Select one of the story ideas presented in your memo. Research and write a 400- to 500-word story on that subject for publication in the chapter newsletter.

Case 32: Communicating with Kids' Club Members (Part B)

A few weeks after the Smithville Blue Sox kick-off dinner and the start of the team's season (see chapter 7, case 23), you meet with Carol Kaiser, the team's public relations and marketing director, to have a follow-up discussion about the team's Kids' Club for youth 12 and under. Kids' Club members get free admission to six Blue Sox games during the season as well as other benefits, such as exclusive autograph-signing sessions with the players and discounts on team clothing. There is no cost to join Kids' Club.

"I've noticed that some of the other teams with Kids' Clubs have a special newsletter for Kids' Club members, and I'm wondering if that's something we should be thinking about," you say.

"Possibly, but do you think children will read a newsletter?" Kaiser asks. "I'd hate to see us spending a lot of time on a project like this, if members are just going to end up getting this in the mail, looking at it quickly, and then just throwing it away."

"I had the same concern, so I called some of the teams that do these kinds of publications. What I found out is, the members tell them that they do read the newsletter. Some of the teams do a hard-copy version and an online version, which they say is working pretty well. Even better, the parents say they read the newsletter, too, so it serves a dual purpose."

"Interesting," Kaiser says. "What about producing a piece like this? We don't have too much extra money in the budget. How would we pay for it?"

"This doesn't have to be an expensive project," you reply. "We could do the newsletter on a quarterly basis to start. I could write all the articles, and most of the articles should be short anyway, considering who our primary audience is. And, I could do all the design and layout on the computer. I take many of the photographs for the team, so we could scan some of those into the newsletter."

"If you think you have the time to do this, then I say, let's try it," Kaiser responds. "The real challenge, I think, will be to make this something the kids will look forward to getting in the mail. It needs to have information in it, but it also needs to be fun, and interactive—a piece that the children can get engaged in somehow."

"I also think we should do more than just write about the team," you add. "Sure, club members will be interested in what's going on with the team, but I think some of the content could be general interest articles on youth sports and fitness. Children are getting into organized sports at much younger ages now, not just in school but in community leagues, for example. Why not include information that will help children be better athletes, or give parents advice about some of the issues they'll face as their children get more involved in sports?"

"I like the sound of this. What you're suggesting gives the newsletter more of a public service flavor, besides being a good promotional tool. Plus, it gives us a way to communicate with members during the off-season. Organize your thoughts and get back to me with more specifics."

Assignments

1. In a memorandum to Kaiser, present your ideas for the Kids' Club newsletter. Include the following information:

   ● Goals of the newsletter and a recommended name for the publication.

- Key content areas. Suggest some of the general types of stories that could be published in the newsletter as well as any ideas for regular features. Also, suggest general photo ideas or other visual elements.
- Eight to 10 specific story ideas for the first issue. List, briefly explain, and justify. Make sure to include ideas for general interest stories, as discussed in the case.

2. Select one of the recommended general interest stories from #1. Research and write a 300-word article on that subject for the Kids' Club newsletter.

10

Brochures, Fliers, and Posters

Pop superstar Madonna once said, "I've written my best things when I'm upset. What's the point of sitting down and notating your happiness?" That's probably not the best way for public relations professionals to approach brochure writing, since it is best to "think positive" when creating these important communication tools.

Brochures are written to inform a target public about a subject that public has an interest in and describe that subject in some detail. The underlying goal of most brochures is to encourage the reader to consider doing something—purchasing a product or service, getting involved in an event, or taking a certain stand on an issue. That means brochures are written in a more persuasive and promotional tone than other public relations pieces such as news releases and backgrounders.

Brochures don't "make the sale" on their own; they are normally used as one tool in a coordinated program of communication activities. Businesses mail brochures to prospective customers to make them aware of a new product and to pave the way for a future sales call. Fund-raising professionals leave brochures behind after meetings with would-be donors as a reminder of the most important reasons to give money to their cause, and also so the information can be shared with other decision makers who didn't attend the meeting. All kinds of organizations send brochures to consumers who call 800 numbers and make requests via Web sites for information on products and lifestyle concerns.

The fundamentals of brochure development and copywriting are discussed in this chapter. This includes guidelines for designing and formatting brochures, planning content, writing cover headlines, and preparing copy. The basics of writing and producing other printed pieces, such as fliers and posters, are discussed at the end of the chapter.

Brochure Format, Content, and Writing

A popular brochure format is the *pamphlet*, often printed as a single sheet folded twice (like a business letter) and inserted into an envelope or mailed by itself. This common size pamphlet is printed on both sides and has six pages or panels; each panel is 8½"

long by 3⅝" wide. If you held a standard pamphlet in front of you and opened it up to
see each panel, this is what it might look like:

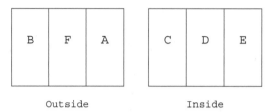

Outside   Inside

- Front cover (A)—a headline, a photo, or illustration, with the organization's
  name and logo. Make sure that the most important information is placed in the
  top-third of the cover panel. That way it will be seen if placed in a brochure
  holder.
- Back right panel (B)—this is folded over and is the first panel you see on your
  inside right after opening the pamphlet. It should include background information on the organization, or additional information about the product, service or
  issue that you want to highlight.
- Inside panels (C, D, E)—introductory copy and a visual on the inside left panel;
  subheads and a few paragraphs of copy under each subhead on the inside center and right panels that further explain the subject, along with a visual on each
  panel.
- Back center panel (F)—brief text that reinforces the main idea or selling point;
  contact information (mailing address, phone numbers, Web site address) and
  the organization's logo.

Many product brochures are printed in color with larger individual panels and more
folds than the traditional pamphlet. Some informational brochures are produced in
booklet form with many bound pages. You can package a brochure in many ways. Your
approach to developing brochure content and writing effective copy, however, should
not vary too much from brochure to brochure:

- Outline your key messages. Have a single, main message that you want readers
  to comprehend. Have additional messages focus on other important product
  features and benefits, or on common questions about an issue to which your
  reader needs answers. The main message in a brochure produced by eWatch, an
  Internet monitoring service, is that eWatch is a valuable service that makes it
  easy for organizations to track news and public opinion on the Internet. Specifically, the service helps "protect corporate reputation," "safeguard shareholder
  value," "monitor the competition," "pinpoint anti-corporate activism" such as
  boycotts, and "improve customer service." These five benefits provide the basis
  for the main text and appear as subheads in the printed brochure.

- <u>Make graphic design a priority.</u> Involve graphic designers early in the process. Make sure they understand the purpose of the brochure, who it targets and what their reading habits are, and what distribution methods will be used. A fund-raising brochure sent to a busy corporate executive, for instance, has to be special to demand attention. That executive might decide to take a second look at your piece because its design made a positive first impression. That was the case with Loaves & Fishes, a Charlotte, NC, emergency food assistance program. The oversized "Making Ends Meet" piece resembled a brown grocery bag, and it was cleverly bound with a mock grocery store receipt listing some of the basic items that many families in the area could not afford to buy. The creative design made people take notice and helped generate a 24% increase in donations.

- <u>Establish benefits on the cover.</u> The cover headline immediately lets your readers know why this subject is important to them and gives them a good reason to open the brochure and continue reading. Some examples:

A pamphlet on a new cellular service that targets cellular phone users:
Headline: "Double Your Minutes, Free Calls, Cellular One to One."

A brochure on a new office software program that targets restaurant managers:
Headline: "Pretty soon, you'll wonder how you ever managed without it."

As these examples show, effective headlines talk directly to the reader by using personal terms such as "you'll" and "your." They stress a benefit or indicate that there is valuable information inside targeted to the reader's interests. More advice on writing good headlines is offered in Exhibit 10.1. Copywriters also craft headlines that indirectly state the benefit of a product or service by presenting a thought-provoking fact or idea that persuades the reader to keep reading. The eWatch brochure takes this approach and uses creative headlines on the cover and on an inside panel that work together to convey one idea:

Cover

Visual: A tiny drop of water making a small splash in a pool of blue water
Headline: 1 Customer Tells Their Bad Experience to 20 Other People . . .

Inside right panel

Visual: A big splash in that same pool of water
Headline: . . . Imagine 50 Million People Reading about it on the Internet

- Introduce the subject. After you hook the reader, begin with some copy that sets the tone and builds reader interest. The eWatch brochure begins with the story of a consumer who used the Internet to let others know about her difficulties in dealing with a specific company. This is followed by two short paragraphs

Exhibit 10.1   Writing Brochure Headlines that Sell

How do you write brochure headlines that make your audience take notice and motivate them to keep reading? Tony L. Callahan, president of the Internet marketing company Link-Promote and publisher of *Web-Links Monthly*, a newsletter offering tips and techniques for successful Web site promotion, has these suggestions:

- Include dynamic headline words that get the audience's attention such as "advice," "save," "rewards," "security," and "protect."

- Use the direct approach. Write in first and second person. Don't write that a product will help "customers" save money; write that it will help "you" save money. Use active, present-tense verbs for greater immediacy and impact.

- Make it believable. Too many adjectives (e.g., great, sensational, superior) in the headline can lead the reader to think your product is too good to be true.

- Keep headlines short—no more than 15 words—and present them in simple, easy-to-read type.

- When creating a headline, write as many different headlines as you can and write variations of the same headline. Evaluate each headline based on three primary criteria—is it honest, does it grab the reader's attention, and does it state a clear benefit for the reader?

- Test market headlines. Get reactions from co-workers, friends, and family. Run a few versions of a free classified ad, with each one featuring a different headline. Track the response you get to each ad. Did one ad and headline prompt more phone calls, requests for information, or sales than the others?

■

explaining this trend in consumerism and Internet use and how corporations are responding to it, along with a summary of how eWatch can help. The opening copy for ParTech, Inc.'s restaurant management software brochure reads:

> Restaurant management is a time-consuming business. But we know how to make it easier—so you can have more time. Time to spend with family. Time to build your business. Time to spend on the golf course. inform™, the back office software from Par Tech, Inc. . . .

The writer's style is relaxed and conversational and blends complete and incomplete sentences that are short and easy to read. The focus stays on the interests of the reader. This introduction also points out a key advantage of this new program—its ability to save busy restaurant managers valuable time—and this major theme is repeated throughout the brochure copy.

- Feature testimonials. Support your product's claims or convince readers that your program is making a difference. One way to do that is by including favorable comments—testimonials—from other satisfied customers or program participants. The eWatch brochure includes testimonials from major corporate executives whose companies have used eWatch and seen its benefits firsthand. Professional organizations include testimonials from longtime and well-regarded members in recruitment brochures that emphasize the networking and professional development activities that membership provides, and how these activities contribute to professional and personal growth.

- Tell the reader more about you and your history. Devote a panel of your brochure to a description of your organization, how long it has been in existence, what it does, and who it serves. Emphasize achievements and results. A not-for-profit group can mention how many people the organization has helped since its founding and the critical services it provides to make lives better. A manufacturing firm could note some of the well-known companies that use its products and highlight how its products help customers save money and achieve their goals. Brochures do more than sell a product, service, or issue; they sell the organization and its capabilities and reputation.

- End with a key selling point, and request reader action. Leave the reader with a final, motivating thought. The Par inform™ brochure does this simply:

    inform™ works overtime . . . so you don't have to.

    The eWatch brochure concludes with this call to action:

    If you need a reliable way to find the intelligence that is critical to you.

    If you need it fast, with enough time in which to respond.

    You need eWatch.

    Subscribe Today.

    Some brochures include tear-off cards that can be sent back to the company requesting more information. Make sure street addresses, 800 numbers, e-mail addresses, and Web sites are printed on the piece.

- Write in "brochure style." Brochure copy needs to do more than just relay information in a matter-of-fact way. It should have some flair and promotional style. It needs to stress targeted benefits and tell readers how your product, service, or company stands apart from the competition:

    Adequate Brochure Style: Our company has been in business for 30 years and manufactures several medical products used by doctors and health care providers.

    Better Brochure Style: Our company has served the medical community for 30 years by providing a variety of products that improve efficiency and respond to the changing needs of physicians and health care providers.

    Also, make sure your copy is written in a language that your public can appreciate. Use words and expressions, in moderation, that are part of their everyday vocabulary, and indicate in the copy that you understand their interests and lifestyle.

Brochures should be designed and written to stand alone; however, they may be part of a series. If an organization provides several services, you might consider developing a separate brochure for each one. In this case, make sure the information in each brochure is inclusive to that one service, while at the same time sharing a similar design. The consistent look will reinforce the organization's corporate identity. A creative concept for a fund-raising brochure is shown in Exhibit 10.2.

Fliers and Posters

Fliers and posters are informational pieces used to announce and promote meetings and public events, rally support for a cause, or get someone to think more carefully about an important health, social, or political issue. Fliers and posters are single sheets with type and visuals printed on one side of the page only. Many fliers and posters are put up on bulletin boards or displayed in other high-traffic areas such as store entrances and hallways. A typical flier is 8½" × 11" in size, while posters tend to be larger. Here are some writing and design tips:

- Use a large headline and a single visual. The message has to jump out quickly to readers and catch their attention instantly. This is especially true of fliers and

Exhibit 10.2   Brochure: Jewish United Fund

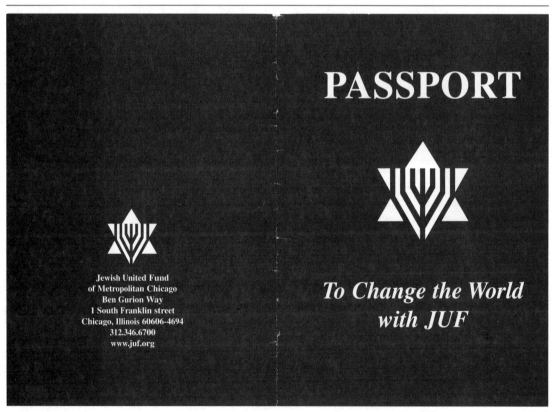

PASSPORT

To Change the World with JUF

Jewish United Fund
of Metropolitan Chicago
Ben Gurion Way
1 South Franklin street
Chicago, Illinois 60606-4694
312.346.6700
www.juf.org

(continued)

posters that a passerby has just a second to see, and that are surrounded by many other pieces on a crowded wall or bulletin board. A bold headline that targets the reader's interest, a compelling photo, and a short sentence or two of copy with a strong call to action are generally the rule.

- Mention necessary details and keep body text brief. Event fliers must have all the relevant facts such as the location, date and time, notable people who will speak or attend, topics of discussion, and a person and phone number to call for more information. If complimentary food and drink is available, mention that, too. Include the names and logos of the sponsoring organization(s) at the bottom of the page, large enough so that readers can identify the sponsors, but not so large that they overpower the key message. It is fine to have more text in targeted leaflets mailed to someone's home about vital neighborhood and community issues, such as the need for school district improvements or changes to a curbside recycling program. Break up large blocks of text with subheads and bulleted items.

Note: Reprinted with permission from the Jewish United Fund of Metropolitan Chicago.

- Adopt a familiar and consistent look. When people receive one of your fliers or see one of your posters, you want them to identify the layout and copy presentation with your organization. Using a consistent color scheme, typeface, logo, and slogan on all promotional pieces are some of the methods for building your organization's identity.

References and Suggested Reading

Carter, D. E. (1999). *Brochures that work*. New York: Hearst Books International.

Gedney, K. & Fultz, P. (1988). *The complete guide to creating successful brochures*. Brentwood, NY: Asher-Gallant Press.

Madonna. (n.d.). Madonna. In *80s rock star quotes*. Retrieved September 7, 2003 from http://80music.about.com/library/weekly/aa070198.htm

CASES

Case 33: A Report on Lactose Intolerance (Part B)

It is now one year after the launch of Dairy-Good, a lactose-reduced milk for people who are lactose intolerant (see chapter 5, case 16). Lactose intolerance is a condition that makes it difficult for someone to digest lactose or milk sugar; it causes gas, stomach cramps, and other discomfort. Dairy-Good is real milk with some of the lactose removed so people who are lactose intolerant can drink it without any discomfort. The product is sold in grocery store dairy cases and has experienced respectable first-year sales.

Aaron Weinstein, a senior account executive who manages the Dairy-Good account for his public relations firm, and you, an assistant account executive who also works on the account, are called to a meeting with the president of Dairy-Good and the company's senior vice president of sales and marketing. The Dairy-Good executives, while pleased with the success of the product so far, tell Weinstein and you that they suspect that supermarket dairy case managers may have some misconceptions about the Dairy-Good product. The Dairy-Good sales force reports that they have heard some dairy case and store managers refer to the product as "artificial milk." Their presumed lack of knowledge could be misleading customers and preventing Dairy-Good from achieving even greater sales. Weinstein and you are asked by the client to survey dairy case managers and investigate this potential awareness problem further.

The firm's research confirms what Dairy-Good's executives suspected: many dairy case managers lack a complete understanding of the product. Many said they thought Dairy-Good was "synthetic milk" that "probably doesn't taste good." Some remarked that they thought customers needed a doctor's prescription to purchase the product, and others did not completely grasp what lactose intolerance is and how this product helps that condition. In actuality, Dairy-Good is 1% real milk with a slightly sweet taste. The product has all the calcium, protein, and nutritional benefits of real milk. People can drink it, put it on cereal, and cook with it, just like they would with non-lactose-reduced milk. After going over the findings with the client, Weinstein and you devise strategies to help correct the perception problems.

"One tool we definitely need is a brochure for dairy case managers that clearly explains the product and why people buy it and use it. The Dairy-Good sales staff wants to then take this piece on sales calls and go over it in person with each dairy case manager with whom they meet," Weinstein says. "They've used this strategy before and said it works quite well with this audience."

"Is there anything else we need to know about our target audience before we start creating the brochure?" you ask.

"Yes. We need to keep in mind what the key messages are for this audience based on what our research told us. The client also informs me that these store managers are busy people, and they get lots of promotional brochures sent to them. Therefore, our brochure needs to be clever and stand out from the crowd. They don't have a lot of time to read, either, so we shouldn't write too much copy. I'm not sure yet how we're going to lay this out. But Dairy-Good's marketing director thinks a two-fold vertical piece might work best. The finished size would be 8½" × 11". He really wants to keep it simple. Let's write a first draft of the copy and then pass it on to the designers."

Assignments

1. Write the copy for a Dairy-Good brochure targeted to dairy case managers. Begin the copy with a creative headline and a brief description of a visual for the brochure's front cover. Copy should be no longer than two pages, double-spaced.

2. Write the copy for a six-panel fold pamphlet (8½" × 11" sheet folded twice) that informs consumers about lactose intolerance, its causes and symptoms, and possible treatments. The pamphlet will be sent to doctors for display in their offices and distribution to patients. Mention Dairy-Good in the copy, but be subtle. Present copy in Q & A format. Do not exceed two to three pages, double-spaced.

Case 34: The Virtual Volunteering Campaign

More and more not-for-profit agencies, schools, and other organizations that rely on volunteer support are getting involved in virtual volunteering, also known as online volunteering or cyber service. Virtual volunteers use the Internet, or a home or work computer, to complete a wide range of volunteer assignments. This is a convenient alternative to traditional volunteering since it allows people who have time constraints to volunteer and make a difference without having to leave their homes or offices.

Virtual volunteering projects generally fall into one of two categories: technical assistance or direct contact. Technical assistance includes projects such as doing Internet research to help an agency gather information for a newsletter or a grant proposal, using desktop publishing to design a publication, or providing online consulting. Direct contact might involve establishing an e-mail relationship with a homebound individual, offering online instruction to help high school students with their homework questions, or staffing a chat room that gives advice and support to people with problems or questions (similar to a telephone hot line). Virtual volunteers often combine these online activities with on-site or face-to-face contact.

The Volunteer Center in your community wants to draw more attention to virtual volunteering. Funded primarily by individuals, businesses, private foundations, and United Way program fees, The Volunteer Center is a non-profit agency whose primary mission is to promote increased volunteerism and help local agencies fill their volunteer needs. Agencies with virtual or other volunteer assignments can list those positions with the Volunteer Center, which then does outreach to recruit community-wide volunteers. In essence, the center helps agencies extend their individual volunteer recruitment efforts.

You have begun a public relations internship with The Volunteer Center, and the center's director has asked you to help execute a campaign to better inform people in the area about virtual volunteering and its benefits, with an ultimate goal of recruiting more virtual volunteers. Your first assignment is to prepare public relations tools that target two specific audiences.

"Obviously, there are lots of different people using computers today, but we've identified two primary target groups," the director tells you. "One is busy executives and professionals in the 30 to 50 age range. Across the community, this is an age group where the number of volunteers is somewhat low; our research shows that virtual volunteering might be a way to get more of them to volunteer. We're also looking at the college community, not just students but faculty and staff, too. A majority of this audience is using computers and the Internet almost every day, and has become comfortable with the technology. This has the potential to be an excellent pool of virtual volunteers."

Assignments

1. Conduct further research on the subject of virtual volunteering. In a two-page memorandum, summarize your findings and highlight key messages that should be included in public relations materials designed for the virtual volunteering campaign.

2. Write the copy for a virtual volunteering brochure targeted to "busy executives and professionals in the 30 to 50 age range." Recommend an attention-getting cover headline and visual, and suggest visuals to accompany the main copy. Limit your copy to about two pages, double-spaced.

3. Create a series of three to six different posters that promotes virtual volunteering to college audiences. For each poster, suggest a visual element, and write a strong headline and any other copy you think is necessary. Make sure there is a common theme or element that connects each poster in the series.

Case 35: Introducing a New Digital Recorder

DigiNotes, Inc. introduced its first compact, battery-operated digital note recorder in the mid 1990s. Since then, DigiNotes has become a leading manufacturer in this product category. Digital recorders have many advantages over hand-held tape recorders. They store voice data on a computer chip, making it easy to access, play, or erase messages by using simple controls, much like those on a compact disc player. There is no rewinding or fast-forwarding. Messages are stored in memory, so there is no risk of accidentally recording over or erasing a message, which can happen when using a tape recorder. The construction of digital recorders makes them more reliable than tape-based devices, since there are no recording heads to be cleaned or mechanical parts to break.

You work as a marketing communications assistant for DigiNotes at the firm's corporate headquarters. One of your primary duties is writing brochures and other product literature. A major project at this time involves preparation of sales promotion materials for a new product, the DigiNotes Manager. In addition to the general benefits of digital recording, DigiNotes Manager offers more conveniences than the company's other recorders currently on the market. You review the features of DigiNotes Manager as outlined in a product fact sheet:

- Available in two models: the DN-20 with 20 minutes of recording time, and the DN-40 with up to 40 minutes of recording time. Previous models have recording capacities of 40 seconds to eight minutes. The DN-20 model sells for $119.95; the DN-40 model for $159.95.

- Notes can be categorized into five channels or "files"; files can be customized by subject headers like "meetings," "memos" and "things to do." The ability to sort and organize messages when recording them digitally, as opposed to recording taped messages in sequence, makes this product useful for busy executives.

- A contact file allows users to store up to 100 names with three phone numbers per name. Voice notes can be added to the names, making this a handy portable database.

- The calendar and scheduling feature makes it possible to record "reminder" messages and program them to play back by day, week, month, or year.

- A display feature lets the user see which channel is in use, how many messages are in the channel, and when a message was recorded. Phone numbers that appear on the display are dialed automatically by holding the recording unit's speaker next to the telephone mouthpiece.

A few minutes later, you call the vice president of marketing and public relations, to clarify the scope of your assignment. "I just want to be sure about what you're asking me to write. The last time we talked, you mentioned two specific pieces on which I should be working. The first is a brochure for retailers that will let them know about DigiNotes Manager and get them interested in carrying it in their stores. The other is a direct mail piece that we'll send to business executives who already have a DigiNotes recorder and who might buy this new model. Am I on target with this?"

"That's it. The format for the retailer brochure will probably be vertical, with two folds and six panels. The finished, printed size will be 8½" by 11". We haven't decided on the format for the direct mail brochure. Give me your thoughts on what you think would work best for that piece."

Assignments

1. Write the copy for the DigiNotes Manager retailer brochure. Come up with a creative cover headline and visual element. Within the body of your text, recommend other visual elements. Briefly describe any visual element at the start of the accompanying text section.

2. In a one-page memo to the vice president of marketing and public relations, recommend and justify a format for the direct mail piece to business executives. Briefly explain the goals of the direct mail piece, and include suggestions for the size of the piece, number of folds, color, and use and placement of visual elements. Then, write copy for the direct mail piece based on the proposed format, and attach that copy to your memo. Include an attention-getting cover headline and visual element.

Case 36: The Big Brothers Big Sisters Brochure

Your public relations firm and its employees are actively involved with nonprofit groups and charities in the community. Several senior executives serve on the local boards of directors of major human service organizations such as Big Brothers Big Sisters of America (BBBSA), and employees regularly take part in events to raise money for cancer research and other worthy causes. The agency also "gives back" by donating its professional services and expertise. This includes writing, designing, and producing public relations materials free of charge for BBBSA.

Today, at the request of your supervisor who serves on the BBBSA board, you are meeting with Claudia Rivera, executive director of the local BBBSA agency. BBBSA (www.bbbsa.org) has more than 500 local agencies in communities throughout the 50 states. Founded in 1904, BBBSA matches adult volunteers with youth between the ages of 6 and 16 who are looking for an older person with whom to spend time. The adult volunteers, known as Big Brothers and Big Sisters, donate a few hours each week and develop one-on-one mentoring relationships with these youths. Many of the Little Brothers and Little Sisters are young people from single-parent families who have lost a parent to death, or who no longer have contact with a parent due to divorce, separation, or abuse. A Big Brother/Big Sister becomes a positive adult role model and brings balance to a young person's life to help keep him or her on track.

In talking with Rivera on the telephone prior to your meeting, you learn that the local BBBSA agency wants to produce a new brochure aimed at recruiting new adult mentors. Currently, the agency has a waiting list of youth requesting a Big Brother or Big Sister, and it does not have enough adult volunteers to meet that demand. As your meeting begins, Rivera gives you more background on the volunteer shortage and additional details about the brochure project.

"We haven't updated our recruitment brochure in some time, and we thought this would be a good time to do it," Rivera says. "As I told you, there's a real need to get more adults on board as mentors. We're hoping a new, attractive brochure targeted to the right kinds of audiences will help us build our volunteer base."

"Is there a certain kind of person you look for? Can anybody be a Big Brother or Sister? Are there specific requirements?" you ask.

"No, we need men and women of all ages and backgrounds. Some of our Big Brothers and Big Sisters are young professionals, some are older people who have their own kids or grandchildren, and some are college students like yourself. We do have an increasing need for young male professionals and African Americans, based on the requests we are getting," Rivera says.

"So, how does this work? Once you get a volunteer, how do you decide with whom that person should be matched?"

"Good question. First of all, any potential volunteer is carefully screened by professionals on our staff. We get a lot of information about the adult, and then we make a match based on the child's needs and interests and the interests and characteristics of the volunteer. This is a thoughtful process."

"I would guess that one of the common objections you hear from potential volunteers is that they are busy and they don't have enough time to spend with someone."

"That's true," Rivera replies. "But we stress that you only have to spend a few hours a week. And what you do together is really up to you. It can be as simple as just taking a walk in a park or grabbing a bite to eat. The important thing is being there for young people, and letting them know that you are an adult they can count on."

You then ask a few more questions about the preferred design and format of the piece. Rivera tells you to assume that the piece will be a two-fold 8½" × 11" pamphlet with six panels. She also says that BBBSA has many good-quality photographs to choose from, but that she welcomes your thoughts on specific photos or artwork that could be included in the new brochure. Before she leaves, Rivera asks you to get back to her shortly with a project timeline.

Assignments

1. Prepare a brief memorandum for Rivera that includes the following:

    *   Goals of the piece and key message points to include in the brochure copy.
    *   A recommended cover headline that could serve as a recruitment campaign theme, along with a proposed visual element. Justify your copy and visual choices.
    *   Suggestions for other photo/artwork ideas that you think will enhance the piece.
    *   An attachment to your memo that presents a timeline for producing the finished recruitment piece. List the activities in the order that they should occur, and indicate the estimated number of days (or weeks) needed to complete each activity.

2. Using the information provided in this case and any additional information compiled from your own research, write the copy for the BBBSA recruitment brochure. Limit your copy to two to three pages, double-spaced. Indicate where subheads and copy blocks should appear in the brochure (e.g., cover, inside right fold, inside spread, back panel).

3. Write the copy for a BBBSA flier to be distributed on college campuses. The goal of the flier is to interest college-age men and women in becoming Big Brothers and Big Sisters. Your copy should include an attention-getting headline and a few sentences of body copy that convey key messages. Begin the copy draft with a brief description of the flier's visual element.

11

Broadcast Media

Forrest Gump, the lovable guy played by actor Tom Hanks in the 1990s movie of the same name, shared many bits of wisdom about life in the film, including this one: "Do not put stock in newspapers; you can find out more just by lookin' around at what is going on." Broadcast media executives and news staffs would support this statement but also add that radio and television make "looking around" a lot easier since they offer sound and visual elements that print media can't provide.

It's not that broadcast media are better publicity tools than print media; they're just different. Radio and television stations can get information out more immediately than newspapers, magazines, and newsletters that publish once a week, day, or month. When your news is urgent or life threatening, radio and television stations can reach large numbers of people right away. Hot issues that people are talking about and in which your organization has a legitimate interest are good topics for radio call-in shows. Stories that involve well-known people with something important to say or show work well on television.

Broadcast writing and print media writing differ somewhat in their style and approach. Broadcast writers have to consider how words will sound and blend with visual images. A major challenge is knowing how to best integrate broadcast media into the media mix, by taking advantage of the distinct opportunities that only radio and television offer such as live interviews, actualities and video news releases, satellite media tours, public service announcements, and promotions.

Radio and Television: An Overview

At home. At work. In the car. In stores. Radio is all around you. It reaches people at all times of the day and in more places than most other media. Targeting radio is a good way to get your messages to specific groups of people, especially in local markets. Top 40 stations' primary listeners are teens and young adults, while an all-news-and-talk station will appeal more to older adults and professionals.

Television, while it can and does target specific audiences, has the main benefit of reaching large numbers of people. According to the Television Bureau of Advertising, more than 98% of all U.S. households had a television set in the year 2002, and the average household spent 7 hours and 35 minutes watching TV each day. A 2002 Gallup

Poll reported that more than half of adults 18 years and older say that television is their main source of news.

Both radio and television present opportunities for national and local news exposure. On a national level, networks such as ABC, CBS, NBC, National Public Radio and the Associated Press air daily newscasts and news programming. But unless your story is of major significance to a national audience, or highly unusual or controversial, it probably won't make it onto a network news broadcast. National cable TV networks present many opportunities for the creative public relations practitioner whose focus is a defined public with an interest in travel, cooking, golf, or any number of specialized subjects.

Much of the publicity you do will target radio and television news operations in local markets. Radio and television stations in cities large and small across the country have their own news departments, and they are often looking for news and human interest stories for their newscasts. Public relations professionals primarily work with *assignment editors*, who decide what stories are covered and assign stories to reporters each day (media alerts are generally sent to assignment editors); *news directors*, who oversee the entire news operation and are the primary contacts for setting up editorial meetings; and *reporters* who cover specific beats and subjects and can be pitched directly with story ideas.

Writing for Broadcast Media

Broadcast media contacts, like their counterparts in print, have certain expectations of public relations materials. News releases and media alerts must be newsworthy, accurate, clear, and written in simple language. The newspaper editor who finds value in your news release might assign a reporter who does further interviews, adds detail, and produces a half-page article. A television news story on the same subject, however, may last only a half a minute. Broadcast news stories don't have the luxury of space or time, so they need to emphasize the key facts and leave out much of the detail seen in print articles.

Generally, the news release or media alert you write for print media is suitable for broadcast media. Television and radio news staffs, for the most part, aren't looking to use your material word for word. Your release is a starting point from which to develop and write their own story using their own reporter. However, there are times when it is preferable to write a news release specifically for broadcast. If a major story breaks at 5 p.m., writing a shorter broadcast-version of your print news release makes it easier to get the news on the air without much copy revision. What are the characteristics of good broadcast news writing?

- Use simple, one subject-one verb sentences. Radio listeners and television viewers get one chance to hear and understand what you say. The longer the sentence, the more difficult that is to do. If you have the urge to use commas, your sentence is probably too long and should be broken into two shorter sentences.

- Try not to use "who, which, or where" clauses in the middle of sentences. It's okay to use short clauses at the end of sentences, but it still may be smoother to make the clause a second sentence.

- Write it like you'd say it. Broadcast writing is for the ear, not the eye. It sounds natural. Think about the way people talk in everyday conversation. They use contractions (I'm, you're), shorter sentences and, at times, incomplete statements without a subject or verb to express their thoughts. There is one exception to the rule, however. Do not use "doesn't" for "does not" or "aren't" for "are not." If listeners don't hear the "t" sound in the contraction, the meaning of the word changes and then alters the story content.

- Keep the verbs active. This rule applies to all good writing but broadcast media is more immediate than print.

- Don't lead with the hard news. Instead write what is referred to as a *soft* or *throwaway lead* that will attract the listener's attention, but not provide important details that can be missed during the first few seconds of an aired story.

- Attribute up front. Articles in print often note sources at the end of sentences. Broadcast writers tend to identify the source at the start of a sentence, often by title on a first reference. Again, this is more natural sounding since in conversation, you would say "the director said," not "said the director."

- Spell out numbers and hard-to-pronounce words. Put *pronouncers* (phonetic spellings) of unusual or unfamiliar names in your scripts. You can spell out unfamiliar words but if they are that unfamiliar, they shouldn't be in your script at all. Exhibit 11.1 lists some of the most common pronouncers.

Interviews

Watch any national morning news show or entertainment program on television, or listen to any afternoon call-in or talk show on radio, and you'll see and hear medical experts, authors, business leaders, and celebrities talking about many subjects. It's likely that some of those interviews have been scheduled by public relations professionals. Many local news broadcasts aired between 4 and 6:30 p.m. are one and two hours long and produce regular segments on health, consumer news, and the Internet. Your organization's experts can be excellent sources for interviews that help local stations fill time with interesting features on these and other subjects.

Arranging interviews is a step-by-step process:

- Identify individuals within your organization who have special expertise and are comfortable talking on air or in front of the camera.

- Listen to radio shows and watch television news programs to get a feel for their formats and possible interview segments.

- Call or send a pitch letter to the appropriate news contact, program producer or talk show host. Explain your idea and why it's timely and newsworthy. Identify your spokesperson and point out his or her credentials.

Exhibit 11.1 Associated Press Pronouncer Guide

Pronouncers are used as phonetic guidelines for reading broadcast copy. They should be used with foreign phrases, unusual names and words, and familiar spellings that are pronounced differently than usual. Pronouncers are placed in parentheses immediately behind the word to which they apply. Using the Associated Press guidelines below, spell the word the way it should sound in lower case letters. Use hyphens to separate the syllables and write the accented syllable(s) in all capital letters.

     Here are some examples:
The French phrase for "without worry"—sans souci (SAHN-soo-CEE)
The abbreviation for the State University of New York—SUNY (SOO-nee)
A different spelling of a common surname—Smyth (SMITH)

Vowels		Consonants	
a	bat, apple	g	got, beg
ah	father, arm	j	job, gem
aw	raw, board	k	keep, cap
ay	fate, ace	ch	chair, butcher
e, eh	bed	sh	shut, fashion
ee	feel, tea	ch	vision, mirage
i, ih	pin, middle	th	thin, math
oh	go, oval	kh	guttural, k
oo	food, two		
ow	scout, crowd		
oy	boy, join		
u	curl, foot		
uh	puff		
y, eye	ice, time, guide		
yoo	fume, few		

Note. Reprinted with permission of the Associated Press.

- Follow up by telephone a few days after sending the pitch, and have some dates in mind for scheduling an interview. If a show or segment airs once a week, remember that guests are probably being booked several weeks in advance.
- Send thank yous and get tapes of interviews for your files. In addition, suggest other story ideas that don't involve your company or clients from time to time to build relations with producers and program staffs.

Radio News Releases

Organizations can also record interviews on audiotape and send them to radio stations. Radio news releases are normally 60 seconds long and include three components: a brief lead that introduces the subject and the spokesperson; the spokesperson's taped comments, which are called *actualities* or *sound bites*; and a closing that highlights a key aspect of the subject. Because the taped comments are in the middle, radio news releases are sometimes called "donuts." The length of actualities has become shorter through the years. Most stations prefer them to be 8 to 12 seconds long.

Radio news releases should avoid promotional language and only mention the sponsoring organization once or twice. While you can have the spokesperson read a pre-pared script, this is not advisable. It is best to conduct a face-to-face interview to ensure getting sound bites that sound natural and similar to those you would hear in broadcast news stories.

Video News Releases

For television, taped interviews can be combined with interesting visuals in a video news release or VNR. VNRs are produced to help companies get widespread exposure for themselves and their people, products, and services. But they cannot be TV com-mercials. Instead, they must present the company's key message in a more subtle way. VNRs can be produced in a variety of lengths, although 90 seconds is the most popular. They are mailed to newsrooms in videotape format or delivered by satellite. A single VNR can cost, on average, $20,000 to $25,000, so you need to think carefully about some critical questions before starting production:

- Does the VNR have mass appeal? VNRs target a wide audience with informa-tion of general interest. If the target public is more narrowly defined, a VNR is probably not the best tool. VNRs on health, entertainment, technology, new products, food, and fashion are popular with television news producers.

- Is there a news hook, and are there credible sources and strong visuals? VNRs that feature comments from third-party sources—experts and specialists not affiliated with your company—may have more credibility; however, it is wise to position the organization's representatives as the experts, especially when the producer of the VNR is spending so much money to develop and distrib-ute it. When you can, include footage that the media would otherwise have difficulty getting, and keep visuals of company logos or products to a bare minimum.

- Have we assembled a complete package? In addition to the fully-produced VNR (also referred to as *a-roll*), include scripts written in broadcast style (see Exhibit 11.2), separate sound bites, and b-roll. *B-roll* is the raw footage— just the visuals—with natural sound and no voice-over. Because of its flexi-bility, b-roll is becoming the favored format over the already-assembled VNR; if news producers want to use the story, but not in its entirety, they can read some of the script and use a sound bite, or they can show several seconds of the b-roll while an anchor reads an edited portion of the copy. Adding a Spanish version or sound bite to the package is a good idea, depending on the subject.

Exhibit 11.2 Video News Release Script: Ben & Jerry's

	STORY: 12629 **TITLE:** "Dave Matthews Band: 'One Sweet Whirled'" **CLIENT:** Ben & Jerry's **TIME:** VNR (1:52) B-ROLL (3:10)	

Contacts:	Tammie Coyman, GCI Group, 212-537-8107
	Chrystie Heimert, Ben & Jerry's, 802-846-1500
Broadcast:	Heather Harrison, West Glen, 800-325-8677, ext. 231

SUGGESTED ANCHOR LEAD		
Studio Anchor on-camera		**STUDIO ANCHOR O/C:** GLOBAL WARMING, MUSIC AND ICE CREAM? WHILE THEY MAY SEEM LIKE AN UNUSUAL COMBINATION, GAYLE JACKSON HAS THE SCOOP ON A NEW CAMPAIGN THAT KICKED OFF AT A PRESS CONFERENCE TODAY (TUESDAY) IN WASHINGTON THAT MAY HELP SAVE THE ENVIRONMENT.

VIDEO	TIME	AUDIO
1. Open with press conf. Footage or a shot of the planet, then concert footage and website.	:00-:10 (:10)	**REPORTER V/O:** *(Nat Sound Band Music)* "ONE SWEET WHIRLED" IS NOT ONLY THE NAME OF THE ENVIRONMENTAL HIT SONG BY THE DAVE MATTHEWS BAND, IT'S ALSO THE NAME OF A NEW CAMPAIGN – AND ICE CREAM -- TO FIGHT GLOBAL WARMING.
2. Band on-camera **SUPER:** **The Dave Matthews Band**	:10-:28 (:18)	**BAND O/C:** "That's why I'm involved because we all need to know about it. We all need to act in the little ways that we can that have such a profound effect. We need to act, and we need to act now to reverse or at least prevent further global warming".
3. Press conference shots segue into shots of ice cream, OSW logo and planet image from website. Continue with shot of traffic, and band footage. Shot of the Capitol in DC. Band shots SUV's, website pledge, earth as seen form space	:28-:54 (:26)	**REPORTER V/O:** DAVE MATTHEWS BAND IS WORKING IN CONCERT WITH BEN & JERRY'S AND SAVEOURENVIRONMENT.ORG TO URGE PEOPLE TO PERSONALLY REDUCE THEIR CARBON DIOXIDE EMISSIONS BY 5% OR 2,000 LBS A YEAR. ONE SWEET WHIRLED ALSO AIMS TO GET THE PUBLIC TO VOICE THEIR CONCERNS TO CONGRESS ABOUT GLOBAL WARMING. THE CAMPAIGN HITS THE ROAD WITH THE BAND'S UPCOMING TOUR WITH AN INTERACTIVE EXHIBIT DESIGNED TO EDUCATE FANS NATIONWIDE ABOUT PRACTICAL SOLUTIONS TO GLOBAL WARMING.
4. Expert on-camera **SUPER:** **Howard Ris** **President, Union of** **Concerned Scientists &** **Member,** **SaveOurEnvironment.org**	:54-1:11 (:17)	**RIS O/C:** "Scientist and environmentalist together agree that global warming is the most pressing environmental problem of the 21st century. Fortunately, there are solutions to this problem. If we're smarter about the way we use energy, if we buy the right kinds of automobiles and take mass transit, we can all contribute to the solution."

VNR #12629   Dave Matthews Band: "One Sweet Whirled"   BEN & JERRY'S   (Page 2 of 3)

5. Family eating ice cream. Ice cream packages on belt. Wind turbines.	1:11-1:21 (:10)	**REPORTER V/O**: AND NOW THERE'S A DELICIOUS WAY TO PUT YOUR MONEY WHERE YOUR MOUTH IS. A PORTION OF EVERY SALE OF DAVE MATTHEWS BAND ONE SWEET WHIRLED GOES TO SUPPORT GLOBAL WARMING INITIATIVES.
6. Ben Cohen on-camera – at podium **SUPER:** **Ben Cohen** **Co-founder of Ben & Jerry's**	1:21-1:36 (:15)	**COHEN O/C:** "As part of the one sweet whirled campaign we are proud to be partnering with the Dave Matthews Bands, and save our environment in a way the makes it easy, incredibly easy to make your voice heard in Washington."
7. Montage sequence of traffic shots, dishwasher, recycling, cars, polar ice caps melting.	1:36-1:52 (:16)	**REPORTER V/O**: DRIVING MORE-FUEL-EFFICIENT CARS, REPLACING WORN OUT APPLIANCES WITH NEW ENERGY-EFFICIENT MODELS AND RECYCLING ARE JUST A FEW OF THE EASY STEPS WE CAN EACH TAKE TO REDUCE CARBON DIOXIDE EMISSIONS AND FIGHT GLOBAL WARMING. THIS IS GAYLE JACKSON.

SUGGESTED ANCHOR TAG		
Studio Anchor on-camera		**STUDIO ANCHOR O/C:** TAKE THE 2,000 POUND PLEDGE AT DAVE MATTHEWS BAND CONCERTS, ON THE WEB SITE, www.onesweetwhirled.org OR BY VISITING BEN & JERRY'S SCOOP SHOPS.

B-ROLL (3:30+)		
1. Dave Matthews Band	:00-:23 (:23)	**BAND O/C:** "This issue should be almost a purpose of the international community today, of the world today. The fact that we're not talking about this everyday, the fact that we're not obsessed by this is almost unforgivable".
2. Dave Matthews Band	:23-:42 (:19)	**BAND O/C:** "There are important issues whether it's hunger, or it's poverty that are out there, but all those issues fall under this. This issue affects all those things. This issue is so central, because it's about the whole planet".
3. Howard Ris	:42-1:03 (:21)	**RIS O/C:** "Global warming is a problem that has real practical solutions available. If we choose the right kinds of automobiles, if we use mass transit more frequently, and if we upgrade the appliances in our home to use less energy we can solve this problem."
4. Howard Ris	1:03-1:18 (:15)	**RIS O/C:** "SaveOurEnvironment.org is a unique coalition of 19 national environmental organizations. We're very pleased to work together with Ben & Jerry's and the Dave Matthews Band on this One Sweet Whirled Campaign to fight global warming".
5. Ben Cohen	1:18-1:50 (:32)	**COHEN O/C:** "The whole world is feeling the effects of global warming.

West Glen Communications, Inc. ◆ 1430 Broadway, New York, NY 10018 ◆ TEL: 212-921-2800 ◆ FAX: 212-382-0718 information@westglen.com   ◆   http://www.westglen.com

(continued)

VNR #12629   Dave Matthews Band: "One Sweet Whirled"   BEN & JERRY'S   (Page 3 of 3)

		Now it's time for Washington to feel a different kind of heat. The heat from the true majority of citizens who demand that our government work to reverse global warming now. Take it from a couple of old ice cream guys, if It's melted it's ruined".
6. Jerry Greenfield	1:50-2:13 (:23)	**GREENFIELD O/C:** "I'm also happy to say that Ben & Jerry's as a company is committing to reducing its emissions. It's committing to reduce its CO2 emissions by 10% from manufacturing facilities over the next 5 years".
7. Jerry Greenfield	2:13-2:33 (:20)	**GREENFIELD O/C:** "I urge everybody to take the pledge. Sign up either on the website or the Ben & Jerry's site. I should probably mention that there's an ice cream flavor involved with this, but you know it's just sort of ancillary to the global warming initiative".
8. Jim Jeffords **SUPER:** **Senator Jim Jeffords (I-VT)** **Chairman of the Senate** **Environment & Public Works** **Committee**	2:33-3:10 (:37)	**JEFFORDS O/C:** "As the Chairman of the Senate Environment Committee, I can tell you that there's no more pressing issue to the environment than global warming. Global warming is no longer just a theory or a distant threat. It's here. The overwhelming agreement among the world's preeminent climate sciences is that impacts are already being seen today and they will only grow worse in the future, if action is not taken now".

MISC. B-ROLL FOOTAGE: Earth Shots, Various land and water scenes, Windmills, House, SUV, Cars traveling, One Sweet Whirled website, press conference shots of all players, Various extra shots of Ben, Jerry & DMB scooping, scoop truck, letter to congress

West Glen Communications, Inc. • 1430 Broadway, New York, NY 10018 • TEL: 212-921-2800 • FAX: 212-382-0718
information@westglen.com   •   http://www.westglen.com

Note. Courtesy of Ben & Jerry's.

- How will we evaluate? You can hire a video clipping service, or use Nielsen Research's SIGMA electronic tracking system. VNR tapes are encoded with SIGMA, which can provide data on stations that used the spot, date, and time of usage, total viewing audience, and how much of the encoded video was used.

When a nationwide hoax fostered reports of syringes found in cans of Diet Pepsi®, the soda company relied on b-roll as a major component of its crisis response plan. Shortly after the first news report (the story would lead newscasts for four days), the Federal Drug Administration (FDA) conducted an exhaustive inspection of Pepsi's manufacturing procedures and ruled out any internal tampering. In an effort to capitalize on the FDA's report and calm the public's fears, Pepsi went inside one of its bottling facilities and videotaped the canning process–footage that was beamed by satellite to hundreds of televisions stations across the country and viewed by 296 million people.

While VNRs are popular tools that can be used effectively by public relations practitioners, they are not without controversy. VNRs were introduced at a time when newsrooms were being downsized; reporters turned to the ready-to-go stories as a convenient source of news, which led to the following questions:

- Is it appropriate for a VNR to appear in a newscast with the news station's logo superimposed?
- Should a VNR be aired without identifying the organization that produced it?
- How credible are the sources of VNRs and the footage in them? "NBC Nightly News" once ran a story on the environmental dangers of logging in Idaho's Clearwater National Forest. The story included footage of dead fish in a stream—a stream that was actually located 400 miles away. An environmental group dedicated to ending logging of ancient forests on public land had given the tape to NBC.

Satellite Media Tours

Although they can cost twice as much to do, satellite media tours (SMTs) have a clear advantage over VNRs. They make it possible to ask questions of a spokesperson live, via satellite hookup. Each station that takes part in the SMT can choose to pick up the satellite feed and do an exclusive interview with a designated spokesperson during a pre-arranged timeframe.

Celebrities, CEOs, and national experts who are not easy for producers to book on their own are excellent choices for SMT spokespersons. Media contacts typically receive a b-roll package as well, so they can have additional footage to air during the interview or prepare a background piece in advance of the SMT. The simplest form of SMT involves a spokesperson sitting in a television studio doing the interviews. More companies are opting to take their spokespeople out of the studio and put them in a visually interesting location that has relevance to the story.

For example, Sarah Ferguson, the Duchess of York and U.S. spokesperson for Weight Watchers, participated in a New Year's Day SMT on location at the Pasadena

Tournament of Roses parade. Weight Watchers had participated in the parade for three years and thought it would be a good place for Ferguson to talk about the new 1-2-3 Success diet plan with some exciting and colorful visuals in the background. In addition, the timing was good since people think about resolutions, one of which is losing weight, as a new year begins. "Good Morning America" and network affiliates in Los Angeles and Chicago picked up the tour, and Weight Watchers classroom attendance increased 20% that month.

Public Service Announcements

It's a television image that many people remember. The shot opens on a frying pan. No sound. Then you see an egg and hear a voice saying, "This is your brain." The egg is cracked into the pan, you hear a sizzling sound for a few seconds, and the voice comes in again to say, "This is your brain on drugs." The egg continues to cook, followed by a brief closing remark: "Any questions?"

This is an example of a classic public service announcement, or PSA. It uses simple visuals, minimal voice-over, and the element of surprise to communicate a single, powerful message—drugs can "fry" your brain. Not-for-profit organizations create PSAs to inform and educate audiences about important health, social, and public interest issues. Although the Federal Communication Commission no longer mandates stations to provide a certain amount of airtime to PSAs, the media still donates time to air these spots as a public service. Many stations have public service directors to coordinate PSAs and public service programming. Competition for PSA placement is stiff. A station may only air a few PSAs a day out of the many it receives each week. Attention to some fundamentals can help your PSAs succeed with the media and your target audiences:

- Come up with a strategic plan for your public service campaign that includes research of the issue, public attitudes, and media interest in the subject; goal setting and targeted message development; production techniques and costs; and distribution and evaluation methods.

- Create and send a variety of formats and lengths—:10, :15, :20, :30, and :60 spots. For radio, you can create prerecorded spots with voice-overs and sound effects (see Exhibit 11.3) as well as simple announcer scripts that cost nothing to produce and can be read on-the-air by deejays between songs to fill time.

- Focus on one main idea and reinforce that idea a few times in the spot. Use a memorable theme line (e.g., Friends don't let friends drive drunk). Do something at the start of the spot using voice, visuals, or sound that will get the audience interested and make them ask, "What's coming next?" Exhibit 11.4 is an example of a television PSA that uses the simple, yet effective, theme of "tools" to demonstrate the many services of the Salvation Army.

- Include a call to action such as a phone number or Web site where people can get more information. Don't ask for money; it's better to be less pushy.

Exhibit 11.3   Radio PSA/Prerecorded Spot: Catholic Campaign for Human Development.

Note. Reprinted with permission from Catholic Campaign for Human Development.

- Incorporate a local angle, such as a local phone number to call or a statistic that relates to the geographic area targeted. Many nationally-prepared PSAs provide room at the end to include local information. Keep minority audiences in mind, and prepare scripts with content that will appeal to diverse groups and ethnic media.

Exhibit 11.4   Television PSA Script: Salvation Army

:60	
1. Woman embracing flood victim; woman showing hands to the camera	**ANNCR V/O:** THE TOOLS NEEDED TO RESTORE FLOOD RAVAGED LIVES AREN'T ALWAYS SHOVELS AND SANDBAGS
2. Homeless person sitting against a wall; Salvation Army worker helping homeless person; Salvation Army worker smiling into camera	**ANNCR V/O:** THE TOOL NEEDED TO SHELTER THE HOMELESS ISN'T ALWAYS A HAMMER.
3. CU of father's face; son hugging father; CU of son's face	**ANNCR V/O:** THE TOOL THAT WILL SAVE A PARENT LOST TO SUBSTANCE ABUSE DOESN'T COME IN A BOX
1. Boy standing against chain linked fence; CU of boy's face behind fence; Salvation Army worker showing hands; young boy showing hands to camera; Salvation Army worker hugging a woman; father playing with his son	**ANNCR V/O:** WHEN LIVES NEED REBUILDING, THE SALVATION ARMY KNOWS IT TAKES MORE THAN TOOLS THAT COME FROM THE HARDWARE STORE. IT TAKES TOOLS THAT COME FROM THE HEART
4. Old man smiling into the camera **SUPER:** The Salvation Army Logo salvationarmyusa.org	**ANNCR V/O:** NEED KNOWS NO SEASON.
:30	
2. Woman embracing flood victim; woman showing hands to the camera	**ANNCR V/O:** THE TOOLS NEEDED TO RESTORE FLOOD RAVAGED LIVES AREN'T ALWAYS SHOVELS AND SANDBAGS
3. Woman helping homeless person	**ANNCR V/O:** THE TOOL NEEDED TO SHELTER THE HOMELESS ISN'T ALWAYS A HAMMER.
4. Boy standing against chain linked fence; CU of boy's face behind fence; Salvation Army worker showing hands to camera; young boy showing hands to camera	**ANNCR V/O:** WHEN LIVES NEED REBUILDING, THE SALVATION ARMY KNOWS IT TAKES MORE THAN TOOLS FROM THE HARDWARE STORE. IT TAKES TOOLS THAT COME FROM THE HEART.
5. Salvation Army worker hugging a woman **SUPER:** The Salvation Army Logo salvationarmyusa.org	**ANNCR V/O:** NEED KNOWS NO SEASON.

Note. Courtesy of Young & Rubicam Inc., Dearborn, MI.

- Track PSA usage. As with VNRs, SIGMA encoding can be used. Send reminder cards or make follow-up phone calls to the media to build interest.

Promotions

Broadcast media, especially radio, offer some unique promotional opportunities that can extend your publicity in original ways. Organizations that sell tickets for sports events, concerts, shows, and other activities, for example, can do *giveaways* with radio stations.

The sponsoring group donates tickets to give away on the air prior to the event. The prospect of winning tickets is an incentive for listeners to tune in, and stations are receptive to getting free items that their listeners would want. In return, the station's deejays make repeated mentions of the group and its event when giving away the tickets, which helps build public awareness of the event.

Stores and businesses celebrating an anniversary or grand opening, and not-for-profit organizations sponsoring popular charitable events might arrange for a radio or TV station to do a *remote* broadcast. During remotes, radio and TV personalities broadcast live from the site of the event and publicize the remote's sponsor during commercial breaks. This helps build traffic at the remote location and gives the media good exposure to passersby who see the station's signage, banners, and mobile vans. Remotes can be expensive because they are considered advertising time; however, a station may occasionally reduce or waive the price for frequent advertisers and charitable organizations. A *trade* may also be arranged where the remote sponsor trades its product or services for the remote.

Another possibility is media *sponsorship* of an event. Media sponsors can help fund the event, but their primary role is often to create and air announcements and provide publicity support, in exchange for visibility at the event and the goodwill this kind of community sponsorship creates.

Contests are a creative way to reach key audiences. Nestle partnered with radio stations to relaunch its *100 Grand* candy bar and position it as a brand of choice among funny and "hip" teens. Stations popular with teens helped Nestle promote America's Biggest Class Clown contest by talking about the event frequently on the air and sending their radio vans to schools where they distributed free candy samples and event flyers. The contest created a new level of excitement about the *100 Grand* candy bar and culminated with the naming of the grand prize winner the day before April Fool's Day.

Regardless of which type of media promotion you choose, make sure the demographics of the radio or TV station match your target audience.

References and Suggested Reading

Bliss, E. & Hoyt, J. (1994). *Writing news for broadcast* (3rd ed.). New York: Columbia University Press.

Boyd, A. (2000). *Broadcast journalism: Techniques of radio and TV news* (5th ed.). Woburn, MA: Focal Press.

Brown, L. (2002). *Your public best: The complete personal appearance and media training guide.* New York: Newmarket Press.

Carroll, V. M. (1997). *Writing news for television: Style and format.* Ames, IA: Iowa State University Press.

Kerchner, K. (2002). *Soundbites: A business guide to working with the media* (2nd ed.). Superior, WI: Savage Press.

MacDonald, R. H. (1994). *A broadcast news manual of style* (2nd ed.). New York: Longman.

Public Service Advertising Research Center, www.psaresearch.com

The Pepsi hoax: What went right. (1993). Purchase, NY: The Pepsi-Cola Company.

Trends in television: Television households. (n.d.). Retrieved December 5, 2002 from http://www.tvb.org/rcentral/index. html

Van Nostran, W. J. (1999). *The media writer's guide: Writing for business and educational programming.* Woburn, MA: Focal Press.

CASES

Case 37: The Humane Society's PSA Campaign

The Humane Society of the United States (HSUS) promotes the humane treatment of animals and encourages people to treat all creatures with respect and compassion. As the nation's largest animal protection organization, HSUS provides educational materials and assistance with policy development to thousands of local animal protection groups and shelters across the country. HSUS is known for its campaigns against pet overpopulation and unnecessary animal testing. It offers many programs and resources to educate people about responsible pet ownership.

Ron Smith works as a public relations specialist for the HSUS and recently has been speaking with staff members in the HSUS's eight regional offices about their public relations needs. Each regional office serves a number of states in a specific part of the country. Local shelters and animal protection organizations seeking educational materials, assistance with animal cruelty investigations, or some other support direct their requests first to their respective regional offices. Smith shares feedback received from regional staff with his supervisor, Della Kraus.

"The regional operations are saying that they're getting more requests from local shelters and humane societies for information on animal cruelty," Smith says. "It seems that many of the local communities have seen an increase in cases involving pet owners who have seriously neglected their animals. There are more reports of malicious attacks on animals—cats that have been set on fire by children who said they were playing a practical joke, dogs beaten and left for dead, things like that. The regional offices told me that they would love to have some new materials to help better educate people about animal cruelty, in hopes that more people will report abuse and neglect and discourage others from committing these acts."

"We've been thinking about creating some new public service announcements," Kraus responds. "This might be a subject on which we could focus. There's an interesting tie-in here, too, with the increase in youth violence that we've seen lately. We know that young people who have been involved in violent acts, like school shootings, often have a history of being cruel to animals. On some level, maybe our efforts could contribute positively to a more serious societal problem."

"PSAs are a good idea. From what I've been told, the local media in these areas have covered many of these animal cruelty cases, and in some instances that coverage got residents to rally around this issue and take a stand. We can talk to some stations in those local markets first, but it sounds like there's media interest in this subject. I'll make a few calls, and start working on some possible scripts."

Kraus continues. "While you're here, I wanted to talk to you about another project. Some years ago, we had a radio program called 'Pet Talk.' We produced a series of one-minute radio actualities on a variety of pet-related topics, and then provided them to targeted radio stations, mainly in some of the smaller markets. Many of the stations we targeted aired the spots on a regular basis, and there's been a renewed interest in getting this series up and running again. I'd like to get your thoughts on topics we might cover and on a new, creative name for the series."

Assignments

1. Prepare scripts for the following HSUS public service announcements. At the top of each script, state the goal of the spot and the audience targeted.
   - 20- and 30-second versions of an announcer-only radio PSA on animal cruelty
   - A 30-second produced radio PSA on animal cruelty
   - A 30-second television PSA on animal cruelty
2. In a memo to Kraus, offer suggestions for the radio series. Include goals and target audience(s); a name for the series along with six to eight topics and possible sources who could be interviewed for the spots; and a completed actuality based on one of those topics. The one-minute actuality should include an opening, scripted comments from a knowledgeable source, and a closing.

Case 38: A Packaging Innovation (Part B)

CreamySmooth Ice Cream, Inc. is getting ready to introduce a first-of-its-kind, environmentally friendly container for its ice cream products (see chapter 6, case 22). Stores will begin selling CreamySmooth in the new "Nature-Safe" pint containers on May 1, and the company hopes other ice cream manufacturers will follow its lead and make this packaging the industry standard.

The new packaging has received some attention in trade publications, on the food pages of daily newspapers, and in the business press, thanks to the publicity efforts of Jamaal Morris, CreamySmooth's public relations director. Now, Morris plans to reach a wider consumer audience by using television to promote the new packaging. He talks over his ideas with Holly Lemos, vice president of communications.

"We might be able to set up some interviews on this subject as we get closer to the official launch date, but I also think we could get some mileage out of a video news release," Morris says. "What's your feeling about that?"

"I think a VNR could have potential, and we've got the budget to do it," Lemos says. "I know I don't have to tell you that we've got to be careful about how we position CreamySmooth within this piece. If it's too promotional, they won't use it. Put together a draft of a script. I'd like to see how you'll develop this VNR so that it has news value, but it also gives us some good exposure for the new packaging."

Assignment

Prepare a one-page memo for Lemos that explains and justifies a good news angle for this video news release. Include your thoughts on sources who might provide sound bites for the piece. Then, write and attach to your memo the draft of a 90-second VNR script. Follow the format shown in Exhibit 11.2 with video ideas presented in a left-hand column of the page, and corresponding audio on the right.

Case 39: Promoting Fire Safety

You are the promotions and public service director for a top 40 radio station whose primary listeners are teens and women 18 to 34. In this position, you coordinate promotional activities such as contests and ticket giveaways to help companies extend their advertising dollars. You also recommend and arrange sponsorships of community events to get exposure for the station in the community, and you work closely with nonprofit groups to create and produce public service announcements.

Olivia Nakano, the station manager, has recently become part of a coalition formed in response to the increasing number of deadly house fires in your city in the past year. Many of the fires were set accidentally by children and teens, and fire investigators determined that more lives may have been saved if the homes that caught fire had working smoke detectors. Members of the coalition include corporate executives, civic leaders, the city's fire chief and director of fire prevention and control, and other media representatives. The coalition has developed a strategic plan that emphasizes public education targeted to children and young families. The goal is to make more people aware of how to prevent fires, thus reducing the number of fires and deaths due to fire in the next year.

Following a meeting of the coalition, Nakano returns to the office and asks for a brief meeting with you. "I've told the members of the coalition that our station definitely wants to do its part to promote fire safety in our community. This is an issue that I'd like to see the station getting involved in all year long. We do have an event coming up, though, that deserves some special attention, and that's National Fire Prevention Week. I've promised the members of the coalition that our station would create and air a public service announcement during that week, but I also think we could sponsor some public relations and promotional activities to get our listeners actively involved with fire safety. We could coordinate some of these activities with other groups or media in the area."

"I think with some creative brainstorming, we can come up with some great ideas. Does the coalition have any activities they'd like us to consider?" you ask.

"We do know that some local companies have agreed to donate smoke detectors, and we can get some of those to give away to our listeners," Nakano says. "I'd like us to think about an interesting way to do that. Otherwise, it's up to us to decide. They've asked each of us to go back to our organizations and begin generating promotional ideas for Fire Prevention Week. We also want to have a single theme that connects all the activities that occur during that week. Then, we'll bring our ideas back to the next coalition meeting and try to come up with a coordinated program."

As your meeting ends, Nakano hands you a summary of research findings from a recent National Fire Protection Association survey distributed at the coalition's meeting. She says the coalition thinks the results may provide some direction as they begin planning Fire Prevention Week. Some of the findings include:

- A majority of Americans have misconceptions about fire and a somewhat passive attitude about fire escape planning.
- Nearly 60% of those surveyed believed they had between 2 and 10 minutes to escape from a house fire after the smoke alarm sounds, but in reality, they only have 2 minutes or less; 24% said they thought they had more than 10 minutes to get out of the house.
- A low number of respondents—only 16%—had developed and practiced a home fire escape plan.

Assignments

1. Write a 30-second radio PSA to air during Fire Prevention Week. State the goal and target audience of the PSA at the top of the script.
2. In a memorandum, present your recommendations for radio promotions during Fire Prevention Week. Include the following information:
   - Goals and target audiences of the Fire Prevention Week program, as well as a theme for the week's activities. Briefly explain why you've chosen this theme.
   - Four promotional activities that the radio station could sponsor. One of those activities should involve the smoke detector giveaways as discussed in the case. List each suggested activity; briefly explain the activity, who it targets and what it involves; justify each activity and how it supports the coalition's and the radio station's goals; and estimate any major costs.
   - Conclusion.

Case 40: Nutrition Education on CD-ROM

Consumers today have access to more detailed information about the important role their diet plays in good health. The media regularly reports on the latest scientific research relating to products and their health problems and benefits. Food labels list ingredients, the nutrients those ingredients contain, and the fat content and calories contained within a single serving. But sorting through all the information can be challenging and confusing. One scientific study says that a certain food is unhealthy, while another reports that same food has nutritional value.

As a result, surveys show a gap between consumers' actual nutrient intake and what they know, or think they know, about nutrition. For example, while the National Cancer Institute recommends that adults have 20 to 30 grams of fiber daily, the average intake is closer to 12 grams per day. To help people make more informed dietary and nutrition decisions, Nutritionals, Inc., a subsidiary of a major pharmaceutical company, has developed a CD-ROM-based program called The Virtual Diet Planner. The self-administered, interactive disc program helps consumers personalize nutrition education, assess individual eating habits, and get advice on dietary changes that will lead to better health.

Individuals who use the program begin by completing a 30-minute dietary questionnaire, with questions on more than 100 food items. Audio and video prompts ask users how much of certain foods they eat in a typical month, and about other health and lifestyle factors such as smoking and dining out. Once the questionnaire is completed, the program does a quick personalized analysis and provides a printout of a nutrition profile. The profile shows comparisons between the user's estimated nutrient intake and several national standards, including the Food and Drug Administration's RDAs, or recommended dietary allowances.

This analysis can then be reviewed with a health professional, who can help the individual create a realistic plan consisting of dietary improvements and lifestyle changes. Currently, the program is being used in physicians' offices, in corporate wellness programs, and in public settings such as health fairs and libraries.

An advisory panel of nutrition educators, medical experts, and health professionals guided development of the program, which is one of the first interactive programs of its kind. In addition to the questionnaire and analysis functions, the program has nutrition education sections including one that lets consumers click on different food groups to learn more about their nutritional content.

You work in Nutritionals' corporate and media relations department, and you have been asked by the department's director to come up with a plan to publicize The Virtual Diet Planner using television. In addition to working on a video news release for distribution to local television stations across the United States, you are considering other tactics to get exposure for the product on national television.

Assignments

1. Write the script for a 90-second video news release on The Virtual Diet Planner. Attach to your script suggestions for two minutes of b-roll to accompany the VNR. List and briefly explain the subject of each b-roll segment, and the approximate length of each segment.
2. Work in two-person teams to prepare a three- to four-page memorandum that presents ideas for publicizing The Virtual Diet Planner on national television. Include:
   - Goals and target audiences of the publicity program.
   - Several key strategies, and a few related tactics for each strategy. Specify media/programs you would target. Note any timing considerations.
   - Evaluation methods.
3. Write a one-page pitch letter to the producer of a national television news or talk program on The Virtual Diet Planner.

12

Online Writing and Communications

Spanish sculptor and painter Pablo Picasso did not like computers much, as you can see from this quote: "Computers are useless. They can only give you answers" (Picasso). American politician and statesman Robert McNamara seems to agree with Picasso about the limitations of computers, but hesitates to write off their usefulness altogether: "A computer does not substitute for judgment any more than a pencil substitutes for literacy. But writing without a pencil is no particular advantage" (McNamara).

There is wisdom in both Picasso's and McNamara's remarks. Computers and the Internet are integral to the work you will do as public relations professionals in the 21st century. On any given day, you can probably expect to send e-mail to a reporter or a colleague, access a search engine, update a Web site, or perform some other online function. But computers don't do the thinking for you. They can't write your e-mail message in good form and style, design your online research strategy, or create a new theme for your Web site. Used effectively, and not as a total substitute for the face-to-face contact that builds strong relationships, online and Web-based communications can have tremendous impact and open your organization to audiences like no other medium can.

Writing for the Internet and the World Wide Web requires an approach that is somewhat different from that applied to traditional print media and public relations literature. This chapter discusses those style differences, and gives direction on developing external and internal Web sites that will engage your audiences and best serve your organization's goals. In addition, some focus is given to the techniques you can use to make the Web a useful publicity and media relations tool.

Writing for the Web

Visitors to Web sites tend to scan text rather than read it word-for-word. A study of Web readability conducted by Sun Microsystems revealed that finding, with 79% of respondents saying they only scan the material. What does that mean for the public relations professional writing copy for a Web site? Keep it short—even shorter than most copy you write for other public relations materials—because most Web readers want to absorb information quickly and they won't labor over every word. Plus, reading text on a computer screen is much harder on the eyes and takes longer than reading the same text on paper. Here, then, are some guidelines for Web-based writing:

- Keep your sentences and paragraphs short. It's better to write many short paragraphs than two or three long ones.
- Use headlines and subheads, and write in a direct and conversational tone.
- Break general text categories down into sub-categories. For example, an "About Us" or "Company Profile" section may be divided into smaller sections on company history, financial data, and senior staff biographies. So, instead of trying to cover all background material on one page, the reader can access the main "About Us" page for a brief summary and a list of bulleted sub-categories. They can click on the sub-categories to go to separate pages with more detailed information about those specific aspects of the organization.
- Think about the computer screen when you are writing. Try to write so that the reader can do minimal scrolling down and see most of a page's content on one screen. Some pages may need to be longer, especially if you know that certain visitors are receptive to reading more on one page.

Conceiving and Designing the Web Site

Your Web site should have style and substance—a writing style that suits Web readers as well as content and graphics that will entice people to read and spend some time at your site. Some critical Web site design factors:

- Establish goals for the site. Have company-wide discussions about the site and what its purpose should be. Will it be an information resource, or will it showcase and sell products and services?
- Target specific audiences. Aiming your site at a large, general audience will attract many visitors who may only come to your site once or twice. Focusing on smaller, defined groups will lead to more return visits by a greater number of people in the long run.
- Size up your competition. Do some research and see what your competitors are doing on the Web. Try to make your site different and consider new and interesting ways to present standard information. In addition to listing and describing its product line, Reebok has included profiles on its Web site of athletes who use certain Reebok products and how those products help them perform well in their respective sports.
- Create and register a short, easy-to-remember address. Many sites use the organization's name, one key part of the name, an identifiable abbreviation (e.g., aspca.com for the American Society for the Prevention of Cruelty to Animals site), or a key word that relates to the site's content (e.g., cancer.org for the American Cancer Society's site).

- Prepare a blueprint of the site content. Organize content into broad categories that include useful information for your audiences and make it easy to navigate your site. As noted previously in this chapter, many organizations include an "About Us" section that includes background on the company, its history, and its people. Other practical categories are "Products and Services," a "What's New" section for recent company developments, a "Press Room" for media personnel with news releases and other background materials, and a "Contact Us" area for visitors to e-mail comments.
- Create a strong home page. The *home page* is the first page visitors see when they access your site so it needs to be attention-getting and attractive. Come up with an original theme for your site and highlight that theme on the home page. Include brief text introducing visitors to the site, and display a table of contents that outlines what visitors will find in the site. Many sites have a navigation device called a *toolbar* at the top or left side of the home page. The toolbar includes two- or three-word descriptions of site content. Visitors can click on an item in the toolbar and be taken to that page or section of the site. Exhibit 12.1 shows the home page for Barbie.com and its creative use of a Web site theme

Exhibit 12.1   Home page: Barbie.com

Note. Courtesy of Mattel, Inc.

that is aimed at young girls. Using bright colors and design, the interactive page makes sounds and uses items in the background scenery as navigational buttons. Exhibit 12.2 shows another Web site home page that targets an audience effectively.

- Think carefully about visuals. Barbie.com is an excellent example of a Web site designed with its target public in mind. Not all audiences will appreciate multicolored and complex visuals, however. Not only may they be inappropriate for your target public, but they also may make it longer to download pages. Include text to let visitors know if certain pages take longer to download. The fewer colors you use, the quicker your pages will come up on the screen.

- Be attentive to smart design. Web designer Roger Black, a former art director for Rolling Stone magazine and the New York Times and author of "Web Sites that Work," suggests that information on Web pages should be presented in small sections for easier reading. Use bigger type and only one or two typefaces for a consistent look, and try to avoid setting type in all caps or in reverse. He also says that black, white, and red—with black type on a white background—are good basic colors that will make your site highly readable.

- Assess the site's impact, and update content regularly. Encourage visitors to give you feedback on the site and how it could better serve their needs. Add fresh content and material as often as you can, and look for opportunities to introduce new sections. Someone who visits your site several times and sees the same material from a month or two before might not return soon, if at all.

Promoting Your Web Site

You want to create a Web site that people will visit, revisit and talk about, and it's logical that you would spend much of your time on content, writing, and graphics. Don't overlook promotion, however, or just assume that people will find your site. Prepare a plan that outlines how you will proactively make target publics aware of your site and what it has to offer.

The simplest way to make your Web site known is to include your **URL** (Uniform Resource Locator, a fancy name for your Web site address) in all publicity and promotional materials such as news releases, brochures, newsletters, advertising, product packaging, company letterhead and business cards. There are a number of inexpensive ways to create visibility for your site using the Internet, as well:

- Register your site with popular search engines. Go to the search engine's home page and fill out the requested information, which includes a brief description of your site and selected search keywords. While some search engines offer free registration, others may charge a fee.

- Use a Web site announcement service such as Submit-It or Web-Promote. For a low fee, these services will register your site for you with major search engines, online directories, and yellow pages.

Exhibit 12.2   Home page: Pro Football Hall of Fame

Welcome to the Pro Football Hall of Fame

Class of 2003
By the numbers

Wide receiver **James Lofton** wore **#80** for most of his career. That included his nine seasons with the Packers. He kept the number when he moved onto Los Angeles and played two years with the Raiders. In 1989, he signed on with Buffalo. During his first season with the Bills, he donned #86 before going back to his familiar #80 the following season.

Then, in 1993, he wore #22 during his one game with the Los Angeles Rams and #80 again during his nine games with the Philadelphia Eagles that year.

Four other members of the Hall of Fame also wore #80 on their jerseys: Tom Fears, Len Ford, Steve Largent, and Kellen Winslow.

▸ James Lofton career capsule

Renovation in full swing
New gallery to open in summer

Construction of the dynamic $1.677 million dollar redesigned exhibit area is under way.

The new enshrinement gallery will feature interactive kiosks that will bring each Hall of Fame member to life.

View of the construction on Wednesday March 5th.

The bronze busts, a mainstay of the Hall of Fame since its opening 40 years ago, will be presented in a most elegant fashion. More>>>

Visit the Hall
Hall of Famers
Pro Football History
Enshrinement/ Hall of Fame Game
Selection Process
Store
Search
>SUBMIT

Update Signup
Sign up now for the latest news and features on the Pro Football Hall of Fame.
○ plain text version
● rich format (html)
>SUBMIT

Museum Store

Original Autographed Hall of Famer footballs
•••••
Give the football fan in your life a ticket to the HOF!

TRIVIA QUESTION
Which Hall of Famer was elected to a record 14 straight Pro Bowls?

○ Ken Houston
○ Ronnie Lott
○ Gino Marchetti
○ Merlin Olsen
○ Walter Payton

Vote

54 Voters
View Results

Note. ©Pro Football Hall of Fame.

- Arrange for other relevant and high-traffic sites to offer free links to your site. You can do this by talking directly with people who manage those sites or by enlisting a service.

- Include the Web site address with your signature on e-mail correspondence. Set it up so people can click on the address and automatically go to your site.

- Create exposure for your site in newsgroups and chat forums. Closely monitor newsgroups and chat rooms for a period of time to make sure they are appropriate, and then look for opportunities to work subtle mentions of your site into related discussions.

Intranets

Whereas the Internet connects the vast area known as cyberspace, intranets work within an organization. Described as an organization's private Web site for employees, intranets provide electronic access to all kinds of information, from corporate bios and company policies to news articles and sales reports. Intranets are designed with electronic devices called firewalls that limit access to employees only. Many companies say that intranets more fully empower employees and increase productivity by providing fast and easy access to information they need to take initiative and do their jobs more effectively. They are especially helpful in facilitating the flow of information within organizations that have more than one geographical location or have employees working off-site.

Internal Web sites can reduce day-to-day operating costs and save companies money, too. Ford Motor Company's intranet has made it possible for project managers from around the country to "meet" and discuss projects online, which has eliminated the need for frequent in-person meetings and reduced corporate travel expenses. Putting the company's policy guidelines online has saved Federal Express almost $120,000 in annual printing costs.

Intranet experts and administrators point to several factors that contribute to good intranet design. These include getting management support at the start of the process and maintaining that support; defining what you want your intranet to accomplish; testing a pilot site to get employee feedback before launching the official site; and making employees aware of the site before its launch and training them on its use. The Q & A at the end of this chapter focuses on the award-winning Ketchum Global Network, the steps involved in creating that site, and the positive impact it has had on Ketchum's internal communications and corporate culture.

Online Media Relations

When you are creating internal and external Web sites, you must consider your publics' information needs and interests. Many organizations create a special area within their site that includes news releases and other content of primary interest to the media. An increasing number of journalists are going online to do research and get story ideas, and public relations professionals are using online techniques more frequently to deliver news and pitch ideas to editors and reporters. How can you make your Web site and online communications "media friendly"?

- Set up your home page with a "Media Information" or "Press Room" button within the toolbar or menu that links media contacts quickly to press materials.

- Give them more than just news releases. Offer other Web site content such as biographies of your executives that highlight their special knowledge and expertise, company and product backgrounders, industry data, and links to industry and related sites. Include artwork that reporters can easily download such as company logos, product shots, and photos of your CEO and senior staff.

- Add an interactive component. Include a form that media contacts can fill out to request an interview with an expert from your organization on a specific topic.

References and Suggested Reading

Black, R. (1997). *Web sites that work*. Berkeley, CA: Adobe Press.

Clark, J. L. & Clark, L. R. (2001). *Cyberstyle: The writer's complete desk reference.* Cincinatti, OH: South-Western College Publishers.

Holtz, S. (2002). *Public relations on the net* (2nd ed.). New York: AMACOM.

Levine, M. & Gendron, G. (2001). *Guerilla PR wired: Waging a successful publicity campaign on-line, offline, and everywhere in between.* New York: McGraw Hill.

McDonnell, S. (1998). *The everything internet book*. Holbrook, MA: Adams Media Corp.

McNamara, R. (n.d.). In *Quotez* (computers). Retrieved December 6, 2002 from http://www.geocities.com/Athens/Oracle/6517/computer.html.

Middleberg, D. (2000). *Winning PR in the wired world: Powerful campaign strategies for the noisy digital space.* New York: McGraw-Hill.

Nielsen, J. (1997). How users read on the Web. Retrieved March 30, 2002 from http://www.useit.com/alertbox/9710a.html

Picasso, Pablo. (n.d.). Pablo Picasso. In *Computers quotations*. Retrieved December 6, 2002 from http://www.wisdomquotes.com/cat_computers.html

Shiva, V. A. (1997). *The internet publicity guide*. New York: Allworth Press.

Web content report. Chicago, IL: Lawrence Ragan Communications, Inc.

Witmer, D. F. (1999). *Spinning the web: A handbook for public relations on the Internet*. New York: Addison Wesley, 1999.

CASES

Case 41: Winery Creates a Web Site

Named for an old steamboat landing, Harvest Landing has become one of the premier wineries in its region. Many of Harvest Landing's wines win top awards and medals in national and international wine competitions held each year. The winery's uniquely designed main building, where visitors can take part in wine tastings and tours, has been honored by The American Institute of Architects as "one of the most notable buildings" constructed in that state in the 20th century.

Much of Harvest Landing's success as a first-class winery is attributed to location and tradition. Grapes are grown on land with superior soil content that has been recognized since the 1800s as ideal for grape cultivation. The vineyards are positioned on gently sloping hills, close to the deep waters of Romulus Lake and exposed to ample sunlight. Harvest Landing's owner, Cole Meaney, comes from a family of grape growers and has spent most of his life working with grapes.

One method the winery uses to build customer loyalty and establish on-going sales is the Harvest Landing Wine Club. Wine club members sign up to receive automatic shipments of two bottles of specially selected wine four times during the year, and they are given exclusive notice about opportunities to purchase limited release wines. They also get special discounts on Harvest Landing promotional items, such as tote bags and wine accessories, and on the purchase of wine by the case. Wine Club members don't pay fees; the club is strictly a promotional strategy designed to provide additional incentives and convenience to Harvest Landing customers. In addition, the winery attracts visitors to its site by sponsoring several holiday and seasonal events, including a "Chocolate and Wine Lovers Weekend" in February, during which visitors sample chocolate delights paired with Harvest's fine red wines.

You are called to a meeting with Meaney to talk about setting up a Web site for the winery. Your agency assists with the production of the winery's quarterly newsletter and with publicity efforts. "We need to have a presence on the Web," Meaney says. "Our most recent marketing studies tell us that our typical customers are professional men and women, 30 to 45, college educated, with higher-than-average incomes. They like to entertain in their homes and they frequently dine out, and many have families as well as busy work and social schedules. We also know that a large percentage of our customers own home computers and use e-mail and the Internet almost every day. It stands to reason, then, that we could be making better use of technology to communicate with them, as well as with potential customers."

"Do you see this site being more marketing- and product-focused, or should it be more of a public relations tool?" you ask.

"I think it should do both," Meaney responds. "I definitely like the idea of making it possible for people to order our wine online. Having a Web site makes it possible to introduce our wines to more people across the country and the world, which can open up some new markets for us and do it cost effectively. But I'd really like to see the site be something more than just a big fact sheet about us. We need to include that kind of material, but I'd also like the site to give people information that makes their lives outside of work richer and more satisfying. Maybe even a little easier. Our wine club members tell us they enjoy reading those kinds of articles in the newsletter, and we could be doing much more of the same on a Web site."

Assignment

Working alone or with a partner, prepare a memorandum for Meaney that presents your ideas for the Harvest Landing Web site. Include:

- Goals and target audiences of the site.
- Recommended content areas. Identify each by a few words or a short phrase, and describe the information that would be included in that section. Justify your content ideas.
- Specific thoughts on the site's home page. Write one brief paragraph of introductory copy, and suggest other content and visuals that should appear on the home page.

Case 42: Primo Pizza Advocates Safer Driving (Part B)

You are the director of public affairs and community relations for Primo Pizza, a chain of more than 50 pizza shops in your state. Anthony Roe, the president of Primo Pizza, has asked you to create and implement a public relations campaign to generate support for a new driver licensing bill, which would change the system for granting full driving privileges to young drivers in that state (see chapter 8, case 30). Primo has aligned itself with this issue because many of its employees are younger drivers who deliver pizzas, and it wants communities to see that the company is committed to the safety of those drivers and the local residents it serves.

One day, after assessing the company's current Web site, you approach Roe with an idea. "Right now, our Web site is pretty basic. It has some sections on the company, its history, and our employees, and it includes our annual report and a section for company news where we post our news releases. But I was thinking, wouldn't it make sense to use the site to tie in with the safe driving campaign? The site has the potential to reach the people we want to reach with our safe driving messages, younger people and their parents, and many of these people are Primo customers."

"Are you suggesting we totally redesign the site, or that we just add some content and a few new pages?" Roe asks.

"For now, I think we could create one new section that focuses on the legislation but also on driving and driver safety issues. We'll add a button to the home page that our Web site visitors can click on. We'll call it "Primo and Driver Safety," or something like that. When visitors get to that first page of the new section, they'll read a few short introductory paragraphs and they'll see several sub-categories they can link to within our site that provide more detailed information on the subject and on driving safety in general. Each of those sub-sections could be a page or so long."

"Could we include some information in this new section that would interest our primary customers, men 25 to 40? This is the audience that accesses our Web site most often, as well," Roe says.

"Sure, that would be a sensible thing for us to do," you add. "I also think we should consider links to related sites on driver safety, and include those on our site, if people want to learn more. We could ask those sites to add Primo's site as a link, too. I'll organize my thoughts and get back to you in about a week or so with my specific suggestions and some proposed copy for the site."

Assignments

1. Prepare a memorandum for Roe that includes the following information:
   - Goals of the "Primo and Driver Safety" Web site section.
   - Descriptions of the content you would include in this new driver safety section, including the first page of the section and all other linked pages within the site. Each linked page should be identified by a few words or a short phrase that summarizes the content on that page.
   - Recommendations for links to 10 other Web sites on driving and driver safety.

2. Write copy, and suggest appropriate visuals, for two pages of the "Primo and Driver Safety" Web site section:
   - The first page, which introduces visitors to the section and summarizes the content that follows.
   - Another linked page that provides information on driving and driver safety that would interest men 25 to 40, Primo's primary customers.

Case 43: Inner Peace Urbanwear Goes Interactive

A few years ago, high school seniors and former graffiti artists Khalil Grant and David Christian raised $300 and began designing their first line of T-shirts, which they sold in the lunchroom of their New York City high school. The shirts were created out of concern for the increased racial tension and violence in their schools and inner-city neighborhoods; the T-shirts helped them express those concerns and send a message promoting greater harmony among culturally diverse people.

The shirts are designed in the style of graffiti art and carry the "Inner Peace" logotype. Soon after the initial success of the shirts, local retailers took an interest in the clothing, and Grant and Christian expanded their Inner Peace line to include sweatshirts and caps. A year later, they made it official and established Inner Peace Inc.

Recently, Grant and Christian signed a deal to sell their clothing in two major retail stores. To further support the company's growth, they established a partnership with StyleZone International, a Los Angeles-based sportswear manufacturer. StyleZone will manage the financial aspects of the business and handle administrative functions such as manufacturing and shipping, which will allow Grant and Christian more time to focus on clothing designs and marketing. The company is now poised to become a major player in the urban wear industry and will soon be adding jeans and sweat outfits to its product line.

You have been hired by Inner Peace to help create the company's first Web site. In a meeting with Grant and Christian, you learn that the company's primary target audience is African American and Latino men in the 15- to 29-year-old age range, although their clothing is building a following among men and women of all races and ages.

"We know a little something about Web design, and David and I have some ideas for visuals and the graphic look of the site," Grant says. "We'd like you to focus on the structure and content of the site. What kind of information should we include and why? The theme of our clothing should come across in the site somehow, and I'd really like us to have a Web site that stands out from the others in our industry."

Assignments

1. Working alone or with a partner, prepare a five-page memorandum for Grant and Christian that includes your recommendations for the structure and content of the Inner Peace Web site. Include:

   - An introduction that states the goals of the site and identifies a theme/strategy that will help distinguish the Inner Peace site from competitors' sites.
   - A proposed structure for the site. Offer suggestions for the home page and its content, along with links to other pages or sections within the site

and why those pages should be included. In one or two paragraphs, summarize the content of each page or section of the site.

- Five specific ideas for promoting the new site to Inner Peace's primary audience to make them aware of the site and encourage site visits.
- Evaluation methods to measure the site's effectiveness.

2. Assume that you are ready to introduce the new Web site. Write a news release announcing the launch of the site for distribution to key consumer magazines and specialized media that reach African American and Latino men ages 15 to 29. Attach a media list to your news release.

Case 44: Building Traffic to homesweethome.com

Your agency has been hired by homesweethome.com, a new Web site where individuals can do one-stop, online shopping for the home. It is the latest in a small but growing number of e-commerce sites focused on the home products and services market, which in 1999 was a $200 billion industry. Visitors to the site can purchase quality furniture and accessories from leading manufacturers, and get information and advice to help them design and decorate every room of their home. The top management team of homesweethome.com has decades of experience in the home products, retailing, and merchandising fields; the president of homesweethome.com founded the business after many years as the chief executive officer of a national chain of retail home stores.

In addition to corporate and media information, the site has four major components:

- A gallery where visitors can view a wide selection of home products for the bedroom, dining room, living room, kitchen, bathroom, and home office. This includes everything from furniture and rugs to wallpaper and other accessories. Any of the products shown can be ordered online.
- An interactive area where people can design a room on their computer screens. Unique imaging technology allows customers to pick the size of the room, add and change furniture, and select different colors and fabrics until they've created a room that suits their preferred style and tastes.
- An online magazine with how-to articles on decorating and design, regular columns written by design experts, and other pieces relating to trends in home design and furnishings. The e-zine also runs feature stories on a variety of topics such as decorating your first apartment, selecting the best kitchen countertops, and mastering the art of decorative home interior painting.
- A "Gifts for Every Occasion" section that offers innovative and affordable ideas for birthday, anniversary, and holiday gifts.

At the first meeting, your client gives you more background information on the company, takes you on a virtual tour of the site, and gives you details of the soon-to-be-launched homesweethome.com national advertising campaign. The company wants your agency to come up with publicity and promotional strategies that will complement the print and television advertising; help create greater awareness of and encourage visits to the site; and position homesweethome.com as the ultimate online store and resource for home products, services, and design advice.

Assignment

Working with a partner, design a publicity and promotional plan for homesweethome.com that includes the following elements:

- Introduction/Situation Analysis.
- Goals and target audiences.
- Publicity strategies and related tactics. Be specific about media that should be targeted. Recommend and justify any other promotional activities that would effectively target your audiences. Note timing and budget considerations; estimate any major costs that would be incurred.
- Evaluation methods.

Tips from the Top

"Developing the Ketchum Global Network"
John R. Kessling

As director of knowledge strategies, John Kessling worked with Ketchum clients and account teams to develop knowledge-based services and capabilities and is now an independent consultant helping organizations apply communications and technology to achieve their business objectives. He served on a four-person Ketchum team charged with developing the agency's first intranet, called the Ketchum Global Network. The site played a vital role in helping the growing number of worldwide Ketchum employees stay connected, and it received awards and national recognition for its innovation and excellence. Ketchum has since upgraded it to an interactive portal providing additional capabilities such as a document repository and collaborative work environments.

Q: Why did Ketchum develop the Ketchum Global Network (KGN)?

A: Ketchum's mission—the foundation of its business strategy—is to deliver extraordinary value to its clients by developing smart, creative communications solutions to their most pressing business challenges. Ketchum accomplishes this by bringing together the best resources—the most qualified people—from throughout the organization to work on client problems. This "Best Teams" approach requires a culture or environment in which people freely collaborate and share ideas.

It became more complex as the company grew and added new offices around the world. Part of the solution was to create vehicles that make it easier to share information across a broad network of offices. The intranet is one of those vehicles.

Q: Who was on the intranet planning team, and why was each person selected?

A: The development team included myself; Katie Jennings, a corporate communications coordinator; Pete Donina, a specialist in Ketchum's Information Technology Group; and Dan Madia, a senior partner and the firm's chief administrative officer.

I had been with the agency for 10 years, worked with a variety of account teams, and had relationships with people who we would need to help develop specific areas of the site and provide content. Katie worked in internal communications, helped maintain agency information, and was knowledgeable of Web-based communications. Pete had deep experience in Web-based technology, and his role was to see that the intranet would be sophisticated, accessible, reliable, and easy to use. Dan, as a member of the company's leadership team, ensured that the intranet continued to have the support of senior-most management.

Q: What research did the team do at the start of the process?

A: Corporate intranets were new at the time (December 1996) and there was precious little published information to help guide us. Our first step was to invite representatives of each Ketchum office to meet in an all-day strategy development session to help determine overall objectives for an intranet. We were able to tap the experience of Crescent Communications, a high technology and Internet communications firm that Ketchum had recently acquired. Crescent's staff brought us a lot of know-how and helped us develop a good [intranet]organizational structure. We also scheduled meetings with Ketchum's executive committee at key points along the way to keep its members apprised of our progress, get feedback, and build their interest.

Q: Briefly, what were the main objectives of the Ketchum Global Network?

A: To support the development and implementation of Ketchum's Best Teams strategy, foster collaboration and coordination among account teams and service areas, enhance the flow and quality of information, facilitate Ketchum's corporate communications, enhance professional and consultative skills among Ketchum's staff, and improve business processes and procedures. Another important objective was to help maintain the culture of the agency during a time of rapid growth and increasing geographic diversity.

Q: Give me a general idea of the site's content and layout.

A: The home page changed every day to highlight company news, new content, and announcements. Major areas included "At Headquarters" where agency information is housed including staff biographies, office listings, and client case histories. There was an area for local offices to put up their own sites. "Practices in Focus" provided each global practice a place to maintain its own site.

A similar area contained sections for major services such as media relations, crisis management, and research and measurement. Another major area, Human Resources, housed information on employee benefits and policies, evaluation forms and job listings.

A popular area of KGN was called "Channel Z," which contained links to external Web sites that have helpful information for people to better organize their lives. We developed Channel Z to help people cope and cut down on time they may spend surfing the Web for personal information. In one place they can find useful information on personal health, finances, and even entertainment.

Q: Who writes the content, and how often is it updated?

A: You could say that everyone in the company writes the content. KGN was designed so that many people write content for their specializations. For example, global practice leaders are responsible for their own areas and rely on members of their practices to prepare summaries of client projects and information about their services and specialties. Ketchum professionals are responsible for writing their own biographies and submitting updates when needed.

KGN had no Webmaster. Instead, the site was maintained on a daily basis by a managing editor responsible for working with practices, services and local offices to keep their respective areas current. She also received and edited contributions from local offices. At first, the managing editor had to serve as a reporter and seek out stories. Over time, the vast majority was e-mailed to her by others.

Q: How was KGN received by employees, and how did you measure its impact?

A: Since its debut, usage of KGN increased steadily. We used tracking software to prepare weekly usage reports. Almost three quarters of the company's employees now visited the home page on a daily basis. We also conducted an in-depth user survey annually to collect more detailed feedback about usage habits and general attitudes about KGN. This was professionally administered by Ketchum's research and measurement department. A survey conducted after the site had been up for nine months indicated that an overwhelming majority thought KGN was an important way to stay informed about the agency and a good forum for employees to share their expertise.

Another important form of measurement is individual feedback. The address editor@ketchum.com was established, and highlighted all over the site. More than a dozen e-mails are received each week and all receive a response within hours or at the outside, within a business day. Additionally, an important indication that KGN helped us maintain our collaborative culture was the finding that more than eight in 10 professionals had visited local office sites other than their own.

Q: If someone asked for your advice on developing an intranet, what words of wisdom—and words of caution—would you offer?

A: Senior management must commit to using the intranet as an important communications vehicle. Usage will increase if employees understand that the intranet is the way they'll stay abreast of company developments and if they hear it straight from the top.

Also, treat the intranet as a journalistic vehicle. You'll build repeat visits by placing emphasis on company news and announcements and changing them frequently. Internal marketing is also important. Consider releasing major new content areas several times a year. The intranet also should be well integrated into employee orientation.

Companies need to be realistic about "ratings." Tracking software can be used to measure visits, but often there are no benchmarks to go by. For example, how many times did employees look up internal telephone numbers before the intranet? What's more, measuring hits doesn't necessarily provide context about how much an intranet is valued as a resource.

Q: Anything else you would want people to know about developing an effective intranet?

A: An intranet needs to mirror the company's culture. If knowledge sharing is readily practiced, the company may be able to rely on a voluntary spirit to maintain the intranet's vibrancy. If there is a lot of internal competition, the company may require a larger central staff and incentives to encourage [content] contributions.

Finally, companies should remember that intranets are only one way to collaborate. They should not be used as a substitute for other important ways employees meet and exchange information—from informal hallway conversations to company meetings.

13

Events

Bruce Springsteen, Harry Connick Jr. and even Rosie O'Donnell, like many popular singers and entertainers, have performed the Christmas song "Santa Claus is Coming to Town." Like the song says, Santa is "making a list and checking it twice," and efficient event planners need to do the same.

Public relations professionals who plan events (that's most of them at some point in their careers) are aware of the need for detailed checklists. They also know that when organizing events, you should have a disciplined planning team, ample time and resources to do the event well, the ability to think quickly on your feet, and backup plans since something is bound to go wrong.

This chapter focuses on events that public relations people arrange and coordinate, from news conferences and media parties to major special events that celebrate history, enhance a company's image, and advance marketing goals. You will also get more information on the critical factors that planners need to consider before, during and after events, as well as suggestions for publicizing events to maximize your media exposure.

News Conferences

News conferences are held to make news announcements that have great impact on a community or an industry, or that have significant public interest. A company planning a major expansion might hold news conferences in its hometown and in expansion cities to announce this development and talk about its positive effect on the job market. When Viacom Inc., owner of the MTV and Nickelodeon cable stations, acquired its former owner, CBS, the CEOs of Viacom and CBS took part in a news conference to discuss the merger. A university hosting the appearance of an important person, such as a top government official or an entertainment figure, can arrange a news conference to give the media in the area a chance to ask questions directly of the well-known visitor.

Unfortunately, there are no strict rules or formulas to follow when deciding if a news conference is appropriate. There are some considerations, however, that provide a good rationale for your decision:

- Is this a major, immediate story that has widespread importance?
- Will the media want to hear directly from our CEO and other senior officials, and ask them questions about this development?

- Will reporters be allowed to ask questions or will only a statement be made?
- Does our announcement present many possible story angles, and will the reporter who attends have a chance to discuss some of these angles and, therefore, develop an individualized story?
- Are visuals or demonstrations central to our news announcement?

If your answer to these questions is "yes," then holding a news conference that media contacts will come to is a pretty good bet. But if reporters show up at your news conference and walk away saying, "That was a waste of time, why didn't they just e-mail or fax me a news release?", it may be impossible to ever get them back to another media event.

Press Parties and Media Tours

Public relations professionals also organize press parties and media tours. Press parties use a more informal, party-like atmosphere to generate publicity and to build relationships with key reporters and editors. Media parties are common in the entertainment industry. Motion picture previews, held a day or two before the first public screening, are followed by a lavish party featuring cocktails, hors d'oeuvres or a dinner. Media attending the party can interview the film's actors and other invited celebrity guests, which gives them time to prepare timely stories about the film that can be published or aired the day the movie opens. Press parties are often done in combination with news conferences when an organization opens a new facility or launches a new product.

Media tours take your executives on the road to meet one-on-one with reporters and editors in their offices to discuss company developments and story ideas. These are often well received by trade media and smaller publications that have an interest in your organization, but that lack the travel funds to attend your media events. In addition, media tours help build relationships and personalize your organization's news to key reporters and editors. Media contacts become more familiar with sources important to their beats, and executives become more comfortable with media contacts who may interview them in the future.

Planning Media Events

Each news conference and press party you plan has several common elements that are critical to its success: location; timing; budget; invitations; program; media kit; and follow-up activities.

First, select an appropriate *location* for the event. The nature of the event may dictate the site you choose. Your organization's main offices are one possibility for news conferences, parties and briefings, but many media events are scheduled at hotels and conference centers that have ample facilities with which the media is familiar and can get to easily. Those facilities book events months to a year in advance, so have some alternate sites in mind if your first choice is unavailable.

In addition, the nature of the event can present logical and, in some cases, more creative location possibilities. If you are planning a media event around the grand opening of a store or some other building, it makes sense to hold the event at the site so reporters can see the new facility. The organizers of a winter festival in a Northeast city held a kick-off news conference at a local ice packing factory to attract media interest. Sun America, a Los Angeles financial services firm, launched a campaign to boost its name recognition and target Baby Boomers with advice about saving money and planning for retirement. The company held a kick-off media party at the Museum of Television and Radio in Beverly Hills. The location tied into the campaign strategy—using former child stars from television programs that Boomers grew up watching—to teach Boomers how to save money. The stars spoke with reporters about how they squandered their fortunes and what they learned about financial management from their experiences.

As with most publicity activities, good *timing* will help boost turnout at your media event. If your news announcement relates to a major, breaking story, your goal is to arrange the news conference as quickly as possible. In other situations, such as a media event to introduce a new product, do some research first to find out if other events are planned that may draw media attention away from your event. Consult the chamber of commerce in the area where your event will take place and access city Web sites to get information about scheduled events. The best day of the week and time of day for a media event really depends on the media you most want to attend your event and what their deadlines are. A mid-to-late morning news conference, for example, gives TV crews adequate time to prepare their stories for evening newscasts. Many public relations professionals say that midweek and even Sundays can be good days for media events, but again, let your media's needs drive the selection of the best day and time.

When planning the *budget*, there are obvious costs to consider. Hotels, conference centers, and other non-company-owned facilities may charge room rental fees. There will also be expenses for food and drink and the use and set-up of audio-visual equipment supplied by the site. Don't forget to factor in tax and gratuities to your food costs. You may need to cover travel costs for non-company experts who agree to speak at your event, not to mention airline and other travel expenses for company personnel, if the event is held in a location away from the organization's main headquarters city.

You may also need to budget for printed *invitations*. Invitations to your media event can take many forms. When your event focuses on important hard news, a one-page media alert, such as the one in Exhibit 13.1, will suffice. But for other events, such as media parties, you may want to make the invitation more formal or creative to capture the media's interest. All invitations, regardless of form and format, should be individually addressed and include the date, time, and location of the event, and a brief explanation of the event and its news value. Include the names of dignitaries and other top officials who will be available to answer questions, and let the media know how long the event is expected to last so they can plan their day accordingly.

The media event *program* is the itinerary that outlines who will speak and in what order, what each person will say and how long each person will talk, and any other activities. The program for a basic news conference or briefing can be simple: a brief welcome and introduction by a company official (sometimes this is a public relations person), followed by prepared statements from a designated spokesperson and a question-and-answer period with reporters. Media parties are usually less rigid in their

Exhibit 13.1   Event Media Alert: Albright-Knox Art Gallery

ALBRIGHT**KNOX**
ART GALLERY

1285 Elmwood Avenue   Tel 716.882.8700
Buffalo, New York   Fax 716.882.1958
14222-1096   www.albrightknox.org

News Advisory

Media Preview for Resplendent Installation of _Modigliani & the Artists of Montparnasse_ Set for Friday at Albright-Knox Art Gallery

Works from Top Museums Worldwide, Including London and Paris, Highlight Landmark Modigliani Exhibition, First in U.S. in 40 Years

Exhibition Organized by the Albright-Knox is Already Garnering International and National Media Attention

WHAT: **Media Preview and Briefing** for the international banner exhibition _Modigliani & the Artists of Montparnasse_. The briefing will include interview opportunities and a first look at the resplendent installation of the exhibition completed this week.

The exhibition showcases the works of Italian master Amedeo Modigliani and his contemporaries, such as Matisse and Picasso, who helped spawn the birth of modern art while working in the Montparnasse section of Paris in the early 20th century. The Albright-Knox and curator Kenneth Wayne organized the exhibition, gathering masterpieces from some of the world's top museums and the Gallery's own distinguished collection. The exhibition has its world premiere at the Gallery in Buffalo October 22 to January 12 before traveling to prestigious museums in Fort Worth and Los Angeles in 2003.

The exhibition is garnering international media attention, with preview articles by The Associated Press, in _The Wall Street Journal, Harper's Bazaar, Town & Country, Vogue, The Art Newspaper, Miami Herald, Detroit Free Press, and_ Canada's national newspaper, _The Globe and Mail,_ which called it one of the top 12 art exhibitions in the world this fall. _The Washington Post, Boston Globe, ARTnews, and The Burlington Magazine_ of London are among the media planning reviews.

WHERE: The Albright-Knox Art Gallery, 1285 Elmwood Ave., just off of Route 198 near Olmsted's Delaware Park in Buffalo's Museum District.

WHEN: **10 a.m. to Noon (Briefing at 10:30 a.m.), Friday, October 18, 2002**

WHO: Albright-Knox Art Gallery Director Douglas G. Schultz will be joined by Curator Kenneth Wayne. The exhibition is made possible in Buffalo through the generous support of M&T Bank.

CONTACT: Cheryl Orlick, Gallery Public Information Officer, 270-8204.

■

Note: Reprinted with permission from Albright-Knox Art Gallery, Buffalo, NY.

program approach, although time should be set aside for someone from the sponsoring organization to make remarks, and provisions should be made for the media to conduct group or one-on-one interviews. Refreshments should be available at all media events. Coffee, pastries, and bagels are often served at morning news conferences, while elaborate media parties require more extensive catering.

When reporters arrive at a media event, especially news conferences, give them some background material that will help them better understand the subject and write their stories. This material can be as simple as a news release, or it can be organized into a larger packet of information known as a *media kit.* Prior to the start of a news conference, a busy reporter who had little time to prepare for your event can look through the media kit and get a quick overview of the subject and formulate some questions for your spokespeople. The media kit also allows you to make sure media contacts receive your key messages in writing. Facts, statistics, and historical data included in the media kit prove valuable to reporters who may have to return to their offices and file their stories under pressing deadlines. Among the standard elements of a media kit:

- A general news release summarizing the main news announcement. The Albright-Knox Art Gallery news release in Exhibit 13.2 illustrates how a good lead creates excitement and introduces the body of the release, which sets the stage for the event.
- Backgrounders and fact sheets that further explain the subject and offer more information on the organization sponsoring the event.
- Sidebars and features that focus on specific newsworthy aspects of the subject in more detail; sidebars can give reporters ideas for possible story angles.
- Biographical sketches and head shots of key company personnel who participated in the media event.
- Visual aids such as architectural designs, maps, charts and graphs, and photographs.

At the conclusion of your media event, there are several *follow-up activities* that bring closure to the event and help you measure its success. These include:

- Getting back to reporters who had questions that require more complete answers. It is important to brief your spokespeople before the event and anticipate questions, but there are going to be times when a question pops up for which you aren't totally prepared. Right after the event, get the answer and call the reporter back as soon as you can.
- Making follow-up calls to media contacts who didn't attend, and delivering or sending media materials by fax or e-mail at their request. You can also include those materials on your Web site, and refer media contacts to that site.
- Paying site and catering fees and taking care of any other expenses.
- Tracking media coverage. For local media events, make sure someone from your staff is assigned to collect newspaper clippings and tape broadcast stories.

Exhibit 13.2   Event News Release: Albright-Knox Art Gallery

	1285 Elmwood Avenue	Tel 716.882.8700
	Buffalo, New York	Fax 716.882.1958
	14222-1096	www.albrightknox.org

NEWS RELEASE

FOR RELEASE: Upon Receipt
October 18, 2002

CONTACT: Cheryl Orlick
Public Information Officer
716.270.8204
corlick@albrightknox.org

THE ART OF AMEDEO MODIGLIANI, RENOWNED ARTIST OF THE EARLY 20TH CENTURY, OPENS AT ALBRIGHT-KNOX ART GALLERY OCTOBER 22

BUFFALO, N.Y. – The Albright-Knox Art Gallery will present a major international exhibition of works by Italian master Amedeo Modigliani, who helped spawn the modern art movement in early 20th century Paris. The exhibition will premiere in Buffalo on October 22, 2002 and be on view through January 12, 2003. For additional information visit www.WhoIsModi.com.

Modigliani & the Artists of Montparnasse—the first major Modigliani exhibition in the United States in 40 years—will feature approximately 60 paintings, sculptures, and works on paper by Modigliani, as well as 22 works by his contemporaries from the Montparnasse section of Paris, artists such as Matisse, Picasso, Brancusi, and Soutine.

Organized by the Albright-Knox, a leading international center of modern and contemporary art, the exhibition will include masterpieces from renowned museums and private collections in America, Europe, and Japan. Many of the works have never been seen in the United States.

In addition to the Albright-Knox, the lenders include Solomon R. Guggenheim Museum of Art, New York; The Art Institute of Chicago; Hirshhorn Museum and Sculpture Garden, Smithsonian Institution, Washington, D.C.; Los Angeles County Museum of Art; The Metropolitan Museum of Art, New York; Art Gallery of Ontario, Toronto; Centre Georges Pompidou, Paris; Musée Picasso, Paris; and Tate Modern, London.

-more-

(continued)

-2-

Modigliani (1884-1920) was born into a Jewish family in the cosmopolitan port town of Livorno, Italy, near Pisa. He moved to Paris in 1906 and became a central figure of the Parisian avant-garde. Modigliani was part of the first real international group of artists, a group that forever changed the art world by using non-Western influences such as African art in modernizing traditional subjects. Their works paved the way for the next generation of modern artists. The exhibition will show how Modigliani's art and life epitomize the diverse, multi-cultural artistic approach that developed in Montparnasse, a bohemian Paris neighborhood at the beginning of the twentieth century.

A master portraitist and sculptor, Modigliani is widely considered one of the great modern European artists. He is known for his elongated and sensuous portraits of women, including many exquisite female nudes. He exhibited with Picasso at least eight times and was often the "headliner" of their exhibitions. Modigliani accomplished much despite personal struggles and a tragically short life, dying of tuberculosis at age 35.

Modigliani's inspiration came from a variety of western and nonwestern sources, including African and Oceanic art, symbolism, fauvism, and cubism, among many others. He also made a major contribution to modern sculpture, producing carved stone heads that were influenced by African masks, Egyptian art, medieval sculpture, and Michelangelo. Several of these sculptures are included in the exhibition.

The exhibition will allow the Albright-Knox to feature several works from its distinguished collection of modern art, including Modigliani's *Servant Girl*, 1918; Marc Chagall's dream-like *Peasant Life*, 1925; Robert Delaunay's dynamic *Sun, Tower, Airplane* from 1913; and *Woman's Head*, 1909, a boldly-modeled sculpture by Pablo Picasso.

Following the premiere in Buffalo, ***Modigliani & the Artists of Montparnasse*** will be presented at two prestigious museums: the Kimbell Art Museum, Fort Worth, Texas, February 9 - May 25, 2003; and the Los Angeles County Museum of Art, June 29 - September 28, 2003.

"He took traditional subjects in art history and modernized them, thereby underscoring their enduring appeal," said exhibition curator Dr. Kenneth Wayne. "Like other avant-garde artists, Modigliani avoided naturalistic depictions in favor of making something more imaginative and creative."

-more-

(continued)

-3-

Albright-Knox Art Gallery Curator Dr. Kenneth Wayne organized the exhibition and wrote the accompanying catalogue published by Harry N. Abrams, Inc. in association with the Albright-Knox Art Gallery. The 224-page volume includes approximately 200 color and black-and-white illustrations and three essays: *Modigliani and Montparnasse; Modigliani and the Avant-Garde; and Modigliani's Lifetime Exhibitions.* The catalogue includes extensive new material drawn from Dr. Wayne's more-than 15 years of research. He was also very fortunate to interview one of Modigliani's last models, Paulette Jourdain and to gain new insight into the artist's life and work.

Modigliani & the Artists of Montparnasse is made possible in Buffalo through the generous support of M&T Bank. This exhibition is supported by an indemnity from the Federal Council on the Arts and Humanities and in part by a grant from the National Endowment for the Arts. The exhibition is organized by the Albright-Knox Art Gallery, Buffalo, New York.

The Buffalo Philharmonic Orchestra recorded the compact disc, "Rhapsodie," in celebration of the exhibition *Modigliani & the Artists of Montparnasse.* The CD includes compositions by Ravel, Debussy, D'Indy, and Massenet, all contemporaries of Modigliani.

The Modigliani exhibition reinforces the Albright-Knox Art Gallery's position as a leading arts institution committed to the acquisition and exhibition of dynamic modern and contemporary art. In addition, it fulfills an objective of the Gallery's new strategic plan to continue to originate special exhibitions for national and international tours.

The Albright-Knox Art Gallery enjoys a worldwide reputation as an outstanding center of modern and contemporary art. Its permanent collection, which includes works by most of the great artists of the late 19th and the 20th centuries, has been cited as "one of the world's top international surveys of modern and contemporary painting and sculpture."

# # #

Note to Editors: Photos are available by contacting Cheryl Orlick at the Gallery or the Agency contact below. For additional information visit www.WhoIsModi.com/

AGENCY CONTACT: Glen White   716.831.1500
                    Carr Marketing Communications
                    gawhite@carrmarketing.com

Note: Reprinted with permission from Albright-Knox Art Gallery, Buffalo, NY.

You may want to hire a clipping service for events expected to generate more widespread media coverage (more on clipping services in chapter 15).

- Compiling a final report that summarizes the media coverage received and assesses the planning and execution of the event. Note those aspects of the event that went smoothly and not so smoothly, and suggest any new approaches that would make similar media events run more efficiently in the future.

Before planning a media event, consider the appropriateness of doing so and make sure that the event does not violate any ethical standards of the public relations or media professions. PRSA's Member Code of Ethics uses the following examples of such violations:

- A public relations practitioner entertains a government official beyond legal limits or in violation of government reporting requirements.
- A public relations representative for a ski manufacturer gives a pair of expensive racing skis to a sports magazine columnist in an effort to influence a positive review of the equipment.

Audioconferences and Videoconferences

Some news announcements must reach multiple audiences in several different locations at the same time. In those cases, it may be best to do an audioconference, also known as a teleconference, or a videoconference using satellite technology. Reporters can participate in audioconferences and videoconferences without having to travel to your location, which saves time and adds convenience.

First, you select an appropriate central location for your spokespeople, whether that be in an office board room or a hotel conference room that can accommodate the necessary telephone or satellite hookups. Prior to the conference, you send a media alert to media contacts to let them know the subject, date and time of the conference, along with information on how to get connected to the conference. For audioconferences, reporters are asked to call a specific telephone number to log in to the conference; for videoconferences, they are asked to go to a designated site in their city equipped with satellite technology and with phone lines to call in questions.

The cost of audioconferences and videoconferences varies, from a few thousand to a few hundred thousand dollars, depending on the size and length of the event, the number of locations involved, and the technical complexity. Many video news conferences use *one-way video* (reporters see your spokespeople, but they don't see the reporters) and *two-way audio* (both sides can ask and receive questions). Two-way video is available but for a much greater cost.

Webcasts

Another technique that will allow you to reach multiple audiences while enhancing your online media relations and publicity efforts is the Webcast or Internet videoconference. Webcasts make it possible for journalists, investors, or other key audiences to attend videoconferences without having to leave their desks. Technology allows for live video to be converted into a digital signal as the event is taking place. The video is then "streamed" on the Internet so media contacts can view the conference on personal computers as it happens. A special Web site is created for Webcasts, and passwords can be provided if there are security concerns.

Before the Webcast, notify your media contacts by phone, fax, or e-mail and let them know the Web site address they will need to access. Those viewing the Webcast will need a sufficient modem or Internet connection, and a multimedia player such as RealOne™ Player. Give reporters access to the player, which costs nothing to download, on the Webcast's Web site. Webcasts can be stored on the Web site after the event, too. Individuals who couldn't log on at the time of the event can go to the Web site at their leisure and see and hear recorded video and audio. You can hire a specialty company, such as Medialink Worldwide, West Glen Communications, or Orbis Broadcast Group to plan, execute, and coordinate Webcasts and SMTs. Most video production companies that arrange videoconferences can add a Webcast for a reasonable cost.

Other Public Relations Events

Public relations professionals organize many other types of special events including:

- *Celebrations* such as company anniversaries, employee recognition dinners and holiday parties. Zale Corporation, the diamond and jewelry company, used its 75th anniversary to show it had rebounded from bankruptcy five years before. On April 15, the company celebrated its anniversary in New York City by using Marilyn Monroe look-alikes dressed in diamonds—Monroe is known for her version of the classic song "Diamonds are a Girl's Best Friend"—who passed out diamond-shaped chocolates to employees entering the New York Stock Exchange building. Some of the look-alikes joined Zale's chairman and CEO in ringing the opening bell at the stock exchange that day, and the company later held a meeting with financial analysts to report record profits and recent successes. The Marilyn Monroes helped draw attention to Zale's financial story, which led to media interviews with Zale's CEO and many business stories on the company.

- *Marketing communications events* such as trade shows (see Exhibit 13.3) and consumer contests. Maalox®, advertised as a fast-acting antacid that works in less than a minute, sponsored a national contest called the "One-Minute Maalox Awards Program." The contest asked consumers to nominate everyday people who used quick thinking to save a life or perform some other heroic task. *Cause-related marketing events* support marketing goals, earn goodwill, and strengthen reputations by aligning companies with a worthy cause. Maxwell House™ coffee partnered with a natural not-for-profit partner, Habitat for Humanity, on the "Build a Home America" project. Volunteers built 100 homes for 100 families in 100 weeks, helping Maxwell House strengthen its century-old image as a brand that cares about home and family.

Exhibit 13.3   Excerpts from *Tactics* article: "Trade Shows: Make Them Worth the Investment" (September, 1999)

Trade Shows: Make Them Worth The Investment
by Kathy Burnham, APR

Trade show involvement can consume the bulk of a marketing budget. How will your organization realize the most value from your trade show participation? Careful planning and seamless execution can convert exhibit dollars to sales.

Public relations practitioners often take responsibility for trade shows. If you're not coordinating logistics, you likely will be a member of a planning or a media relations team. This article provides tips to help companies transform budget-intensive trade show efforts into lead-generating and brand-building successes.

Start With A Road Map

Selecting the appropriate shows requires research. Review key trade publications for your industry. Which shows do your customers attend? Which events do your competitors attend? Which shows have been positive experiences? Which shows are advertised?

With answers to these questions, narrow options by compiling more detailed information about each show, including: show size (average number of exhibitors and attendees), location and date, frequency and exhibitor investment. This information can be obtained from the show Web site or sponsor.

Next, analyze survey data provided by show sponsors to attract exhibitors. Data can tell you who, by title, previously attended the show, what they liked or disliked about what they experienced, and whether they made a purchase decision based on what they learned at the show.

Now it's time to develop the look or design of your booth.

Most booths feature a wide range of booth designs. At the low end, booths include modest graphics and an inquiry stand to collect leads. Larger booths include areas for holding private or semi-private meetings, theaters for live presentations, and product demo space. Watch for special restrictions for booth height, noise and signage. It's one thing to stand out among competitors. It's another to be tagged for a violation by the show police.

The near-final steps in planning are assembling the show team and staffing the booth. The show team is responsible for logistics, including booth transportation, equipment delivery, and setup. The team also schedules booth staff assignments, arranges staff travel and hotel accommodations, creates pre-show and on-site promotion activities, trains the booth staff, manages lead gathering and follow-up, and coordinates media relations.

Clearly outline all team member responsibilities and hold periodic meetings to share progress. The ideal show team includes a mix of staff from different disciplines: sales and marketing, production or design, management (for key customer visits and other business) and public relations.

Traveling Your Course

Promotion tactics for trade shows are virtually unlimited. As a general rule, pre-show promotion can help get prospects to the show, on-site promotion gets them to your booth, and post-show promotion gets them in front of a sales rep.

Editorial coverage, direct mail sent to pre-registered show attendees, advertising in trade publications and electronic promotion on your Web site are all examples of pre-show promotion. Regardless of the vehicles you select, time it early enough for recipients to make arrangements to attend, and leverage the show's theme, graphics and key messages.

On-site promotion options include: editorial coverage and advertising in trade publications and the "show daily" (a newspaper published by the show sponsor); signage, banners, flyers, bus wraps, billboards, hotel video ads and other advertising near or at the show site; sales collateral; theater/stage shows in the booth; give-aways and other attention-capturing tactics. All serve the same purpose—steering prospects to your booth.

Post-show promotion helps streamline the sales process. Targeted at prospects who visited your booth (or those who should have), direct mail, sales calls and Web site references help lead customers to purchase decisions. The success of these tactics depends significantly on the strength of the lead-capturing system.

Activities away from the booth are events within an event. Because the booth environment can be loud and cramped, meetings held off-site or after show hours can be more productive. These events are generally geared toward existing customers and leading prospects, and they require advance planning.

Event options include: hosting a hospitality suite at a nearby hotel; sponsoring customer events at location-appropriate venues; conducting tours at local customer sites to show-case products in action; and conducting customer/prospect focus groups to gather opinions used in product development and marketing programs.

Trade shows offer an opportunity to meet face-to-face with the media, which allows editors to get a firsthand look at your products. Because editors generally have limited time, it is important to contact the media early.

Assuming you have already generated and verified media lists and assembled an informative press kit, consider using one or more of these media relations tactics; one-on-one booth appointments to introduce editors to key people and demonstrate new products; press conferences to launch groundbreaking news to all press simultaneously; editor events to make smaller announcements in a more informal atmosphere; and editor boot camps promoted as training sessions for junior reporters to learn more about your products and the industry.

Was It Worth It?

Determining whether your trade show was worth the investment can be time-consuming. The process involves counting, qualifying and following up on leads generated, as well as looking at other intangibles to determine if you met marketing objectives.

For example, did promotional efforts draw more people to the booth? Was the customer event memorable? Did you attract media coverage?

The bottom line: Did one or more of the leads generated or contacts made at the show result in a sale? If you're lucky, some purchase orders will be placed at the show. Others take time to develop. With effective lead-capturing and follow-up mechanisms in place, you can answer this question much more efficiently.

However you choose to evaluate your investment, don't forget to establish for management that participation is worth the effort and cost. Along the way, you'll also identify elements that should be improved, dropped or modified for future shows.

Note. Copyright 1999 PR Tactics. Reprinted with permission from the Public Relations Society of America (www.prsa.org).

- *Fund-raising and public service events*. The Muscular Dystrophy Association (MDA) is known for its annual Jerry Lewis Labor Day Telethon, which raises millions of dollars for muscle disease research and creates national media exposure for MDA's mission. AT&T sponsored the AT&T CARES Community Service Program and invited all of its employees to donate one paid work day volunteering for a community organization of their choice.

- *Informational events* such as conferences, workshops, and presentations to community groups. As part of Bayer® aspirin's 100th anniversary, planners arranged a conference for health and women's magazine writers on the special pain needs of women and the new uses of aspirin. The conference featured presentations by and discussions with renowned medical experts and provided targeted media with substantial information for health stories.

Event Planning

While each event has its own unique set of challenges, most require attention to some general planning principles before, during, and after:

Before the Event

- Develop a plan including goals and objectives, target publics, strategies and tactics for organizing and promoting the event, a budget, and a timetable of activity. Assemble an event planning team, delegate responsibilities, and assign weekly deadlines. As mentioned, research the market to make sure your event doesn't go head-to-head with others in which your target public may have an interest.

- Start promoting the event to the target publics right away; send a postcard announcing the upcoming event to prospective attendees several months in advance so they can mark their calendars early. Follow up with regular, strategically timed mailings, e-mail and other personalized communication to continue building interest, but don't overdo it.

  In addition, some events have news value and the potential to receive media coverage. The media will likely cover your event, for example, if it features an appearance or speech by a well-known person, focuses on a timely issue that people are talking about, involves a notable business advancement, is designed to help the less fortunate in your community, or has a unique theme.

  Let's say you are a business association and you are planning a conference for business professionals in your area that spotlights a keynote speech by an internationally known corporation president. The smart public relations person knows that in a situation like this, there's more to publicizing the event than just sending out a single news release a few weeks before the event. A better strategy is to supply the media with information about the event in several stages to get media exposure:

  - Send a general announcement release one or two months before the event to inform the business community about the upcoming conference and its focus, when and where it will be held, and how people can register.

  - Send a second news release announcing your keynote speaker, a few weeks to a month before the event. This gives you a second opportunity to share details about the event and boost attendance, while giving the media another legitimate news hook.

  - Distribute a media alert a few days before the event that invites the media to a news conference with the industry leader, or that invites them to attend the conference and cover the speech.

- Maintain activity checklists, have weekly meetings to discuss progress and obstacles, and adjust timetables as needed. A template of an activity checklist is located in the Appendix.
- Anticipate problems and establish backup plans. When planning outdoor functions, event planners should secure a tent or indoor site in case of bad weather. Conference planners need to think about guest speakers or presenters canceling at the last minute and identify others in advance who could speak in their place. Fund-raising events that involve running or some other physical activity by participants require on-site medical care.
- Confirm final attendance and make sure there is adequate space, food, and parking for the expected crowd. Hotels and caterers want to know the expected attendance several days to a week before the event, and they will bill you for that number, even if that minimum number of people doesn't show.

Day of the Event

- Do a final walk-through of the space you are using and check on details such as room setup (are there enough chairs and are they arranged properly?), sound and lighting (do microphones work?) and equipment (are VCRs functioning? Will PowerPoint slides or computer programs operate without difficulty?).
- Make sure there is adequate and visible signage to direct people to the event site.
- Have a formal registration area set up and adequately staffed for people to officially check in. Have name tags, extra pens and pencils, and notepads available.
- Distribute a brief survey or comment card at the end of the event to get feedback from participants.

After the Event

- If the event had news value, send out a follow-up news release or photo release to the appropriate media later that day or the day after the event.
- Hold a meeting with your planning team to assess the event and critique the event plan. Did you achieve your goals and get the desired response from the target audience? If problems came up, were they handled efficiently? What lessons did you learn from planning this event?
- Compile participant survey results and gather any media clippings.
- Send thank you letters to participants, guests, speakers, vendors, and any others who contributed to the success of the event.
- Prepare a final report for clients and senior managers summarizing all the information above; attach a summary of participants' survey responses.

Exhibit 13.4 shows the work that is involved in hosting an award-winning event.

Exhibit 13.4   2002 PRSA Silver Anvil Award, Special Events: Compaq's "Give Thanks America"

2002 PRSA Silver Anvil Award Winner: Special Events

Give Thanks America
Compaq Computer Corporation with Hill and Knowlton, Inc.

OVERVIEW

September 11, 2001 is a date forever burned into America's collective psyche. On that horrific day, five Compaq Computer Corporation employees lost their lives in the terrorist attacks on the World Trade Center. In response to the many Compaq employees asking "What can I do?", Hill and Knowlton created the "Give Thanks America" program. Give Thanks America provided an opportunity for families of military personnel, as well as the general public, to record and send digital video e-mail messages via the Internet to troops deployed in harm's way, as well as to American heroes in every uniform - police, fire fighters, and emergency medical technicians.

RESEARCH

For primary research, Compaq first conducted an e-mail survey of employees to determine their interest in a volunteer program. This was overwhelmingly positive (1,234 respondents), so we engaged Hill and Knowlton to identify appropriate venues through a telephone survey of Chambers of Commerce and Convention and Visitors Bureaus in major metropolitan areas. Based on this information, we selected New York City and Washington, DC as kickoff venues, with nine other cities to follow a few days later. In addition, Compaq conducted telephone and e-mail surveys of Internet technology professionals to determine the technological feasibility of the initiative. Responses indicated that Compaq should seek partners that could provide Web-casting and hosting/management services.

Secondary research included an Internet search and media audit of other military outreach programs. Based on this, Compaq partnered with the Department of Defense, which provided research into marketplace competition. They advised that 24 other similar programs had been proposed, but none could send digital video messages to the troops via e-mail. Given the impact of Anthrax on the U.S. Postal Service, this was a key factor in our choosing an online solution.

Compaq also analyzed previous internal surveys and archival research, and conducted interviews with industry analysts. Compaq technical experts were brought in for a focused evaluation of the hardware, software and system architecture needed to run the program. In terms of the promotion of Compaq equipment through Give Thanks America, data analysis showed that customers would be willing to pay more for computers if attractive services and features/capabilities beyond the box were included.

My Movie Studio, promoted through Give Thanks America, would provide Compaq with a strong differentiator. In short, research showed there was interest in Americans thanking people in uniform; Compaq had unique technology to enable this; the military would support us; there was a place in the market for Compaq to carve its niche; and Compaq employees strongly supported the program.

PLANNING

We began planning in late September for a target launch the week of Nov. 12. We purchased Internet URLs for givethanksamerica.com and org. However, negative publicity over the announced pending merger of Compaq and Hewlett Packard required a delay until Dec. 4.

(continued)

The mission of Give Thanks America was to develop a public service program that would portray Compaq in a positive light while enabling Americans to show their appreciation and support of men and women in uniform. The goal was to raise consumer awareness of Compaq technology. The objectives were to generate more than 2,000 video messages, more than 200 media hits and at least 300,000 Web hits in December.

Program strategies were: (1) position Compaq as an innovative technology solutions provider, especially under the merger's negative media cloud; (2) position Compaq as a caring corporate citizen; (3) showcase My Movie Studio and Compaq's solutions stack.

Challenges: (1) developing a technology solution that made it easy to send digital video-streamed messages; (2) coordinating with the Department of Defense during war time; (3) not overburdening military e-mail systems; (4) not appearing mercenary or commercial; (5) competing against other initiatives; (6) coordinating efforts in 22 markets that would involve 700 people.

Tactics: (1) Identify key audiences: families of military; military; fire, police departments; general public; Compaq employees. (2) Create a program task grid/timeline to ensure that all components would be completed in a timely manner and people assigned specific responsibilities. (3) Design and produce collateral materials (brochures, pocket folders, buttons, stationery, T-shirts, and Polo shirts). (4) Identify venues. (5) Develop and test technology solution. (6) Develop media plan and conduct outreach. (7) Launch the event. (8) Evaluate results.

Budgets of $30,000 for support and $10,000 for out-of-pocket expenses were established for 10 venues (Salt Lake City's budget was handled by Sorenson Media), New York City and Washington, D.C. were scheduled to launch the event on Dec. 4 and run three days. The other nine markets would follow Dec. 7 (Pearl Harbor Day) through Dec. 9. The mobile tour of the Southwest would launch on Dec. 8 at The Alamo in San Antonio - and continue for two weeks.

EXECUTION

Team Development: Give Thanks America public relations teams were formed in each market. A central committee provided regional leaders with instructions and guidelines regarding venues, hardware and software support, volunteers, staffing, media relations, and security. Agencies and Compaq recruited volunteers and conducted training. One agency person served as a media relations liaison for the three-day event at each venue.

The media plan called for significant, broad, sustained outreach through December. Targets included national and local broadcast, print and Web outlets. National and local news releases were developed. Additional media relations efforts included the production and distribution of radio & TV celebrity PSAs, a Video News Release, and video b-roll. Media relations guidelines included pitching all local media, soft-sounding PSAs with radio stations, pitching remote broadcasts for TV and radio, pitching morning shows, weather remotes, scheduling interviews for Compaq spokespersons, and conducting short media training refresher/messaging reviews with spokespersons. Media kits were developed and distributed. A Video News Release was produced and marketed to TV stations in target cities.

Event Management: Security guidelines required regional leaders to obtain volunteer assistance from local military/reserve units or police. A national event design vendor was contracted to provide consistent pipe-and-drape in each venue. Compaq computer equipment was acquired and shipped to each location.

(continued)

Technology: Per initial research, we identified technology partners (Sorenson Media and Digital Island) to ensure a workable technology solution. They created a Web site at www.givethanksamerica.com so generic messages to the military, police, fire, and EMT professionals would be posted and available for viewing. Messages of celebrities and politicians were identified for easy reference.

Spokespersons: Local leaders and celebrities were recruited in each market. Celebrity radio and TV PSAs were produced and marketed to broadcast outlets in all venues. Celebrities recording messages included Craig T. Nelson, Scott Glenn, Randy Travis, Burt Reynolds, Bo Derek, Maria Conchita Alonso, Diahann Carroll, Andy Garcia, Shaquille O'Neal, Michael Bolton, Kobe Bryant, Esai Morales, Rick Fox, Ann-Margret, Buzz Aldrin and B.B. King. Travis granted use of his "America Will Always Stand" song as GTA official song. Launch events were conducted in New York and Washington, D.C. on Dec. 4; in Atlanta, Boston, Chicago, Colorado Springs, Dallas, Houston, Salt Lake City, San Diego and San Jose on Dec. 7-9. In Washington, D.C., two recording sites were created: one at the VFW Building and a second at The Pentagon. Subsequent GTA venues included the United We Stand event in Washington, D.C. for Bush family members; VFW pilot site in Greensboro, NC; the Galleryfurniture.com Bowl football game; and a celebrity thank-you luncheon at the Digital Media Summit in Hollywood.

EVALUATION

All measurable objectives were exceeded. Some 1,200 Compaq employees volunteered and 600 actively participated. 3,000+ digital video messages were recorded with 600,000 Web hits in the first 20 days. 350+ media hits were documented. Measurable results -- 11-city launch: Radio PSA audience: 7,138,200; 300+ media hits. 11-city Southwest Mobile Tour: VNR audience: 488,279; Radio PSA audience: 450,231. TV PSA audience: 851,938; 50+ media hits; TV coverage audience: 2,798,298.

National media coverage: CNN, CNET, The Today Show. Bloomberg Radio, Associated Press.

Note: "Give Thanks America" was developed under the leadership of Roger Frizzell, who heads up HP's Public Relations for the Personal Systems Group.

References and Suggested Reading

Armstrong, J. S. (2001). *Planning special events*. San Francisco: Jossey Bass.

Coons, P. (1999). *Gala!: The special event planner for professionals and volunteers*. Dulles, VA: Capital Books.

Hoyle, L. H. (2002). *Event marketing: How to successfully promote events, festivals, conventions, and expositions*. Hoboken, NJ: John Wiley & Sons.

Levy, B. R. & Mairon, B. (1997). *Successful special events: Planning, hosting and evaluating*. New York: Aspen Publishers.

PRSA member code of ethics 2000. (2000). Retrieved January 19, 2003 from http://www.prsa.org/_About/ethics/index. asp?ident=eth1

Salzman, J. (1998). *Making the news: A guide for nonprofits and activists*. Boulder, CO: Westview Press.

Skinner, B. E. & Rukavina, V. (2002). *Event sponsorship*. Hoboken, NJ: John Wiley & Sons.

Special events magazine. www.specialevents.com

CASES

Case 45: Boy Scouts Honor Local Hero

The Boy Scouts of America presents the National Meritorious Award for life saving each year to 150 youths and adults across the country involved in Boy Scouts. You work as a public relations specialist for a local Boy Scout council, and today you learn that a scout from your area will receive the national award for heroism this year.

Eleven-year-old Grady Reynolds successfully performed the Heimlich maneuver on his friend, Joshua Walker, last year after Walker started choking while eating a piece of pizza during lunch hour in their Grant Middle School cafeteria. Reynolds, who was 10 and a Cub Scout at the time, learned the Heimlich maneuver at a Cub Scout meeting. In selecting Reynolds for the award, the Court of Honor at Boy Scout National Headquarters in Dallas, Texas cited his success in performing the Heimlich and his ability to keep a "cool head when facing a life-and-death situation." Reynolds is now one of the youngest scouts to ever receive the National Meritorious Award.

Kent Humphries, executive director of your local Boy Scout council, calls Reynolds and his parents to give them the good news. Later, he talks with you about planning a local event to recognize Reynolds for his achievement. "We don't often have a local scout who wins this award, especially one who's so young. I talked with Grady and his mom and dad about having some kind of media event in his honor, and they were thrilled about the idea," Humphries says.

"The local media will probably love it, too," you add. "This is the kind of human interest story I could see the TV stations running on their 5 or 6 p.m. newscasts. I'm thinking that we could set this event up in any number of ways. What did you have in mind?"

"I haven't really thought too much about the format," Jeffries responds. "I'll let you handle all those details. Whatever we do, I want people to know that we have a local hero in our community of whom we can all be very proud. If we can get some positive media exposure for the Boy Scouts at the same time, that would be great. I'd like to hold the event some time in the next two or three weeks or so, before the news of his national award gets too dated."

Assignments

1. Assume that you work for the Boy Scouts in the area where your college is located or in a city designated by your instructor. In a memorandum to Jeffries, present your plan for the Grady Reynolds recognition/media event. Include:

   ● Goals of the event.
   ● Suggestions for the location, day, and time of the event (pick a specific day in the next two or three weeks). Justify your choices.
   ● Program/format. Explain the structure of the event—who will speak and in what order, and what will they be asked to say. Note any other activities that will take place.
   ● Media kit. Provide a list and brief description of written and visual materials for distribution to reporters at the event. Be specific about the format and content of written materials, and justify your choices.
   ● Evaluation. Present a brief summary of recommended evaluation methods—how will you measure the success and impact of this event?

2. Write a media alert inviting local media to cover the Grady Reynolds recognition event. For this assignment, assume that your city has one morning and one evening daily newspaper; three television stations (ABC, CBS and NBC affiliates) that air noon, early evening (5 to 6:30), and 11 p.m. local newscasts; a dozen FM and AM radio stations of various formats; and several weekly/community newspapers.

Case 46: The MP3 Player Product Launch

MP3 is a software system that makes it possible for digital music to be sent over the Internet and then downloaded to a computer hard drive or directly to a portable MP3 player. The player connects by cable to the computer and once the music is recorded, the player is unplugged and becomes a portable stereo with headphones. MP3 players are smaller than compact disc players, making them easier to transport. Because the music is downloaded digitally from the Internet, sound quality is much better than the quality achieved from copying music from a CD to an audiotape.

Many musical performers have MP3 samples available on their own Web sites or on other Web sites. People who have MP3 players can go to those sites, choose preferred tracks from different albums by different artists, download those tracks, and assemble an individualized library of MP3 audio. Some artists use MP3 technology to preview songs from new albums or to deliver bonus songs that are only available for download from the Internet. Rock musician David Bowie was one of the first to offer a complete album as a computer download, and more artists are taking his lead.

Electronix, a major electronics company, is getting ready to introduce the first in its line of MP3 players, the Digi Player 2000. This tiny MP3 player fits easily in a pocket or purse, uses two AAA batteries, holds 40 to 60 minutes of music, and works with Windows software. The suggested retail price is $179.95. Additional postage-stamp-sized computer chips that store 30 minutes or more of additional music can be purchased for $70 to $90 each. The company has future plans to introduce two other models that are Macintosh-compatible and have greater memory to allow the user to download more minutes of music.

You work in media relations for Electronix and report to Jenna Saltzmann, the brand manager for audio products. Saltzmann meets with you to talk about setting up an event to introduce Digi Player 2000. "We're not the first company to introduce an MP3 player, but ours will be the smallest and most portable player on the market. Plus, this is our entry into the MP3 market and our upcoming line of MP3 players will be designed to hold more memory than competitive products. That might count for something and help us get some press for Digi Player 2000."

"But do you really think we can interest the media enough in this product to get them to come to a news conference? It just seems like it would be more sensible and cost effective to send them a media kit and do some follow-up calls. That might get us the same kind of results," you say.

"True. The traditional news conference may not be the way to go here. But the company's senior executives want to create some media buzz with the introduction of this product and really get consumers excited about it. They're expecting to see some kind of creative product launch that will help introduce the product to consumers in grand style, get the media to take an interest, and give us some good exposure. With some thought, I believe we can come up with something that will help us cut through the clutter and make this new product stand out."

You respond: "Here's a suggestion. Let me bounce this idea off some people. I'll call some of our media contacts and get their thoughts about the news value of the Digi Player 2000 and how they might cover it. Then I'll recommend a couple of approaches—a few different kick-off events that would help us make an initial splash with Digi Player 2000 and get the press and the public talking about it. We'll follow-up in a week and I'll present my ideas to you then."

Assignments

1. Prepare a memorandum for Saltzmann that presents three different ideas for a Digi Player 2000 kick-off event. Include:

   - Goals of a Digi Player 2000 kick-off event.
   - Description of each event. Summarize the nature of the event, what it involves and who it targets, where and when it will be held, and why you think it will have impact. Specify budget considerations and estimate major costs that would be incurred.

- Conclusion. Recap the three events and their individual strengths. Recommend one event that you think has the greatest potential to generate media exposure and consumer interest, and justify your choice.

2. Compile a list of key consumer magazines and trade media that should receive media materials on the Digi Player 2000 MP3 player. Specify the name and address of the publication; summarize its content and target audience; and include the name of key contacts and their titles. In a memorandum, recommend written and visual components of a media kit on the new Digi Player 2000 MP3 player. Identify each piece and briefly explain its content. Support your choices.

Case 47: The Great American Smokeout Events (Part A)

Established by the American Cancer Society (www.cancer.org) in 1977, the Great American Smokeout is dedicated to helping people quit smoking. On the third Thursday in November, the Smokeout invites smokers to give up cigarettes for one day, in hopes that it will motivate them to stop smoking completely. Through the years, millions of Americans have quit smoking as a result of the Great American Smokeout, and more people try to quit on that day than on any other day of the year, including New Year's.

You work as a fund-raising and community relations specialist for a local office of the American Cancer Society in a city of 100,000. Each year, you plan and coordinate activities for the Great American Smokeout in your area. After reading a current article in the Journal of the National Cancer Institute, you talk with your executive director about some ideas for this year's Smokeout.

"I don't know if you saw this article in the journal. It reports the results of a study that was done to find out how often doctors counsel their adolescent patients—adolescents being people between the ages of 11 and 21—on tobacco use. They tracked more than 16,000 office visits to 5,000 physicians across the country and discovered that counseling was provided to adolescents at only 1.6% of those visits."

"Wow, that's an incredibly low number. Any other interesting findings?" asks Nick Copanas, the executive director.

You continue: "They also analyzed extensive data to find out if physicians determined if their patients smoked and, if so, if they counseled teen smokers on the dangers of smoking and how they could quit. What they found was physicians identified if their adolescent patients smoked in 72% of the visits, but only 17% of those patients were counseled on ways to quit. Any way, I think this study might give us a strong hook for the media this year and help us get some good publicity for the Smokeout."

"That's a great idea," Copanas says. "We've been doing the Smokeout for so long that we have to give the local media some fresh story angles every year, if we expect any kind of substantial coverage. Besides the publicity, have you given any thought to some special events we could organize to get the community involved in the Smokeout?"

"Well, something else really stood out in the journal article, and it got me thinking about events we could plan. The researchers also found that younger and non-White adolescents were less likely to be counseled than older and White teens. I'd like to look at targeting some events to those two audiences— younger kids in the age 5 to 11 range, and non-White teens. This ties in nicely with the changing focus of Smokeout during the last few years. It's no longer just a day where we ask smokers to quit smoking, but a time when we put the focus on younger people and we try to educate them about the reasons they shouldn't start smoking in the first place."

"Going into schools and just talking to children and teens about how bad smoking is for them doesn't seem to work well, though," Copanas adds. "We've got to do something different and fun, something that will get them interested, without trying to lecture or force a lot of information on them. We have to make our point in such a way that they don't even realize that they're learning something, do you know what I mean?"

"Yes, I do, and as you said, we should try to come up with some fun and interactive events that will interest younger people. I'll start working on this project today and we'll sit down again in a week to talk about some preliminary ideas for the events."

Assignments

1. Working alone or with a partner, prepare a memorandum with recommendations for two Great American Smokeout events—one that targets children ages 5 to 11, and a second for non-White teens. Include:

   - Introduction/Situation Analysis.
   - Description of each event. Summarize the nature of the event, what it involves and who it targets, when and where it will be held, and why you think it will have impact. Support your ideas. Specify budget considerations and estimate any major costs that would be incurred.
   - Conclusion.

2. Select one of the events detailed in #1 that you think has the greatest potential to generate media coverage. Write a media alert inviting the local media to cover the event.

Case 48: Celebrating Ketchup's 125th Anniversary

For many people, it's hard to truly enjoy a burger and fries without ketchup. The origins of ketchup have been traced back many centuries, and it is still going strong today as one of America's favorite condiments. Ninety-seven percent of Americans keep ketchup in their kitchens, and each person eats about five bottles of ketchup per year. A tablespoon of ketchup has 16 calories and no fat. Four tablespoons of ketchup, which is close to the amount you might eat with an order of fries, has the nutritional equivalent of a ripe medium tomato.

The Fuller's Company is one of the leading manufacturers of ketchup, with worldwide net sales of $9 billion and just over half of the total U.S. market share. The company sells a wide variety of food products including baby food, juices, canned fruits and vegetables, a line of low-fat frozen dinners, and pet foods. In the mid-1990s, as consumers began purchasing more salsa, ketchup sales started to drop, as did Fuller's market share. Fuller's lowered ketchup prices and increased its advertising budget to stay competitive and stimulate sales. The result—ketchup regained the lead and started outselling salsa once again in the late 1990s.

Now, Fuller's plans to celebrate its 125th year of making and bottling ketchup. To mark that milestone, the company has decided to sponsor special anniversary events and promotions that support increased ketchup sales and help rebuild the brand as the most popular ketchup in the United States and the world. Your public relations agency has been hired to plan and coordinate the 125th anniversary campaign. You are an assistant account executive and a member of the planning team led by Gerald Kaplan, an account supervisor in the agency's food and beverage division.

"I met with the client today, and we discussed some of his ideas for the Fuller's Ketchup anniversary," Kaplan says. "He is interested in doing some kind of consumer contest that would create renewed excitement about Fuller's Ketchup and drive sales. He wants us to give him some recommendations, not only for a contest but also for other anniversary events and activities that target consumers and help generate media coverage."

"When you say 'consumer,' to whom are you referring?" you ask. "I mean, people of all ages buy ketchup, but I'm sure there is a target audience the company wants to focus on."

"The main audience is families who have children and teens between the ages of 6 and 18 living at home. Women tend to be the primary purchasers. They're also hoping to position ketchup as being more 'hip' with teens and young adults. This is a group that helped make salsa a big seller. They've grown up on salsa as a condiment of preference so there's an interest in reintroducing them to ketchup and starting to build their loyalty as future ketchup buyers."

Assignment

1. Working with a partner, prepare a 125th anniversary plan for Fuller's Ketchup that includes the following:
   - Introduction/Situation Analysis.
   - Goals of the Fuller's Ketchup 125th anniversary.

- A proposed consumer contest. Specify the target audience, and suggest a creative name for the contest. Explain the design of the contest, what activities are involved, and why this contest will have impact and help the company achieve its goals. Note timing and budget considerations.
- Three or four additional recommendations for consumer and media events to celebrate the 125th anniversary. For each event or activity description, include details similar to those outlined for the consumer contest.
- Evaluation Methods/Conclusion.

Tips from the Top

"Coordinating a First Lady's Visit"
Kimberly MacLeod

As she began preparing for a U.S. Senate run, former first lady and now Senator Hillary Clinton (D-NY) traveled across New York state on a "listening tour." She made a stop at Bassett Heathcare, a rural network of primary and specialty health care providers who practice at three hospitals and 20 community centers in a 10-county region. Kimberly MacLeod, formerly Bassett's director of public relations and now communications and alumni relations coordinator at the State University of New York at Delhi, handled many details of the event and assisted the media on the day of Mrs. Clinton's visit.

Q: Why was Bassett chosen as a stop on Mrs. Clinton's New York state tour?
A: When Bassett was first contacted, the hospital really didn't know why Mrs. Clinton selected us, other than the fact that it's a unique health care organization in the region. Bassett provides high-quality health care while maintaining the status of a teaching hospital and research facility. Her advance people told us they were looking for a good setting where Mrs. Clinton could discuss upstate New York health care issues on a broader level.

Q: When you say her "advance people," what do you mean?
A: The advance people are members of Mrs. Clinton's staff. They were responsible for arranging many of the details of the event prior to the first lady's arrival at Bassett—everything from setting up the agenda for the day to managing the traffic flow. And they were at the event making sure things went as planned.

Q: What was the agenda for her visit?
A: The plan was that Mrs. Clinton would be at Bassett for about an hour and a half. First, she would meet with business and community leaders for about 15 or 20 minutes, and the rest of the time would be spent taking part in a panel discussion of health care issues with Bassett employees and patients. After that, Mrs. Clinton would meet with some key members of the press selected by her advance team, and then she would leave for her next stop on the tour.

Q: Did the advance team impose any restrictions relating to the event?
A: Her advance people told us they did not want word of Mrs. Clinton's visit to get out until just before her arrival. They wanted us to keep the situation under our hats, so to speak, and under control as much as possible to avoid dealing with any disruptive forces—like protesters, for example—who might have time to get organized and create problems at the event. So, we gathered a select group of

Bassett people including myself, the vice president of external affairs, the vice president of facilities, our chief operating officer, and our CEO. Bassett staff members were briefed on the agenda and then we took it from there.

Q: **Even though the advance team specified how the event should be laid out, then, your staff was responsible for handling certain details.**

A: That's right. Bassett only had one week's notice, which really put some limits on our planning time. On the other hand, the event was so well orchestrated by the advance people, we weren't at too much of a loss. Bassett was responsible for:

- Selecting the five members of the panel discussion, and organizing an audience of about 50 to 75 people for that discussion.
- Deciding which VIPs would greet Mrs. Clinton prior to the discussion.
- Determining how and when our CEO would meet Mrs. Clinton and formally welcome her.
- Helping to coordinate Mrs. Clinton's arrival with the arrival of the media, and thinking about the security issues involved in all this and how we would officially greet the media when they showed up.
- Contacting the local media in our area to make sure they were informed, and putting together a press packet with useful information.
- Making arrangements for a file room for the media, where they could work on their stories, and making sure there were extra phone lines in that space for them.
- Providing refreshments for the media.

Q: **How about your employees? Did you open this event up to them?**

A: Mrs. Clinton's advance people were also adamant about keeping the audience to a minimum. Bassett wanted its employees to have the opportunity to see the panel discussion, so they were invited to an auditorium in one of the hospital buildings where they could see a live telecast of the event. Bassett also made its teleconferencing equipment available to allow our outreach health centers to view the discussion, too.

Q: **There was tremendous media turnout on the day of Mrs. Clinton's visit. What were some of the challenges you faced with the media?**

A: First, I should tell you that the advance people made all the arrangements with the press, complete with a press bus to take them from location to location. Our role at the event was to work with the advance team and pretty much follow its instructions. Bassett's public relations staff was limited to meeting and greeting the media and seeing that they had what they needed from Mrs. Clinton's people.

The public relations staff had to deal with many different personalities, from those journalists who were polite and grateful for the information we could provide to those who were far more demanding. One challenge involved the area behind the audience that the advance people designated for the media at the panel discussion.It was really much too small to accommodate all the reporters that someone would expect to show up at a major event like this. They may have done this for effect—to make it look on camera as if they were "breaking down the doors to see Hillary." I'm sure that's the image they wanted to portray.

Q: Overall, how did you evaluate the success of this event? What lessons did you learn?

A: All mentions of Bassett were tracked through the media clippings provided by a clipping service, and the staff took the best of those clippings and shared them with senior managers to show that Bassett did receive national coverage and mentions in national stories. As far as the public relations impact, it's hard to tell. Bassett did get wider exposure than it normally gets, and Mrs. Clinton offered a great quote for use in future promotions. She called Bassett the "crown jewel of health care."

It would have been nice to have more control, but it would have been hard to gain more control without jeopardizing the event. The staff chalked it up to the unique situation it was. It's not every day that the first lady comes to visit.

Q: This was, as you say, no ordinary event. When a celebrity is involved, how does this affect the event planning process?

A: When a celebrity is involved, I would say your best bet is to work with his or her [public relations] people as best you can, while trying to work on your own agenda. Bassett, of course, had its own agenda and topics it wanted to bring to the table, but quickly found out that the advance people were simply looking for a good health care setting for Mrs. Clinton. At that point, it was necessary to take a step back, focus on giving them what they wanted—a setting for the panel discussion—and then just allow Bassett to shine in the media spotlight and get some great exposure.

14

Crisis Planning and Communications

"To be successful you have to be selfish, or else you never achieve. And once you get to your highest level, then you have to be unselfish. Stay reachable. Stay in touch. Don't isolate." This is a quote from Michael Jordan, a true artist on the basketball court and now a sports legend. Organizations in crisis also have to be unselfish and put the needs of others first. They cannot isolate themselves and hide from public view or the media. People affected by the crisis need to receive constant communication. Companies and their senior managers need to "stay reachable" and "stay in touch" during those tough times. If communication is handled correctly, damage to the company will be lessened, even if the company is at fault.

Certainly, every crisis is a problem, but not every problem is a crisis. Problem situations affect a limited number of people, can be handled rather quickly with limited resources, and usually do not attract attention from the media and other outside groups. Public relations professionals encounter all kinds of problems in their daily routines—executives who are upset by media stories that aren't totally positive, conference speakers who cancel visits at the last minute, printers who can't finish a job on deadline. It's up to the public relations professional to put problems in perspective and not make "mountains out of molehills." What's important to people within the organization may not be important to anyone outside the organization.

Crises, by contrast, are serious unexpected events that have long-term implications for an organization and can threaten its survival. When a crisis hits, it disrupts the business routine and has the potential to significantly impact many of the organization's audiences. Crises include natural disasters (hurricanes, floods), on-site emergencies (plant fires, industrial accidents), other unpredictable events (workplace violence, sudden resignation or termination of a top executive), as well as predictable events (performing poorly on a health department survey or financial audit).

How an organization plans and prepares for crisis situations, effectively communicates with internal and external publics during and after the crisis, and presents itself to the media will have a dramatic effect on corporate reputation. Allen H. Center and Patrick Jackson, in their book *Public Relations Practices: Managerial Case Studies and Problems,* make this point about crisis management: "The term 'crisis management' does not imply that an organization or its public relations staff can manage external influences. What can—and must—be managed is the response."

Preparing for Crises

Organizations can never be fully prepared for a crisis when it strikes. But public relations professionals can help companies with *risk assessment*, identifying the types of emergencies they could realistically face and determining how they might respond effectively should those situations occur. A food product manufacturer, for example, has to consider the possibility of product tampering, product recalls, consumer boycotts, and product liability lawsuits. Having a blueprint in place before a crisis hits can better prepare organizations so that their reactions to emergencies are quicker, more efficient, and based on sound strategies that the organization and its senior managers have already discussed and agreed upon.

It is also important to organize in advance a *crisis team* that is responsible for managing the crisis from start to finish. Members of the crisis team should have designated responsibilities and be properly briefed beforehand on the roles they are to play during the crisis. Deciding who serves on the crisis team can depend on the nature of the organization and the type of crisis you face. A chemical company may want to have an environmental expert on the crisis team assembled in response to a chemical spill. Many crisis teams include:

- Senior official, often the CEO, who makes the first formal statement about the crisis and whose visibility during the crisis makes a strong statement about the organization's commitment to rectifying the situation;
- Public relations director, who oversees crisis communications efforts and is often the first contact for the media;
- Chief financial officer, who helps secure the funds needed to manage the crisis;
- Legal advisor, who counsels the team on liability issues and other legal matters;
- Human resources manager, who acts as a link to employees and keeps them informed about the crisis.

Another preparedness step is creation of a *crisis communications plan*, which details how information will be provided to key publics during the crisis and specifies who will be responsible for specific crisis communications duties. Most public relations professionals will tell you that the best plans are the ones that never have to be used. The crisis communications plan should contain the following information:

- Goals. Crisis communications efforts generally aim to provide open and truthful information to key publics throughout the crisis. It is important to communicate with key publics quickly after the crisis hits and to communicate consistently with these groups; show the organization's concern about the situation and compassion for those affected; and protect the company's reputation and maintain a positive image by demonstrating the company's willingness to take responsibility for resolving the situation.

- Publics and communications channels. List all internal and external publics who require information during a crisis and specify preferred methods for getting information to those audiences. For instance, bulletin boards, voice mail, and e-mail are good tools of choice for communicating with internal audiences. Be sure to designate a secondary way to communicate in case the crisis has affected the preferred method of relaying information (for example, there is no telephone service or the computer server is down).

- Crisis directory. This contains contact information for crisis team members, company management and board members including home addresses and phone numbers, cellular phone numbers, e-mail addresses, and fax numbers. Similar contact information should also be included for police and fire officials, hospitals, regulatory agencies, community leaders, and the media.

- Media information. Identify the primary media spokesperson. Include company backgrounders, biographies of company executives, product fact sheets, and other information useful to media contacts.

- Prepared statements. Draft initial statements that can be made for different crisis and emergency scenarios and get approval of those statements from legal counsel.

Communicating During the First 24 Hours

First reactions to a crisis are critical. The speed at which you move will make or break the organization's reputation. Moving too slowly to address the situation or refusing to comment about what is happening can create the perception that your organization simply doesn't care. There are some vital first steps to take in a crisis:

- Set up a crisis communications headquarters. Have one central location—often the public relations office—at the organization's headquarters where all inquiries about the crisis are directed to and from which all company information is distributed. This helps to ensure that your messages are consistent. There should also be a system in place to quickly alert all employees to the situation. Ask that they refer all phone calls and questions from reporters and others outside the company to the public relations office. If media are expected to gather at the site of the emergency, set up a separate *media information center* to supervise crisis coverage and facilitate the flow of information.

- Get top officials to the scene. When a crisis hits, notify the CEO immediately and get him or her to the disaster site as soon as possible. If the CEO is unable to get there right away, send the next highest company official. This shows that senior management is concerned about the situation and leading the effort to manage the crisis. The importance of who represents the company at the disaster site and how quickly he or she gets there cannot be underestimated. For example, USAir was lauded for its quick and visible response when one of its planes crashed outside of Pittsburgh, killing 132 people. The airline's CEO immediately rushed to the site. On the other hand, when a Pan American World Airways jet exploded over Lockerbie, Scotland, the airline's CEO was criticized for not responding quickly, and when the Exxon Valdez ran aground in Alaska, the CEO's initial absence at the scene helped to confirm Exxon's place in public relations history as how *not* to handle a crisis.

- Prioritize audiences. Think carefully about the people most affected by the crisis and consider their interests and communications needs first. In most cases, employees should be the first to be informed about the crisis. Not only are employees directly affected by a crisis situation, but also, if properly informed, they can assist the organization in implementing its crisis plan. For example, immediately following a plane crash, an airline needs to concentrate on the victims and their families and work closely with law enforcement officials investigating the accident. In order to meet the needs of these publics, employees must be informed promptly. Then, attention can be placed on communicating more fully with other audiences such as the media and government agencies. Understand that all of these audiences must be brought into the loop as soon as possible, but those most impacted by the event should always be foremost in the company's mind as it deals with the crisis.

- Issue an initial statement within the first few hours. The sooner you can say something about the crisis, the easier it is to gain control of the message. This helps prevent rumors from spreading and keeps the media from speculating too much about what is going on. That statement you make in the first few hours doesn't need to be too specific. You will probably not have all the facts, which makes it difficult to comment in great detail anyway. Simply acknowledge the situation and let people know when they will hear more about it from you:

> At 10 a.m., there was an explosion at our Milltown plant. Our CEO and other top officials have been rushed to the scene, and we are working closely with authorities to assess injuries and damage. We will make a more complete statement about the situation at 8 p.m.

- Make a more formal announcement as soon as possible, and definitely within the first 12 to 24 hours. When it comes time to make a more complete statement, organize a news conference at which the CEO shares facts about the situation and fields reporters' questions. Make sure that this announcement expresses regret about the situation and sympathy for those affected, and explain what is being done now to handle the situation. Consult with your legal staff to review and approve written materials, especially before publicly acknowledging fault. Prepare and distribute a news release including facts that you know to be true and that have been confirmed by the police or other authorities investigating the situation. Note in Exhibit 14.1 how a crisis communications news release is straightforward, shares hard facts, does not speculate about cause, and focuses

Exhibit 14.1 Crisis News Release: New York Power Authority

1633 Broadway
New York, New York 10019

News

For Further Information:
January 14, 1999
WOODY BERZINS
(315) 349-6681

 **NewYork Power Authority**

FOR IMMEDIATE RELEASE

OSWEGO—A fire broke out shortly before 1 p.m. Thursday in a hydrogen storage tank area at the New York Power Authority's James A. FitzPatrick Nuclear Power Plant.

Fire officials declared the fire under control about one hour later, but continued to apply water to extinguish it.

The fire was confined to the tank area, 250 feet northwest of the closest part of the plant and several hundred feet farther from the building that houses that nuclear reactor.

Three local fire departments responded to the event, and a valve from the tanks to the plant was closed to prevent the spread of the fire. Plant staff was evacuated from the area of the storage tanks.

A fireman who was struck in the leg by a hose and a plant worker who was slightly burned were taken to Oswego Hospital.

The hydrogen stored in the tanks is used to cool the electric generator in the non-nuclear portion of the plant and to adjust feedwater chemistry.

The cause of the fire, which broke out in a valve cabinet near the tanks, was not immediately determined.

The 820,000-kilowatt plant has continued to operate at full power.

The Power Authority declared an unusual event—the lowest of four categories for events at nuclear power plants—and activated response facilities at the plant. State and county officials were notified, along with the U.S. Nuclear Regulatory Commission.

-30-

■

Note: Reprinted with the permission of the New York Power Authority.

on key messages the organization wants to make about the crisis being "under control" and an "unusual event."

- Be responsive and responsible. Do not hide behind "no comment"; if you can't answer a question, explain why—"I don't have that information now, but will share it with you as soon as I get it." Abide by a policy of openness and cooperation. Take responsibility for resolving the situation, but if you are unsure of the cause, be careful not to assume blame for the problem. If it has been determined that your organization is at fault for an accident, let people know what you are doing to make amends and help the victims and their families, and talk about the steps you are taking to make sure situations like this don't happen again.

Ongoing Crisis Communication

Most crises are not resolved in one day. It is essential that you respond quickly and stay on top of the situation early on, but you also need to keep lines of communication open with your audiences until the crisis has stabilized. Niagara Mohawk (NiMo), an energy services company, learned that lesson well. Following an early morning Labor Day storm that killed two people and severely damaged electrical wires and transmission lines, the upstate New York company faced the daunting task of restoring power to more than 250,000 people. NiMo quickly sent out crews to assess the damage, and then formed a crisis team comprised of NiMo officials and representatives from the company's public relations firm. That team met twice a day during the crisis period to discuss strategy and decide on the important messages that audiences needed to receive. NiMo sent out its first news release about the storm at 9:30 a.m., just hours after the storm hit. While all media was targeted, radio and television stations were especially important since many people were relying on battery-powered radios and televisions to get storm information. The first news release:

- Focused on public safety issues and explained what people should and should not do in this kind of emergency situation.
- Stressed that people should avoid walking under downed power lines or touching downed lines and wires.
- Recommended that customers unplug appliances and electrical equipment that might cause a power surge or circuit overload as repairs were being made.
- Urged people to call a toll-free storm emergency line, if they thought NiMo may not be aware of a particular situation.

By noon, NiMo made its first official statement about the storm and storm damage and gave customers their first sense of how long repairs would take:

"We are still assessing storm damage," said Edward J. Dienst, vice president of NiMo's Electric Delivery. "However, it is clear that many customers will be without power for several days, and overall restoration will take more than a week."

In that statement, and in subsequent releases, NiMo also clarified its restoration policy, which involved first addressing problems with "transmission lines, substations and critical customers such as hospitals, fire departments, and law enforcement agencies" and that once those problems were resolved, it would "focus on repairing primary and secondary circuits that affect local neighborhoods." At all times, the company wanted to be "up front" with customers about the situation and when their power might realistically be restored. Later that same afternoon, radio PSAs began airing once an hour. The spots provided safety tips and mentioned the toll-free hotline. Television PSAs started airing a few days later, and regular newspaper ads and stories kept people up to date on restoration efforts and gave target dates for restoring power to specific areas. NiMo continued to send out daily news releases until all customers got their power back by Sept. 15. Many of these releases focused on concerns customers might have in the aftermath of the storm such as how they should prepare for power to return, who is responsible for disposing of storm debris, and what questions to ask if they needed to hire an electrical contractor.

When the crisis ended, NiMo ran "thank you" ads in local newspapers to thank customers for their patience and cooperation during the storm recovery period. In response, people sent hundreds of letters to the editor to local newspapers and praised NiMo on call-in radio shows for the outstanding job done to restore power as quickly and efficiently as possible. Honest, regular communication throughout the crisis period—from shortly after the storm struck to the day all power was restored—created positive public opinion and bolstered NiMo's reputation with customers and the communities the company serves. Exhibit 14.2 provides more tips for communicating during a crisis.

Handling the Cybercrisis

Organizational crises resulting from unexpected natural disasters and the damage they cause have always been around. Today, however, companies are contending with a newer kind of crisis that gained momentum in the late 20th century—the cybercrisis. Dissatisfied consumers and employees can enter an Internet chat room and, within minutes, begin airing complaints and spreading rumors about a company and its products and services. Quick support has been rallied online for major boycotts and protests. Negative Web sites crop up that are solely devoted to criticizing an organization and its policies.

When a college professor felt he didn't receive good customer service after complaining to Intel that there was a flaw in its Pentium computer chip, he took his complaints to the Internet. Despite growing negative publicity, Intel decided not to acknowledge the problem and chose not to notify its customers or offer a recall. The cybercrisis continued to escalate and, six months later, IBM announced it was halting shipments of PCs containing the faulty Intel chip. Finally forced to respond, Intel ran full-page newspaper ads apologizing for not handling customer complaints properly; the company also offered a free replacement Pentium.

Dissatisfied customers, disgruntled employees, and activist customers may turn to the Internet for more than just posting negative comments—they may create a rogue

Exhibit 14.2   Crisis Lessons Learned from a Tragedy

CRISIS LESSONS LEARNED FROM A TRAGEDY

Prior to September 11th, when was the last time you heard of a politician having an 85-90% approval rating? Probably never.

Former NYC Mayor Rudy Giuliani achieved this because of his strong yet compassionate leadership in the aftermath of the terrorist attacks on his city.

Through my tears for the human tragedy that was unfolding just 50 miles from my home, I watched from the perspective of a crisis management consultant. I was interested to see how the Mayor would communicate during this period of monumental crisis. Now that it is some months after that horrific event, I'd like to share some thoughts on what I observed. Perhaps it will help you prepare yourself for less catastrophic but still distressing crises that could occur in your company.

In my workshops, a major topic is entitled "The 10 C's of Good Crisis Communications." I will touch briefly on each of them as exemplified by the Mayor.

1. Be COOPERATIVE: The Mayor knew from years of experience that he had to make himself personally available to the press immediately. Any attempt on his part to avoid or delay meeting with reporters who were under the gun to relate the latest news would have led to miscommunication, rumor, and possibly panic.
2. Maintain CONTROL: He and his staff quickly set up a room for the media where they could be assured he would come to report the latest news. You do not want the media wandering around, getting in the way of emergency responders or officials trying to do their jobs.
3. Demonstrate CARING AND CONCERN: Expressions of compassion for those who have been victimized by an incident are always in order. Don't let your lawyers talk you out of this because they are afraid it will be interpreted as an admission of legal liability. Work with your legal advisors to find the best ways to word your expressions of condolence and comfort, but be sure to show kindness. Judges tend to throw the book at organizations that appear callous and uncaring.
4. Display COMPETENCE: Some executives and managers believe that, because they have achieved a position of authority, they somehow know instinctively what to do and say in a crisis. Many have learned that, sadly, this is not necessarily the case. Planning, preparation, and practice promote competence. When David Letterman asked the Mayor how he seemed to always know the right things to do and say, Rudy's answer was, "We DRILL on these things."
5. Be CREDIBLE: There are two major components of credibility.

(continued)

The first is to never lie. Hiding or even shading the truth will come back to haunt you. Some days after September 11th, even when the families of the victims did not want to hear the truth, the Mayor had to tell them the chances of rescuing anyone alive were extremely remote. The other aspect of credibility has to do with not speculating. Even though the media pushed for definite answers to important questions, if the Mayor did not have certain knowledge, he refused to be stampeded into an answer just to satisfy them.

6. Be CONSISTENT: Speak with one voice. Be on the same page. Get your story straight. These are ways to express this vital component of crisis communications. If a situation is long-term, where several spokespersons must be used, they must all coordinate their messages to prevent confusion or the impression that things are not quite as represented. Even slightly different versions can damage credibility. The Mayor and his deputies/department heads obviously briefed each other prior to appearing in front of the media.

7. Speak with CLARITY: Several things come into play here. Even when exhaustion is inevitable due to lack of sleep, try not to mumble. Do not use jargon or technical language. If a 5 cent word expresses your thought well, do not use a 50 cent word because you think it will impress people. Your goal is to communicate clearly.

8. Be CONCISE: This is a skill that comes with practice. The public does not want long drawn-out detailed explanations in the first throes of a crisis. They want the basic facts - as many as you can provide. The media is looking for "sound bites" - concise, memorable descriptions that conjure up a mental picture and lead to understanding. If your major message is buried among unimportant details, it may all end up on the editor's cutting room floor. Rudy was excellent in his ability to respond with answers that were to the point.

9. Keep CURRENT: Reporters have to know for a fact that they will be kept up to date with the latest developments if they stay in the designated media center. If too much time passes between briefings, they will become impatient and wander off to talk to other sources - anyone who will grant an interview.

10. Act with CALM: Note this does not say "BE calm." In a serious crisis, it would be a rare individual who would not be anxious. But a person who can demonstrate a steady confidence is highly regarded.

If your company experiences a crisis of any kind, you would be well served to remember the example set by Mayor Giuliani as he led New York City through some of the darkest days anyone could ever imagine.

Judith Hoffman is a crisis communications consultant, president of JCH Enterprises and author of *Keeping Cool on the Hot Seat: Dealing Effectively with the Media in Times if Crisis*.

■

Note: Reprinted with permission from Judith C. Hoffman, Principal, JCH Enterprises. www.judyhoffman.com

Web site. Ford Motor Co. found itself the victim of an Internet attack when the Association of Flaming Ford Owners posted a site demanding the recall of 26 million cars and trucks. McDonald's also was the target of a cyber-attack when the McInformation Network created a Web site called McSpotlight to provide the media and public with information on a lawsuit McDonald's had brought against two people who published a fact sheet featuring negative comments about the fast food chain on the Internet.

Managing the cybercrisis begins with actively monitoring what people are saying about you on the Internet. In addition to the daily chat room monitoring you can do sitting at your office computer, consider hiring an automated online monitoring service such as eWatch or CyberAlert to do a lot of the work for you. eWatch, for example, monitors more than 44,000 Usenet groups and electronic mailing lists, hundreds of public discussion areas hosted by services such as AOL and CompuServe, and nearly 6,000 Web publications for information on topics you designate. What should you do when faced with a cybercrisis?

- As with any crisis, have a plan. The Internet provides instant communication, and damaging comments can spread fast, not just to other consumers but to reporters and the financial community as well. Responding quickly, then, is critical. Having prepared strategies in place for potential cybercrises makes that quick response much easier.

- Defend yourself, but don't aggressively attack. If you know for a fact that claims being made online about your company are misinformed or false, make every effort to educate people and set the record straight. Don't go on the attack or try to shut down a negative site. Investigate the situation, open a dialogue to find out exactly what people are thinking, and then post information on your Web site and use listservs and third party experts to help correct misperceptions and regain support.

- Be ethical, and admit to mistakes. Never go into a chat room and pose as someone else to get information or try to influence people. If anyone finds out that you actually work for the company, this will certainly make the situation worse. And, keep an open mind. There may be times when a legitimate concern is brought to your attention in cyberspace. Do the right thing and work to solve the problem.

- Keep a watchful eye, even after the crisis is over. Once someone puts negative material on a Web site, it can stay up there for a long time. After the first crisis dies down, it is possible for the controversy to get reignited when new visitors access the information. Stay alert to those possibilities.

References and Suggested Reading

Barton, L. (2001). *Crisis in organizations: Managing and communicating in the heat of chaos* (2nd ed.). Cincinnati, OH: South-Western Publishing Co.

Center, A. H. & Jackson, P. (2003). *Public relations practices: Managerial case studies and problems* (6th ed.). Upper Saddle River, NJ: Prentice Hall.

Coombs, T. W. (1999). *Ongoing crisis communication: Planning, managing and responding*. Thousand Oaks, CA: Corwin Press.

Fearn-Banks, K. (2002). *Crisis communications: A casebook approach* (2nd ed.). Mahwah, NJ: Lawrence Erlbaum Associates.

Henry, R. A. (2001). *You'd better have a hose if you want to put out the fire*. Windsor, CA: Gollywobbler Productions.

Lukaszewski, J. E. (1995). *Communication standards: The principles and protocols for standard-setting individual and corporate communication*. White Plains, NY: The Lukaszewski Group.

Lukaszewski, J. E. (2000). *Media relations strategies during emergencies: A crisis communication management guide* (3rd ed.). White Plains, NY: The Lukaszewski Group.

Middleberg, D. (1996, November). How to avoid a cybercrisis. *Public relations tactics, 1,* 15.

Mitroff, I. I. & Anagnos, G. (2000). *Managing crises before they happen: What every executive and manager needs to know about crisis management*. New York: AMACOM.

Pinsdorf, M. K. (1999). *Communicating when your company is under siege: Surviving public crisis* (Rev. ed.). New York: Fordham University Press.

Seitel, F. (1994, November). Dealing with deadly disaster. *Public relations tactics, 1,* 13.

Seitel, F. (1995, January). 'No-tell' Intel learns silence isn't golden. *Public relations tactics, 1,* 13.

Wilson, S. (2002). *Real people, real crises: An inside look at corporate crisis communications*. Winchester, VA: Oakhill Press.

CASES

Case 49: Law Firm Launches PR Program (Part B)

Lisa Chen is a marketing assistant with the Fleischman, Craig, Gurdak, and Heasley law firm. She recently worked with Margaret Bogan, the firm's marketing and client relations director, to develop and begin executing a public relations program for the firm to help raise its visibility in the community (see chapter 5, case 13).

A few months after initial activities are approved and program implementation begins, Chen is called to Bogan's office to discuss a media opportunity. "I just spoke with Rebecca Foster. She's the managing editor of a group of eight community newspapers that circulate weekly throughout the area. We've worked on a few projects together in the past. Anyway, she tells me that they are planning a special section on financial and estate planning, and I suggested we could put together a by-lined piece on some of the important legal issues surrounding wills and estate planning, especially for people nearing retirement age. She liked the idea, since many of her readers fit this profile. She asked me to get back to her with more specifics on the content of the piece before we submit anything."

"I'd be happy to work on this, if you'd like," Chen says. "It strikes me that Jonathan Pomeroy would be the best person to work with on this article, since he heads up the wills and estate planning section and has a solid background in finance and retirement planning. Do you want me to set up a meeting with him?"

"Let me run the idea by him first and make sure he's okay with it," Bogan replies." He and I can also talk about some of the main points we might want to cover in an article like this, and I can share those with Rebecca before we go any further. Once she gives me the go-ahead on our approach, you can interview Jonathan and start writing a first draft. Rebecca told me that if she likes what we send her, she may be receptive to having us write a monthly guest column on legal issues, so I want to make sure we do this right."

That day, Bogan talks to Pomeroy and he agrees to take part in the project. He also tells her that he has met Foster before since their children go to the same school. Bogan then contacts Foster with more information about the by-lined article. Foster tells Bogan she likes the direction of the piece and that there's a good chance they would publish it. At the end of their conversation,

Bogan confirms a deadline for submission of the piece, and she lets Foster know that Chen will be coordinating the project from this point on. Foster says that Chen can use e-mail to correspond with her and to submit the final draft of the article.

Later that week, Chen interviews Pomeroy and begins preparing a first draft. After several rewrites, based on comments from both Pomeroy and Bogan, Chen prepares a final draft of the article for submission to Foster. It is approved by Bogan and Pomeroy and sent to Foster by e-mail, with a cover letter, several days before the agreed-upon deadline. The letter summarizes the content of the article and confirms details of Bogan's previous conversations with Foster about the piece. The next day, Chen calls Foster to confirm that she received the article. Foster tells Chen that she got the article and "it looks good," and they plan to publish it in the upcoming special section in two weeks.

Two weeks later, Bogan comes to Chen's office with the financial and estate planning special section in hand. "I think we may have a problem, Lisa. I just picked up the special section and I've looked through it from cover to cover, and I don't see Jonathan's by-lined piece anywhere. On top of that, Jonathan just stormed into my office and he wants to know why the piece didn't run. He insists that he's going to call Rebecca and ask her why, as he put it, 'she stiffed us.' He's involved in a conference call with a client right now, which should last another half hour or so, but there's no telling what he'll do after that. Frankly, I've never dealt with anything like this so I'm not sure what to do next."

Assignments

1. In a memorandum to your instructor, present an action plan in response to this situation. Specify the next steps to take, in sequence, and justify each step. (Or, the instructor can set up a role-playing exercise, with one student assigned to play the role of Chen and another to act out the role of Bogan. Pick up the conversation from the last line of the case. The student playing the role of Chen should advise Bogan on the next steps to take, in sequence.)

2. In the aftermath of this situation, Bogan asks Chen to prepare a media relations checklist for the attorneys that offers practical tips on dealing with reporters and conducting interviews. Prepare this checklist, using at least five sources. Explain how each tip or guideline is important for effective media relations. Attach a list of sources to your checklist.

Case 50: The Controversial TV Star

Tamara Rawlins is the community relations director for a major school district in her city. Students from Percy Junior High, a school in her district, recently won a contest sponsored by a local television station. Junior and senior high school students in the area were invited to collect cans and bottles during a two-week period. The school that raised the most money from the redemption of cans and bottles collected received the grand prize—several new computers donated by a local company, and a visit to the school by Shannon Steele, the hot new star of the popular "Rescue Beach" television series. All the money raised from the can and bottle drive was donated to a shelter for homeless and runaway youth run by the local Salvation Army.

A week before Steele's appearance at the school, Rawlins leaves for an education conference. The day Rawlins returns from the conference, she arrives home in the late afternoon to a number of messages on her answering machine. One of these is an urgent message left about an hour ago from Sandra Cassidy, who is the principal of Percy school. In her message, Cassidy asks Rawlins to call her as soon as she gets in "to talk about a serious problem we have with the Steele visit." As she is about to pick up the phone and call Cassidy, Rawlins gets a phone call from Ken Simmons, a reporter for the city's morning daily newspaper. She knows Simmons quite well and has worked with him on many stories.

"Hi Ken, what can I do for you?" Rawlins asks.

"I'm working on the story for tomorrow's paper about Shannon Steele and the contest that the Percy students won," Simmons says. "It seems that several kids from Percy have stumbled on some adult magazines with nude pictures of Steele, and they started circulating the magazines around the school. We've also found out that Steele spent some time a few years back as a model on one of those interactive pornography sites on the Internet. Did your school know about her background when you arranged this visit?" Simmons asks.

"Ken, to be honest, I just got home and I need to get more information about this. Can I ask you, is there proof that these pictures actually exist?"

"Apparently, a parent got a hold of one of the magazines earlier today and took it to the school principal, Sandra Cassidy. I've seen the photos so there's no question they exist. You should know that we're definitely running a story on this, and we'd like to have some comment from the school. I'm planning to file my story in about three hours or so."

Rawlins says: "Let me get back to you, okay? I'll try to call you back in about two hours."

Assignments

1. Compile a list of five to 10 questions to which Rawlins needs to get answers in the next few hours. Write each question exactly as it should be asked, and briefly state the importance of each.

2. In a memorandum to your instructor, specify the steps that Rawlins should take in the next two hours. Begin with the first step you would recommend, and explain why that should be the first step taken. Then, indicate and explain the sequence of steps to follow that first step, and justify the order of those steps.

3. Assume that a decision has been made to cancel Shannon Steele's visit in response to the strong objections voiced by parents and to avoid the negative attention this event would bring to the school, the students and their fund-raising efforts, and the other groups involved. Write a news release announcing the cancellation of the visit for distribution to the local media. Include a quote from an appropriate spokesperson.

Case 51: Workforce Reductions at Century Insurance

Century, Inc. is one of the largest U.S. insurance companies with revenues of $25 billion. It specializes in personal-lines insurance such as automobile, homeowners, and life insurance. As the company's director of corporate communications, Alicia Parenti has been involved in high-level management discussions regarding a proposed restructuring of the company and the elimination of 4,000 jobs. The reorganization will reduce Century's annual expenses by about $600 million and allow the company to finance a new service that makes it possible for consumers to buy insurance policies through the Internet. Today, the company's board of directors approved the proposed restructuring. Shortly after the meeting concludes, Parenti talks with Carter Hutton, Century's president and CEO, about communicating this decision to important audiences.

"This is a critical time for us since we've never had a layoff of this magnitude," Parenti says. "I want to make sure that I have all the facts about who will be losing their jobs and where those job cuts will take place."

"Right now, the plan is to eliminate about 500 jobs at corporate headquarters," Hutton replies. "The rest of the job losses will come from closing four regional offices in Kansas City, MO.; Columbus, OH; Orange, CA.; and Farmington, CT. There also may be some natural attrition, like early retirements. These are all non-agent jobs, mostly administrative and staff support positions. We need to stress that we won't be laying off any of our 15,000 insurance agents, so our customer service won't suffer at all during this time."

"It's my understanding that our goal is to start making the new Internet services available in 16 states in six months, and the rest of country will be able to tap into the service in about two years. Current customers will be able to use the Internet service, right?"

"Yes, that's right. Any new customers who purchase a policy over the Internet also will have access to an agent in their area, if that's important to them. I think we should make the point that while it's never easy to let people go, this is the only way for us to take better advantage of electronic commerce and to stay more competitive. In the end, our customers will benefit from the changes because more and more of them want to do business this way. We're responding to the marketplace, basically, and this is a move that's long overdue. As you know, last month our operating income dropped 35%, mainly because we've had to lower auto insurance rates to stay on a (level playing field) with all the new competition out there. Obviously, the company can't keep experiencing that kind of financial loss," Hutton says.

"Everything you're saying makes good sense, and it's a message we need to make sure the public and our customers hear. It won't make the people who are losing their jobs feel any better, so we should be sensitive about the way we share this news with them," Parenti adds.

"Agreed. Why don't you put together a plan that outlines how we should make this announcement, both to employees and the media. In this situation, I think I should be the primary spokesperson. The people affected need to hear this from the CEO; I'm sure you would agree. And let's move on this quickly. I don't want to risk any leaks or internal rumors starting. That could create serious problems for us."

Assignments

1. Prepare a communications plan, in memorandum form, for the employee and media announcements of Century's layoffs and office closings. Include the following in your plan:
   - An exact date and time in the next two weeks for the announcements and the order in which the announcements should occur. Support your choices.
   - The location for the announcements and the method/format to be used when making the announcements. Support your choices.
   - Any other key audiences to consider and the methods for communicating this announcement to those audiences.
   - A list of questions that employees and the media may ask, and speaking points for Hutton in response to those questions.

2. Write a news release on the Century layoffs for distribution to the media on the day of the announcement. Include a quote from the CEO.

Case 52: The Questionable Coffeemaker

Work-Rite is a national manufacturer known best by consumers for its high-quality power tools. In the past two years, Work-Rite's sales have leveled off, prompting management to conduct intensive marketing studies aimed at identifying a profitable new product category that will logically expand the company's current product line and appeal to new market segments. After months of research, Work-Rite is launching a line of household items designed for the "person on the go." The first product in that line, the Java-Flo under-the-cabinet coffee maker, is now being developed for distribution to key test market areas. The company hopes to make Java-Flo available in stores in time for the Christmas shopping season.

In preparation for the product's launch, Work-Rite's vice president of marketing communications, Nora Frazier, calls a meeting with her staff to discuss the development of a campaign to support the Java-Flo introduction. The day before the meeting, Frazier distributes background materials on the new product to each member of her six-person staff. This includes Guy Thomas, Work-Rite's consumer and media relations manager.

At 8 a.m. the next day, Frazier's staff gathers in the department's conference room for a brainstorming and strategy session. "Our main task is to start getting the word out about Java-Flo and to get consumers interested in the product before its makes its way into stores. There's a lot at stake here since this is a new venture for the company. If Java-Flo flops, it could mean a rough road ahead for all of us, and some of our jobs might even be on the line. We have to give 200% to this project since the work we do out of this office has the potential to make this product a success. This is a chance for our department to increase its value to the company and make some points with top management. With that said, where do we start?"

"Before we start throwing promotional ideas around, Nora, I'd like to talk about something I saw buried in the background materials that really bothers me," Thomas says. "It seems that one of the members of the product development team had some concerns about Java-Flo and how safe it is. He went on record saying that there are problems with Java-Flo's design, specifically its thermostat which he says, and I quote, 'has the potential to malfunction and start a fire.' Do we know anything else about this?"

"Here's what I can tell you," Frazier says. "The CEO and executive vice presidents are well aware of this man's claims. Apparently, this person has had a gripe with the company for some time about being passed over for a promotion, and he's not exactly well-respected by his colleagues. As a matter of fact, he's no longer employed by Work-Rite. He was let go because his supervisor said his work was not up to company standards. We consulted the other members of the product development team about this issue, and they said Java-Flo poses little risk, and the chance of a fire starting is something like one in 50 million. The company decided to move forward with the product based on the opinions of all the other team members. It's a bit late to turn back now, anyway, since production has kicked in and millions of dollars have already been invested."

Frazier then steers the discussion away from the product development report and begins the planning session. An hour and a half later during a break in the meeting, Frazier talks in private with Thomas. "You've been rather quiet today, Guy, so my guess is you're still worried about the safety allegations. Let me just say that I really don't believe the company would do anything that might harm consumers. I was there, and I heard the other product developers tell us, quite clearly, that this is not an unsafe product. What we need to do now is put this issue aside and start thinking about how we're going to get the media to write about Java-Flo. I'm relying on your expertise to help us do that. After our break, I'd like to hear your ideas on how we can get lots of publicity for Java-Flo."

Assignments

1. Assume you are Thomas. In a memorandum to Frazier, identify and explain any ethical, legal, and public relations problems related to this case. In addition, present your recommendations on the course of action Work-Rite should take regarding the Java-Flo product introduction.

It is now one year after the launch of Java-Flo. The product surpassed its sales goals for the first year; the company is satisfied with Java-Flo's market performance, and with the positive response from consumers. One afternoon, Guy Thomas receives a call from a television consumer reporter who is located in a major city in a nearby state. The reporter tells Thomas that a local woman contacted the station after her Java-Flo coffee maker caught on fire. He adds that the accident left the woman with second-degree burns, and that initial reports seem to indicate the coffee maker had a faulty thermostat, and this may have been the cause of the fire. The reporter asks for the company's reaction to this incident and to comment on Work-Rite's responsibility in this situation. Thomas tells the reporter that this is the first he's heard of the incident, and that he will call the reporter back once he's had a chance to look into the situation further.

Thomas informs Nora Frazier about the call and after a brief discussion, they call an urgent meeting with Work-Rite's CEO. During their discussion, Thomas mentions the previous report that claimed Java-Flo posed possible safety hazards to consumers. The CEO says, "We don't have to worry about that report since it has been destroyed. Basically, there's no record of that report ever existing. Frankly, I'd like to keep this as low-key as possible. Java-Flo is selling well for us, and getting too involved in this situation, or even commenting about it, could really set us back. We don't need a crisis like this right now. It could mean financial disaster for us. But you're my public relations counsel. What do you think we should do?"

2. What advice would you give the CEO about how to handle this situation? Present a plan of action in response to this situation. Begin with the first step you would recommend, and explain why that should be the first step taken. Then, indicate and explain the sequence of steps to follow in the next 24 hours.

15

Evaluation

As a preface to this final chapter, here are two quotes worth pondering from Socrates, the ancient Greek philosopher, and talk-show host and celebrity Oprah Winfrey, who some might call a modern-day prophet: "The unexamined life is not worth living," Socrates once said. And according to Winfrey, "Luck is a matter of preparation meeting opportunity."

How do these words of wisdom fit into a chapter on public relations evaluation and measurement, you might ask? Because like an unexamined life, a public relations program that is not examined and evaluated has little value to an organization. And, you can't leave the success of a program to chance or luck. You must think about how you will measure success during the initial stages of campaign planning, not as an afterthought once the campaign has ended.

Evaluation cannot be overlooked in the public relations process. Public relations professionals must provide hard evidence of their accomplishments, and how the work they did helped further the organization's business plan. Success has to be measured based on legitimate criteria, not personal feelings ("We think this was a good program.") or superficial judgments ("That story about us in the newspaper looked great, didn't it?"). The CEO expects marketing, sales, finance, and other key departments to show tangible results, and public relations must do the same to earn respect and justify the value of the function to the organization.

Because public relations involves a broad range of activities and many different approaches, there isn't "one right way" to measure public relations effectiveness. As this chapter points out, you measure public relations success by using a number of techniques that consider the specific public relations objectives you establish, the exposure created by communications tools and public relations activities, and the influence your work had in changing public perception or motivating people to do something that supports your organization and its mission.

The Components of Public Relations Measurement

A 2003 report published by the Institute for Public Relations titled "Public Relations Research for Planning and Evaluation" (Lindenmann, 2003b) recommends that public relations professionals consider four components of the evaluation process:

- Setting specific measurable public relations goals and objectives—have specific goals and objectives been established at the start? After a project is implemented, you can measure its success against predetermined goals and objectives. When goals and objectives are stated in specific terms, they are much easier to measure. For example, a public information campaign can aim to generate 1,000 phone calls or requests for information within a certain time period. The goal of an annual fund raiser might be to increase donations by 10% as compared to the previous year. Or, a professional organization hopes to double the number of attendees at its national conference.

- Measuring communication output—what public relations materials did you produce and what activities did you execute, and how much exposure or attention did you get as a result? Outputs are the most immediate and most visible results of a public relations program. Typical public relations outputs include quantities of brochures and other printed materials produced and distributed, the extent and content of media coverage gained through publicity, and the number of community events held and the total number of people who attended those events.

- Measuring communication outgrowths and outcomes—what impact did your public relations programming have on target publics' attitudes, behaviors, and actions? While outputs are short-term in nature, outcomes relate to the more lasting effect that public relations efforts had on your publics. Focus groups, audits, and other scientific research techniques are used to measure if a public received and understood messages contained within internal and external communications tools, or if a public felt more positively about an organization or situation following a public relations campaign. Also, consider changes in behavior that led to a desired action, such as endorsing a new organizational policy.

- Measuring institutional outcomes—how did public relations programming support the mission and profitability of the organization? Public relations programs that contribute on some level to increased sales or a better market share will carry more weight than those that don't. Public relations efforts alone cannot often be tied directly to improved sales. But the number of new business leads generated by a direct-mail brochure produced by the public relations department, and the number of those leads that turned into new clients or customers, are valid measures of public relations' impact on the bottom line.

Goals and objectives were discussed in detail in chapter 4; however, we should take a closer look at measuring output and outcomes.

Measuring Output

Public relations professionals are responsible for a variety of outputs. Output relates to exposure, so one way to establish how much exposure a program produces is to analyze media coverage. Conduct a ***content analysis*** that generally looks at how many media placements you received and the types of media (i.e., print, broadcast, online) in which those stories appeared; how many people potentially read, heard, or viewed those stories; and how effectively those media placements conveyed your organization's key messages. If your organization generates extensive media coverage, you may want to hire a ***media clipping service*** (see Exhibit 15.1) to handle this for you. For each media placement, consider these content analysis criteria:

- Name of each newspaper, magazine, radio station, television station or electronic publication, and the publication or broadcast date. The reach and frequency of the media outlet's distribution should also be included. ***Reach*** refers

Exhibit 15.1   Clipping Services

Burrelle's (www.burrelles.com)
Monitors 18,000 nationwide publications, which includes all daily and non-daily newspapers and more than 7,000 magazines and newsletters. Provides word-for-word transcripts of network and local radio and TV segments, as well as Web monitoring. News clip analysis of article type and size, editorial slant, impressions and key word mentions.

PRtrak (www.PRtrak.com)
Calculates audience impressions and advertising dollar equivalency for TV, radio, newspaper, and magazine stories in all major U.S. markets. Allows user to input data related to a media placement at his or her desktop and get quick information on media values and content analysis.

CyberScan (www.clippingservice.com)
Provides clipping service and online issues tracking. Webscan service monitors millions of Web sites and all major online publications based on a keyword search. Opinion Monitoring service tracks issues and what's being said about an organization in Usenet groups, listservs, bulletin boards, and forums.

Luce Press Clippings (www.lucepress.com)
Reads more than 15,000 publications daily including all daily newspapers; most weekly newspapers; and consumer, business, trade, and professional magazines. Also monitors network radio and TV coverage and local TV coverage in more than 150 cities.

WebClipping.com
Key word searches of 20,000 online news sources and publications, 63,000 Usenet groups, 1.5 billion Web pages, and 90 live streaming newswires. Provides 600-word e-mail summaries of each clip, and a link to the actual text or online location of text.

to how many people are exposed to the medium during a specific time period (such as "sweeps weeks"). *Frequency* refers to the number of times those people were exposed.

- Type of placement (i.e., news or feature article, op-ed piece) and length of each story in total column inches, paragraphs, pages or seconds/minutes of air time. Consider figuring out how much the coverage you received would have cost if it had appeared as advertising. Also, look at the source of each story. For example, did it result from a news release or pitch letter you sent or a media event you held? Tracking the source of each story will help you assess the effectiveness of specific publicity tools in generating media interest and make adjustments when developing future media campaigns.

- *Media impressions* refer to the total circulation of a newspaper or magazine, or the total number of people listening to or watching a radio or television program. If a daily newspaper has a circulation of 500,000 readers, and two stories are published in that newspaper, then that coverage produces 1 million impressions. Such numbers can be impressive, but don't mistake impressions with impact. Impressions represent the number of people who may have been exposed to your message at a given time. They don't tell you if desirable target groups received the message, understood it, or acted on it.

- Subject, tone, and key message points. Summarize the editorial focus of the story and total mentions of your organization by name in the headline and body copy. Identify individuals from your organization quoted or referred to in the story. Look at how often your organization and its officials are mentioned in comparison to your competitors. Also, determine if the story portrays your organization in a favorable light and if it positions company officials in a desirable way (i.e., as industry experts or thought leaders.) The tone of a piece can be open to interpretation. What some view as a positive story, others may see as a neutral or even slightly negative piece. You should, however, examine how clearly and accurately the story conveys your key message points and attempts to give a balanced view of the topic.

When evaluating outputs, you also need to think about *events*. Events designed to generate media coverage are assessed based on the media turnout and interest in your announcement, and the number of stories produced as a result of the event. It is also smart to assess the logistics of the event. Was the room or facility where the announcement was made large enough to accommodate the media? Were there any questions asked for which your spokespersons could have been better prepared? Was videoconferencing or Webcasting technology used without any glitches?

For community and other special events, a primary evaluation measure is attendance. Did you get the turnout you hoped for? For annual events, event planners often try to increase attendance, participation, or monies raised based on the previous year's numbers. Give participants a brief evaluation form, either in a registration packet handed out at the start of an event, or at the end of the event. Ask them to let you know what they learned or gained from attending the event, and get their comments on the quality of speakers, activities, facilities, and food. This feedback can be useful as it will help you redesign future events with publics' concerns and interests in mind.

Newsletters, Brochures, and Other Publications

You should do more than simply look at how many publications are distributed and to whom they are being sent. Conduct periodic readership studies to find out if your target publics are taking the time to read your newsletter, what content they are reading most often, and the kinds of stories they would like to see in comparison to the types of articles you are publishing. A simple questionnaire can assess readership preferences, while interviews and focus groups are good techniques for examining readership habits in more depth.

Build response mechanisms into your brochures such as reply cards, toll-free numbers, and Web site addresses. Track how many reply cards you receive requesting more information. Tabulate the number of phone calls and Web site visits you get as a result of brochure distribution. Always ask new customers if they received a printed piece that prompted them to call your company or visit its Web site.

Web Sites

One way to measure how well your Web site is doing is to monitor the site's *traffic*—that is, the number of people who make daily visits to your site. Even more critical is the number of return visits a person makes, if those visitors include a large percentage of potential customers you hope to reach, and if those customers are making more specific product inquiries or placing orders online. Also monitor the pages that are visited most and least often, and adjust the site content accordingly. As with media impressions, don't be fooled by a large number of hits. They don't tell you if desirable target groups received the message, understood it, or acted on it.

If overall traffic is low, you may need to expand your promotional strategies or re-think the content of the site to make it more appealing. Always include a "Feedback," "E-Mail Us" or "Tell Us" section for visitors to give you suggestions for improving the site to make it more useful and more user friendly. Respond quickly to people and let them know you've received their e-mail and that you appreciate their feedback.

Measuring Outcomes

Evaluating output helps you to see if your communications materials and activities have been well received, and if a target public took notice of what you had to say. But it is critical to go further to find out if the information you shared increased audience under-standing, led to a change in their thinking, or inspired them to take action.

You cannot assume that people became more aware of something based on the number of stories they may have read in the media, or that they have become more supportive of an issue because a few of them wrote positive letters to the editor.

Benchmarking is used to help accurately measure changes in awareness levels or changes in public opinion. Before implementing a public relations program, conduct interviews, focus groups, or surveys to clearly identify what people know or think about an issue. This provides a benchmark or a point of reference at the start of the campaign. After the campaign concludes, do follow-up focus groups or surveys and compare your findings at that time with previous research results. If awareness levels are higher or public opinion has shifted more in your favor, then you can say more definitely that your public relations programming elevated awareness or influenced opinion.

You also need to ask yourself, did our public relations efforts produce action-based outcomes and support the organization's goals? The Department of Health Services for the State of California wanted to reduce the escalating costs incurred by state and local governments for emergency health care provided to uninsured children. To deliver health care to that audience, the Department of Health Services launched the "Healthy Families/Medi-Cal for Children" public relations campaign to deliver preventive, low-cost health care to uninsured California children. Working with Hill & Knowlton in Los Angeles, the department set up a toll-free phone line. The hotline made it possible for callers to get information on low-cost health care and to be put in touch with community-based organizations in the state that could assist them in securing this coverage.

The hotline, which handled calls in more than 10 different languages, received more than 270,000 calls, and 60,000 of those callers got referrals to local "Healthy Families" enrollment sites. In the end, the campaign was credited with enrolling more than 90,000 uninsured children in the "Healthy Families" program. Public relations strategies, then, had a positive impact because they motivated the target public to take a desired action—to call the hotline and enroll in the program—but they also contributed significantly to the organization's goals of providing low-cost health care to uninsured children, reducing government spending on health care, and improving the overall health care of California residents.

An Evaluation Case Study

The Puget Sound Environmental Quality Agencies and Elgin DDB launched a campaign aimed at getting residents of the Seattle and King County areas to change their lawn-mowing habits and reduce the amount of grass clippings being left for curbside trash pick-up. By doing this, they would alleviate the extra burden on the region's landfills and composting facilities in the spring and summer months.

Several events were organized and targeted to male homeowners 25 to 65 years old during late March and early April in 1999. The events not only focused on educating people about the problem but also on getting them to trade in old lawn mowers for new electric mulching mowers that are better for the environment and that lessen the amount of grass clippings left on the lawn after it is cut.

The key objectives of the campaign were to sell 3,000 mulch mowers at special sales events, draw at least 5,000 people to these events, remove 1,500 high-polluting gas lawnmowers from the market, and see a 5% reduction in the curbside disposal of grass clippings. Publicity and media advertising created exposure for the events, resulting in

22 television news stories and 17 newspaper articles, with an average audience of 150,000 per story. The media coverage helped build awareness of and bring people to the four events, which attracted 12,000 people. At the events, 5,000 mulch mowers were sold and 2,600 gas mowers were traded in and recycled. In the end, curbside disposal of grass clippings dropped by 17%, more than three times the level that was hoped for.

This example illustrates how the four components of public relations evaluation are incorporated into a single campaign. Clear and specific public relations objectives were set, and outputs such as media coverage and event attendance were tracked and measured. In the end, public relations outcomes were positive—the events and media strategies motivated a targeted group of people to take action and change their behaviors. They changed the way they cared for the lawns by trading in gas mowers for mulch mowers. This, in turn, satisfied city, county, and environmental agencies that wanted to ease the strain on over-extended landfills and improve air quality in the area through the use of more environmentally friendly mulch mowers.

References and Suggested Reading

Alexander, J. E. & Tate, M. A. (1999). *Web wisdom: How to evaluate and create information quality on the web*. Mahwah, NJ: Lawrence Erlbaum Associates.

Anderson, F. W. & Hadley, L. (1999). *Guidelines for setting measurable PR objectives*. Gainesville, FL: Institute for Public Relations Research and Education.

Daymon, C. & Holloway, I. (2002). *Qualitative research methods in public relations and marketing communications*. New York: Routledge.

Li, Hairong. (2002). Advertising media. *Encyclopedia of advertising*. Chicago: Fitzroy Dearborn Publishers.

Lindenmann, W. K. (2003a). *Guidelines and standards for measuring and evaluating PR effectiveness*. Gainesville, FL: Institute for Public Relations Research and Education.

Lindenmann, W. K. (2003b). *Public relations research for planning and evaluation*. Gainesville, FL: Institute for Public Relations Research and Education.

Patterson, J. G. (1996). *Benchmarking basics: Looking for a better way*. Menlo Park, CA: Crisp Publications.

Socrates. (n.d.). Retrieved December 15, 2002 from http://www.yokemonster.com/quotes/quotes/s/q101168.html

Winfrey, Oprah. (n.d.). Quotes worth repeating. Retrieved December 15, 2002 from http://www.womenwhonetwork.com/Quote.asp

CASES

Case 53: Evaluating the United Way Campaign (Part B)

It is four months after the series of articles on United Way agencies began running in the daily newspaper in your area (see chapter 8, case 27). You are a public relations intern with the local United Way, and it has been your responsibility to write and submit the articles each week to the newspaper. During the three-month period, the newspaper published a weekly profile of a United Way agency on the community page of its Sunday edition.

Two days ago, the United Way completed its annual fall fund-raising campaign. A large percentage of the monies distributed to local United Way agencies each year is raised during this critical period. This year's campaign has been one of the most successful in the local United Way's history. Langston Hill, the director of communications, calls a meeting with United Way staff to begin assessing the campaign.

"I'm happy to report to everyone that we reached our fall campaign fund-raising goal, and the board is also happy about that. We received excellent support from the local media, and the series on United Way agencies that the newspaper has been running gave us some prime visibility leading up to and continuing through the campaign period. Another positive result is all the new donors we've seen this year. There's been a big jump in the number of people who gave to the United Way for the first time, which is very encouraging."

Hill continues. "As is usually the case, I want to prepare a report for the board that gives them a wrap-up of the campaign and evaluates what we did well and what didn't work so well. I'm especially interested in the surge in new donors. I'm curious about the reasons behind this increase, and what we might have done this year to contribute to the increase. What we learn from examining the new donor audience and our communication with that group could be extremely valuable when we start developing materials for next year's campaign."

Assignment

1. You have been asked by Hill at this meeting to assist with the campaign evaluation process. He wants you to focus specifically on the increase in new donors.

(a) Identify 10 specific questions you would ask at the meeting that will guide the United Way in its efforts to evaluate the fall fund-raising campaign as well as the increase in new donors. Write each question exactly as you would ask it, and briefly explain why that question is important to the evaluation process.

(b) Prepare a memorandum for Hill that presents recommended methods or techniques for evaluating the United Way's success in recruiting new donors. Specify each evaluation method and clearly explain the steps or activities that would be involved in carrying out each method. Justify your recommendations.

Case 54: Assessing the Value of a Community Sponsorship

For three years, your company has been a major corporate sponsor of a road race held each July in its headquarter's city. The RoadRunner race is regarded as one of the top running events in the country. Hundreds of local, national, and international runners take part in the annual race, which generates millions of dollars in tourism revenue in that area. Last year's race attracted more than 100,000 spectators and national media attention; attendance is expected to be even higher this year.

In your role as media and community relations director, you developed the initial proposal recommending that your company sponsor the event and now manage all details of the sponsorship. This includes serving on the RoadRunner planning committee, promoting the company's sponsorship to key audiences, and evaluating the exposure and other public relations benefits gained from sponsoring the race.

After this year's race, which takes place in one month, your company completes its three-year sponsorship contract. This has led some members of senior staff to raise some hard questions about the value of the sponsorship and whether it is worth the money spent. Sponsorship costs are approximately 40% of the annual community and media relations budget. The company's vice president of marketing and public relations, to whom you report, calls a meeting to discuss the company's concerns about continuing the sponsorship.

"Both the CEO and the board have generally been happy with all the attention we've received from this event in the community and in the media. But they've got some questions about the real value of this sponsorship. Are we getting something substantial for all the money we're spending, outside of just feeling good about it and showing our community spirit? That's all fine and good, true, but how much is this helping our bottom line? Do our customers really care? I have to admit, I share some of the board's concerns about all of this."

Hart continues. "So, we have to think more carefully about evaluating the event this year. Besides the usual criteria we look at when we evaluate the success of an event, let's look more closely at public opinion and what people think about our company's sponsorship of the race. I'd like some thoughts from you on some of the specific issues we need to address in this evaluation process, and how we might go about getting the information we need."

Assignment

Prepare a five-page proposal in memorandum form that recommends evaluation methods for assessing the value of the RoadRunner race sponsorship. Include:

- An introduction that summarizes the challenges you face in this situation. In this section, identify specific questions that you would like the evaluation process to answer. In one sentence, state the question. Then, briefly explain why that question is important to the evaluation process.
- Goals of your evaluation program and the key audiences you will target.
- Specific methods and techniques to be used in evaluating the event itself, as well as the value of the sponsorship to the company. Each method should be clearly stated, explained, and justified.

Case 55: The Great American Smokeout Events (Part B)

You work as a fund-raising and community relations specialist for the American Cancer Society. It is several weeks before the annual Great American Smokeout (see chapter 13, case 47), and you have two events planned on that day—one for children ages 6 to 11, and one for non-White teens in your community. This morning, you sit down with executive director Nick Copanas to begin mapping out an evaluation plan for the day's activities.

"I'd like us to give some thought now to how we will measure the success of the Smokeout this year," Copanas says. "Obviously, there are the usual techniques that we use to evaluate what participants thought of the events we sponsored, and to examine the media coverage we got. But I want to go deeper with the evaluation this year. I'd like to look more closely at the specific reactions teens had to the Smokeout. Did they even hear about it? What kind of impact did the day have on their attitudes about smoking? You had suggested before that we do some more formal research in this area, and I think the time is right to do just that."

"I'm glad to hear that we're finally ready to get this kind of feedback," you reply. "One of the concerns I've had with the Smokeout is that we've been relying mostly on national studies and statistics to guide what we do locally. That's fine, and it's smart to use any legitimate research to help you design good programs. But we just never seem to have the time or the resources to do public opinion research locally."

"The difference this year is that I've hooked up with one of the local colleges, and we've arranged to work with some public relations students on some post-

Smokeout research. They'll work closely with us to develop and execute research methods and to put together any questionnaires or other research materials we'll need. Getting the students involved will save us some time and money, but still give us some quality work," Copanas says.

"I'm assuming that I'll be the key contact here working with the students. It would probably be smart if I started thinking about research strategy and some of the options we have for getting feedback from the teen audience."

"Good, I was going to suggest that," Copanas responds. "I'd like the two of us to have a chance to discuss some of the different research approaches we could take before our first meeting with the students. And while you're doing that, jot down some specific ideas for evaluating any media coverage we get related to the Smokeout. I want to take a careful look at the how the local media covers the Smokeout, and then use that information to fine tune next year's publicity and media relations efforts."

Assignments

1. In a memorandum to Copanas, present a plan for evaluating the impact of the Great American Smokeout on local teens and their attitudes about smoking. Include the following information:

   - Goals of post-Smokeout research directed to teens.
   - Possible sample selection methods. Recommend and justify a preferred method.
   - Three or four public opinion research methods that could be used to target teens. Explain the pros and cons of each method. Recommend the research method you think will produce the best results, and justify your choice.
   - Ten questions that should be asked of the teen audience when conducting the post-Smokeout evaluation. Write the question exactly as you would ask it, and briefly explain the importance of that question to the evaluation process.

2. In an attachment to the above memorandum, specify techniques for evaluating media coverage of the Great American Smokeout. Clearly identify and describe each technique, and explain the importance of that technique to the evaluation process.

Case 56: Measuring the Impact of an Image Campaign

Top Flight Airlines has been providing service to a major U.S. city for almost 60 years, and it recently signed a 30-year lease at that city's newly-renovated international airport. Top Flight employs thousands of people and supports 200 charitable causes in the area. Despite its positive impact on the local economy and its contributions to the community, Top Flight has a serious image problem and is not fully recognized for all the good it does in the area.

Public opinion surveys show that a majority of residents have negative perceptions of the airline. Many feel that Top Flight, which now has a 70% market share, drove a well-liked competitor out of the city. The competitor was highly visible and respected for its community outreach and corporate philanthropy. Shortly after this development, Top Flight increased its ticket prices, as did other major carriers at hub airports across the country. Top Flight received much negative publicity following the price hikes. To further complicate the situation, malfunctions in critical airport operations contributed to many delayed openings of the new international airport, and Top Flight received bad press in connection with this story, even though the airline had no control over the problems.

Top Flight management realized that something had to be done to change negative public opinion and more firmly demonstrate the airline's commitment to the community. Your agency was hired to develop and implement a major public relations campaign targeted to 1) the local media, 2) business, civic, and other community leaders, 3) consumer groups such as frequent fliers and business and leisure travelers, and (4) local employees. The campaign's objectives:

- Educate the media and business community about the benefits of being the primary carrier in that city, in an effort to reverse the negative media coverage and establish Top Flight as the "hometown airline."
- Better publicize philanthropic activities to produce more positive stories.
- Place more executives on major community boards to create a stronger local leadership position for the airline.
- Build relationships and alliances with key business and civic organizations.
- Identify additional corporate sponsorships that further support the airline's established corporate philanthropy.

Your agency recommended multiple public relations and communications strategies including proactive media relations; more focused community relations and greater outreach to community influencers; and special events and sponsorships, including a signature event that Top Flight could call its own in the community. The agency decided on and implemented the following tactics:

- Create a local news bureau to research and place more positive stories about the airline's employees, local philanthropy, innovations, and passenger benefits.
- Conduct media training with executives to sharpen their abilities as company spokespeople; hold ongoing media briefings with local media to keep them updated about operations, issues, etc.
- Use your agency's contacts to place local Top Flight executives on influential community boards.

- Organize and sponsor business breakfasts and secure speaking engagements directed to community and business leaders, in an effort to align Top Flight's interests with the local community's needs and goals.
- Write and distribute a monthly newsletter to community leaders and customers to communicate the advantages Top Flight brings to customers in that hub city, the positive contributions it makes to the area, and other key messages.
- Establish a signature corporate sponsorship to redesign the planetarium at the city's museum of science and technology and provide continued financial support for its upkeep; the planetarium is now known as the Top Flight Planetarium.
- Organize a week-long series of pride events to celebrate the new airport's first anniversary and Top Flight's first-year employee accomplishments, which included one of the best on-time records for flights anywhere in the country.

Assignment

You have been charged with measuring the effectiveness of Top Flight's image campaign. In a memorandum to your instructor, recommend the evaluation methods and techniques you would use to assess the impact of this campaign. Identify each method, describe the method and what it would involve, and be specific about the information or insight you would hope to gain.

Tips from the Top

"Assessing the Impact of Online Publicity Tools and Web Sites"
B. L. Ochman

B. L. Ochman, president of whatsnextonline, describes her New York City-based firm as a "positioning agency" that helps Internet companies build traffic to their Web sites and then convert that traffic to greater sales by using a variety of techniques including public relations, cyber marketing, direct marketing, events and other marketing tools. In this piece, she suggests ways to get more mileage from online publicity efforts and how to best evaluate your organization's Web site.

Q: When doing online publicity, you believe that using traditional news releases is a "colossal waste of time." Why is that?

A: Too many companies are simply taking the 8½" × 11" print news release and putting that version online. But on an e-mail screen, a traditional print news release is too long and takes up too much space. Editors have to scroll past contact information and long and wordy headlines before they can get to the real point of the story.

Q: What format do you recommend for news releases that are sent to the media online?

A: I prefer to use more of a media advisory format, with "who, what, when, where, and why" headings. Any online release should be 200 words or so, about five short paragraphs. Use a strong subject line and headline, and keep those short and sweet. Avoid using long words. Be provocative in the subject line, but not too cute. For a story on former welfare mothers who had gone on to become successful entrepreneurs, I used a subject line that read "A story about Cinderella entrepreneurs." If it takes more than one sentence to say it in your subject line or headline, then you haven't figured out what you have to say.

Q: I read in one of your whatsnextonline newsletters that you like to use pitch letters, too.

A: Yes, I think a pitch letter is better. Everyone else is writing a news release, but editors will end up writing their own stories. You have to get editors interested first, and a strong pitch can do that. Once they're interested, then you can send them more information. In that first pitch, you need to leave out extraneous information and give editors something they can use. I interviewed 30 editors to find out what they looked for in pitches. They said they looked for stories about trends, or a new model for business, or something that has impact on a lot of readers. Or, as I like to say, a story that can pass the "Hey Martha" test. It would make someone say, "Hey Martha, come look at this story."

Q: **What about promoting Web sites? Talk about methods you think are most effective for promoting traffic to sites.**

A: You have to begin with the content of the site. It needs to have marketable features built in, some way to get people engaged, and for people to interact. When you have something interactive in place, then you can say, "What can I do to promote this site?" Surveys and polls are good ways to get people involved, and the media likes to publish the results of surveys, which can create more exposure for a site. What you do to promote a site depends on the subject of the site, but we have a lot of success with cross promotions.

Q: **Cross promotions? What do you mean by that, and how are they used? Can you give me an example?**

A: One of our clients is a company that makes home colon cancer testing kits. This is an embarrassing subject and we had to ask ourselves, how do we make this something people would want to know more about. We did some cross promotions and built alliances with other Web sites to help build traffic from one site to another. For example, we wrote copy about colon cancer and the testing kit and provided it to other relevant health sites. Those sites also included a link to our colon cancer site. Some of the company's experts were made available to other health sites, too.

We also worked with an African American chef who developed some easy recipes for colon cancer prevention and he featured those on his Web site. African American men were an important target audience so this made good sense from a marketing perspective. And we set up radio and television appearances to promote the chef and the recipes, and this helped build awareness of his site and our client's site.

Q: **I'd like to shift the discussion to evaluation of Web sites. Let's start with content. How do you know if the written content is doing the job?**

A: This has to start at the beginning. When we create a Web site for a client, we do a competitive site anaylsis to give us an idea of the kind of content to include. We look at the presentation of competitive sites, features, navigation ease, things like that, and then ask ourselves, what could we do differently or better with our site. A lot of people put their site up and say "Thank goodness we got that up," but an Internet site needs to change. There should be at least one area of the site where information changes on a regular basis. When a regular visitor returns to the site for a third time, he should see something new on the site.

Q **When looking at how well the overall site is performing, you can track the total "hits" or visits to the site but you say this is not enough, right?**

A: No. The real issue is, what percentage of traffic converted to sales. Take a close look at site logs. Site logs indicate how much traffic has come to the site and where it came from. The site log can tell you what someone's path to the site was. It can tell you the number of people that came to your site from time.com, for example. This is useful since it can tell you how well your Web site publicity and promotion is working. The log tells you where visitors came in to the site and where they came out; what are the most popular times of the day and night to visit; and how many people came to the order page, but didn't complete the order. This might lead you to take a second look at the order form and maybe make changes to the form to make the process easier.

Q: **You say that a good online news release or pitch should summarize the story in two sentences. In two sentences, then, what would you say are the most important criteria for measuring the impact of a Web site?**

A: A Web site is doing the job if you find that you're getting repeat traffic and the conversion rate to sales is going up. So if 100 people come to a site and three people buy products, that's a 3% conversion. If you do some kind of integrated marketing campaign and after six months 400 people have visited the site and 75 of those people bought products or made inquiries, then your conversion rate is going up.

Q: **Is there any other advice you would give to people working in the public relations field about Web sites and using the Internet?**

A: The most important information on a site is on the first page above the fold. If people have to click three or four times to get to the good stuff, they will never get to it. And, the most important information visitors can give you on the Internet is their e-mail address and permission to send e-mail.

It's not easy to hide information with the explosion of the Internet. There are sites now where people can put in their opinions about companies—one of those is opinions.com. You need to be aware of forums, chat rooms, and discussion groups that affect your client or company. You can't ignore what customers and potential customers are saying; this can translate to important opportunities since you have the chance to respond to a criticism and do it instantly, not in a few months. You can't just keep track of what people are saying, either. Someone has to look at what people are saying and analyze and report on what they are saying and how this can impact your company. This is an important job for public relations people.

The Public Relations Process

Research

- ☐ Conduct primary research
- ☐ Review secondary sources
- ☐ Include situation analysis

Planning

- ☐ Identify goal(s)
- ☐ Identify target publics
- ☐ Write measurable objectives
- ☐ Develop strategies
- ☐ Outline tactics
- ☐ Develop budget
- ☐ Establish timetable

Execution

- ☐ Develop message(s)
- ☐ Determine channel(s) of distribution

Evaluation

- ☐ Measure communication output
- ☐ Measure communication outgrowths and outcomes
- ☐ Measure institutional output
- ☐ Compare measurements to objectives

Message Development

- ☐ Identify purpose of piece
- ☐ Identify and analyze target audience
- ☐ Determine how piece will be used and/or distributed
- ☐ Determine what information is needed
- ☐ Determine best way to obtain information

Interviews

Before

☐ Make appointment
☐ Confirm time, place, and purpose
☐ Provide prep questions to interviewee
☐ Research interviewee and topic
☐ Prepare questions
☐ Get permission to tape record interview
☐ Check tape recorder for batteries and adequate tape
☐ Bring notepad and extra pens

After

☐ Review notes immediately
☐ Send thank you

Memo

Format

☐ Company letterhead

☐ Heading (to, from, date, subject)

☐ Single space between lines; double space between paragraphs

Content

☐ Clearly state purpose in first sentence

☐ Include important points in body

☐ Suggest follow-up action in closing

Writing

☐ Brief

☐ Short sentences and paragraphs

☐ Personal language ("I," "you," "we")

Planning Memo

Format

☐   Company letterhead
☐   Heading (to, from, date, subject)
☐   Subheads
☐   Single space between lines; double space between paragraphs
☐   Numbered items
☐   Graphics

Content

☐   Introduce plan
☐   Summarize research
☐   Include situation analysis
☐   Identify goal(s)
☐   Identify target publics
☐   Include measurable objectives
☐   Outline strategies and tactics
☐   Include budget
☐   Include timetable
☐   Explain evaluation methods to be used
☐   Reinforce strengths and benefits of plan in conclusion

Writing

☐   Easy to read
☐   Informative but persuasive

Business Letter

Format

- ☐ Company letterhead
- ☐ Heading (date; recipient's name, title, company, and address)
- ☐ Salutation
- ☐ Closing and signature
- ☐ Single space between lines; double space between paragraphs

Content

- ☐ Clearly state reason for letter in first paragraph
- ☐ Present key ideas in subsequent paragraphs

Writing

- ☐ Brief
- ☐ Personal language ("I," "you," "we")

Response to Complaint Letter

Format

☐ Company letterhead

☐ Heading (date; recipient's name, title, company, and address)

☐ Salutation

☐ Closing and signature

☐ Single space between lines; double space between paragraphs

Content

☐ Acknowledge complaint in first paragraph

☐ Don't make accusations

☐ Show concern

☐ Outline specific steps to correct problem

☐ Offer apologies, if appropriate and cleared by legal counsel

☐ Stress value of customer and his/her business

Writing

☐ Brief

☐ Personal language ("I," "you," "we")

E-mail Message

Format

☐ Strong subject line
☐ Formal closing (sender's name, title, company, phone, fax, e-mail, Web site)
☐ Check to see if attachments are welcome by recipient

Content

☐ Clearly state purpose in first paragraph

Writing

☐ Brief
☐ Personal language ("I," "you," "we")
☐ E-mail etiquette used (proper use of capitalization, no smiley faces, etc.)

Research Report

Format

☐ Cover page (title, names, date)
☐ Table of contents
☐ Executive summary
☐ Introduction
☐ Narrative
☐ Supporting information
☐ Charts/graphs/graphics
☐ Bibliography

Content

☐ Detail findings
☐ Interpret and analyze data
☐ Discuss implications
☐ Propose recommendations

Writing

☐ Short sentences and paragraphs

Grant Proposal

Format

- ☐ Narrative
- ☐ Supporting information
- ☐ Budget
- ☐ Timetable
- ☐ Credentials of key staff
- ☐ Authorized signatures

Content

- ☐ Clearly state proposal at beginning of narrative
- ☐ Present background on problem
- ☐ Use statistics and hard evidence
- ☐ Include reasons why proposal should be funded
- ☐ Address short- and long-term benefits
- ☐ Identify target publics
- ☐ Include goals and measurable objectives
- ☐ Include budget
- ☐ Include timetable
- ☐ Explain evaluation methods to be used
- ☐ Emphasize cost efficiency
- ☐ Express confidence in idea

Writing

- ☐ Concise, persuasive language
- ☐ Appeal to self-interest of all parties
- ☐ Tailor to reader

Annual Report

Format

- ☐ Theme
- ☐ CEO letter to shareholders
- ☐ Detailed financial facts, figures, and statements
- ☐ Company information
- ☐ Photos, charts, or other visuals

Content

- ☐ Review previous year
- ☐ Examine current or potential critical issues
- ☐ Show connection with company goals

Writing

- ☐ Factual, straightforward, honest
- ☐ Positive tone
- ☐ Simple, easy-to-understand language
- ☐ Avoid technical terms
- ☐ Active voice
- ☐ Visually creative and interesting

News Release

Format

☐ Company letterhead

☐ Minimum 1-inch margin on all sides

☐ 1½- to 2-line spacing between sentences; no double spacing between paragraphs

☐ Indent paragraphs

☐ Contact information: name, title, phone number, e-mail

☐ Date release is distributed

☐ Release information

☐ Headline

☐ Dateline

☐ End mark

☐ For additional pages: "more" and slug

Content

☐ Lead with news

☐ Emphasize local angle

☐ State why news is significant

☐ Include details: who, what, where, how, when

☐ Provide background information

☐ Include boilerplate

☐ Use strong quotes that are not obvious or too self-serving

Writing

☐ Short sentences and paragraphs

☐ Objective

☐ Active voice

☐ Few adjectives

☐ AP style

E-mail Version

☐ Address individually (avoid group mailings)

☐ Include strong subject line

☐ Include headline

☐ Include contact information

☐ Summarize important information

☐ Direct reader to full release on the Web

Broadcast Version

☐ Avoid hard news or details in first sentence

☐ Use simple, one-subject, one-verb sentences

☐ Avoid clauses that begin with "who," "which," or "where"

☐ Write for the ear

☐ Use conversational tone

☐ Use active voice

☐ Attribute information up front

☐ Use pronouncers (phonetic spellings)

☐ Radio: consider including actuality (8 to 12 seconds)

☐ TV: consider a-roll (90 seconds) and b-roll

Media Alert

Format

☐ Company letterhead
☐ Minimum 1-inch margin on all sides
☐ 1½- to 2-line spacing between sentences; no double spacing between paragraphs
☐ Indent paragraphs
☐ "Media Advisory" label
☐ Contact information: name, title, phone number, e-mail
☐ Headline

Content

☐ Summarize why event is newsworthy
☐ Include only necessary details: who, what, where, when
☐ Avoid too much information

Writing

☐ Brief
☐ Clear and concise
☐ AP style

E-mail Version

☐ Address individually (avoid group mailings)
☐ Include strong subject line
☐ Include headline
☐ Include contact information
☐ Summarize important information

Pitch Letter

Format

- ☐ Company letterhead
- ☐ Heading (date; recipient's name, title, company, and address)
- ☐ Salutation
- ☐ Closing and signature
- ☐ Single space between lines; double space between paragraphs

Content

- ☐ Begin with attention-getting first paragraph
- ☐ Introduce story angle
- ☐ Suggest credible sources
- ☐ Share key facts, statistics, anecdotes, and details that legitimize story
- ☐ Clearly state what you want (interview, feature coverage, etc.)
- ☐ Indicate follow-up plans
- ☐ Reinforce willingness to provide additional information
- ☐ Include contact information: name, title, phone number, e-mail

Writing

- ☐ Creative
- ☐ Address editor's interest
- ☐ Avoid being self-serving
- ☐ Avoid being pushy
- ☐ Brief

E-mail Version

- ☐ Include strong subject line
- ☐ Include headline
- ☐ Include contact information
- ☐ Summarize important information
- ☐ Keep it brief

Photo Caption

Photos

- ☐ Show action
- ☐ Look natural
- ☐ Avoid clutter
- ☐ Avoid overly promoting the company
- ☐ Ensure high-quality
- ☐ Use preferred format for media

Format

- ☐ Company letterhead
- ☐ Contact information: name, title, phone number, e-mail
- ☐ Date being sent
- ☐ Headline
- ☐ Dateline

Content

- ☐ Describe action in photo in first sentence
- ☐ Write first sentence in present tense
- ☐ Use past tense for rest of caption
- ☐ Refer to company only once
- ☐ Identify people based on action

Writing

- ☐ Avoid "obvious" references
- ☐ Brief
- ☐ Straightforward

Fact Sheet / Backgrounder

Format

- ☐ Name of company
- ☐ Contact information: name, title, phone number, e-mail
- ☐ Headline
- ☐ Subheadings
- ☐ Q & A, bullet, narrative

Content

- ☐ Summarize important information
- ☐ Highlight interesting, provocative facts

Writing

- ☐ Factual and informative
- ☐ Objective

Organizational History

Format

- ☐ Name of company
- ☐ Contact information: name, title, phone number, e-mail
- ☐ Headline
- ☐ Q & A, bullet, narrative

Content

- ☐ Introduce history in first one or two paragraphs
- ☐ Provide chronological account
- ☐ Highlight significant years and notable achievements

Writing

- ☐ Factual
- ☐ Objective

Biography

Format

☐ Name of company

☐ Name and title of person

☐ Photo (optional)

Content

☐ State job description in first paragraph

☐ Provide specifics of job duties and activities

☐ Include special knowledge or practice areas

☐ Summarize career history

☐ Highlight professional activities

☐ Summarize education

☐ Include community/public service work

☐ Include personal information, if appropriate

Writing

☐ Factual

☐ Objective

Feature

Format

☐ Name of company
☐ Headline

Content

☐ Begin with attention-getting lead
☐ Clearly state focus of story
☐ Include colorful details
☐ Use revealing quotes
☐ End with strong conclusion that reconnects with focus of story

Writing

☐ Imaginative
☐ Descriptive language

Technical Article

Format

- ☐ By-line
- ☐ Headline

Content

- ☐ Offer general advice
- ☐ Support claims and/or predictions
- ☐ Attribute statistics
- ☐ Avoid promotion of company or products

Writing

- ☐ Factual
- ☐ Objective

Letter to the Editor

Format

- ☐ Company letterhead
- ☐ Salutation ("Dear Editor" or "To the Editor")
- ☐ Signed (name, title)
- ☐ Follow other guidelines provided by newspaper

Content

- ☐ Refer to issue or specific article (headline and date) in first paragraph
- ☐ Identify why issue is important and timely
- ☐ Provide background on subject
- ☐ Use facts and statistics
- ☐ Express opinion
- ☐ Summarize main point

Writing

- ☐ Brief (250 to 300 words)
- ☐ Maintain positive tone
- ☐ Avoid name calling and harsh criticism

Op-Ed Article

Format

☐ By-line
☐ Follow other guidelines provided by newspaper

Content

☐ Identify key points or arguments
☐ Include facts, statistics and other supporting evidence
☐ Summarize main points
☐ Offer solution
☐ Provide reasons why solution should be enacted or supported

Writing

☐ Concise (600 to 800 words)
☐ Persuasive language

Public Relations Advertisement / Announcement

Format

- ☐ Creative headline
- ☐ Simple body copy
- ☐ Variety of formats and lengths

Content

- ☐ Expand on headline in first paragraph
- ☐ Focus on one idea in body
- ☐ Use supporting information
- ☐ Recap main point at end
- ☐ Emphasize desired action

Writing

- ☐ Memorable theme
- ☐ Short sentences and paragraphs
- ☐ Active voice
- ☐ Simple language

Newsletter

Planning

- ☐ Identify purpose
- ☐ Create mission statement
- ☐ Select editor and contributors
- ☐ Determine frequency of distribution
- ☐ Establish budget
- ☐ Determine length and format
- ☐ Develop content formula
- ☐ Choose "look and feel" that reflects organization
- ☐ Create attractive cover page

Format

- ☐ Nameplate
- ☐ Strong headlines, subheadings and captions
- ☐ Masthead
- ☐ Clean, highly readable fonts
- ☐ Reader-friendly design
- ☐ Photo/graphic on each page

Content

- ☐ Follow content formula
- ☐ Use a variety of writing formats and styles (news, feature, etc.)
- ☐ Keep consistent with mission statement
- ☐ Focus on news, not promotion
- ☐ Emphasize reader benefits
- ☐ Provide two-way communication and encourage feedback
- ☐ Be aware of copyright infringement

Writing

- ☐ Reader-focused
- ☐ Simple language
- ☐ Concise and crisp
- ☐ Short sentences and paragraphs

E-zines

Format

- ☐ Table of contents
- ☐ Strong headlines
- ☐ Links to full text

Content

- ☐ Lead with substance, not promotion
- ☐ Include helpful tips
- ☐ Use bulleted lists

Writing

- ☐ Brief articles (less than two paragraphs)

Brochure

Format

☐ Enticing cover (focus on top third)
☐ Strong graphic design
☐ Visuals on each panel
☐ Reflect organization

Content

☐ Focus on benefits to reader
☐ Highlight key points
☐ Explain features and benefits
☐ Use testimonials or other supporting information
☐ Include background information on organization, product, or service
☐ End with selling point
☐ Request action from reader
☐ Include contact information
☐ Include company mailing and Web address, phone, fax, e-mail, and logo
☐ Information should be inclusive so brochure can "stand alone"

Writing

☐ Persuasive and promotional
☐ Flair
☐ Personal language ("I," "you," "we")
☐ Copy should set tone
☐ Easy to understand

Flier / Poster

Format

☐ One-sided, single sheet
☐ Large headline
☐ Single visual

Content

☐ Focus on important details only
☐ Include call to action
☐ Identify sponsor(s) by name and logo

Writing

☐ Brief

Web Site

Planning

- ☐ Establish goals
- ☐ Target specific audience
- ☐ Monitor competition
- ☐ Develop site map
- ☐ Create short, easy-to-remember Web address
- ☐ Determine how site will be evaluated

Designing

- ☐ Reflect character of organization
- ☐ Create strong home page
- ☐ Develop creative, efficient toolbars
- ☐ Develop short, easy-to-read sections
- ☐ Include headlines and subheads
- ☐ Avoid small type, all caps, reverse type, and multiple typefaces
- ☐ Be cautious of visuals that take a long time to load

Writing

- ☐ Short sentences and paragraphs
- ☐ Aim for minimal scrolling
- ☐ Direct, conversational tone

Promoting

- ☐ Register site with search engines
- ☐ Register with Web announcement service
- ☐ Take advantage of free links
- ☐ Publicize URL on organizational materials
- ☐ Promote through news and chat forums

News Conference

Before

- ☐ Select location
- ☐ Determine best date and time
- ☐ Develop budget
- ☐ Prepare invitation or media alert
- ☐ Outline program
- ☐ Draft welcome and introductions
- ☐ Write opening news statement/announcement
- ☐ Brief speakers; anticipate questions and prepare answers
- ☐ Assemble media kit
- ☐ Arrange for refreshments
- ☐ Prepare background visuals

After

- ☐ Provide any follow-up information that is requested
- ☐ Contact media that were not in attendance
- ☐ Track media coverage
- ☐ Write final evaluation report

Audioconferences / Videoconferences

- ☐ Include connection information in media alert

Webcast

- ☐ Provide media with access to multimedia player

Special Events

Initial Planning

- ☐ Set goals and objectives
- ☐ Identify target publics
- ☐ Select theme
- ☐ Develop strategies and tactics
- ☐ Develop budget
- ☐ Develop timetable
- ☐ Check for competing events
- ☐ Assemble event planning team
- ☐ Delegate responsibilities

Logistics

- ☐ Visit potential sites; check for:
  - ☐ Handicapped accessibility
  - ☐ Kitchen access
  - ☐ Bathrooms
  - ☐ Parking area
  - ☐ Coat check
- ☐ Confirm floor plan
- ☐ Book valet service
- ☐ Book caterer
- ☐ Select menu
- ☐ Arrange for bar service
- ☐ Rent tables, chairs, linens, dishes, flatware, stemware, serving dishes, tent
- ☐ Arrange for security
- ☐ Arrange for insurance
- ☐ Obtain permits
- ☐ Determine type of music (band, DJ, "piped" in) and book
- ☐ Determine audio/visual needs; arrange for:
  - ☐ microphones and speakers
  - ☐ podium
  - ☐ projectors and screens
  - ☐ lighting
  - ☐ staging or risers
  - ☐ Internet connection
- ☐ Conduct final walk-through day of event to check on details

Special Considerations

- ☐ Hire décor consultant
- ☐ Order centerpieces, corsages/boutonnières, and decorative arrangements
- ☐ Order balloons
- ☐ Buy candles
- ☐ Book photographer
- ☐ Order table favors
- ☐ Order "goody bags" for guests
- ☐ Assemble hospitality baskets for bathrooms

Program

- ☐ Arrange transportation, accommodations, and meals for speaker/emcee
- ☐ Order gift/awards for speaker/award recipients
- ☐ Obtain guest list from award recipients
- ☐ Write script
- ☐ Prepare visual presentation and test all A/V equipment beforehand

Publicity

- ☐ Send news release announcing event
- ☐ Send news release announcing speaker or award recipient
- ☐ Send media alert

Printing

- ☐ Hire graphic designer
- ☐ Select printer

- ☐ Assemble mailing list
- ☐ "Save this Date" card
- ☐ Invitations
- ☐ Program
- ☐ Signage (directional, registration, recognition, tables)
- ☐ Banners

Staffing

- ☐ Recruit and train volunteers
- ☐ "Go to" person day of event
- ☐ Checkbook chief
- ☐ Registration
- ☐ Greeters
- ☐ Escort for speaker/emcee
- ☐ Set up/clean up
- ☐ Order or make special nametags
- ☐ Arrange for snacks
- ☐ Arrange for "thank you" gifts

Registration Table

- ☐ Arrange for table, chairs, linens, décor, etc.
- ☐ Easel
- ☐ Wastebasket
- ☐ Printed nametags
- ☐ Blank nametags
- ☐ Pens/markers
- ☐ Reservation list
- ☐ Table diagram/seating arrangements
- ☐ Cash box/change

Follow Up

- ☐ Send thank you notes to:
  - ☐ Speaker/emcee
  - ☐ Sponsors
  - ☐ Volunteers
  - ☐ Event planning team
- ☐ Send follow-up news release
- ☐ Write evaluative report

Crisis Communication Plan

☐   Conduct risk assessment to identify crisis scenarios

☐   Explain goals of organization during crisis

☐   Draft initial statement for each scenario

☐   Obtain approval from legal counsel

☐   Identify crisis team

☐   Designate responsibilities

☐   Identify internal and external publics

☐   Specify preferred and secondary methods of communicating to publics

☐   Identify primary media spokesperson

☐   Keep organizational materials (bios, backgrounders, etc.) up-to-date

☐   Maintain crisis directory

Responding to a Crisis

- ☐ Set up crisis communication headquarters
- ☐ Inform employees
- ☐ Refer all media calls to headquarters
- ☐ Establish separate media headquarters, if necessary
- ☐ Get top officials to scene
- ☐ Prioritize target publics
- ☐ Issue initial statement as soon as possible
- ☐ Issue subsequent statements as information is made available
- ☐ Organize news conference for formal statement(s)
- ☐ Prepare and distribute news release(s)
- ☐ Be responsive, ethical, and responsible
- ☐ Provide open and truthful information
- ☐ Keep communication consistent
- ☐ Show concern and compassion
- ☐ Protect company's reputation and image
- ☐ Monitor after-effects

Author Index

Note: Numbers in italics indicate pages with complete bibliographic information.

Subject Index